BEATRICE AND SIDNEY WEBB

Fabian Socialists

Lisanne Radice

M
MACMILLAN

First published 1984 by
THE MACMILLAN PRESS LTD
London and Basingstoke
Companies and representatives throughout the world

ISBN 0 333 36183 0 (hardcover)
ISBN 0 333 37888 1 (paperback)

Printed in Great Britain at
The Camelot Press Ltd, Southampton

The extracts from Bernard Shaw's *Sixteen Self Sketches*, *Bluffing the Value Theory* and his letters to Sidney Webb and Beatrice Potter are included by permission of the Society of Authors on behalf of the Bernard Shaw Estate.

To Giles, without whose help and endless patience this book would never have been published

Contents

Acknowledgements

Most of the material for this biography is deposited in the British Library of Political and Economic Science catalogued under the Passfield Papers. However, I have also had occasion to discuss the Webbs with those who either knew them or have written about them. I would like to thank in particular the following who so kindly gave of their valuable time: John Parker, Robin Page-Arnot, Malcolm and Kitty Muggeridge, Professor Norman Mackenzie and the late William Robson. I also wish to thank Dr John Hurt, who read an early draft of some chapters and made many helpful comments. The present Lord Ponsonby kindly allowed me to quote from his grandfather's unpublished diary.

I should also like to thank Dr Angela Raspin and the staff at the British Library of Political and Economic Science for always being unfailingly kind and helpful; Mrs Irene Wagner and the staff of the Labour Party Library; the staff of the British Museum; the staff of the Bodleian Library, Oxford; Nuffield College, Oxford; Corpus Christi College, Oxford; the Public Record Office; and the staff of Transport House.

I wish to thank the following for permission to quote: the London School of Economics for permission to quote from the diary of Beatrice Webb and the papers in the Passfield Papers; the Society of Authors for quotations from the writings of Bernard Shaw; Frederick Muller Ltd for quotations from *The Webbs and their Work*.

I am also grateful to Yvonne South, who has toiled over the typescript cheerfully typing and retyping it, and to Nancy Williams who advised me on the illustrations.

There are, however, two people to whom I owe a particular debt. The first is Maureen Gilbert, who was my research assistant during the early part of the book. She accepted the daily grind of reading the Diary and the letters with an astonishing cheerfulness while at the same time skilfully and patiently extrapolating the most significant passages.

The second is to my husband Giles Radice. He not only encouraged me whenever I faltered but also by a skilful combination of editing and rewriting greatly improved the text. I am particularly grateful for his contribution to Chapters 4, 8, 10, 11, 13 and 14. Without his help this book would never have been published.

L. R.

List of Illustrations

Introduction

It is one of the puzzles of modern historiography that, despite the immense contribution of Beatrice and Sidney Webb to the development of British social sciences and politics, no full length biography of the partnership has yet been attempted. Beatrice's niece Kitty Muggeridge, produced a sympathetic study of her aunt some years ago, and the Webbs play a major part in Norman and Jeanne Mackenzie's brilliant encapsulation of the early Fabians – but this unfortunately ends in 1914. There is, also, Professor Mackenzie's outstanding edition of the Webb letters and Beatrice's Diaries which gives an outline account of their lives, as well as, of course Beatrice's two autobiographical studies, *My Apprenticeship* and *Our Partnership*, the latter of which was edited after her death by Margaret Cole. Apart from these studies, articles and papers have been written on their philosophy and on their impact on the world of politics, social administration and education. But there has been no overall assessment of their life and work.

Why have the Webbs been so neglected? Probably one of the major obstacles has been a hostility to their personalities and ideas, best epitomised by Anthony Crosland's famous remark that 'total abstinence and a good filing system are not now the right signposts to the socialist Utopia'. Or, as David Caute in his book *The Fellow Travellers* said of them: 'The Webbs were excellent examples of the type which prefers mankind to people; which originally intends to sacrifice a few to save everyone and ends by sacrificing everyone to save a few.'

It was H. G. Wells who made the first public attack on the partnership. He quarrelled with them over the direction of the Fabian Society and, more personally, over his love affair with one of their friends' daughters which he conducted in an indiscreet and selfish manner. His reply was to try and stir up the Fabians against them – but he was no match for the politically astute Sidney. After his defeat in the Society, Wells vented his spleen in *The New Machiavelli* published in 1910. In it the Webbs, thinly disguised, are described as 'two active self-centred people excessively devoted to the public service' living in a 'hard little house'. Sidney was depicted as having a 'mind as orderly as a museum and an invincible power over detail', while the vision they displayed was seen as 'hard, narrow'. According to Wells they wanted things 'more organised, more co-related with government and a collective purpose'. And 'if they had the universe in hand I know they would take down all the trees and put up stamped tin green shades and sunlight accumulators.' The book came out at a time when their popularity was low and when the 'firm of Webb', as Beatrice remarked, was 'out'. So Wells's brilliant caricature of the Fabian partnership slipped into folk myth and became an uncritically accepted truth.

But determined biographers have written histories about the most unattractive personalities; Bullock on Hitler, Deutscher on Stalin. A bigger stumbling block is the sheer breadth of their range and achievement. It is no exaggeration to say that the Webbs were polymaths. To give a full account of their work their biographer would have to be knowledgeable in economics, social administration, labour and social history, social policy, political philosophy and political science. I have no pretensions to having a mastery over so many specialist fields and like all biographers have given priority to those parts of my subjects' lives which interest me most. An example of what might be felt to be a major *lacuna*, for instance, is the briefest of descriptions of the Webbs' writings on local government, even though they spent over twenty years on their fourteen volumes. There is a further point. To do full justice to all the events which crowded these long and fascinating years (their lives span nine decades) would need two volumes. Inevitably, a one volume work means compression and omissions.

The main themes of my book are three: first that the Webbs were a unique political and intellectual partnership; second that their achievements were so great that it is no exaggeration to say that they were among the most influential architects of modern British society; third, that their philosophy is more profound, less doctrinaire and more democratic than their detractors would have us believe.

The key to an understanding of the strength of the partnership is that together they were greater than the sum of their parts. Character faults were compensated for, individual strengths were enhanced, and a common purpose developed. Superficially, the Webbs appeared an ill-assorted couple. In fact they were remarkably suited.

Beatrice, beautiful, intelligent but highly neurotic came from a successful line of upper middle class entrepreneurs. Despite being one of nine sisters, she led a solitary and introspective early childhood which 'was not on the whole a happy one. Ill health and starved affection and the mental disorders which spring from these . . . and its loneliness was absolute'. Denied a formal education, she single-mindedly set herself the task of extending her knowledge by a thorough mastering of the classics, philosophy, history and economics. Subconsciously she aimed at discovering order and certainty, what amounted to a secular faith. It was this almost desperate search which possibly gave rise to her six years obsession with the charismatic radical reformer, Joseph Chamberlain, whom she met in 1883 when she was in her middle twenties, and whose powerful personality seemed for a time to offer that stability which Beatrice was so anxiously seeking. The failure of the relationship crippled her emotionally for a considerable number of years, so much so that she convinced herself that she would never love any man as she had loved Chamberlain.

She accepted Sidney's courtship for a number of complicated psychological reasons. In Sidney she could at one and the same time seek her subconscious revenge on Chamberlain for spurning her, and yet gain a much needed companion. Sidney's adoration, coupled with his inferior social status, made her feel that she was bestowing a benefit on him – an altruistic action which proved to herself the superior quality and goodness of her character. On the other hand, his undoubted cleverness and intellectual self-assurance gave her the strength she had sought. At times a psychosomatic depressive given to melancholia, Beatrice needed the steadying influence that Sidney provided. Frequently suicidal before her marriage, the inner peace produced by Sidney's loving affection enabled her to overcome successfully even her deepest mental crises – without that support it is quite conceivable that she might have committed suicide by early middle age. Without Sidney, Beatrice was unsure of herself and her own powers; he gave her purpose and self confidence. Though she claimed to have married him not for love but for the sake of their 'common cause', it was a feeling which lasted a short time. A year after her marriage she joyously recorded in her diary, 'I am triumphantly happy'.

The partnership with Sidney was also vital to the development of Beatrice's work. Although imaginative and often able intuitively to see through a problem, she was not, unlike her more gifted husband, a natural writer, spending an excessive time in drafting and redrafting. Her only book prior to her marriage was a short account of the Co-operative Movement, and even the devoted Sidney was moved to write rather testily that she had taken too long over something that would not, as he put it somewhat unkindly, be 'a *very* great work'. All the same, she had a quick grasp for hidden truths buried beneath mountains of facts and layers of accepted dogma, as her seminal work on the East End sweating trade amply demonstrated. But it was Sidney who provided the partnership with the brilliant analytical powers and the political and economic knowledge without which Beatrice would never have risen out of the ranks of the gifted amateur social observer. More important, his deeply-held faith in socialism replaced the religion she had lost in early childhood; she now had both a goal and a creed. Beatrice's marriage to Sidney turned the elegant Miss Potter from a quasi-social worker of the normal Victorian breed into one of the most formidable social scientists of the late nineteenth and early twentieth century, and the other half of a great research and writing partnership.

Marriage also profoundly changed Sidney's life. Brought up in a lower middle class London family (Beatrice described him as an 'ugly little man with no social position') he had won a place at the Colonial Office through his superb performance in the Civil Service examinations. But his duties at the Colonial Office failed to stretch the powers of 'the ablest man in England', as Shaw once called him. Marriage released him from bureaucratic drudgery. The acquisition of Miss Potter's private income ensured that he need never live the often desperately uncertain life which the reliance on journalism that Shaw endured would have entailed; it also meant that he could now devote his entire time to the London County Council and the Fabian Society – to the gain of both.

The 'Member for Potter', as he once wryly described himself, had however to pay a price for his financial independence. Sidney left no record of his personal thoughts but it is quite clear from both his letters and Beatrice's diary that he was inclined to try for Parliament early on in their married life, and that a number of winnable constituencies had, even before their marriage, invited him to stand. There is no doubt that he was tempted – but Beatrice would have none of it. Her reasons were mixed. She believed that he would never make an effective House of Commons man, a judgement which turned out to be correct. She also considered that, as a political writer, Sidney needed administrative experience which would be best gained at the LCC. However, perhaps the predominant motive was that, for selfish though loving reasons, she hated the thought of losing his daily companionship and knew that life at Westminster, with its many ties and inconveniences, would take him too much away from her. Always fully aware of his debt to Beatrice, Sidney allowed personal political ambition to take second place, although in the end, and much to his astonishment, he became a Cabinet Minister in both the interwar Labour governments.

Marriage into the Potter family also brought with it other advantages. It is true that Sidney had little in common with Beatrice's sisters, the complacent and self-assured daughters of a wealthy captain of industry. But there were compensations. The daughters had married prominent barristers, politicians and industrialists. There were brilliant and famous friends, such as Asquith, the two Balfours, Haldane and Dilke, who could be invited to the Webbs' austere table. Fabians and ministers, socialists and bishops, intellectuals and civil servants, rubbed shoulders over the cold boiled beef at 41 Grosvenor Road. Both the partnership and their guests benefited. The Webbs could 'permeate' the Establishment; the Establishment could gain from their ideas.

The generosity of their help to and concern for others goes far to dispel the popular image of the Webbs as a desiccated, soulless couple concerned only with their own ideas and interests. There are many examples. Even though Herbert Spencer refused to allow Beatrice to remain his literary executor after her marriage to Sidney, she would frequently travel down to Bournemouth to visit the old philosopher in his gloomy retirement. When Alys Pearsall Smith's marriage to Bertrand Russell began to disintegrate, Beatrice immediately suggested going abroad with her, despite considerable inconvenience. The Webbs did as much as they could to ease the anger and hurt left behind by the débâcle of the Reeves-Wells infatuation. They always encouraged the younger generation; many an academic or political hopeful was offered advice and friendship at Passfield Corner (as John Parker and Lord

Longford have both confirmed to the author). They also never forgot their debts to those who worked for them – they even went so far as to make one of their most faithful secretaries, Galton, the General Secretary of the Fabian Society.

Gradually the partnership lost their separate identities. People referred not to Sidney Webb or Beatrice Webb but to 'the Webbs'. This fusion of personality was actively promoted not just by outside observers but by both Sidney and Beatrice. It would have been less remarkable if it had been Beatrice alone who encouraged the idea. But the fact that Sidney was also insistent on their duality underlines the crucial point that this was a unique partnership of equals in a male dominated society.

Their towering reputation rests partly on their writing. Here the achievements of the partnership are awe inspiring. Their *History of Trade Unionism* (1894) and *Industrial Democracy* (1897) remain standard works to this day, while the *History of the Co-Operative Movement* (1892) is still widely read. *A Constitution for the Socialist Commonwealth of Great Britain* (1920) brilliantly sums up their ideas on the development of a democratic socialist state. They also produced innumerable pamphlets for the Fabian Society and the Labour Party which are a model of careful research and clear presentation.

However, their accomplishments were not merely intellectual. Above all they were practical reformers who helped to change the face of British society.

The Webbs' earliest successes were educational. Sidney was chairman of the prestigious Technical Education Board of the LCC for 16 years. As chairman, he set up the first scholarship scheme for bright working class children as well as establishing polytechnics and technical institutions which opened up opportunities for self improvement for poor London children. He also supported Haldane in setting up Imperial College, and, together with Beatrice, helped to promote the far-reaching educational reforms of 1902 and 1903 which, by placing education under the county councils, gave a logical structure to a system which was beginning to disintegrate.

The creation of the London School of Economics alone would have made the Webbs famous. According to Graham Wallas, the Webbs woke up one morning and decided to use part of the money which the Fabian Society had been left by a rich member to set up a School in London on the lines of the *Ecole Libre des Sciences Politiques* in Paris. Through their determination this vision of a centre of excellence devoted to the study of the social sciences (virtually ignored by the older universities) became a triumphant reality.

With Lloyd George and Beveridge, Beatrice and Sidney Webb can justly be said to be the founders of the modern welfare state. They were lifelong exponents of the concept of the National Minimum which they first discussed at length in *Industrial Democracy*, as well as in innumerable Fabian tracts and pamphlets. They believed that it was the duty of the state to provide a safety net of basic welfare services, from education through to housing and health for all its citizens. They carried the argument further in their 1909 Minority Report to the Royal Commission on the Poor Law, of which Beatrice was a member. In it they laid down a blueprint for the development of welfare programmes to cater for the sick, the aged, and the unemployed. This and their subsequent Campaign for the Prevention of Destitution helped create a climate of opinion which made the demand for the establishment of a welfare state one of the main objectives of the Labour Party.

Educational reformers, propagandists for the welfare state, the Webbs also played a crucial role in the development of British socialism. Their name has been most closely associated with the Fabian Society. Sidney Webb and George Bernard Shaw moulded the early character of the Society, but it was due to the former that it changed from an idiosyncratic middle class debating society into the most influential research and policy discussion body of the Labour Party, whose members (Attlee, Gaitskell, Wilson, Crosland and Crossman) have been among the most famous within the labour movement. Sidney's approach became the Society's; ethical in character and evolutionary in practice, its socialism was firmly based on a systematic presentation of the facts – a novel and immensely powerful method of political argument and propaganda which still retains its persuasiveness.

They also founded the *New Statesman* in 1913, and encouraged the establishment of the *Political Quarterly* in 1930. The purpose of the *New Statesman* was to gain support for their ideas among a wider circle of radical opinion; the *Political Quarterly* was aimed at a more academic audience. Linking the two was their belief in the need for informed discussion of new political and social ideas.

Recent historians such as J. M. Winter and Ross McGibbin have rightly argued that Sidney's influence on the Labour Party's development was crucial. It was mainly due to his and Henderson's insistence that the Party became socialist in character and a genuine political alternative to the established parties. During the 1914–18 war Sidney was the most powerful member of the two most prestigious and influential committees of the labour movement – the War Emergency Committee and the policy sub-committee of the National Executive Committee. Out of these came the 1918 constitution and election manifesto *Labour and the New Social Order*.

Most historians accept that Sidney was the chief architect of the 1918 constitution by which the Labour Party opened its doors to individual members, accepted a new grass roots organisation and, through Clause 4 Part 4, established its socialist credentials. As to the manifesto, which Sidney wrote, it was not only a clear restatement of Webbian objectives – a national minimum, democratic control of industry, and increased municipalisation – but it also provided the Labour Party, for the first time, with a blue print for changing society. Although Sidney was a prominent Cabinet Minister in both the 1924 and 1929 governments, the Webbs' main contribution to the rise of labour was ideological. They captured the labour movement for their ideas, and helped prepare the Labour Party for power.

What links the Webbs' different achievements is a profound belief that society needed to be changed, and that its individualistic and selfish attributes could be transformed into a moral order. Their philosophy was also based on a belief in a meritocracy to be achieved through the provision of equal opportunities for all, while public service was seen as an intrinsic duty. Their approach was pragmatic, evolutionary, and collectivist and founded on a deep commitment to a democratic, pluralist state.

However, Beatrice and Sidney have been called elitist. Is this a fair description? If by elitist is meant that some individuals are born natural leaders as of right, then neither of the Webbs can be accused of accepting the notion of a chosen few. They were, nevertheless, passionate believers in the rights of individuals to better themselves, and that opportunities had to be provided, as of right, for those who were disadvantaged. Sidney quite consciously hoped to replace the old aristocratic élite with a new meritocratic one based on talent, but his meritocracy was founded on a wide definition of equality of opportunity and environment. Later Socialist generations have developed the argument; Anthony Crosland in *The Future of Socialism* pointed out: 'No one deserves either so generous a reward or so severe a penalty for a quality implanted from the outside and for which he can claim only a limited responsibility.'

The 'spirit of public service' was also a crucial element in the Webbian concept of the future socialist state. It was certainly partly for this reason that the Webbs founded the LSE. Bright young men and women trained in the right principles would work with selfless dedication and devote themselves to the new democratic state. The creation of a new body of 'Samurai' – public spirited guardians of a democratic society – had meritocratic overtones, but it was also very much tied to their belief that the 'working of democratic institutions means . . . one long training in enlightened altruism' and that 'we must reconstruct society, on a basis not of interest but of community of service . . . and of that willingness to subordinate oneself to the welfare of the whole.' Perhaps it was misguided of them to believe that others could have the self same altruistic devotion to duty that they had. Occasionally they came across high ranking civil servants who proved their point; on the whole they set their fellow humans an impossible task. But their objective was an honourable one. What they wished to establish was a society where merit would be rewarded not by materialistic gain but by service to the community.

In his interpretation of socialist objectives Sidney was a pragmatic collectivist rather than the dogmatic hardliner which he has occasionally been made out to be. This misconception of Webbian socialism is in part based on misinterpretation of Clause 4, Part 4, of the Labour Party constitution. The issue will be discussed at greater length later in the book. Here it is only necessary to make what might be seen as a somewhat controversial statement; Clause 4, Part 4, particularly its references to common ownership, has always been misunderstood. Sidney spelt out the implications of the new constitution in his short but important pamphlet entitled *The New Constitution of the Labour Party*. He had this to say about 'common ownership':

> it is [he wrote] socialism which is no more specific than a definite repudiation of the individualism that characterised all the political parties of the past generation . . . this declaration of the Labour Party leaves it open to choose from time to time whatever forms of common ownership . . . may *in particular cases* commend themselves.

In the view of this author Clause 4 is neither the 'fig leaf' that Professor Ralph Miliband has so scornfully called it, nor a recipe for out and out state ownership as those on the hard left would have us believe, but more a pragmatic collectivism which covers all types of common ownership and is to be used with discretion.

The Webbs' socialism was evolutionary not revolutionary; a mixture of Positivism, Radicalism and collectivist socialism. In a phrase which later became famous – 'the inevitability of gradualness' – Sidney explained to the 1923 Labour Party conference the nature of socialist aspirations. This has usually been thought to imply a reaffirmation of the old Webbian belief in the eventual triumph of Fabian permeation. Professor Norman Mackenzie, however, in *The First Fabians* argued that Sidney was merely putting forward the thesis that the Labour Party would inevitably come to power. There is a third interpretation which is more credible. Sidney believed it was essential for the Labour Party, particularly after 1917, to disassociate itself from all revolutionary, including Syndicalist, tendencies; to show itself both respectable and responsible. It had to assure the voters that any changes it made when once in power would be both democratic and parliamentary. Beatrice and Sidney were always passionately concerned with the manner in which democracy would evolve in a socialist state. Collectivists they might be, dedicated democrats they certainly were.

This brings me to the final element of their political philosophy; the Webbs' dedication to the pursuit of democratic socialism. This dedication provides a vital clue both to their written work and their political achievements and is a direct refutation of those, like Caute and Wright, who accuse them of totalitarian tendencies.

When discussing their *History of Trade Unionism*, Beatrice recorded in her diary that she and Sidney hoped to provide a framework for 'a new democratic state'. However, it was not until the last forty-three pages of *Industrial Democracy* (their second major book published some three years later) that the Webbs first examined this question in some detail. What they then aimed to solve was the seemingly intractible problem of combining administrative efficiency with popular control. As libertarians they were aware of the pitfalls of unrestrained power:

> not even the wisest of men can be trusted with that supreme authority which comes from the union of knowledge, capacity and opportunity with the power of untrammelled and ultimate decision. Democracy is an expedient . . . for preventing the

> concentration in any single individual or in any single class of what inevitably becomes, when so concentrated, a terrible engine of oppression.

And they went on to argue that only democracy was compatible with the freedom of all to develop.

The Webbs' earliest arguments for a democratic state were based on a belief that 'the average sensual man' could only, given his lack of political education, play a passive role – though in time, the process of democracy would encourage participation. To compensate for this passivity, the Webbs argued for a new breed of professional representatives who would keep closely in touch with the electorate and act as pressure points against the state apparatus.

In 1912 the Webbs were forced into a new consideration of democracy by outside events. The years between 1909 and 1911 had been years of industrial unrest, growing unemployment and trade union expansion. One of the by-products of the unrest was the growth of the syndicalist movement whose main purpose – the overthrow of parliamentary government by the workers using the general strike as a political weapon, and its replacement by a government based on industrial unions – was anathema to the Webbs. Aware of the increasing power of syndicalism within the trade unions, and afraid of the consequences for democracy, the Webbs launched a vigorous counter attack in support of their type of democratic socialist state. They believed that, now the manual workers had the vote, 'the ballot box has made obsolete the barricades.' At the same time government by the Syndicalist National Unions would result in a new authoritarianism; as trade unions were now to become part of the structure of government they would no longer be able to represent employees. In addition, whole groups of citizens, such as women, professional people, pensioners and so on, who were not producers and therefore not in trade unions, would lose their political rights. In their view, Syndicalism was narrow, authoritarian, and based exclusively on producer rather than community interests.

However in an important article entitled 'A Stratified Democracy' (published in 1919), influenced now by G. D. H. Cole and the Guild Socialists as much as by the Syndicalists, Sidney admitted that producers needed to have more power than they had previously allowed. But the Webbs' main quarrel with Cole remained unresolved: they believed that his form of industrial organisation was too narrow – there ought not to be one overriding authority, even if it were that of the producers. Otherwise, 'presbyter is apt to be old priest writ large.' So a diffusion of interests was necessary so 'you do not have one sovereignty, you have a number of separate sources of authority and each authority has to restrict itself and be restricted by all the other authorities simultaneously.'

'A Stratified Democracy' was followed a year later by the Webbs' only major book on democratic theory: *A Constitution for the Socialist Commonwealth of Great Britain*. This was both a critique of the British parliamentary system and an attempt to develop a blueprint for democratic change which took into account recent developments. Given the complexity of modern industrial society, there could be no 'model constitution for a Utopian community' and therefore no single democratic solution. The Webbs based their new democratic theory on three major factors, man as producer, as consumer, and as citizen. What they hoped to achieve was a democracy in which no one stratum would hold the monopoly of power and where the individual enjoyed the maximum amount of liberty as was compatible with his place in a complex, interdependent society. At the same time democracy, they firmly warned,

> cannot afford to dispense with the complication in its administrative machinery because only by an extensive variety of parts in a deliberately adjusted relation between those parts, can there be any security for the personal freedom and independence and initiative in the great mass of individuals, whether as producers, consumers or as citizens.

The diffusion and variety which they advocated was reflected in their democratic model. Two Parliaments, political and social, were envisaged to reflect the two sides of man's interests. The organisation of industry in a socialist commonwealth was to be democratic, with worker participation at all levels. Consumer interests were to be safeguarded as well as 'the permanent welfare of the community as a whole'. The new democratic structure would be underpinned by the 'disinterested professional expert' who would provide that 'searchlight of published knowledge' which the Webbs regarded as the 'cornerstone of successful Democracy'. As to local government, they believed in extending its scope,

> the very differences among localities, with the different local administrations that they involve provide an increase in the scope of individual choice, a widening of personal freedom and a safeguard against the monotonous uniformity and centralised tyranny over the individual.

They therefore aimed for a complex and varied democratic pluralistic society in which liberty would be protected and individual rights and opportunities increased. The structure of the new socialist commonwealth was based on a system of countervailing checks and balances, a considerable dispersal of power and genuine participation – a model which is as relevant today as it was in the 1920s.

The myth, however, has persisted that the Webbs were bureaucratice collectivists at best and totalitarians at worst, a reputation which is mostly based on their last major work, *Soviet Communism – A New Civilisation?* The book, which was published in 1935, was the product of a visit Beatrice and Sidney made to the Soviet Union in 1932. Discouraged by the slump and other failures of Western capitalism, the Webbs went to Russia disposed to applaud: 'without doubt we are on the side of Russia', Beatrice recorded in her diary before their voyage. And they were: they extolled the virtues of the Soviet regime, laid stress on the virtues of the Communist Party and the Komsomols, and appeared to underwrite what was even then considered to be one of the most oppressive regimes in existence.

There are those like David Caute, in his *Fellow Travellers*, who put their approval of Soviet communism down not only to their pessimism and lack of understanding but, more important, to their own totalitarian tendencies. Confronted by the power of a strong collectivist state, they could no longer hide their anti-democratic views. Professor George Feaver, in an interesting article in *Encounter*, put forward a different and more persuasive hypothesis. He argued that the reason why Beatrice and Sidney were enthused by the Soviet system was not because they were undemocratic collectivists but because, as devout pilgrims, engaged in a hitherto barren voyage in search of a secular faith, they found in the apparent altruism and dedication of the Communist Party the faith which they had been seeking. Certainly Beatrice wrote enthusiastically, if inaccurately, that Russian communists had 'voluntarily pledged themselves to two out of three of the characteristic obligations of the religious orders of Christianity, namely to proverty . . . and to obedience'.

However, my own conclusion is that their misrepresentation of Soviet society was more than the blindness of the religious convert. The Webbs genuinely believed that in the Soviet Union they were witnessing the birth of a democratic state in which all citizens were encouraged to participate at every level of society. Participation had been a crucial element of their own model in *Socialist Commonwealth*; their view of the Soviet system was that they had encountered 'the personal participation in public affairs of an unprecedented proportion of the entire adult population.' Here is the clue to their embrace of the Soviet regime.

It is not difficult to criticise the Webbs for their eulogy of the Soviet Union. Never at their best abroad, they failed to see that Soviet grassroots democracy was only effective if the Communist leadership allowed it to be, and that the lack of competing political parties of independent sources of power, and of the checks and balances (so central to the *Socialist Commonwealth*) made a mockery of their argument in *Soviet Communism* that democracy could ever be equated solely with participation. Instead they mistakenly believed that the discussions which took place at all levels of Soviet society would provide an effective check on a centralised state and that the Communist Party was a selfless vanguard which would eventually produce an environment in which individual freedom would flourish. However, their espousal of the Communist regime should be seen not as a rejection of their life-long support for pluralist democracy, expressed most forcefully and convincingly in *Socialist Commonwealth*, but as the misjudgement of two disillusioned and tired' septuagenarians, who characteristically saw in Russia only what they wanted to see.

I
1858–1890
A Victorian Apprenticeship

'The Elegant Miss Potter.'

Beatrice Potter was born on 2 January 1858 at Standish House, a white barrack-like mansion set in the rolling Cotswold Hills. She was the eighth of the nine daughters (a son, Dicky, was born when Beatrice was four, but died suddenly two years later) of Richard and Lawrencina Potter.

The Potters and the Hayworths, Lawrencina's family, were typical examples of the new, vigorous entrepreneurs thrown up by the Industrial Revolution. Both her grandfathers were men of action and initiative who grasped the opportunities provided by the new age of machinery and bettered themselves rapidly. Beatrice's paternal grandfather, who came from Yorkshire tenant farmer stock, took advantage of the boom in the Lancashire textile industry, amassed great wealth, and then, as a seal on his new-found prosperity, entered Parliament as a Radical after the 1832 Reform Act. Her maternal grandfather, who was descended from a family of domestic manufacturers in Rossendale, made his money as a merchant in another part of the flourishing north-west, Liverpool, and also became a Member of Parliament, standing for Derby in 1847.

In contrast, Beatrice's paternal grandmother was of Jewish extraction, read Hebrew and loved music. She was eventually put away in a lunatic asylum after being brought back from Paris, where she had gone in her obsession to lead the Jews back to Palestine. Later, Beatrice sometimes feared the effects of her influence.

Richard Potter, her father, was sent to Clifton, one of the new public schools then sprouting up to accommodate the growing demands of the upwardly mobile middle classes, and later to University College, London, which his father had helped to found, as well as Queen's College, Cambridge. He was called to the Bar but decided not to practise on the grounds that he would always have the money to lead the life of leisure which his father's energetic application to capitalist enterprises had earned for him. Richard Potter was an easy-going, good-humoured man, with catholic tastes, intellectual interests and a wide circle of eminent friends among whom were included the evolutionist Thomas Huxley, the philosopher Herbert Spencer and the positivist Frederick Harrison.

Lawrencina Potter had a more difficult, introverted personality. An only daughter, she was brought up by her father, who was widowed early, as 'a scholar and a gentlewoman'. Both her father and brothers regarded her as a paragon of 'virtue, beauty and learning', and were inclined to indulge her. Beatrice always claimed that she was

> cursed with a divided personality; she was not at peace in herself. The discords in her nature were reflected in her physiognomy. In profile, she was, if not ugly, lacking grace . . . Looked at thus, she was obviously a managing woman, unrelenting, probably domineering, possibly fanatical. But her full face showed any such interpretation of her character to be a ludicrous libel. Here the central feature, the soul of her personality, were the eyes, soft hazel brown . . . eyes uniting in their light and shade the caress of sympathy with the quest of knowledge . . . clearly a woman to charm, perhaps to inspire.[1]

Beautiful and efficient, Beatrice's mother had a puritanical streak which caused her to suppress her emotions and appear forbidding to her children. Her inability to relate to her own sex made living with her difficult for her daughters, particularly Beatrice whom she dismissed as the least intelligent of the family. When her son, on whom she had centred all her emotions, died, she retired more and more into herself. She left her daughters to run the many Potter households whilst she immersed herself in an eccentric programme of self-improvement which consisted of mastering foreign grammars in languages other than their own, so that she learnt Greek grammar in French, Hebrew grammar in German and Spanish grammar in Scandinavian. A strict follower of the Utilitarian economists, she believed it was the duty of every individual to better himself and in so doing the whole of society would prosper. She longed to accept religious orthodoxies but found it impossible to do so.

Beatrice's parents met in romantic circumstances. Both were making the Grand Tour with younger relatives when, by chance, they met in Rome and immediately fell in love. They married soon after their return to England in 1844 and moved to Herefordshire. Inheritors of substantial wealth, they had hoped for a pleasant and leisurely life of country pursuits, but the financial crisis of 1847 and 1848 swallowed up their fortune. Four years after his marriage Richard Potter was forced to look for a living. His path, however, was smoothed by his father-in-law: within a short time he was both a director of the Great Western Railway, and a partner in a prosperous timber business.

The crash of 1848 proved the making of Richard Potter. He turned out to be a brilliant planner, an imaginative and pragmatic negotiator and an excellent administrator. As a promoter and speculator, he was remarkably successful, amassing great wealth from the Crimean War by supplying both the French and the British with wooden huts for their armies. He became involved in a 'maze of capitalist undertakings', becoming a director of two famous railway companies, the Great Western Railway, and the Grand Trunk Railway of Canada, as well as of the Hudson Bay Company. He was also involved in smaller enterprises such as the manufacture of railway signals. The Radical tradition of his family was much weaker in Richard, who began as a Liberal but ended up by failing to get elected, by twenty eight votes, as a Conservative Parliamentary candidate for Gloucester. However, after the 1867 Reform Act he came to dislike Disraeli as much as Gladstone. Until he died, Richard Potter believed that a paternalistic form of government, made up from the leisured, and therefore least partisan, classes, was the best way to rule the country.

But, despite his conservatism, Richard Potter accepted change. As Beatrice noted

> once the suffrage had been lowered he became enthusiastic about working class education. 'We must educate our masters', he was never tired of asserting. 'If necessary we must send our daughters to educate the masses', was an indiscreet remark at a political meeting which shocked the Conservatives and infuriated the Radicals.[2]

If anything, Richard Potter's exhortation 'to send our daughters to educate the masses' was a demonstration of his belief in female ability. Beatrice once said that he was the only man she knew who genuinely believed that women were superior to men. In his family life, he freely discussed religion, politics, philosophy and sex with his wife and daughters as if they were equals. The most important influence in the life of his nine daughters, it is clear that Beatrice derived much of her love of intellectual pursuits from the stimulating atmosphere inspired by her father.

The peripatetic nature of the Potter household must have been very unsettling for Beatrice. Her parents moved from mansion to mansion, seldom staying long in one place, spending some months in Gloucestershire, moving to London for the season, and then going on to either Westmoreland or Monmouthshire for the summer months. It was a nomadic existence with no one person or place that was permanent. 'The world of human intercourse in which I was brought up was in fact an endless series of human beings, unrelated one to the other . . . a miscellaneous crowd who came into and went out of our lives, rapidly and unexpectedly.'[3] It meant that Beatrice (whose formal education was perhaps most neglected of all the Potter girls) was left very much to her own devices. Looking back on her early life, she later claimed that she spent much of her childhood among domestic servants 'creeping in the shadow of my baby brother's birth and death', with the only compensating factor the stimulus she derived from her father's intellectual houseguests. Beatrice found no solace in the succession of nurses and governesses, so typical of middle and upper class Victorian homes; but she was fortunate enough to discover a much loved confidant in 'Dada', Lawrencina's companion and distant relative with whom the lonely and ignored little girl experienced some of the warmth and companionship lacking in her relationship with her mother. Beatrice adored Dada – the only saint, she later wrote, she ever knew. She mothered the entire household, nursed and comforted the children and spoke up for them when they were in disgrace. Most important of all, she taught Beatrice the importance of the 'overpowering consciousness of love' which she bestowed on any person in need.

Beatrice, whose ethereal good looks and sweet smile can already be seen in early photographs, grew up as an introspective child much given to fits of gloom and despair, as well as such minor ailments as nervous headaches and neuralgia which she later admitted were psychosomatic. She looked back on that period with little affection recalling that it,

> was not on the whole a happy one, ill-health and starved affection and the mental disorders which spring from these: ill-temper and resentment marred it . . . long dreary times of brooding and resentfulness, sharp pangs of mortified vanity and remorse for untruthfulness, constant physical discomfort and frequent pain, absorbed the greater part of my existence – and its *loneliness* was absolute. (8 April 1884)

Her intellectual curiosity was encouraged by her father from a very early age so that, even though she had very little formal teaching, she took her educational studies seriously. Indeed, one of her first entries in her diary, written at the age of eleven, shows that she was able to look at girls' education with remarkable detachment but also with a priggish self-consciousness. She recorded that, in her opinion, not enough thought was given to the problem; girls were encouraged to read novels which, she claimed, destroyed the young mind and encouraged the habit of make-believe – so much so that 'it is a habit that is so thoroughly inured in me, that I cannot make a good resolution without making a castle in air about it' (1869).

Beatrice began to write her diary regularly in the last months of 1872, when she was still fourteen, and continued to do so until her death seventy years later. She poured into it all her longings, her emotional frustrations and her deep anxiety; the diary was the confidant she never really had. She imagined marvellous death scenes of repentence, hid chloroform (which evaporated) in case she should want to commit suicide and agonised over her attention-seeking. 'I am very disgusted with myself', she wrote at the beginning of the diary. 'whenever I am in the company of any gentleman, I cannot help wishing and doing all I possibly can to attract his attention and admiration . . . I am *very very* wicked' (23 December 1872). From the first the diary shows a mind infused by guilt, intent on sublimating natural feelings, filled with religious doubt. Despite resenting and even disliking her mother, she and Lawrencina had much in common. Beatrice fought a continuous battle between her sensual emotions and her puritanical self-criticism, a battle which troubled and tormented her throughout her life.

At fifteen she went with her father and her sister Kate to America, a journey which stimulated her and took her out of herself although she fell ill towards the end. It was then that she began to write her diary on a regular basis. Back in England her previous anxieties returned. Beatrice was worried and unhappy about her personal relationships with her family, particularly her mother, with whom she was conscious that there was 'a kind of feeling of dislike and distrust which I believe is mutual' (24 March 1874). She began to search more earnestly for some aim in life. 'Perhaps I shall find some day' she wrote bleakly, 'a solution to this great difficulty of how I ought to employ my time' (24 October 1873).

Beatrice's introspection led her towards religion. She had 'gone off the path of orthodox religion' by the time she was sixteen, and now began to look for a 'firm belief of my own'. She sought a religion which was unselfish and demanded the highest duties from the self, 'the power of self-sacrifice in the individual for the good of the community'. Her studies included Catholicism, Buddhism and the 'Religion of Humanity'. Revealingly, the latter with its firm appeal to selfless duty, only partly caught her imagination – there was too little mysticism for Beatrice. Anxiously searching for a faith which might satisfy her, she read the Bible and Plato, translated Faust, immersed herself in Jewish history and even took up spiritualism.

She began to believe that she might become a novelist, avidly reading George Eliot, whose moral stance she approved, while at the same time dismissing Charlotte Brontë for her emotionalism.

Beatrice was very much aware that she had two sides to her character; that of her severe 'gloomily religious' mother and that of her more open and emotional father. The battle between moral duty and worldly passion she fought secretly, her diary being the only recipient of her confidences. She was not always the studious bluestocking. Partly because her mother had more or less opted out, her sisters allowed her to take part in the round of dances of the London season when Beatrice was in her middle teens. Most of them were as beautiful and intelligent as Beatrice and found no difficulty in getting married, so that year after year successful Potter engagements were made to rising young men. Lallie, the eldest, married Robert Holt the shipowner in 1867; she was followed three years later by Mary who married a mill-owner, Arthur Playne; Georgie and Blanche the next two sisters in line, married respectively a banker, Daniel Meinertzhagen, and a surgeon, Will Cripps, in 1873 and 1877. Sometimes Beatrice regretted the empty, hectic, frivolity of the summer months; at other times she was carried away by the excitement and glitter of the round of balls and dinner parties. But usually her high moral sense of purpose tinged the rapture with guilt.

It was in 1877 when she was nineteen and the year after she had 'come out', that Beatrice, still anxiously pursuing her search for personal salvation, seriously began to study the work of a great family friend, Herbert Spencer, 'the incessantly ratiocinating philosopher', perhaps the most eminent of living Victorian thinkers. He was a frequent visitor to the Potter household and from the first had encouraged the young and rather shy Beatrice:

> Memory recalls a finely sculptured head, prematurely bald, long stiff upper-lip and powerful chin, obstinately compressed mouth, small sparkling grey eyes, set close together, with a prominent Roman nose – altogether a remarkable headpiece dominating a tall, spare, well articulated figure, tapering off into diminutive and well-formed hands and feet.[4]

He became the intellectual confidant she had never had, taking her for long walks, earnestly explaining evolution and philosophy to his intelligent pupil, who was particularly affected by the harmony in nature that Spencer claimed to have discovered. Initially, his *First Principles* opened up new hopes for one who had so far found no substitute for orthodox religion. Duty, she understood, but she, like so many other Victorians in the age of the scientific revolution, needed more. 'One has always feared', she wrote on 15 December of that year, 'that when the orthodox religion vanished, no mystery could and would be explained and become commonplace – but instead of that each new discovery of science will increase our wonder at the Great Unknown, and our appreciation of the Great Truth'. Although Beatrice was ultimately dissatisfied with his emphasis on rationality, she gained much from Spencer, for whom she had 'an unmeasured admiration' and from whose evolutionary theory of society she learnt to understand the significance of empirical evidence and its importance to a scientific method of reasoning. 'What he taught me to discern was not the truth, but the relevance of facts.'

Soon after her twentieth birthday, Beatrice was sent to Germany (partly as a cure for her nervous tension) with her sister Mary, whose husband, Arthur Playne, also accompanied them. She found that she had little liking for the Germans, 'dirty, slovenly creatures, so underbred and rowdy-looking', she criticised sharply in a tone typical of her later comments when abroad. Beatrice, like so many of her Victorian contemporaries, travelled frequently to Europe, mostly to Germany and Italy, the latter for culture, the former for its combination of culture and open air exercise. Like her compatriot fellow-travellers, Beatrice, although remaining abroad for considerable lengths of time, rarely took any interest in the inhabitants of the countries she visited, judging them by English standards and usually finding them wanting. This narrowness of vision was to handicap the Webbs considerably when they journeyed abroad for serious social investigation.

Back in England, Beatrice returned to the opulent and gay life of the Potter family. Purposelessness constrained and irritated her. Her spirits fell, physically she grew listless and anaemic; headaches, neuralgia and other psychosomatic symptoms plagued her days. It was all due, she wrote, to a 'want of employment, which makes life almost a torture, a silent misery, all the more painful because apparently causeless' (30 March 1879). Her reaction 'to the restless and futile activities of society life' was to return with greater determination to her self-imposed studies. She read widely, finding particular comfort in Ruskin and Goethe. She also escaped from her family with her favourite sister Maggie in the summer of 1878 on an enjoyable reading holiday in the Lake District which she described as one of her happiest memories. Maggie brought her the friendship that had long eluded her in her early childhood; 'warm hearted and self-sacrificing', she was a witty, erudite and stimulating companion on the long rides and walks with which the Potter girls wiled away the dull months in the country between 'bouts of London society, country-house visiting and foreign travel'.

Sadly for Beatrice, her new relationship only lasted a short time. In 1880 Maggie married Henry Hobhouse – a man of 'cultivated refinement' with 'a sense of social obligation' who later became an MP. Her remaining unmarried sisters followed Maggie's example. In 1881, Theresa married Charles Alfred Cripps, a brilliantly successful barrister, who later became a Conservative attorney-general, although as Lord Parmoor he joined the first Labour government in 1924; and in 1883 Kate, the second oldest sister, married Leonard Courtney, later Liberal Deputy Speaker of the House of Commons, whose 'massive intelligence' and 'amazing memory' were 'combined with the intellectual integrity and personal disinterestedness of a superman'.

By the age of twenty three, Beatrice found herself head of a household consisting of her mother, who was leading her own eccentric and withdrawn existence; her father, for whom, as befitted a great captain of industry, she had to entertain lavishly; and the younger sister, Rosy, who had been much affected by the death of Dicky, the little brother, and whose subsequent rejection by Lawrencina stunted her emotionally for many years. For Beatrice the social requirements of a rich industrial household, even one as liberal as that of Richard Potter, were an irksome constraint. Her dilemma was that she was an intelligent female whose accepted duty lay in the home but who yearned secretly to practise 'the craft of the social investigator'. Or, at any rate, to perform some kind of useful research which would help in the advancement of society. There seemed to be no escape – hence her growing despair and bitterness, and the strange and prolonged bouts of fever.

In May 1882, her mother, with whom she had begun to have a better and more understanding relationship, died suddenly, and Beatrice was now left in sole charge of the Potter households. She felt a deep sense of loss at her mother's death and regretted that she and her mother had grown to know each other too late; 'I never knew how much she had done for me,' she wrote sadly a few months after her death, 'how many of my best habits I had taken from her, how strong would be the impress of her personality when the pressure had gone' (27 August 1882). Her remorse tinged her days with added sadness, so that, looking back, she could see only the pain and the frustration. In search of consolation, Beatrice turned once more towards religion for help and began going to church. As a form of atonement, she also vowed that she would give up her intellectual pursuits and take up society life in order to gain the full-hearted support and affection of her family, who, she felt, had little regard for her efforts at self improvement.

But Beatrice was too committed to her inner life for the mood of self-abnegation to last. It was not long before she was at her studies, even though she was much occupied with the running of the various households. Indeed, her mother's death had one surprising and unexpected result. Because she now had so much less time for herself, she began to get up at five in the morning so that she could squeeze three extra precious hours out of the day. This addition to her duties had the beneficial effect of making her less neurotic. She became more energetic, less inclined towards self-criticism, and, at least temporarily gave up her moods of depression.

The months following her mother's death were crucial in other ways. After the shock had worn off, the weight of her new responsibilities began again to seem unbearable. 'At present I feel like a caged animal,' she wrote towards the end of March, 'bound up by the luxury, comfort and respectability of my position. I can't get a training that I want without neglecting my duty' (31 March 1883). She realised that her seven married sisters had little understanding of either her intellectual curiosity or her desperate need for some sort of 'craft'. They would have been far-sighted Victorians had they done so. Beatrice, therefore, 'silently withdrew' all her hopes and plans for 'self-culture and self-expression from family discussion – a reserve which entailed isolation and loneliness'.

Privately, however, she turned to new subjects as if to push herself to her utmost intellectual limits. She now began a course of reading on political science – much more taxing than previous literary and historical excursions. She was attempting, she admitted, to work out means whereby what she called the 'imbalances of society' could be redressed. It was the first time that she had interested herself in the problems of the modern world.

Her initial reactions were Malthusian; she came to the conclusion that reproduction of the working class had to be arrested, judging that emigration, that particular favourite of some sections of the upper middle classes, was unworkable. 'Perhaps one of the strongest arguments for further intellectual education of the masses' she wrote, 'is that the direct physical effect and the indirect moral effect (making life unbearable without certain conditions) will, in all probability, arrest the increase of the population up to their means of bare subsistence'. Her argument at this time was simple: the more the poor could be educated to accept middle class mores, the more likely they would be to wish to raise their standard of living by cutting back on family size.

In early spring 1883, Beatrice backed up her new intellectual interest with practical experience and joined the philanthropic Charity Organisation Society. The COS was founded by, among others, the well-known philanthropist Octavia Hill. The main purpose of the Organisation (and one extremely fashionable in the nineteenth century) was to make the poor more self-dependent, by cutting out indiscriminate charity, which was seen as a means whereby the 'average sensual man' was demoralised and made incapable of steady work. On her charitable visits to Soho, she came for the first time into contact with the poor and the destitute. Her reactions were interesting. Unlike most middle class do-gooders, she questioned the usefulness of the COS and boldly came to the conclusion that the giver of charity to those they believed were 'deserving' of it gained more than the recipient. 'One thing is clear in my mind', she noted 'it is distinctly advantageous to go among the poor. We can get from them an experience of life which is novel and interesting; the study of their lives and surroundings gives us the facts where-with we can attempt to solve the social problem' (18 April 1883). She concluded that charity was irrelevant unless backed-up by statistical data which would pin-point accurately those in greatest need. The type of philanthropy practised by the COS was, she concluded, actually damaging in that it failed to tackle the roots of the problem of poverty.

The year 1883 was also important emotionally. On 3 June Beatrice was introduced to Joseph Chamberlain at a dinner. Regarded as the most brilliant Radical politician of his day, he was also one of the most eligible. Now forty seven and twice widowed unexpectedly, his good looks, handsome figure and masterful oratory, created a powerful impression on all those who met him. An ambitious and successful municipal reformer, his reorganisation of the Liberal Party made him one of the most influential Liberal politicians, while his advocacy of social reform earned him the leadership of the growing radical elements in the party.

Beatrice's reactions on their first meeting were guarded but she was also fascinated. 'I do and I don't, like him', she recorded. 'Talking to "clever men" in society is a snare and a delusion as regards interest. Much better read their books' (3 June 1883). It was clear, however, that they were immediately attracted to each other, even though Beatrice was very much aware that a gulf might exist between the fantasy of a brilliant and successful marriage to someone whose ideas she admired, and the realisation that Joseph Chamberlain was looking more for a helpmate than an intellectual equal. From the beginning of their acquaintance he made his views known to her: 'It pains me to hear any of my views controverted,' he told her. Nevertheless, Beatrice found him 'a curious and interesting character' and though they saw each other rarely, she thought of him constantly, fascinated and, at the same time, repelled. She always acknowledged that she would never be able to accept a subordinate role and yet she could not help being attracted by the idea of being married to a charismatic and famous politician.

The months that followed the June meeting were ones of torment. Beatrice was unsure of herself and unsure of Chamberlain's feelings towards her. In the autumn she was invited to spend a week at his London house by his daughter, Beatrice, with whom she had become very friendly. Advice on the suitability of Chamberlain as a suitor was freely given by her sisters. Mary Playne felt that Beatrice's 'social and practical powers' made her a perfect candidate as the wife of a famous politician. Theresa, however, enjoined Beatrice to 'look at the man himself as a man'. In turn, she invited him in the New Year, with his family, to the Potters' Monmouthshire home, The Argoed. She had had high hopes of the visit and felt 'as if I were dancing in a dream towards some precipice' (12 January 1884). She awaited his arrival with something akin to panic: 'my tortured state cannot long endure – the to be or not to be will soon be settled' she wrote. She felt herself in the midst of a terrifying dilemma, 'principle versus feeling' to which there seemed no solution. She became tense and anxious, unnecessarily so, she later admitted, as Chamberlain was only feeling the ground, in that he had not yet made up his mind about Beatrice.

Drawn to his politics, fascinated by his personality, ready to be swept off her feet, Beatrice nevertheless found herself in immediate argument with him – over the question of authority. She asked him whether he would allow differences of opinion to be expressed in his house. 'No', he said firmly, 'and that little word ended our intercourse' wrote Beatrice. His stay had proved a near disaster and the visit finished on a cool note. 'He was simply determined to assert his convictions', Beatrice recalled bitterly. He was, she complained, a totally political animal, an 'enthusiast and a despot', with a

> keen, calculating intellect, admirable in manipulating practical detail and in adapting the means to the end, considerable diplomatic power and personal influence over men . . . And now that is all over, I have a stunned feeling as I gradually wake up to the old surroundings. (12 January 1884)

Even so, tempted by his attraction for her, his magnetic personality, and perhaps by the role of influential political hostess, Beatrice, against her better judgement, could not bring herself to break with him.

At the end of January she went to stay with the Chamberlains at their 'gloomy and richly overpowering' Birmingham mansion.

Watching him at a political rally, seeing him play with the emotions of the crowd, she was disturbed but once again fascinated. She now accepted that she had fallen in love with Joseph Chamberlain but was not sanguine about the outcome. 'I don't know how it will all end', she noted sadly in her diary.

> Certainly not in *my happiness*. As it is, his personality absorbs all my thought and he occupies a too prominent position for me not to be continually reminded of him . . . if the fates should unite us (against *my* will) all joy and lightheartedness will go from me. I shall be absorbed into the life of a man, whose aims are not my aims, who will refuse me all freedom of thought in my intercourse with him; to whose career I shall have to subordinate all my life, mental and physical, without believing in the usefulness of this career whether it be inspired by earnest conviction or by ambition. (16 March 1884)

And yet she could not break away. 'I have loved and lost; but possibly by my own wilful mishandling, possibly also for my own happiness; but still lost' (9 May 1884).

There is no doubt that the affair affected Beatrice both physically and mentally. She became gloomy and introspective once more, given to melancholia and severe bouts of mental depression. Afraid that if she married Chamberlain she would lose her personality and independence, she was still drawn towards him. His 'temperament and his character are intensely attractive to me. I feel I could relieve the gloom, could understand the mixed motive and the difficulties of a nature in which genuine enthusiasm and personal ambition are so curiously interwoven', she wrote in spite of herself (22 April 1884). And yet at the same time she understood that marriage to Chamberlain would mean the end of her independence. Love, hero-worship, pride and anger fought each other and left her exhausted. Bitterly she came to the conclusion that Chamberlain did not love her and that she should try not to see him again.

Finally matters came to a head. Kate Courtney invited them both to a picnic among the Burnham Beeches in Buckinghamshire – the most painful day of her life, Beatrice later wrote. Chamberlain behaved with 'marked rudeness and indifference' and Beatrice understood that whatever had been between them had now vanished. In November came a further blow. Chamberlain's sister, Clara Ryland, invited her to come and stay during her brother's absence. Beatrice, overwhelmed by past memories, could not contain her feelings, only to be sharply informed by Clara that her 'brother had never thought of me'. The pain of her deeply felt emotion and rejection was too much.

One result of her obsession was a new interest in politics. She took to considering the nature of government, returning to her father's own line of argument that a 'correct diagnosis' by the ablest minds was infinitely to be preferred to democracy. Her self confidence, never strong, dropped to its lowest ebb: 'I see clearly', she wrote bleakly, 'that my intellectual faculty is only mirage, that I have no special mission, to discover and tell ought to mankind' (9 May 1884). Six months later she still despaired: 'I get up and look at myself: a strong healthy body – looking as if it had centuries before it. No release yet; years of health before you. How is it that anyone cares for life? I have always hoped for better – and better has never come' (26 November 1884).

Even though (in itself surely an additional hurt) Chamberlain had never actually proposed nor declared himself in love, Beatrice's passionate nature had received a shattering blow. 'I am constantly weary;' she confessed in November, 'life is a continual struggle . . . Still . . . there is interest enough in life – and affection too – and this gnawing pain will cease – in time. I have not yet fully realised the *uselessness* of it' (8 November 1885). The following year she received a cool letter from Chamberlain.

> And so the agony of two years ends . . . Is it ended now? I think so. Double-mindedness has run right through – a perpetual struggle between conscience on the one hand and feeling on the other – not had the courage to follow either to the bitter end – hence my misery. And on his side hatred of insubordination and personal attraction possibly tinged with pity, for I believe the man believed I loved him – so I did! Anyhow, these last words from me close it. God help me. (6 March 1886)

But it was another three years before Beatrice, who had cared for Chamberlain so passionately, was to feel at peace with herself.

Her mainstay during these long months was her continued studies. She began an attempt to synthesise what she had learned from Spencer with the positivist theory she had begun to assimilate from reading Comte. In 1883 Beatrice had come to the conclusion that a study of science was imperative for those who wished to examine the workings of society – the harmonies of nature might give direction to social scientists. She had even asked one of her brothers-in-law, the famous surgeon, Willy Cripps, to give her lessons in biology. She, like other Victorians before her, had begun to believe that the clue to human progress lay in the sciences – and Beatrice, always thorough, felt she ought to master at least the simpler concepts. Despite her keenness, however, she discovered that the study of natural sciences bored her, and became convinced that the subjects she was really interested in were those dealing with the social conditions of man: 'from the flight of emotion away from the service of God to the service of man and from the current faith in the scientific method', she wrote later, 'I drew the inference that the most hopeful form of social service was the craft of a social investigator'.[5]

That same year, when she was twenty five, Beatrice undertook her first piece of social investigation. She had reached the conclusion that the cases of extreme destitution, dealt with by the Charity Organisation, were not characteristic of the working classes in general. Beatrice, therefore, decided to see for herself how other areas compared. She persuaded her old nurse, Margaret Jackson, ('Dada'), to allow her to accompany her on a visit to distant relations in Bacup, a cottonmill town in Lancashire. Beatrice had discovered that Dada was also a far-flung cousin of the Potter family herself, so that the visit would be to her own Potter kinsmen. She decided to go in disguise simply because she felt that a Miss Jones, a Welsh farmer's daughter, would be that much easier accepted by her artisan cousins than the rich Miss Potter. A bold and imaginative gesture for a rich, middle class girl, the journey had momentous consequences. She managed for a few weeks to live as a member of the artisan classes and the impressions she gained remained with her for life, radically altering its direction.

She was impressed by both the simplicity and earnestness she found among the people of Bacup as well as by their kindliness and spirit of self-reliance. She found the visit 'less amusing and much more interesting' than she had expected. 'I was surprised at their fair-mindedness', she wrote in a letter to her father soon after she arrived. 'And at the kindliness of their view of men and things; now they all recognise that men get on from having certain qualities, and that "no makin' of laws can alter that".'[6] Their way of life, particularly their involvement in the Co-operative Movement, was a revelation to Beatrice whose immediate reaction was to conclude that it was in such communities that a new basis of society could be found. Now that religion mattered less, it 'seems to me', she wrote to her father, 'of great importance that the political thought should take a practical instead of a theoretical line; that each section of the community should try experiments on a small scale, and that the promoters should see and reap the difficulties and disadvantages of each experiment as it is executed'.[7] And what she glimpsed was 'the difference between trying to alleviate poverty and seeking to eliminate it'.

So by 1884, when she was twenty six, Beatrice had begun to lead a strange double existence, combining the empty life of a fashionable society hostess with the discipline and stimulus of intellectual studies, backed up by the occasional investigative foray into the life of the destitute. But because she was lonely and also because she could not rid herself of her obsession with Chamberlain, Beatrice was wracked by self-doubt. She began to question earnestly what she called 'my small attempts at self-culture', deciding that it would be wiser to direct her energies into a more suitable field – that of community work. Here, apart from being a recognised occupation for the spinster daughters of the rich middle classes, she felt she might at least be useful. A chance came when her sister Kate, who had married Leonard Courtney, barrister and rising young politician, gave up her unpaid job as rent collector and quasi-social worker in St Katherine's Buildings near Tower Bridge. These new dwellings, a part of Octavia Hill's charitable housing schemes, were purpose-built for the more 'deserving poor', who had to be rehoused due to slum-clearing projects.

Evidence of Octavia Hill's severe approach to the problem of the 'deserving poor', St Katherine's Buildings were five-stories high, built as a 'super-economical structure', whose two main requirements were low rents and 'physically sanitary buildings'. The rent collecting entailed administration and general overseeing and, although Beatrice initially found the 'collective brutality' of the inhabitants frightening, and hated the personal emotional involvement, the work soon began to stir her imagination. Though it was not quite what she wanted, by the middle of the following year she finally decided what she would be good at was finding out and understanding 'the conditions of the working class in the way of "Housing", by digesting the evidence of others, testing and supplementing it by my own observation and actual effort in that direction'. She went on,

> to study state interference in its two separate functions is the special question: first of enforcing respect in the individual for the health of others – obliging the individual to fulfil the acknowledged or unacknowledged contract with society – and secondly, that more doubtfully natural function – its attempt to supplement by direct constructive activity the work of voluntary enterprise and of individual effort. (6 October 1885)

Beatrice had now come to accept that the life of a social investigator, whose findings would influence the making of social policy, was her true vocation.

She quickly showed her qualities of imagination and initiative. It was not long before she was proposing to Canon Barnett of Toynbee Hall a scheme whereby all those agencies involved in the housing of the poor should collect data and pool their resources in one central association. Even though the Canon was impressed, Beatrice wrote to her father in a mood of self-doubt that she lacked method and strength,

> both fail me in critical times. I have a much greater *show* of ability than reality, arising from my audacity of mind and plausible way of putting things. My dear old Father, I am a sort of weak edition of you! There is no doubt about it. I enjoy planting but don't care for the tending![8]

It was at this time that Beatrice began quite consciously to form friendships with those involved in either philanthropic work or social investigation. Among those she admired most were Canon Barnett and his wife Henrietta. Rector of St Jude's and founder of Toynbee Hall, with his 'diminutive body clothed in shabby and badly assorted garments, big knobby, and prematurely bald head', the Canon was famous in the East End for his 'fathomless sympathy', humility and inspiring encouragement. The Barnetts broke with the COS in 1886, partly because of its harsh attitude towards the poor. The second couple who influenced Beatrice's life profoundly were the Booths – Charles, Liverpool shipowner and merchant by profession, married to Beatrice's clever and charming cousin, Mary. Tall, abnormally thin, 'garments hanging as if on pegs, the complexion of a consumptive girl . . . the whole countenance dominated by finely-moulded brow and large, observant grey eyes, Charles Booth was an attractive but distinctly queer figure of a man'.[9] His most important attributes were an overpowering intellectual curiosity about the nature of things, originality, and a deeply-held belief in the need for man's service to man. Powerfully influenced by the new ferment raging over the various questions connected with poverty, Charles Booth came to the conclusion that there could be no solution to the problem until an accurate picture was formed on the basis of a closely investigated statistical survey. Hence his famous Inquiry into the Conditions of the East End, which later came out (in seventeen volumes) as *The Life and Labour of the People in London*.

Nevertheless, Beatrice, whatever her inclinations, could spend little time on the rent-collecting or thinking about the problems of the poor, as her duties as a hostess to her father and the growing need to mother the disturbed Rosy took up most of her days. Indeed, generously she decided that a journey abroad might help to calm her sister's neuroses, even though she herself had little inclination for it. The plan was for them to travel towards the end of 1885. However, returning from voting in the November election of that year, Richard Potter had a stroke and was immediately paralysed. There was now no question of Beatrice being able to get away. The prospect ahead of her – long days spent looking after a semi-paralysed parent terrified her. She saw herself, as the oldest unmarried daughter, chained to his bedside for ever, unable to devote herself either to her studies or even her minor career in the East End. She despaired: 'If Death comes it will be welcome, for life has always been distasteful', she wrote dramatically three months later.

Her life seemed to be in ruins. Having at last begun to put a painful and humiliating relationship behind her, the possibility of becoming a social investigator had become more promising. Now it looked as if she would be tied down for ever with only memories to sustain her. 'Life seems to my consciousness a horrible fact,' she wrote in early February 1886:

> Sometimes I wonder how long I shall support it. I am never at peace with myself now – the whole of my past looks like an irretrievable blunder . . . I struggle through each new day – waking with suicidal thoughts early in the morning . . . Eight-and-twenty! living a life without hope . . . no future, but the vain repetition of the breaking waves of feeling. (11 February 1886)

Her father's stroke resulted in a complete rearrangement of her life.

Beatrice took him to Bournemouth to recover and was unable to return to her London commitments. The family now discovered that he had been making heavy losses (for which she, as his companion and business helpmate, was partly blamed by her relations), and it was decided to give up their grand London mansion, York House. It also meant that she would be exposed to a double burden as she would not only have to look after her father, but would also be in continual proximity to Rosy, whom she neither understood nor liked; this now filled her with further apprehension. 'I shall give her love', she wrote 'if she will let me, but not friendship; shall make it a condition that she obeys me' (19 June 1886). There was only one crumb of comfort. In January 1886, Beatrice had written a letter to the Pall Mall Gazette on the subject of unemployment in the East End. Britain was in the throes of a major depression, unemployment had risen so high that a Lord Mayor's fund had been set up to bring aid to the destitute. Beatrice argued against the setting up of relief work in the East End on the grounds that it would attract even more labour to an area in which there were already too few jobs. The Editor, impressed with Beatrice's argument, had asked whether or not he might turn the letter into an article, and 'A Lady's View of the Unemployed' was published that February. It was, as she noted, 'a turning point in my life'.

It also rather unfortunately opened up a new correspondence with Chamberlain, who read the article and asked if he could discuss it with her. A further correspondence ensued which prolonged Beatrice's agony for another eighteen months. It was not until July 1887 that it finally ended – for it was in that month that Beatrice suddenly, and with great passion, 'opened up her heart' to him, when he was once more a guest at the Argoed. Chamberlain's cool reception shamed her; and their letter-writing petered out. It is doubtful if Chamberlain was ever in love with Beatrice but he was plainly attracted to her. Given his need for a subservient partner, pride and self will were obstacles which he appeared unwilling to overcome, probably because by this time he was completely obsessed by his own political career. As to Beatrice, the unhappiness and humiliation caused by the relationship undoubtedly affected her personality.

Her emotional life in ruin, career blighted before it had started, Beatrice turned in that summer of 1886 to a study of political economy, as if the difficulties of the subject would eradicate the misery of her present situation. As was usual, her studies were thorough and she worked her way through every writer's work she could lay her hands on. She disciplined herself severely and for the first time tried her hand at a serious essay: 'The Rise and Growth of English Economics' for which she had publication hopes. However, little came of it – she gave it to Charles Booth whose advice was against sending it to editors of serious journals. But she persevered, mainly because writing was now her only link with the outside world.

Her second work, also unpublished, was a dismissive essay on Karl Marx. 'Karl Marx's analysis not only represents no order of things, but no *conceivable* order of things', she argued fiercely. She took the view that his assertion that labour was the only source of value was too narrow, and concluded that value had to correspond to social consumption. Marx's analysis, Beatrice claimed, took account neither of fashion nor of the difficulties of finding markets; nor of the 'manifold qualities essential' to the successful man of business. But her new interest (she had been invited by Charles Booth to be a member of the Board of Statistical Research) lay in the methodology of social sciences, particularly the question of what was the right relation of personal observation to statistical inquiry.

Her enforced confinement was broken by her other sisters' determination that she should be able to lead her own life, at least for part of the year. A new pattern was therefore evolved – she would spend eight months looking after Rosy and her father and the remaining four would be hers to do with what she would, while her sisters took her place. She opted to continue to work in the East End. However, though still ambitious to make her mark, Beatrice continued to be assailed by self-doubt: 'practical work does not satisfy me', she wrote miserably. 'It seems like walking on the shifting sand with the forlorn hope that the impress of your steps will be lasting to guide others across the desert' (8 November 1886). Nor did she find rent-collecting nor the management of St. Katherine's Buildings any more satisfying. 'The lady collectors', she noted somewhat tartly, 'are an altogether superficial thing . . . what are they in the face of this collective brutality – heaped up together in infecting contact – adding to each other's dirt, physical and moral' (8 November 1886).

However, a new field of study was opening up to her through Charles Booth. He had suggested that Beatrice join his Board of Statistical Research and then in December 1886, she agreed to help with his Inquiry by working on the data on dock labour in Tower

Hamlets. It was a marvellous opportunity for her, particularly as her duties at St. Katherine's Buildings were wearing her down both physically and mentally. She had come to the conclusion that rent-collecting was a waste of time, as it merely skirted round the problem of poverty and was therefore glad to leave it behind. Instead, she went happily to live at the Devonshire House Hotel, the Quakers' Headquarters in Bishopsgate, as soon as her sisters came down to relieve her from her duties in Bournemouth; her freedom was now more considerable than at any time since her mother's death.

Beatrice's earlier determination to become a social investigator, her long hours of study and her interest in methodology fitted her to her new work. The inquiry was one of the most searching of its kind. Charles Booth combined for the first time qualitative and quantitative data and by using numerous interviewers, attempted to cancel out personal biases, inevitable in any survey of that kind. It was a mammoth work whose findings horrified complacent contemporaries. The following extract from the diary gives the flavour of her daily routine in the docks. 'Go to docks early in the morning', she recorded in a revealing passage in May 1887

> Permanent men respectable, sober, clean. Casuals, low-looking bestial, content with their own condition. Watch brutal fight and struggle: then sudden dissolution of the crowd with coarse jokes and loud laughter . . . The mass of the rejected lounge down to another dock to spread themselves over the entrance of the various wharves . . . If a man weary of *ennui* and of an empty stomach drops off to sleep, his companions promptly search his pockets for the haphazard penny. (May 1887)

The inquiry also provided Beatrice with another stepping stone. The prestigious *Nineteenth Century* published an account of her investigation as 'Dock Life in the East End of London', in September 1887. This was followed by three other articles: 'The Tailoring Trade in East London'; 'Pages From a Workgirl's Diary', which gained her a *succès d'estime*; and, finally, 'The Lords' Committee on the Sweating System'. By 1890, Beatrice Potter had become a well-known name in progressive intellectual circles.

Her first article in the *Nineteenth Century* filled Beatrice with delight. She was happier at twenty nine, she now declared, than she had ever been: 'enter promising beginning'. 'It is strange', she wrote in a moment of reappraisal,

> that it is *the* work I have always longed to do – it is the realisation of my youthful ambition . . . I know now that I have no *talent*, that I am almost lacking in literary faculty. But I have originality of aim and method – and I have implicit faith that I am on the right track – and I have the sort of persistency which comes from despair of my own happiness. (30 September 1887)

Her self-deprecation was never far from the surface, even in moments of success.

Reluctantly, at the end of her investigation into dock labour, she came to the conclusion that it was the unchecked individual whims of the consumers that lay behind the serious unemployment of the docks. Tentatively, she suggested a remedy – municipal socialism which 'would facilitate a better organisation of trade and admit the dove-tailing of business'. Her investigations had led Beatrice into at least a partial, if unwilling, acceptance of collectivist principles. The inquiry not only helped establish her as an exceptionally able social investigator (she was a very sympathetic and careful interviewer) but it also gave her her first taste of public speaking. She was invited to attend a meeting of dock labourers in November 1887, where she met Ben Tillett, who was their Secretary. She was the only woman present – a foretaste of things to come – and 'as I made my way up to the platform I enjoyed the first experience of being "cheered" as a Public Character' (27 November 1887).

After the docks came the investigation into sweating in the tailoring trade. To gain as much information as possible, Beatrice described herself as 'a plain trouser hand', obtaining temporary jobs in various Jewish tailoring shops for short lengths of time. 'Settled with Charlie on the autumn's work', she recorded in early August. 'The Sweating System is to be the subject of my next paper. I have it in mind to make it more of a picture than my article on "Dock Life" – to dramatise it . . . I could not get at the picture without living among the actual workers' (8 August 1887). She was nothing if not thorough, interviewing in the months available to her, employers and employees, school board visitors, factory and sanitary inspectors, rent collectors, visiting home workers and small masters. She even trained as a trouser-hand in a domestic workshop of a former tenant of Katherine's Buildings.

First morning learning how to sweat. Mrs Moses 78, Oxford Street, Stepney. Four rooms and a kitchen, one-room let for 3/0s. House 12/-. Deserted street during the daytime. Public House at each corner. Small backyard. Three rooms on ground floor – two used as workshop. Large room with two machinists, Jew and Polish – and master who acts as presser. Back room, mistress, first hand who was a Scotch woman – two girls learning the trade. Coats turned out at 1/2d each, trimmings and thread supplied by the sweater. Button holes 4½d a dozen by woman outside . . . Evidently these people worked tremendously hard – women working from 8 to 10 without looking round and master working up to 2 o'clock and often beginning at 5 the next morning. (19 October 1887)

It was her first experience of real poverty and the conditions she encountered horrified her. Her analysis of the rationale behind the sweating system was surprisingly original. She showed that, paradoxically, the sweater was not the rich middle-man he had always been depicted, but as poor as his own hands. Beatrice described sweating as a mode of work carried out in overcrowded and insanitary workshops with long and irregular hours, constantly falling prices and a consequently low rate of wages for the mass of workers. It was not profits, which did not exist, that had to be attacked, but the conditions and wages of the workers. Sweaters, she unexpectedly concluded, were more the victims of the industrial system than the exploiters.

On 11 May 1888, Beatrice was called in front of the House of Lords Select Committee on the Sweating System. 'An inquiry into the sweating system', she told the Committee, was 'practically an inquiry into all labour employed in manufacture which had escaped the regulation of the Factory Act and trade unions'.[10] She stressed that pauper immigration, which had always been thought to have caused many of the problems, had little effect on the tailoring trade, even though it was often said that because Jews could live on less than their Gentile counterparts, they brought down the wages. Beatrice argued against such a narrow interpretation, pointing out that the trade was, in any case, divided into watertight compartments, so that neither Jews nor Gentiles affected each other's working conditions. She went on to suggest two remedies: that the landlord should be made responsible for his property and that better sanitation should be provided for the workshops.

Beatrice's appearance before the Select Committee caused a mild sensation. It was not often that a beautiful and intelligent young woman appeared to give evidence. 'A few Peeresses came down to stare at me!' she noted with amusement (12 May 1888). But what was more important to her was the fact that she had exaggerated the length of time she had worked as a trouser hand. Her conscience, always active, caused her sleepless nights. However, when the proofs of her evidence arrived for her to correct, she discovered how to remedy her earlier falsehood. She decided to tamper with her own words. But this falsification of her evidence caused her more despair and wakeful nights. As usual, Beatrice felt passionately about her wrong deeds, even contemplating suicide. The publicity she had gained from her articles and appearance before the Select Committee worried her. 'I brood over what will be thought or said about me', she wrote in an anxious mood of self criticism. 'Now feel elated by appreciation and praise, then down in the depths of misery from a sense of indifference or blame: think one day I am a genius, another day an utter failure' (21 July 1888).

The Select Committee published its findings in 1890. Its report skirted over the major issues within the sweating trade. Beatrice, asked to comment on its conclusions, reiterated her earlier impressions: 'It will be through awakening the sense of this responsibility', she wrote in the *Nineteenth Century*, 'through insisting on the performance of this duty by legislative enactment, by the pressure of public opinion and by all forms of voluntary combination that we can alone root out and destroy those hideous social evils known as the Sweating System.'[11] She had become firmly convinced that state intervention coupled to unionisation, alone could cure the evils of the tailoring trade. The strong impression that sweating made on her at that time is shown in a paper that she gave to the Co-operative Society a few years later.

> The sweater is, in fact, the whole nation. The mass of struggling men and women whose suffering have lately been laid bare, are oppressed and defrauded in every relation of life; by the man who sells or gives out the material on which they labour; by the shopkeeper who sells them provisions on credit, or forces them under the truck system; by the landlord who exacts, in return for the four walls of a bedroom, or for the unpaved and undrained backyard, the double rent of workshop and dwelling; and, lastly, by every man, woman and child who consumes the product of their labour.[12]

Through her work on Charles Booth's inquiry, Beatrice, whose capitalist background had taught her to believe in the power of individualism, had swung round to a growing realisation of the need for state intervention. Her new philosophy as yet had nothing to do with socialism – which she dismissed as 'catastrophic' – but it made her more receptive to new ideas. From a social investigator, fascinated by statistics and methodology and confirmed in her faith in the application of scientific methods to social organisation, she was gradually forced into discussing political questions. If the weaknesses of the capitalist world were to be rectified, its devastating results had somehow to be investigated.

Yet, while she began to develop new opinions about poverty and ways to deal with it, she still displayed attitudes which were typical of her class. In 'The Jews of East London' (published later with Sidney Webb and based on her experiences of this time), there is more than a hint of antisemitism. In an aside she appeared, even though applauding the Jews for their energy and initiative, to castigate them for their lack of social morality in that they seemed to wish to pursue only their own self-interest, irrespective of the needs of society as a whole; they were, she said, 'deficient in that highest and latest development of human sentiment – social morality'.[13] Antisemitism was linked to a general dislike of foreigners. In the article on dock labour published by the *Nineteenth Century*, she remarked that 'the presence of the foreigner is the only unpleasant feature common to East London which is omitted from the composition of dock and waterside life'.[14]

Although Beatrice was beginning to make her way in the world outside, she was still tied to her home. In August of that year, Rosy married, and Beatrice, at the age of thirty, found herself the last remaining unmarried Potter daughter. She began slowly to come to terms with her predicament. Her bouts of suicidal depression grew less frequent and she became conscious for the first time that she had what she called 'a marketable talent'. She realised that she was getting better known as invitations slowly trickled in; in November she was asked to give a paper at a trade union meeting at Oxford and Charles Booth again suggested that she should do more work on his Survey, this time on women's work in the East End. Beatrice could feel, with satisfaction, that, in spite of all the obstacles in front of her, she had begun to carve a niche for herself. The end of the year, which had started off with such success was, however, marred by Joseph Chamberlain's announcement of his forthcoming marriage, which sent her spinning into a nervous collapse. 'I walked about with a bit of cold steel in my heart – and at nights I tossed about with the heat and discomfort of feverishness from a festering sore' (10 November 1888). But at least, as she came to realise, the black cloud which had hung over her for six years was gone, having burst 'with a terrific flash and peal of thunder' (29 December 1888). She could now be at peace with herself.

Although Charles Booth had suggested she work for him again, Beatrice now had the self-confidence gained from her work in the East End to follow her own line of investigation. Her Bacup visit, which she had twice repeated, had stimulated her interest in the Co-operative Movement. She wondered whether it might provide a new alternative to the capitalist system. Although she had come to accept the need for state intervention, she felt herself alien from current socialist ideologies. The Social Democratic Federation alarmed her with their talk of revolution, and she had so far not come across the Fabian Society. Perhaps, she now felt, the answer might lie in a society based on self-governing workshops which by eliminating the capitalist entrepreneur would enable the workers themselves to own their own capital.

Such a field of enquiry, however, would mean a complete change of life-style. Not only would it entail breaking away from the Booth team but, given the thoroughness of her own approach, it would also mean long investigative visits away from her father, with whom she had recently moved to Box House in Gloucestershire, to be near her sister, Mary Playne. She would also now be involved in totally independent research unsupported by a team of investigators. Beatrice as usual doubted her own capacities and hesitated for some time before refusing Charles Booth's offer.

However, a visit to Cambridge in March 1889, when she was thirty one, hardened her resolve. She met Professor Marshall, then the leading English economist, at a dinner and asked his advice as to which course she ought to pursue. He immediately settled for the Booth enquiry on the grounds, he told her firmly, that it would be a waste for her to work on the history of the Co-operative Movement. Marshall pointed out that she not only had more facts about women workers at her command than anyone else, but, he added, she had, unlike most women

> a fairly trained intellect and the courage and capacity for original work . . . To sum it all up with perfect frankness: if you devote

> yourself to the study of your own sex as an industrial factor, your name will be a household word two hundred years hence; if you write a History of Co-operation, it will be superceded or ignored in a few years. (6 March 1889)

But the ambitious Miss Potter, nettled by Marshall's discouraging advice, decided for an inquiry into the Co-operative Movement.

There was a second reason why she rejected Charles Booth's suggestion. Earlier that year she had agreed to sign a famous anti-suffrage manifesto drafted by the novelist Mrs Humphrey Ward. It was a gesture she came to reject and was publicly to recant twenty years later. Her motives for signing were complex; she was genuinely prejudiced against politics and therefore saw little point in her own sex participating in it, either as voters or as politicians. She felt herself reacting against what she thought was her father's excessive over-evaluation of women. In addition, she herself had never felt discriminated against. Having by sheer determination made herself into that rare bird, 'a competent female writer on economic question', she found it easy to place her work and so did not understand the need for female emancipation. However, she accepted that the consequence of signing the manifesto was that her standing as an authority on problems of female labour would be suspect – another argument for the Co-operative project.

Beatrice's new studies began badly. On 7 March 1889, her father had another slight stroke and she found herself once more completely tied to his bedside. Filled with depression, she longed for his death. Even the weight of her spinsterhood seemed a deep burden: 'God knows', she wrote in despair, 'celibacy is as painful to a woman (even from the physical standpoint) as it is to a man – It could not be more painful than it is to a woman' (7 March 1889). She could not work and only found relief when her sister took over from her for a short spell.

By May she was back at The Argoed, their summer house in Monmouthshire, looking after her father, getting up at six to study the endless journals which the Co-operators had begun to send her. She managed to slip away to the Co-operative Congress at Ipswich on 6 June where she met up with friends she had made during her research; men like Benjamin Jones, the General Manager of the London Co-operative Wholesale Society, John Mitchell, the Chairman, and John Burnett, Labour Correspondent to the Board of Trade; even Professor Marshall was there. As usual she was much impressed, as she had been at Bacup, with the quality of the Co-operators who were very much the kind of working class men she approved of:

> Benjamin Jones [she noted] is a sort of combination of the high-minded grocer, the statesman and the wire-puller – in the Co-operative movement he is all three. Burnett has the dignity of a skilled mechanic, the self-reliance of a general, and the massive power of a leader of great strikes based on broad claims. (18 June 1889)

By August, however, in spite of the encouragement of the Co-operators, she was finding the work far more tedious than she had ever anticipated: 'A grind and no mistake'; she wrote complainingly. 'Six hours a day reading and note-taking from those endless volumes of Co-operative News' (20 August 1889). But she persevered. During 1889, she found time to travel through the midlands, the north and the Scottish lowlands, attending special meetings and sectional conferences, spending a few days in the great industrial towns, such as Manchester, Leeds, Glasgow and Newcastle, visiting the small stores as well as the grander emporia.

As she travelled, she began to draw unexpected conclusions. 'It seems to me', she wrote after she had been working on her investigations for some months, that the Co-operative Movement appeared

> to have been a movement not towards the sharing of profits by workers but towards an unconscious realisation of the socialist ideal of officially-managed business on the basis of voluntary (consumer) association . . . that it has embodied in its creed the ethics of industry, purity of goods, equal payments, and care for the workers. (And yet I am slow to accept a theory which ignores the whole idealism of the actual leaders.) (30 October 1889)

Another original conclusion which was to lead the Webbs into their great investigations into the trade union movement, was that the democracy of consumers represented by the Co-operative Movement needed to be balanced by the democracy of producers, represented by trade unions, because of the bias of the Co-operative

Movement towards the production of cheap goods for the consumers, without consideration for those that produced the goods. The Board of the Co-operative Wholesale Society, she claimed, absent-mindedly forgot about the conditions of employment of their staff and, therefore, had to be reminded by those who represented the workforce. The process by which wages and conditions should be decided she called 'collective bargaining' which she described as 'the social relation which will supercede the individual relation'. Here, even in her use of technical terms, Miss Potter was breaking new ground.

Apart from its originality, the book on the Co-operative Movement had one other result. She was convinced from that time on that self-governing workshops (which, she pointed out to the co-operators, whatever their originators believed, their societies were not) had no chance of success. This was one of the main reasons why the Webbs were later to reject the arguments of the Syndicalists and the Guild Socialists.

There is also no doubt that Beatrice's research among the co-operators, unique for a woman of that time, earned her not only respect and admiration but, more important for their later work, also enabled the Webbs to gain an entrée into the trade union world. It is therefore as much to Beatrice as to Sidney that the Webbs were to owe their more practical approach to the formation of the coming socialist state.

Although she spent eight months of the year by her father's bedside, Beatrice, even though isolated in the country, was affected by outside events. The late 1880s were a time of recession and industrial unrest, which resulted in such outbreaks of violence as Bloody Sunday in 1887, when a march organised by the Social Democratic Federation was brutally broken up by the police. Beatrice had barely noted it but the growing militancy of the dock workers in the summer months of 1889 had, not surprisingly given her interest in the East End, caught her imagination, and the solidarity of the dockers was a revelation to her. She noted shrewdly that it was vital to harness public opinion to ensure trade union victory and that a strike in the capital was infinitely more crippling than one in the provinces.

A month later, in September, she went to the TUC Conference at Dundee which was held while the dock strike was still on. Here she met not only the older unionists, men such as Henry Broadhurst, the major figure on the Parliamentary Committee of the TUC, but the new militant socialists like Will Thorne and Ben Tillett, bent on reforming the older institutions. Beatrice had little sympathy with the new unionists, whom she described in a telling aside as men with 'dirty personalities with which they pelt each other, with their envy and malice against any leader and with their ignorance, one might almost say their contempt and hatred for facts' (1 September 1889). She saw in them all the qualities which she most disliked – lack of moral fibre, selfish class preoccupations, no interest in the common good – and was therefore all the more pleased that their demand for an independent working class political party was defeated.

Dundee was a short interlude and immediately afterwards Beatrice returned home to her sick father and the arid mass of print 'and interminable volumes' of the Co-operative journals. Her isolation whetted her appetite for a greater involvement in the stirring events taking place around her. She felt

> exiled from the world of the thought and action of other men and women. London is in a ferment: Strikes are the order of the day, the New Trade Unionism with its magnificant conquest of the Docks is striding along with an arrogance rousing employers to a keen sense of danger and to a determination to strike against strikes.

She was intensely moved by the excitement around her:

> The Socialists, led by a small set of able young men (the Fabian Society) are manipulating London radicals . . . I, from the peculiarity of my social position, should be in the midst of all parties – sympathetic with all – allied with none . . . And the whole seems a whirl of contending actions, aspirations and aims out of which I dimly see the tendency towards a socialist community in which there will be individual freedom and public property in the stead of class-slavery and private possession of the means of subsistence of the whole People. At last I am a *Socialist*! [she exclaimed triumphantly] This is where observation and study have led me, in spite of training, class bias. (1 February 1890)

Beatrice may have been surprised by her discovery that she was a socialist but she had been moving in that direction, albeit slowly and tentatively for a number of years. As early as 1885, she had talked of 'taking from a whole class that which had been stolen' (7 August 1885), but it was her work as a social investigator from 1887 which caused her to examine more critically the functions of the state and the role of the individual within society. Beatrice came to believe that state intervention was a necessary supplement to individual effort and that she was a 'true socialist through my willingness to sacrifice the individual to the community' (15 March 1887). She also considered that state regulations of working conditions should be buttressed by what she called 'the provision of a "national minimum" for all citizens, which would include free education, health, leisure amenities and public provision for the aged and infirm, to be paid out of rates and taxes'.

Her research on the Co-operative Movement persuaded her that the profit-making employer who most Victorians, including her family, thought vital to the health of the British nation, could in fact be superceded by 'democracies of consumers' complemented by 'democracies of producers'. Beatrice, however, believed in evolution and not revolution. She thought that the new socialist state would come about through gradual state intervention rather than sudden explosion. She therefore mistrusted the Marxist Social Democratic Federation as well as those trade unionists like Will Thorne, Tom Mann and Ben Tillett, who were influenced by its revolutionary precepts. Essentially her socialism was based on ethics and morality. She rejected selfish materialism and believed that only by giving up class prerogatives and sectional interests would the common good be advanced. She concluded that,

> only under the communal ownership of the means of production, can you arrive at the most perfect form of individual development . . . at the greatest stimulus to individual effort; in other words complete Socialism is only consistent with absolute individualism. As such, some day, I shall stand on a barrel and preach it. (15 February 1890)

NOTES

1. B. Webb. *My Apprenticeship*, Penguin, p. 38.
2. Ibid, p. 35.
3. Ibid, p. 64.

4. Ibid, p. 49.
5. Ibid, p. 165.
6. B. Potter to R. Potter, 2nd letter Nov 1883, Passfield Papers.
7. Ibid, 3rd letter, Passfield Papers.
8. B. Potter to R. Potter, Nov 1885, Passfield Papers.
9. B. Webb, *My Apprenticeship*, p. 228–9.
10. Ibid, p. 334.
11. 'The Lords and the Sweating System', *The Nineteenth Century*, June 1890.
12. Paper given to 24th Congress of Co-operative Societies, Rochdale 1892. See *Problems of Modern Industry*, S. and B. Webb 1898, pp. 140–5.
13. Ibid, p. 21. See also W. J. Fishman, *East End Jewish Radicals, 1875–1914*, p. 82.
14. 'Dock Life of East London', *The Nineteenth Century*, October 1887.

2
1859–1890
Intellectual Cockney

'A Remarkable Little Man.'

Sidney Webb came from a very different background to that of Miss Potter. He was lower middle class, had a pronounced Cockney accent, and was also far from handsome, being rather small and rounded, with a large head and tiny hands and feet. 'Homely and plain' Beatrice once described him. But he had an equable temper, amazing stamina and determination and a formidable intellect. He was also a brilliant examinee, winning prizes as other boys collected butterflies.

Sidney was born on 13 July 1859 at 44 Cranbourne Street near Leicester Square, the second of three children. Although only a few records survive, we know that his father's father was an innkeeper in Kent, while his mother's father was for a time a small farmer in Suffolk. The latter, sent to Australia by his family, died there, and his four children were transported back to England and scattered among their relatives. Sidney's mother, Elizabeth Mary Stacey, was brought up by aunts in Essex. The young Miss Stacey proved herself a tough, energetic and independent woman. In 1848 she borrowed money from a brother-in-law, travelled down to London and set herself up in Cranbourne Street in what soon became a relatively prosperous, though unassuming, hair dressing and millinery establishment.

Sidney's father, whom his mother married somewhat late in life, was her former employee. After marriage he worked in a modest way as an accountant and tax collector, which provided a supplementary income to that of the shop. He had however considerable outside interests; he was not only a keen vestry man, and a member of the local Board of Guardians, but also had considerable intellectual curiosity and a reputation for being a radical in politics.

The Webb parents believed strongly in the benefits of good education. Their two boys, Sidney and Charles, went to a good middle class educational establishment in St. Martin's Lane. Unusually for their class, they were also sent abroad, first to Switzerland for three months to learn French and then later, for a period of nearly two years, to the home of a Lutheran pastor in Wismar on the Baltic Sea to perfect their German. Thus soundly equipped for commercial life, Sidney became at seventeen a junior clerk in a colonial broker's office in the City.

Sidney grew up in a relatively happy climate of religious fervour, good works and radical politics. The only thing his home lacked, he recollected later, was a quiet atmosphere. From his early youth he was a passionate lover of his own native city: 'Very early on declaring that no place on earth (I knew nothing of any other place) would content me for habitation other than the very middle of London.'[1] He also exhibited that delight in the amassing of information which was to stand him in such good stead in later years:

> It used to take me a full hour to get the whole length of Fleet Street, so absorbing were the pages of the periodicals there exposed to view. I found more instruction in the reputedly arid pages of Kelly's London Directory, then already a ponderous tome, than in any other single volume to which my childhood had access.[2]

Despite having to earn his living, the young Sidney was intent on bettering himself. Between the ages of seventeen and twenty one he attended evening courses at four different establishments: the City of London College, the London Society for the Extension of University Teaching, the Society for the Encouragement of Arts, Manufactures and Commerce, and Birkbeck Institute. He won many prizes, including awards for German, bookkeeping, geology, logic and political economy. In one year of evening classes at Birkbeck, Sidney went off with ten prizes; in December 1879, when he was twenty, he was awarded seven.[3] By 1884, Webb calculated that he had earned £450 in prize money – then a considerable sum.

Two years earlier, he had been awarded the Whewell Scholarship in International Law at Trinity College, Cambridge. However, as the scholarship did not cover the cost of a three-year period of full-time study, and as he had no private means, he was unable to accept it. He decided instead to take an external LLB at London University and three years later was placed fourth in the Honours List.

It was at Birkbeck that Sidney first demonstrated his radicalism. He attacked the committee of the Institute for having altered the rules so that a majority of two-thirds would be needed for any change to be made in the constitution, which, given the conservative composition of the committee, made it practically impossible to achieve any reforms. The letter which he wrote to the committee bore Sidney's hallmark – clarity and a reasoned and objective approach: 'The Committee,' he declared, 'must believe that we are acting simply on the principle we think, will, in the long run, conduce the greatest permanent benefit to the Institution'.[4] Little came of his protest, so he tried a different and novel approach – student representation on the body of the Institute. In October 1880 he put forward the names of three candidates who had agreed to stand as student representatives, but the committee rejected the idea out of hand.

Sidney's outstanding ability in passing exams provided him with a means of escape from the City life for which he was obviously unsuited. He decided to sit for the Civil Service which, following the Northcote-Trevelyan reforms, was now open to all candidates who passed the Entrance Exam. He was immediately successful. In 1881 at the age of twenty two, he came second of all the candidates in the Lower Division and joined the Inland Revenue; a year later he was again second in the much tougher examinations for the Upper Division. He was offered a place in the War Office, which he declined to accept. In 1883 when he was twenty four he sat the exam again. He was second for the third time running (an outstanding achievement for one who was mainly self-taught) having this time been beaten by a brilliant Oxford graduate, Sydney Olivier. Both young men joined the Colonial Office.

Sidney's formidable scholastic achievements won him a job with a steady income at the Colonial Office and, equally important, a short working day, which gave him the opportunity to use his energies elsewhere. Like other young men of a Nonconformist background, brought up in the last half of the nineteenth century, he needed a substitute for religion. His mother had dragged him from one church to another to find a preacher 'free from sacerdotalism'. But Sidney, under the influence of Darwin and Huxley, became an agnostic. It was however an agnosticism which needed the support of some other kind of inspiration – a personal philosophy which would make sense of his environment.

It was a time of great uncertainty – social and political as well as religious. The optimistic days of unrestrained, capitalist expansion were now a thing of the past; recession was hitting major British industries and unemployment began to rise steeply. The gentlemanly, cautious conduct of the 'new model unions' seemed irrelevant when the mass of the unemployed were unskilled, unrepresented and living in near famine conditions. In this insecure world, economic individualism lost much of its attraction, and young intellectuals began to explore new ideas and consider new solutions. An important forum for these discussions was the debating club so characteristic of the London of this period. These clubs formed and reformed as their young, intellectually curious, religiously and politically ambivalent participants were swayed excitedly by first one idea and then another: papers they discussed ranged from 'Is Happiness generally attainable? And if so How?' to 'The Future of India' and 'Was Shakespeare a Democrat?' Whatever the fate of these societies, a hard core of members remained and, through their constant debates, got to know each other intimately.

Sidney joined most of these clubs – the Argosy Society, the Zetetical Society, the Karl Marx Club (which later became the Hampstead Historical Society) and the radical clubs – and usually became either secretary or a member of the steering committee. To a young man who had not been to university it provided a crucial element in his education. He not only met such stimulating companions as the Reverend Stewart Headlam, a radical curate famous for his eccentricities, Annie Besant, left-wing writer and pamphleteer, who was later to turn to theosophy, H. H. Champion, secretary of the Social Democratic Federation, Helen Taylor, stepdaughter of John Stuart Mill and a devotee of many progressive causes, as well as Sidney's two closest friends, Bernard Shaw and Graham Wallas; he was also able to try out his own ideas on them.

Despite his many activities, Sidney read prodigiously; by the time he was twenty one he had mastered the work of the major philosophers including Kant, Hegel, Fichte and Mill. He then decided to explore the ideas of living thinkers, particularly Herbert Spencer, then at the height of his influence. He was much impressed with the latter's writing and in one of his earliest essays, later given as a lecture, 'The New Learning of the Nineteenth Century: Its Influence on Philosophy', he conceded that the Spencerian synthesis had superceded, except in economics and logic, the ideas of his radical hero, John Stuart Mill.[5]

However Spencer's individualistic philosophy was too anti-social for Webb. By 1880 he had begun to turn to Positivism. He told the Zetetical Society (whose 'primary object was to search for truth in all matters affecting the human race') in a lecture entitled 'The Ethics of Existence' that man's salvation lay not in a selfish individualism but in selflessness: 'A happy life was only to be attained by an absorption of self in some pursuit, leaving the pleasures to be picked up by the way. Only in this way did it seem that perfect happiness was to be obtained'.[6] The pursuit, spelled out in further lectures, was the service of mankind.

Sidney owed his introduction to positivism to his friendship with Sydney Olivier, his fellow Resident Clerk at the Colonial Office. Olivier came from a different background from that of Sidney. The son of a harsh, narrow, Anglican cleric, he found it impossible to accept the rigid teaching of his father. At Oxford he had been influenced by the secularism of Graham Wallas (who had also rejected his father's Evangelical faith, though not his strong moral sense and his dedication to service). Olivier and Webb's far from taxing duties at the Colonial Office allowed them many hours of discussions over games of chess. These conversations had a great impact on Sidney. Olivier, who had been tutor to the son of a positivist, Henry Crompton, and was much under Comte's spell, persuaded Sidney to follow the same path.

It is hardly surprising that Comte was attractive to Sidney. Comte's belief in a professional elite dedicated to mankind appealed to an altruistic civil servant who had turned from an earlier desire to serve God to a commitment to the idea of devoted service. Sidney, who was feeling his way towards a theory of social unity and reconstruction, was drawn towards Comte's view that this dedication would bring social harmony. Sidney also accepted the Comtean notion of progress, an important ingredient in the development of his socialism. In his lecture 'Heredity as a Factor in Psychology and Ethics'[7] he concluded that human potential was unlimited, and that history was on the side of mankind provided that each generation recognised its responsibilities. He also suggested that industrialisation had created a new community of interest: 'The progress of industrialism has bound everyone of us into one great army of workers . . . We fight the battle of life shoulder to shoulder throughout the whole universe.'[8] Everyone was, therefore, involved in a collective effort to improve the lot of mankind.

Sidney was also influenced, as were many Fabians, by the economic theories of Ricardo; they found the Ricardian 'law' of differential rent more intellectually satisfying than Marx's theory of surplus value. The idea of a rent on land had been successfully popularised by Henry George in his *Progress and Poverty*; while the idea of a rent on capital was even then being put forward by the Social Democratic Federation. Sidney took the argument a step further by suggesting a rent on ability.

He argued that all three types of rentier – the landlord, the capitalist, and the professional and skilled worker – were trustees who ought to return to society the gains which accrued because of their particularly favourable circumstances. In other words, he expected the rentier to use his surplus for the general good. He put this notion more precisely in an early lecture he gave to the Fabian Society entitled 'The Way Out': 'The skilled labourer', he told his audience,

> is exactly in the position of the landlord or the capitalist; he is a trustee who possesses social force: his brain does not belong altogether to himself but to society at large, and he is bound to use it to the full extent – to use it for all, not for himself and friends only.[9]

The vital question for Sidney was how the monopolist – be he landlord, capitalist or skilled worker – should use his wealth for the benefit of society. Clearly such a change could not be arrived at easily, so that much work had yet to be done. In 'The Way Out', Sidney was hopeful that persuasion would, in the end, win the day: 'we must bring home to the monopolist', he wrote,

> the sense of his trusteeship and no-one need wait for the millenium – each one can begin it for himself. In this, as in an older faith, the Kingdom of God is at hand; not afar off, not

merely as a dim and distantly future world for which we can only wait and hope.

But the immediate practical significance of his argument was to justify progressive taxation on capital and the income of those with exceptional ability, as well as land and its distribution in the form of social services, public investment and increased wages. His acceptance of progressive distributive taxation as the solution for the imbalances of Victorian society did not, however, mean that he saw himself as a follower of the Marxist Social Democratic Federation which was led by Hyndman and expanded rapidly in the early 1880s. Indeed, between 1883 and 1886, Sidney spent much of his time arguing, mainly through the medium of articles and lectures, against their brand of socialism. He believed that his concept of the three rents, combined with progressive taxation, would redress the imbalances of society without the need for the expropriation which was very much a panacea of the SDF and popular at the time. He argued that it was immoral to expropriate either land or capital. What was required was that monopolists should accept that they should only consume what was essential and that the surplus should be left over for the community.[10] His road to socialism led rather through self-denial and progressive taxation than through expropriation.

One influence in his rejection of Marxian socialism was the discussions of a Hampstead debating society. In 1884, Sidney joined a group of earnest young people who met regularly at the Hampstead home of Charlotte Wilson, a rich bluestocking, who was later to edit the Anarchist journal *Freedom*. Initially known as the Karl Marx Club, it was set up for the purpose of discussing Marx. Later, it changed its name to the less forbidding one of the Hampstead Historical Society. It was a club which attracted many of the leading radicals and socialists of the day, including John Burns, then the most famous working class leader, Belfort Bax, the Marxist journalist, Edward Pease, future secretary of the Fabian Society, Graham Wallas, who was a schoolmaster at that time, Sydney Olivier, and Bernard Shaw, most of whom later became Fabians.

The initial meetings of the club began with the reading of *Capital*, followed by argument and rejection of its author. Both Shaw and Webb left memorable sketches of these early disputations. Shaw recalled how a 'young lady used to read out *Capital* in French to us until we began to quarrel, which usually occurred before she had gone on long enough to make us feel seriously fatigued'.[11] The determined group of seekers after truth found little in Marx's writings with which they could agree. Professor Edgeworth, the Cambridge economist who led the discussion at the first meeting, was so contemptuous that he reduced his audience to silence. 'In despair, he appealed to me. I rushed in and the rest of the evening was a kind of Scottish reel *à deux*, Edgeworth and I gaily dancing on the unfortunate K. M. trampling him remorselessly under foot', Sidney wrote to the absent Shaw.[12]

The result of the monthly gatherings, even for Shaw who came most under the influence of Marx, was to propel the small band of self-improvers decisively in the direction of the neoclassical economists and away from Marx and the theory of surplus value. Sidney consistently took the line that there was no scientific basis to Marxism and that its methodological content was weak. Socialists, he wrote in an interesting paper he gave on 'Economic Method' in 1884, were mistaken in their claims to be scientific investigators and had discovered no new truths about either economics or ethics: 'As Economists, they have produced nothing, corrected nothing, discovered nothing, so that . . . the only useful method of Political Economy remains the much abused but still triumphant concrete Deductive Method of Ricardo, Mill and Cairns.'[13] A year later in an unpublished essay entitled 'Rent, Interest and Wages', he continued his criticism of Marx, the weakness of whose arguments, he claimed, rested on too narrow an interpretation of human nature and society, as well as a failure to take into account such factors as population and the part played by savings from income, which, Sidney argued, clearly encouraged production. He also criticised Marx for his treatment of management. Marx, he said, 'habitually ignores, at least underestimates the great difficulty of managing this (work) force which is, at present, performed by part of the class he would abolish'.[14]

Having rejected Marx but nevertheless impelled by the logic of his own analysis, Sidney began to develop a distinctive version of socialism – eclectic, pragmatic and evolutionary. A crucial factor in his emergence as a socialist was his decision in 1885 to become a member of the Fabian Society.

When Sidney joined the Fabians, there was no reason to suppose that the Society would have any more chance of survival than any of the other societies which came and went so abruptly in the ferment of the middle 1880s. It owed its beginnings to Percival Chubb, a Second Division clerk in the Legal Department of the Local Government Board and an acolyte of the itinerant scholar and idealist Thomas Davidson. Chubb, like Sidney Webb, was also a great joiner of societies, although he was more interested in moral improvement than in social reconstruction. He joined the Progressive Association in 1882 together with Havelock Ellis, then a medical student, and Frank Podmore, an Upper Division clerk in the Post Office. As Professor Mackenzie has recently shown,[15] there is 'a strong family resemblance, a likeness that suggests direct inheritance' both in membership and in aims between the Progressive Association and the Fabian Society.

Under the influence of Davidson, Chubb, together with a group of Progressive Society members, was much taken with the idea of setting up a small community committed to a new life of moral simplicity and regeneration. A meeting in October 1883 to discuss the possibility was inconclusive. Subsequent meetings brought out a fundamental disagreement between the moralists and the socialists. The Chubb group demanded 'the subordination of material things to spiritual things' and by January 1884, were prepared to sever relations with those who intended a different path. A separation was amicably agreed on: the followers of Chubb and Davidson met as the Fellowship of the New Life and the second, more socialistic group, became the Fabian Society.

Of the nine people who first joined the Fabians, Frank Podmore, a clergyman's son and civil servant, Edward Pease, a young social reformer then working unhappily in a stockbroking firm, and Hubert Bland, a failed businessman, agreed to run the new Society, christened by Podmore after the Roman General, Fabius Cunctator, who owed his success to cautious rather than brilliant campaigning. Despite their break with the 'New Lifers' the original Fabian members made no clear distinction between moral issues and socialist programmes of reform, as the proposals that Podmore made to the Society that 'the competitive system . . . must be reconstructed for the general welfare' and that 'the reconstruction of society should be in accordance with the highest moral principles' demonstrate. In Professor Mackenzie's words, 'there was a muddle of motives among these genteel radicals'. However they agreed to concentrate on economic and social questions and Bland's wife, Edith Nesbit, the writer of children's stories, described her fellow members as 'quite the nicest set of people I ever knew', and noted with approval that their objectives were 'to improve the social system – or rather to spread its news as to the possible improvements of this said FS'.[16] Although there was no agreement on solutions, the title of their first pamphlet *Why are the Many Poor?* brought out three months after its foundation, indicates the way in which the Society was beginning to go.

It was the arrival of Shaw at the end of 1884 and then of Webb (who quickly joined the executive) in May 1885, which gave the infant society its dynamism and cohesion. In 1885 Sidney was already a formidable figure. He had a keen intellect, the confidence of a man who had worked out his own ideas, a flair for political argument, and a talent for organisation. Bernard Shaw, then a struggling journalist and playwright, described their first meeting, which took place at the Zetetical Society. Webb was, he wrote, 'rather below middle height, with small hands and feet and a profile which suggested an improvement on Napoleon III'. What immediately impressed Shaw was his encyclopaedic knowledge.

> He knew all about the subject of debate; he knew more than anybody present; had read everything that had been written on the subject; and remembered all the facts that bore upon it. He used notes, ticked them off one by one, threw them away, and finished with a coolness and clearness that, to me in my then trembling state, seemed miraculous. This young man was the ablest man in England.[17]

GBS later claimed that he had forced his friendship on the brilliant scholarship boy: 'quite the cleverest thing I did. When we met', he reminded Sidney just before the latter's death, 'you knew everything that I didn't know and I knew everything that you didn't know. We had everything to learn from one another and brains enough to do it.'[18] In short, Shaw and Webb were a complementary partnership; Shaw, fertile in ideas and a brilliant polemicist and publicist, Webb providing the intellectual thrust and discipline required to give direction to the Fabian Society.

In an important lecture 'What Socialism Means' given a year after he joined, Sidney for the first time set out fully his vision of socialism and mapped out a new approach for the Fabian Socialist. His socialism, he told Fabians, dissociating himself from the Social Democratic Federation, was evolutionary rather than revolutionary. He believed that institutions could be changed without revolution. The aim of socialists should be to bring about such a shift in public opinion that it would make socialism inevitable. Socialism, he argued, was 'one of the unforeseen results of the industrial revolution'. Great wealth had been created by the capitalist system but it had failed 'to exterminate or even to alleviate poverty'. In a moving passage, he pointed out that 'in this London, the wealthiest city of the world, there is also the greatest mass of poverty and misery'. The poor had to labour all their lives for a bare subsistence and their existence was considerably shortened in the process.

> We rob the wageworkers of eighteen years of life each; they die before their time, like worn-out draught horses and their innocent children like flies. Even as slaves they would be better off. They die in their own rooms of diseases which we, in our wealth, know how to prevent; one or two will die tonight in London alone of actual starvation.[19]

The Webbian model of socialism was based on the assertion of two leading principles. First, a recognition of man's interdependence: 'by division of labour and mutual exchange, all are sharing in each other's toil'. Secondly, the ethical right of the workers to the whole product of their labour:

> We contend . . . that the whole produce of labour is due to labour alone – whether labour of hand or labour of brain – and that any form of society which enables idle monopolists of certain social products to exact for their personal consumption a toll from helpless fellow citizens, although perhaps useful in the earlier stage of social evolution, is now bad.

These two principles united the different schools of thought: the collectivist which laid stress on the role of the state in achieving equality of consumption; the positivist which, though it understood the need for some government regulation, believed that such equality could only be achieved by an advance in personal morality; and the anarchist school, which, though egalitarian, was totally against government intervention.

Sidney's socialism was pragmatic:

> it does not mean any particular form or scheme of social reorganisation, nor the vain dream of equality of wealth. It means no

> contempt for machinery, no dislike of education or culture, no enmity to brainwork or invention. It is, in fact, because we want more of these that we are socialists.

However the application of his socialist principles had radical implications. Once economic interest and rent were regarded as tolls upon labour by monopolists

> a different aspect is placed upon the public provision of museums, parks, picture galleries, for the multitude; on free education and on universal technical training, so as to secure at least – to the whole people – that real free choice of occupation in life, now enjoyed only by a small class.[20]

Of course, socialism would mean a loss of liberty for the landlords and the capitalists. But they should remember from where their wealth came.

> As you feed the fire, you will see the miner, bent double underground, in his exhausting toil, giving up his life that you may be warmed. As you look upon your daughters . . . you will see behind them the daughters of other mothers, slaving seamstresses, working sixteen hours for sixteen pence.

Once faced by the truth, the wealthy would be compelled to 'come over to us for very shame'. Sidney finished on a warning note. If they did not change their ways, they must not be surprised

> if the long-suffering masses, roused at last from their ignorant patience and deserted by those who ought to have been leaders, shake in their despair the whole social structure about your ears, crying of your class, of its good as of its evil, 'cut it down, why cumbreth it the ground'.[21]

So, Sidney Webb, in a skilful and moving amalgam of positivism, collectivism and neo-classical economics, launched Fabian Socialism.

The next question was how Fabian socialism was most effectively to be pursued. There were two views which, although they overlapped were nevertheless distinct. The colourful and energetic Annie Besant, who was attracted by Marxist ideas, believed that the time was right for the formation of a working class party and that the discrediting of the Social Democratic Federation, following Hyndman's involvement with the Conservative Party at the 1885 election (the so-called 'Tory Gold' scandal), gave the Fabians an opportunity to assume the leadership of an independent socialist party. Sidney saw the role of the society in a different light. Fabians should concentrate on research, education and permeation, so as to bring about 'a slowly dawning conviction in the minds of men for the need of reform'.[22] His view was, in fact, influenced by his belief in non-violent, Parliamentary political methods. The 1886 riots of the unemployed (when London's clubland was partially wrecked after a Trafalgar Square rally addressed by the leaders of the SDF, Hyndman, Champion and Burns amongst others) frightened the majority of Fabians, including Sidney, and encouraged them to separate themselves both ideologically and organisationally from the SDF.

The other main factor in shaping Sidney's ideas for the Society was his optimistic assessment of the possibilities of capturing Liberals for his brand of socialism. The Liberal Party, which had been badly defeated at the 1886 election following the defection of Joseph Chamberlain and the Liberal Unionists, was also deeply divided on the issue of social reform. The solid core of its middle class supporters were against state intervention, while the radical clubs and associations, which were particularly strong in London, took a much more collectivist approach, strongly supporting the reformism of the 'Unauthorised Programme' of 1885. Sidney, who joined the Holborn, Westminster and London University Liberal and Radical Associations, and was elected to the executive committee of the London Liberal and Radical Union, saw the clubs as natural vehicles for Fabian permeation and joint action (including the setting up of joint Democratic Committees of Fabians and radicals to run candidates for the London School Board elections of 1888). 'I believe very much in getting hold of the Liberal caucuses', he wrote to Edward Pease. 'They are just on the turn, without knowing it, and a little push from inside does much to send them in our direction.'[23]

It followed from Webb's conception of the Society as the intellectual powerhouse of British socialism that the Fabians should produce a series of well-researched, clearly-written pamphlets and articles, as well as initiating lecture programmes. The first Fabian pamphlet written by Sidney in 1887 was *Facts for Socialists*, which graphically described the glaring inequalities of late-Victorian society. There was little novel about the remedies except for the advocacy of 'restitution to public purposes of rent and interest of every kind' which 'will be mainly brought about by means of progressive taxation in the shape of graduated death duties, a graduated differentiated income tax, and the rating of land values'. Even so, in its clear presentation of facts and its support for radical reform, the pamphlet broke new ground and became a best-seller, with 25 000 copies sold by 1890.

The next few years were immensely creative ones for both the Fabian Society and Sidney Webb. By 1890, over a 1000 Fabian lectures had been given a year; Sidney was lecturing at least twice a week. Out of the first twenty eight Tracts which established the reputation of the Society, Sidney, still a full-time civil servant, wrote nineteen. His pamphlets included: *Facts for Londoners, Figures for Londoners, English Progress Towards Social Democracy, A Plea for An Eight-Hours Bill, The Workers' Political Programme,* and *Practicable Land Nationalisation.* Though mostly short, they were all well-researched and taken together, presented not only a devastating indictment, all the more telling for being factual, of Victorian Britain, but also provided a reforming programme for Parliamentary socialists and progressive radicals.

Perhaps the most impressive and influential work produced by the Society in that period was the *Fabian Essays in Socialism* published in 1889, the year of great trade union unrest. The popularity of the *Essays*, which were in one sense an alternative to trade union militancy, owed much to the renewed interest in socialism awakened by the Gasworkers' and Dockers' strikes. The *Essays*, which were edited by Shaw and published by the Fabian Society, were an immediate success, with 1000 copies sold within the first month and over 25 000 within eighteen months.

The seven essays, which covered the economic, historic, industrial and moral bases of, as well as the transition to, socialism, were written by Shaw, Webb, William Clark, Sydney Olivier, Graham Wallas, Hubert Bland and Annie Besant. Although there were differences in approach between the essays, a common thread was their belief that progress towards a more collectivised and socially conscious society was inevitable – and partly, because of its inevitability, ought to be gradual rather than revolutionary. The importance of the *Fabian Essays* was that at a time of intellectual uncertainty and political and industrial ferment they provided an optimistic and attractive way forward for progressive radicals who rejected revolution.

Sidney's contribution was to show how socialism had developed as a natural response to the inadequacies of unrestrained capitalism. Much of his essay was devoted to demonstrating that, without knowing it, Britain was well on its way towards socialism. In a whole range of activities, including those performed by local authorities, the State had so increased its responsibilities that 'it may now be fairly claimed that the socialist philosophy of today is but the unconscious and exclusive assertion of principles of social organisation which have been already in great part unconsciously adopted'.[24] Sidney also argued that the coming of democracy was pushing politicians in a socialist direction: 'So long . . . as Democracy in political administration continues to be the dominant principle, Socialism may be safely predicted as its economic obverse . . . every increase in the political power of the proletariat will most surely be used by them for their economic and social protection.' Small wonder that the 'glide into collectivist socialism' was 'irresistible'.

What did socialism mean to Sidney? In an essay published that year, he summed up the Fabian road to socialism:

> On the economic side, socialism implies the collective administration of rent and interest, leaving to the individual only the wages of his labour, of hand and brain. On the political side, it involves the collective control over and ultimate administration of all the main instruments of wealth production. On the ethical side, it expresses the general recognition of fraternity, the universal obligation of personal service, and the subordination of personal ambition to the common good.[25]

Sidney was so optimistic about progress towards socialism and more generally about the power of ideas that he saw no necessity to form a new party. What was needed, he contended, was a small educated elite, 'supplying ideas and principles of social reconstruction to each of the great political parties in turn, as the changing results of English politics bring them alternatively into power'.[26] Fabian permeation, not independent party politics, was the best way to make England socialist.

In January 1890, when he met Beatrice Potter, Sidney Webb was thirty, already a well-known pamphleteer and lecturer and a leading figure in radical circles. What kind of man lay behind the seemingly confident public figure? In personal matters Sidney was reserved, so reserved that it was only after he had been turned down by a girl he hoped to marry that he had revealed his feelings to his two greatest friends, Shaw and Wallas. The unrequited love affair brought out all Sidney's feelings of inadequacy as well as confirming him in his pessimism about personal happiness: 'I want you to bear with me whatever I may do as I feel very desolate indeed. Why *did* God put such a thing into life?'[27] he wrote sadly to Wallas. He concluded that individual happiness was 'not obtainable at all'. The experience left him shaken; he found himself 'distinctly *more* atheistic than before, and I am afraid also more unsettled as to the ethical standard of its application'. However, the episode confirmed him in his previous conviction that 'the idea of devoted service' was 'the noblest of man's inspiration'.[28]

To forget his unhappiness he joined Wallas, who had been sacked from his post at Highgate School for refusing to participate in religious services, in Germany that same year. They stayed in Weimar in the house of a widow whose stoical attitude to the loss of her husband strengthened Sidney in his resolve to forget his own lesser unhappiness. It was on this holiday that he read a novel which had a formative effect on him. The hero of Edward Bellamy's *Dr Heidenhoff's Process*, who was able to overcome his doubts and anxieties by the application of his will-power over his subconscious, was a figure with whom Sidney was able to identify and from whom he was able to draw strength.

In a letter that he wrote in 1889 to Edward Pease's fiancée, Marjory Davidson, a fellow Fabian, Sidney gave a rare glimpse of his feelings and of his views on marriage. The impending marriage of one of his oldest colleagues, he told her, opened an old wound which still embittered him. He wanted, he wrote, her friendship, although 'with the very smallest capacity for acquiring it. I have often envied' he went on

> the ease with which others 'catch on' to congenial spirits . . . where I simply remain outside. I am, of course, very busy; somewhat serious; very analytic and introspective – but, I hope, passably honest, sincere, and not obviously hateful or repulsive. Yet I seem 'left out' in more than one case and in more than one department of life.

He went on somewhat pedantically, to define what he called his 'theory of life' which

> is to feel at every moment that I am acting as a member of a committee and for that committee – in some affairs a committee of my own family merely, in others again a committee as wide as the Aryan race. But I aspire *never* to act alone, or for myself. This theoretically combined action involves rules, deliberation, discussion, concert, the disregard of one's own impulses and, in fact, is Collectivism or Communism.

Marriage, Sidney added, should be a partnership whose sum was greater than that partnership, while the partners should, 'in every detail, act in and for the partnership – except in such sphere as they may severally act in and for larger committees.[29] Prescient words for the future partner of Beatrice Potter.

NOTES

1. 'Reminiscences' S. and B. Webb *St Martin's Review* Dec 1928.
2. Ibid.
3. See list of his successes in the Passfield Papers.
4. *A Short History of Birkbeck College* C. Delisle Burns, 1924.
5. See Willard Wolfe *From Radicalism to Socialism: Men and Ideas in the Formation of Fabian Society Doctrines 1881–1889* for an excellent account of Sidney Webb's political philosophy.
6. 'The Ethics of Existence' Lecture, circa 1880, Passfield Papers VI.
7. *Heredity as a Factor in Psychology and Ethics*, circa 1880, Passfield Papers VI.
8. *Growth of Industrialism*, Passfield Papers VI.
9. 'The Economics of a Positivist Community', *The Practical Socialist*, Feb 1886. See also *The Way Out* circa 1884 or 1885.
10. *The Economic Function of the Middle Class*, Argosy Society, 6 Feb 1885, Passfield Papers.
11. G. B. Shaw. 'Bluffing the Value Theory', *Today*, 1889.
12. S. Webb to G. B. Shaw, 4 Nov 84, Shaw Papers BM 50553.
13. *On Economic Method*, circa 1885, Passfield Papers VI.
14. *Rent, Interest and Wages being a criticism of Karl Marx and a statement of economic theory*, unpublished essay, 1886, Passfield Papers VI.
15. N. Mackenzie: 'Percival Chubb and the founding of the Fabian Society' *Victorian Studies*, Autumn 1979.
16. Quoted in N. and J. Mackenzie *The First Fabians*.
17. G. B. Shaw, *Sixteen Self-Sketches*.
18. G. B. Shaw to S. Webb, 26 Mar 1946.
19. 'What Socialism Means: A Call to the Unconverted', *The Practical Socialist* June, 1886.
20. Ibid.
21. Ibid.

22. *The Transition to Social Democracy*, 1889.
23. S. Webb to E. Pease, 16 Nov 1887, HRCUT.
24. *Fabian Essays in Socialism*, 1889.
25. *Socialism in England*, American Economic Association, 1889, Passfield Papers VII.
26. Ibid.
27. S. Webb to G. Wallas, 22 Aug 1885, Passfield Papers.
28. *George Eliot's Works*, 1882, Passfield Papers VI.
29. S. Webb to M. Davidson, 12 Dec 1888, Passfield Papers.

3
1890–1892
Courtship

'Transform I and I into II.'

Sidney Webb and Beatrice Potter met through Beatrice's study of the Co-operative Movement. She felt that she needed more historical background to her co-operative studies and had asked one of her relations, Maggie Harkness, a journalist with radical connections, to recommend someone with the appropriate knowledge. Maggie suggested Sidney Webb. His name caught Beatrice's attention because she had just finished reading the recently published *Fabian Essays in Socialism* and been particularly impressed by Sidney Webb's contribution, which she thought 'had the historic sense'. She was attracted, too, by Sidney's confidence in the inevitability of his step-by-step socialism. Sidney, for his part, had remarked that, of the contributors to Charles Booth's first volume, Beatrice Potter was the only one with literary talent.

During 1889, Beatrice had little time for extra research as she was busy nursing her sick father who had again become critically ill. She was so worn out with nursing that her sisters suggested that she take a holiday. She decided to go up to London in January 1890 and was introduced to Sidney who, characteristically, provided her with a comprehensive list of all the possible historical sources she might need for her work. A few days later he sent her his newly published pamphlet on the *Rate of Interest*. A memorable, if protracted, courtship had begun.

After their original meeting in January 1890, Beatrice invited him to dinner a month later at the Devonshire House Hotel to meet Charles and Mary Booth. She was stimulated by her conversation with Sidney, though unimpressed by his physical appearance and by his lower middle class background. 'A remarkable little man', she wrote after that meeting,

> with a huge head on a very tiny body: a breadth of forehead quite sufficient to account for the encyclopaedic character of his knowledge, a Jewish nose, prominent eyes and mouth, black hair somewhat unkempt, spectacles and a most bourgeois black coat shiny with wear; regarded as a whole somewhere between a London card and a German Professor. To keep to externals: his pronunciation is Cockney, his H's are shaky, his attitudes by no means eloquent – with his thumbs fixed pugnaciously in a far from immaculate waistcoat, with his bulky head thrown back and his little body forward, he struts even when he stands, delivering himself with extraordinary rapidity of thought and utterance and with an expression of inexhaustible self-complacency. But I like the man. There is a directness of speech, an open-mindedness, an imaginative warm-heartedness which should carry him far. He has the self-complacency of one who is always thinking faster than his neighbours, who is untroubled by doubts, and to whom the acquisition of facts is as easy as the grasping of matter; but he has no vanity and is totally unselfconscious – hence his absence of consciousness as to his neighbours' corns. (13 February 1890)

Beatrice was interested, though hardly swept off her feet. But she enjoyed being in the company of clever men and had admired the Fabians from afar; she was also flattered by the apparent respect with which Sidney listened to her, even though his lower middle class origins might be against him. He was deeply struck by the beautiful and clever Miss Potter; for him it was love at first sight.

The day after the dinner she and the Booths had a long conversation on socialism, presumably inspired by her meeting with Sidney Webb. 'It was in my first conversation with you . . . that it flashed across my mind that I was, or ought to be, a Socialist – if I was true', she later admitted to Sidney on 2 May 1890.[1] If Charles Booth believed in a paternalistic individualism, Beatrice was now prepared to go much further. '*I*, mean by socialism', she wrote,

> not a vague and sentimental desire to 'ameliorate the condition of the masses', but a definite economic form: a peculiar industrial organisation – *the communal or state ownership of Capital and*

> *Land* . . . the transference to the community of the *means* of Production as distinguished from the *faculty* to produce . . . In short, under this system, supposing it could exist, which I do not assert, there would be a perfect exchange of faculty and desire, a rewarding of all services according to their competitive worth to the community. (15 February 1890)

She and Sidney had socialism in common.

Having met a leading Fabian, she was even more interested in the *Fabian Essays* and delighted with their success. She felt encouraged by 'the *delicious positivism* of the authors'. Their confident optimism and their moderate approach appealed to her. It also caused her, on her return to Box House, to question the basis of her family's fortune and to feel uneasy as to their way of life. She invited Sidney down to stay, ostensibly to be guided by him on how to influence the Lords' Commission on Sweating. Sidney was again deeply impressed by her and suggested, hoping to encourage the relationship, that she act as his 'mentor', wooing Beatrice by asking for her advice on Fabian tracts. 'You need not fear', he wrote after the visit 'our taking up any impracticable or sectarian attitude: we are, indeed, constantly seeking chances of translating the crude abstractions of the doctrinaire socialist into the language of practical politics.'[3] Beatrice was as flattered and delighted to pick Sidney's brains in return. It had been a successful first visit. Sidney, already infatuated, could not help in that first letter in indulging in a little boasting. He told Beatrice that he had a belief in his own star and was so carried away by her sympathetic attitude that he felt encouraged to tell her his life history and to reveal his hopes for the future. Looking back on his stay, he wrote, 'You have reduced me to pulp by your sympathy'. But she in turn claimed, 'You have humbled me – by making me a socialist.'

In spite of herself, Beatrice was drawn towards Sidney. Speculations in her diary, although tinged with a dislike for his physical appearance, show an increasing interest. 'I am not sure as to the future of that man:' she recorded after he had returned to London.

> His tiny tadpole body, unhealthy skin, lack of manner, cockney pronunciation, poverty, are all against him. He has the conceit of (a) man who has raised himself out of the most insignificant surroundings into a position of power – how much power no one

quite knows . . . A London retail tradesman with the aims of a Napoleon! a queer monstrosity to be justified only by success. And above all a loophole into the socialist party; one of the small body of men, with whom I may sooner or later throw in my lot for good and all. (26 April 1890)

To Beatrice, then, friendship with Sidney meant primarily an entrée into the world of Fabian politics.

Setting the pattern of their courtship, she responded primly to his more emotional overtures. On 2 May she replied coolly to his second letter. Her feelings of friendliness towards him, she wrote, were those of mere gratitude, her helpfulness simply a woman's reaction. First she outlined her position: 'Friendship between men and women', she stated, could become 'one of the greatest factors in life – so long as it is not blurred by the predominence of lower feeling – when I think it becomes a source of pure evil – whatever the relationship may be.'[3]

Sidney tried another tack. He wrote to tell her that he had been asked to write an article on the Poor Law for the *Contemporary Review* and appealed for her help and sympathy. 'I am now in the throes of building it up', he told her, 'with my usual sinking of heart and feeling of despair. (Yet all the world – except, I hope, you – believe that I am a fatuously self-confident person!)' He then went on to ask for her help and advice, as well as to enclose some articles and to end on a warm note: 'Behind it all I who *am* timid and cursed with looking before and after, fear to hear the "ground whirl of the perished leaves of hope". (Did you credit me with knowing my Rossetti?)'[4] Beatrice remained detached. However, though she disclaimed any knowledge of old age pensions or the Poor Law, her reply gave him hope. She asked Sidney whether he would like to come with her to the Co-operative Congress to be held that year in Glasgow in May.

The Glasgow visit was one of the turning points in their relationship. Beatrice and Sidney travelled up together. Sidney 'squatting on a portmanteau' with 'relays of workingmen friends lying full length' at her feet, earnestly discussing trade unions, co-operation and socialism. Beatrice, who enjoyed a position of trust and friendship with the co-operators – unique for a woman of her class – was obviously delighted to show that side of herself to Sidney. He, in spite of his growing importance in the socialist world, knew little of the trade union movement and eagerly availed himself of the opportunity to discuss 'Trades Unions, Co-operation and Socialism'.

The comradeship and apparent closeness between them emboldened Sidney to reveal his feelings. As they wandered through the streets of Glasgow, 'a long walk by glorious sunset through the crowded streets . . . with glory in the sky, and hideous bestiality on the earth', he declared his love. Beatrice, not attracted to him physically, and still emotionally involved with Joseph Chamberlain, shied away, unable, she told him, to promise anything and instead suggested that they should come to 'a working compact'. She told Sidney she could not reciprocate his feelings and only held out a vague hope. 'You understand', she told him, 'you promise me to realise that the chances are a hundred to one that nothing follows but friendship.' And then went on to state that 'if you feel that it is weakening your life, that your work is less efficient for it, you will promise me to give it all up?'

Whatever happened, Sidney was determined not to lose Beatrice's friendship and assured her that her work would not suffer. 'I will *make* you help me and I will insist in helping you – our relationship shall be judged solely by the helpfulness to each other's work' he told her, and went on to plead, 'Forgive me, if I say that I believe that if we were united we could do great things together' (Whitsun 1890). Beatrice, unhappy about Sidney's passionate outburst, suggested that he think of her as a married woman, the wife of a friend; and though he refused to commit himself, she believed that she had successfully extricated herself from an unacceptable and emotional entanglement. 'One grasp of the hand – and we were soon in a warm discussion of some question of Economics. Finis' (24 May 1890).

An uncompleted letter of Sidney's revealed some of his feelings. 'You tortured me horribly last night by your intolerable "superiority"', he wrote in anguish on 24 May after her rejection.

> Surely an affectation of heartlessness is as objectionable as an affectation of conceit. And you blasphemed horribly against what is highest and holiest in human relations. I could not speak my mind last night, but this agony is unendurable. You will at any rate not be indifferent to my suffering. I do not know how to face another night such [as] I have passed.[5]

Beatrice however, afraid of his passion, unwilling after six years of repressed emotion to consider a new relationship, would offer him nothing but friendship. Nevertheless, although the chances were a hundred-to-one that nothing but friendship would come of the 'working compact', for the first time since her unhappy affair with Chamberlain, she had made a small if tentative commitment. Beatrice understood this; she forced herself to re-read all of Chamberlain's letters (which she had kept carefully sealed) in an attempt to exorcise his ghost which had, she admitted, 'haunted me day and night'. Looking back on her years of suffering, she now vowed to 'forgive and forget'. At the same time, she also resolved to clear the air with Sidney. 'Do not let us misunderstand each other', she now wrote to dampen his ardour. 'I want you to realise that you will be betraying my confidence and trust if you allow yourself to build up a hope . . . if I find that our friendship leads to a constant perplexity and anxiety on my side . . . I shall retire absolutely and entirely from it.'[6]

Sidney's reply, his first love letter, was a skilful appeal to Beatrice's intellectual ambitions as well as her feelings. 'You cannot now, by any noble frankness and friendliness deepen your hold on me', he wrote, saddened by her attitude,

> because I am through and through yours already . . . Now you are to me the sun and source of all my work . . . I am simply and hopelessly dependent on your kindness and courage . . . I could be as great an adjunct to your intellectual life as you are to my moral being. Of course, I stand to gain by far the most, because I gain your intellect too, and cannot give you moral help. *But together we could move the world.*[7]

Beatrice was impressed. 'It is a very solemn thought to feel to have a man's soul in your keeping. This afternoon at Westminster Abbey I prayed I might be worthy of the trust – that it might raise my life and his to a higher level of "service" ' (31 May 1890). The same day, however, she wrote him a reproving reply. 'Your letter has touched me deeply; but it must be the *last word of personal feeling*.'[8] Sidney, duly contrite and anxious not to lose Beatrice, hastened to assure her, 'I promise to write a criticism on your article' (published in June in *Nineteenth Century* on the 'Sweating System'). 'Perhaps I emphasise the fact that I must not go beyond that by using official paper!'[9]

Beatrice went to Austria in June with Alice Green, widow of the historian John Richard Green, author of the *Short History of the English People*, but continued to correspond with Sidney. She was clearly unwilling to break up the friendship. She and Alice Green went to Oberammergau to see the Passion Play and Beatrice wrote to Sidney suggesting that he too should come and see it – the revolt of women and workers 'led by a great socialist'. She was, she also said, worried that he was thought of as a political manipulator, although in her next sentence she apologised for her frankness and asked for his forgiveness. She hoped, she wrote, that he would do the same in return, 'when you see a moral lapse or intellectual failure'.[10] The tone of her letters shows that, in spite of herself, Beatrice was becoming more involved than she had ever anticipated. One of the pleasures of the new relationship was the knowledge that for the first time since her happy days of intimacy with her sister Maggie, she had someone she could both confide in and be intellectually stimulated by.

Sidney accepted her criticisms meekly, and throughout the holiday they corresponded at length. He was always very careful not to go too far, though at the same time remaining optimistic. 'You cannot realise how much you have changed me. Do not let my happiness disquiet you. It gives me no claim on you and it enormously strengthens all the good elements in me . . . As to the future, let us wait.'[11] But it was difficult for Sidney to keep his side of the bargain. At their first meeting alone since her return from abroad, he took her to Epping Forest. Initially, he intended to remain calm and unemotional. They had met the day before on 27 July in Surrey, where Beatrice had been visiting the positivist, Frederick Harrison, and Sidney had gone down to see other friends. They returned to London together but promised to meet the next day. On arrival at his home, however, Sidney found, to his consternation, a note from Massingham, editor of the *Star*, asking him to review Alfred Marshall's *Principles of Economics*. As he and Bernard Shaw were about to go abroad to Germany, he realised that he would have to read the massive tome immediately. He therefore took himself off to the National Liberal Club where he devoured the 600 pages at one sitting. His amazing feat ensured that his initial conversation with Beatrice in Epping Forest began on a suitably impersonal level, particularly as they then turned to discussing the political situation. Towards the end of the afternoon, Sidney, conscious that he would not see her for some time, weakened, and read Keats and Rossetti to Beatrice as they lay under the oaks and hornbeams in the forest. But she refused to allow him any emotion, immediately criticising him for his outburst. 'I give you leave to think of me when you would be thinking of yourself', she told him priggishly, 'but not when you have sufficient power to work' (27 July 1890).

It was Sidney's turn to go abroad. He and Shaw also went off in August to Oberammergau to see the famous Passion Play. He wrote every day to Beatrice, hiding this from Shaw who throughout their holiday believed him to be busy writing an article on municipal death duties. Sidney had been much affected by their idyll in Epping Forest, although it was also there that he had learnt of Beatrice's wealth. 'I feel as if I could never ask you to make that sacrifice for me,' he wrote to her in sorrow. 'Just as I am . . . I should be tempted to despair, tempted to the mad altruism of refusing that sacrifice which perhaps alone can save me. Frankly, I do not know how I can go on without you . . . Do not now desert me. Do not despise me because I am at your feet.'[12] Beatrice's reply showed her at her most brutal. 'I ask you,' she replied on 9 August,

> is it delicate or honourable of you to use the relationship of friends, which I have granted you, as a ground for attack – for a constant and continuous pressing forward of wishes of your own which you know are distasteful to me – and which simply worry distress and rob me of all the help and strength your friendship might give me? . . . If it had not been the outcome of evident emotion – it could, really have been a gross impertinence . . . If you value the continuence of our friendship, exercise a little more self-control.[13]

To which Sidney replied sadly, 'I will not offend again. You shall not need to write me another such letter: a terrible letter.'[14] But Beatrice was careful to continue with the correspondence, having come to the conclusion that she had been too harsh, and wrote from the country to say so to Sidney who was now back in London. He, of course, was delighted. A kind letter, he enthused was deeply appreciated, adding that she could rely on his obedience to her 'signal that I go too far'. They now began to discuss her work – she had been asked by the publishers Sonnenheim (on Sidney's initiative) to write a small book on Co-operation, for his Social Science Series. Sidney gave her advice, for which she was grateful, on the format of her book, on what to read on the subject, and on any other information she wanted. She had also begun to be introduced to some of his friends. She met Graham Wallas, still then a schoolmaster and, of course, a leading Fabian. In spite of herself Beatrice was impressed. 'What charms me is the perfect sort of relationship between your little knot of men–it is singularly trustful; you really care for each other. Such friendship is very precious, it defies cynicism',[15] she told him.

But though their relationship grew closer the couple found it difficult to meet. For Beatrice to ask Sidney down to Box House frequently would have been to invite comment. However, his eloquent and beautifully-expressed sentiments by letter probably did more for his suit than any meeting they might have had, while his support and advice was particularly welcome to one alone with a sick father and starved of intellectual company. It was when they met that their relationship often suffered a setback. Nevertheless Sidney was less happy than Beatrice who had found so generous and loyal a friend. He still longed for more than friendship and his emotional frustration began to affect his work, while Beatrice's habit of fault-finding did nothing to augment his confidence. He could see no clear future ahead of him, for which, he wrote to Beatrice, she was partly responsible, as 'a man in love is weak, and to be weak is miserable'.

As he became filled with self-doubt so she chided him for his weaknesses. Although Beatrice was still tied to her father's bedside she could and did occasionally get away. In September 1890, she and Sidney went to Leeds to the annual meeting of the British Association where Sidney gave a paper. Though stimulated by his clever contribution to the discussion, Beatrice immediately returned to the attack. She had disliked his manner which, she told him, she thought self-important and unpleasant. She later took him to task ungraciously: 'Don't overwork', she demanded. 'Look after the breadth of the English vowel! Do not refuse to recognise the individual existence of oi, ow, a, and confound them all in a common *er*.'[16] But to her diary she admitted 'the tie is stiffening'.

They both worked hard throughout August and September: Beatrice began her book and invited Sidney down to Box House once more. 'You will, of course,' she admonished him 'be very discreet'. Sidney was much in need of a rest. He had already produced five of the Fabian Pamphlets of that year and was in the process of writing a book on the *Eight Hours Movement* with Harold

Cox, brother-in-law of Sydney Olivier. His visit to Box was another success, for while Beatrice might berate him over his vowels, nevertheless she suggested that they should keep up a weekly correspondence.

That September Sidney took part in the immensely successful Fabian Lancashire Campaign. Beatrice suggested that instead of writing letters, he should keep a diary; 'though I am absent,' she wrote in that same letter in which she pronounced on his accent: 'You would then feel that I was by your side . . . you would enable me to feel part and parcel of your life.' So Sidney bought 'a common little book' in which he jotted down his thoughts and then sent them off to her.

His tour took him round most of the major Lancashire towns. It was an exhausting but stimulating experience, especially as it included such memorable occasions as at Rochdale, where he lectured to the SDF on an empty stomach and 'drank beer with a dozen gas-stokers just off work – all virtually Socialists – who were immensely struck by the contrast between my hand and theirs as we clasped hands – and sang the Marseillaise from an English song book of which several had copies!'[17] Even so he found it hard work. It was 'not so much the lecture every night as the irregular life; the perpetual talking to new people, the constant external stimulus'. All the same, the lecture tour, which lasted six weeks was a great triumph and the prodigious energy with which the Fabian lecturers exploited the new situation created by the ferment of the previous year paid off. Pamphlets sold and membership increased rapidly.

It was a highly successful time for Sidney personally. He was much in demand writing books, articles, lecturing. Even his courtship appeared to be gaining ground. Beatrice's invitation for him to stay at Box together with her old friend Alice Green (who thought him 'a dear little man') at the end of September, gave him a breathing space. She was much impressed by his impeccable behaviour and also noted that he had become 'a needful background' to her life, and, encouraged by what he saw as a new and softer mood, Sidney, keen to draw her closer into his circle, planned to introduce her to more Fabians at a party he was to give for Sydney Olivier who was to be posted abroad. Beatrice in her turn invited Shaw and Pease down to the country. But she was turned down by Shaw on the grounds that the journey was too expensive. He added that she might 'reduce the rest of the Fabians to slavery – they prattle from morning to night about Beatrice Potter in a way I despise – but if I am to go through my amusing conversational performance for you, you must come up to town: this lion is untameable'.[18]

If Sidney had hopes that their friendship could lead to something stronger, he was premature; there was as yet no question of transforming 'I and I into II', as he had begun to presume. Beatrice still kept him at arm's length. They met again in London in October and Beatrice, once more intensely disturbed by his deep devotion, forced herself to discuss her six years' love for Chamberlain. She told Sidney, in answer to a sad letter from him, that she had tried to love him but found it impossible:

> I cannot and will not be engaged to you . . . But if you care to wait until the question is a practical one, promise me one thing – that we write frankly to each other under the promise that if it leads to nothing we return each other's letters, or faithfully destroy them . . . Dear Sidney, I will try to love you, but don't be impatient, do not think the world faithless because I fail to do so! What can I do more? I am doing more than I would do for any other man simply because you are a Socialist and I am a Socialist. That other man I loved but did not believe in, you I believe in but do not love. Will it end equally unhappily?[19]

Beatrice's feelings are difficult to interpret. It was not so much that there was no prospect that she would come to love Sidney (her continuous correspondence proved that she was anxious not to lose him) but rather that she was afraid of becoming emotionally attached to another person. Starved of affection in her youth, her unsatisfactory relationship with Chamberlain had undermined her emotional confidence.

Sidney, whose days after her rejection, seemed 'long and dreary', buried himself in his work. Articles, essays, reviews flowed from his pen, as well as evening lectures for the Fabian Society. Beatrice, whatever her dismissal of Sidney's feelings, had not broken their friendship. She was prepared to carry on with their written relationship but to go no further. Sidney, patient and deeply in love, accepted her terms:

> You are quite free, free even from the apprehension that to decide one way would injure me appreciably or permanently. It may and will diminish my usefulness, but that is not for you so much to be responsible for, and it is not in my hands to prevent.[20]

Beatrice confessed that he had made her feel depressed and miserable and that the burden of unreturned affection was too much. She begged him to believe that what was important was their work and not themselves. Sidney would have none of it. 'Don't say too much about our *work*', he replied tartly, 'if it were to be decided on that ground alone, there could be no doubt as to the answer.'[21] Sidney told her that she was living in the past which 'tended to harden your nature and dry-up your feelings'. He implored her to accept his 'blundering devotion' which he knew she found oppressive but, he declared, emotionally 'I have loved enough for two'. Beatrice refused to be drawn any further. Nevertheless she continued to meet Sidney on the odd occasion. She came to Sydney Olivier's farewell party which made him both happy and nervous but a subsequent conversation with the Booths, who were unimpressed with Sidney, simply added to her general state of emotional depression and irresolution.

In November Sidney became very ill with scarlet fever. The illness dragged on for several weeks and left him feeling flat and debilitated; suddenly he could see no future in their relationship. And yet, as he had admitted, he had had such high hopes in October – the 'zenith of his existence' as he put it. Now it seemed clear to him that Beatrice did not love him. Even so, weakened by the long, drawn-out illness, Sidney could not help himself revealing his feelings to Beatrice. He had, he wrote bitterly to her, realised that this was a crisis in his life. He had hoped to leave the civil service and 'carve out a way of public service in some more honoured sphere'. In this, he told Beatrice accusingly, he had been influenced by her support and encouragement. Now he no longer believed that he had a future with her. Nor, he admitted, could he see himself as the husband of the rich Miss Potter. It would be different if she loved him, 'but you have let me see only too clearly that you do not'. It was therefore her duty to tell him if anything at all would ever induce her to marry him.

Beatrice wrote back honestly. 'I do not love you', she replied.

All the misery of this relationship arises from this . . . there is no change in my feeling except a growing certainty that I cannot love you.

To be perfectly frank I did at one time *fancy* I was beginning to care for you . . . but . . . what I cared for was not *you* but simply the fact of being loved.

> Frankly, I do not believe my nature is capable of love. I came out of that six years of agony . . . a bit of steel. I was not broken but hardened – the fire must do one or the other. And this being the case – the fact that I do not love you – I cannot, and will never, make the stupendous sacrifice of marriage.[22]

There seemed nothing that Sidney could do except accept her decision. 'You will not find' he told her, 'that I will cease to love you, but I will cease to regard you as a "marriagable" person'. He begged Beatrice that they should continue as friends 'or I feel I literally have no-one else'.[23]

Beatrice refused to give Sidney any hope. Kindly, but with great firmness, she drew up new rules for their friendship, which was to continue but not on terms of any intimacy. The crisis between them had also left her shaken and deeply distressed. She feared marriage because she might lose her identity and independence and also because she suspected that her nature was incapable of love. There is an interesting note in her diary towards the end of 1890 on a visit Haldane paid to Box House (to discuss a possible alliance between the progressive Liberals and the Fabians) during which, she thought, he looked her over as a suitable wife. 'I cannot bring myself to face an act of *felo de se*', she recorded, 'for a speculation in personal happiness . . . though I am susceptible to the charm of being loved, I am not capable of loving. Personal passion has burned itself out, and what little personal feeling still exists haunts the memory of that other man' (1 December 1890).

She summed up the past twelve months in her diary as was her usual practice at the end of each year: 'a year of Love, accepted but not given. The tie that was tightening between me and another, I have snapped asunder and I am alone again, facing work and the world' (31 December 1890). A courtship of nine months seemed to have ended.

Despite the apparent break, they met early in the new year. Sidney had previously suggested that she join the Fabian Society but Beatrice had been reluctant to do so on the grounds that it would injure her chances as an impartial investigator. Now she finally allowed herself to become a member on the condition that only her initials would be mentioned in the subscription list. Sidney, who had not yet recovered fully from his illness and whom she had not seen for at least six weeks, persuaded her to discuss her decision with him. She found him in a thoroughly weak state, 'excited and jealous, and more deeply involved than ever' (4 January 1891).

Beatrice gloomily wondered whether she should continue with the friendship.

In spite of her doubts and Sidney's demoralised state, they did not break the link, although the tone of their letters became more impersonal. Sidney recounted the difficulties he was having with Haldane, who was refusing to accept Fabian leadership for his political wing of the Liberal Party, and venturing a little nearer to personal matters, he also told Beatrice that he felt that perhaps he ought to leave the Colonial Office and either enter Parliament or at least stand for the coming LCC election. He was sure, he wrote, to be offered a safe seat. If he accepted he thought he would be able to finance himself through journalism, but he was undecided as to what to do. 'I distrust my power to earn money: I distrust my physical endurance:' he told her in a mood of pessimism. 'I am fearful my brain should breakdown. I dislike and shrink from the publicity, the electoral campaigns . . . if only I knew what I *ought* to do.'[24]

Beatrice, although sympathetic, refused to be drawn into a discussion about his future. She knew too little about the chances of life, she wrote to him, to be able to give any assistance. She did however admit that 'you are admirably suited to Parliamentary and Administrative Life, and the LCC would be a splendid training'.[25] Once more their correspondence returned to impersonal issues such as Sidney's negotiations with the Liberals, and a discussion about her book on Co-operation which was nearing completion. Sidney's blunt criticism of her final draft must have hurt Beatrice, whatever her outward reactions. She had sent him the proofs and got an immediate reply. He was, he told her in early March 1891, disappointed; he admitted he had perhaps expected too much. 'You have taken too long over it', he wrote critically. 'The book will not be a *very* great work.'[26] Beatrice accepted his judgement, 'I give it full weight', she replied, 'even if I do not altogether agree with it'.

In April 1891 the situation changed in Sidney's favour. Sidney, having spent a considerable time unable to make up his mind whether to give up the civil service and go into politics, suddenly decided to make the change. If, 'things look clearer as the summer advances', he wrote to a political acquaintance, 'I shall plunge'. And to John Burns, one of the most famous London labour leaders, he offered himself as Parliamentary candidate for Bethnal Green. He made Beatrice aware of the way his mind was going and asked her opinion again. 'You are under some responsibility to *use* your influence and not ignore it' he told her at the beginning of April. 'Help me!' he pleaded. Beatrice, who with her book on Co-operation reaching the proof stage was already discussing with Sidney her next project (a study of trade unionism) and who in any case was already coming up to London to give a series of lectures on the Co-operative Movement, agreed to meet him.

Immediately they met she asked Sidney's advice as to how to draft a press release for *The Times* which needed one for an advance summary. Sidney speedily wrote a précis which was more lucid – she admitted – than her own lecture. This was the first time she had been asked to give a public lecture and felt 'horribly nervous', particularly when she saw the distinguished audience who had come to hear her.

It is difficult to trace the change in her feelings for Sidney. Perhaps a long estrangement from each other, his unfailing kindness and devotion, his tough criticism over her book where he considered it justified, the very simple but vital help he gave her over her press statement, even the success of her own lecture, all must suddenly have combined to make him indispensable. Perhaps she also felt that if he became a fulltime politician, she would lose him. Whatever the reasons, the indecision of the preceding months vanished at the Co-operative Congress in May, and on their return Beatrice acknowledged to Sidney that she loved him. The barriers against her emotion had finally been pulled down. 'I cannot tell how things will settle themselves', she wrote, but then went on to admit,

> I think probably in his way. His resolute patient affection, his honest care for my welfare – helping and correcting me – a growing distrust of a self-absorbed life and the egotism of successful work . . . all these feelings are making for our eventual union – the joining together of our resources – mental and material – serve together the 'commonwealth' . . . if I marry – though I shall be drawn to it by affection and gratitude – it will be an act of renunciation of self and not of indulgence of self, as it would have been in the other case. Perhaps, therefore it will be blessed to both of us. (22 May 1891)

Nothing could mar Sidney's delight. 'I cannot exhaust the present moment', he wrote to her ecstatically, 'which is *délire, extase, ivresse*'.

At the end of May they became engaged, though because of her father whom they knew would never approve, they decided to keep it a secret. Beatrice had a final look at her correspondence with Chamberlain to test herself, and found that she could now do so with calmness. Sidney had won.

The following month they went to Norway with Graham Wallas and a young woman Fabian friend Clara Bridgman. Sidney, at last successful, was happy and content. Beatrice, although now accepting her commitment to Sidney, retained some hesitancy as to her true feelings: 'On the face of it,' she wrote,

> it seems an extraordinary end to the once brilliant Beatrice Potter . . . to marry an ugly little man with no social position and less means, whose only recommendation – so some may say – is a certain pushing ability. And I am not 'in love', not as I was . . . our marriage will be based on fellowship – the common faith and a common work. (20 June 1891)

Having agreed to marry him, Beatrice immediately set about organising Sidney's future. She felt that now that he had the backing of her money, he should give up the Colonial Office as he had planned and stand for the LCC where he would get valuable administrative experience (which she believed he sadly lacked). Sidney had hoped to make about £2000 a year from his journalism which would have enabled him to support Beatrice adequately. She would have none of it; such work, she decided would sap his energies and waste his time, and when Sidney doubted the wisdom of simply relying on her money, he was overruled. 'We are both of us second-rate minds', she told him 'but we are curiously combined – I am the investigator and he the executor – and we have a wide and varied experience of men and things between us. We have also our unearned salary. This forms our unique circumstances' (7 July 1891). It was therefore agreed that he would resign, collaborate with Beatrice on her trades union book, and go into London politics.

On their return to England, though their engagement was still a secret, Beatrice decided to tell the news to the Booths who had remained among her closest friends. They received her announcement coolly – Mary after all had doubted the suitability of Sidney's friendship for Beatrice. She was hurt by their lack of enthusiasm, although they were pleased that she should look 'so young, pretty and blooming'. Other friends however, such as Alice Green, Graham Wallas and Haldane, were delighted, so it was with a good deal of happiness that she returned to her father's bedside and to her new studies.

The following month Beatrice moved into Herbert Spencer's house in St John's Wood. It was a time of marvellous freedom for her. She and Sidney met every day to discuss the format of their trade union project, entertained trade union leaders and worked 'away together, undermining the individualism of the British race, with intervals of 'human nature' (19 August 1891). Sidney, too, was deliriously happy ('surely no one was ever quite so fortunate before'), though his joy was tempered by the sudden death of his father that summer. By August Beatrice was back in Gloucestershire looking after her father once more. She kept her engagement a secret from her sisters which gave her a curious pleasure, as the following extract from a letter to Sidney testifies:

> This morning I had a walk with Kate. She was very friendly and in the course of the talk exclaimed 'I wonder whether you will marry?' I sedately replied that I thought it highly probable . . . She asked me whether I liked Sidney Webb as much after the tour as before? I answered enigmatically, 'I like both those men immensely', and then told her that Graham Wallas was coming to spend a week.[27]

They tried to meet as often as they could but Beatrice was tied down either in the country or by her new researches. However, at the end of September she travelled up to Newcastle for that year's Trades Union Congress. She still disliked the growing influence of the new militant trades unionists and was worried that they would cause the break-up of the Trades Union movement. Sidney joined her later in the north-east and together they continued the round of interviews of local trade union officials which she had already begun. Beatrice worried what effect her marriage would have on her work. 'I love you – but I love my work better!' she wrote revealingly to Sidney. His resignation from the Colonial Office had by then become official and his emergence into political life assured. He was asked to stand for a safe seat for the London School Board and the Shoreditch Radicals suggested that he become their candidate for the LCC. Parliamentary seats were also discussed although Beatrice was against it. 'You will lose sight of the direction the machine should take' she warned him. She was, however, anxious that he stand for the LCC and in December Sidney accepted an invitation to be a

Progressive candidate for Deptford (which he won the following year).

As Sidney could not get away from London, Beatrice was left alone to carry on with their investigations. She now became disheartened by the size of the enquiry, finding it physically and mentally exhausting, and came to the conclusion, in a sudden mood of despondency, that she had not the strength to carry on. Sidney, at his most loving, assured her that all would be well, promising her all the help he could give and persuading her that she should not feel

> any compunction that your work will take you away from me sometimes. We are not going into this union anymore than we go about any other part of our lives, merely to make things pleasant to us. You know, that I know, and I know that you know, that with each of us duty is imperative: and, dearest, our kisses will be all the sweeter when we can afford them . . . My dearest love, don't be despondent.[28]

It was but one of many such comforting letters.

Beatrice, heartened by the stream of loving letters from London, overcame her self-doubts. Instead she turned to organising Sidney from afar. 'Get a new tie and string to your pince-nez!' she admonished. 'And look after your pronunciation. You can't afford not to be careful about externals you can improve!'[29]

While in the north-east Beatrice suddenly saw Chamberlain and his new wife on the same train. She found there were no regrets. 'Now, indeed, I can bless him for his clear understanding of my deficiencies for the great role of "walking gentlewoman" to the play of *Chamberlain*!'

Beatrice returned to Box House in November to find her father very ill; it looked as if he were dying. They made plans to tell her sisters of their engagement in the New Year as her father lingered on, and Beatrice had not the heart to leave him for more than a day. She and Sidney corresponded almost daily in lieu of meetings, analysing their joint work, their future and the faults in their character. 'What you say about one's *success* securing consideration (rather than one's deserts)', Sidney admitted to her,

> is true enough . . . Do you know, I fear we are both a little apt to be *too* fond of success and consideration . . . Secretly conscious of our own imperfections (perhaps morbidly so) we wonder whether

> we are of any use at all; and are glad to be reassured by the kindly praise of our friends.[30]

And although uncertain as to when their future together would be, Beatrice now looked ahead to it. 'When we have finished the Trade Union book', she wrote to Sidney in November, 'I shall also be able to devote myself to getting to know the ins and outs of London government and to getting some personal hold over councillors and officials. We might make our house the centre of London government.'[31]

By the end of the month Beatrice decided that it would be wiser to tell her sisters about her engagement, only kept secret in order to spare her father whom she knew would have been horrified at the thought of her marrying Sidney. Then 'we can begin the New Year openly – and face everything openly and together'.[32] She became very depressed during the long winter evenings as she watched her father weaken slowly. She even hated work and felt dispirited about 'those ugly details of day work and piecework . . . and the squalid fortunes of defaulting branch officers'. The only thing that kept her from giving it all up and turning to novels was the memory of those they investigated. 'That ever-important 30 per cent – with the background of their terrible East End streets'.[33] Sidney, on the other hand, confessed 'to a low taste. I *like* the kitchen of life. Trade unions and details of administration are more to me than art or literature . . . I want to be more "cultivated" and we must try to carve a little time together for pictures and poetry and music, you patiently helping me to comprehend.' And referring to the prospect of standing as an LCC candidate he wrote lightheartedly, 'Yes, you shall give me a cheque for County Council expenses: it won't come to £100 *at most* – and I shall be the "Member for Potter".'[34]

Whatever her father's condition, it was clear that a new life was beginning for them. Beatrice, writing to Sidney on Christmas Day, acknowledged her need of him and her love:

> Dear One, I will try to repay your love and devotion and to make your home and happiness together – in spite of your 'professional' wife. I will try and prove that a woman may be a loving wife and gentle mistress without assuming to be a strenuous public servant. But I shall often stumble and fall – and you must help me up and protect me against self-complacancy or lethargy either at home or in our work.[35]

They did not have long to wait. Richard Potter died on New Year's Eve. 'The end came peacefully this morning', Beatrice wrote sadly to Sidney.

> Kate and I watched till two o'clock and then left and I was with him again about eight. He died a few minutes before nine o'clock . . . It seems a long while to look back on these six years – six years ago at this time . . . I was in the depths of despair. My life seemed finished . . . Now I can with your love look forward to a life of effort and faith and affection. We will try to live our lives with dignity and devotion, as Father did according to his lights in his day.[36]

Beatrice was left with an annual income of £1000 and was therefore free to marry; there was nothing now to stop the announcement of their engagement. She anticipated opposition and wrote to her sisters appealing to them not to turn against her. 'I need not say that, should my marriage mean a break . . . between us', she told her sister Mary, 'I should be genuinely and personally grieved.'[37]

To her eldest sister she sent a long letter elaborating on Sidney's background so as to set her family's mind at rest. 'You will feel assured', she told Lallie sternly after describing Sidney's brilliant examination successes, 'that your new brother-in-law, however below the family standard in means and position, is not different in those substantial qualities of character and intelligence which enable a man to be successful in the line of life that he deliberately chooses.' His warmth, generosity and quick perception, she added, the family would soon come to acknowledge.[38] On the whole her family behaved 'with tolerance and good sense'. It was the old philosopher, Herbert Spencer, who refused to give her his blessing. As an individualist, he told Beatrice, he had little sympathy with one who believed in the collectivist state. And sadly he asked her to relinquish her duties as his literary executor.

In the following weeks Sidney met Beatrice's family, and she in turn met his. When she paid a visit to Park Village East, Sidney's home, the dingy and crowded little workroom where he wrote initially dismayed her, though she liked his mother and 'energetic, warm-hearted, plain body of a sister'. Gradually, she admitted, 'the feeling of unwished for dislike of ugly and small surroundings disappeared in the blessedness of love' (21 January 1892). But both came to the conclusion that they had little in common with either side of the family and that in future they would lead their own lives.

They decided not to marry until Beatrice had completed the major part of her research for their trade union book. The date fixed was the last week in July. The months in between were furiously busy. Sidney spent most of them electioneering in Deptford, while Beatrice attended union and branch meetings all over the country. He was elected on 5 March after a brilliant and energetic campaign and immediately was expected to become a powerful figure in the new LCC. Both hated the separation and were deeply relieved when July came.

Beatrice and Sidney were married on 23 July 1892 in the vestry hall of St. Pancras. To the end Beatrice was reluctant to lose her freedom. On their wedding day she cryptically recorded, 'exit Beatrice Potter, enter Beatrice Webb or rather (Mrs) Sidney Webb for I lose, alas, both names'.

NOTES

1. B. Potter to S. Webb, 2 May 1890, Passfield Papers.
2. S. Webb to B. Potter, 30 Apr 1890, Passfield Papers.
3. B. Potter to S. Webb, 2 May 1890, Passfield Papers.
4. S. Webb to B. Potter, 14 May 1890, Passfield Papers.
5. S. Webb to B. Potter, 24 May 1890, Passfield Papers.
6. B. Potter to S. Webb, 29 May 1890, Passfield Papers.
7. S. Webb to B. Potter, 30 May 1890, Passfield Papers.
8. B. Potter to S. Webb, 31 May 1890, Passfield Papers.
9. S. Webb to B. Potter, 4 June 1890, Passfield Papers.
10. B. Potter to S. Webb, 11 June 1890, Passfield Papers.
11. S. Webb to B. Potter, 24 June 1890, Passfield Papers.
12. Ibid, 29 July 1890, Passfield Papers.
13. B. Potter to S. Webb, 9 Aug 1890, Passfield Papers.
14. S. Webb to B. Potter, 11 Aug 1890, Passfield Papers.
15. B. Potter to S. Webb, 23 Aug 1890, Passfield Papers.
16. Ibid, undated, Passfield Papers.
17. S. Webb to B. Potter, 18 Sept 1890, Passfield Papers.
18. G. B. Shaw to B. Potter, 6 Oct 1890, Passfield Papers.
19. B. Potter to S. Webb, 8 or 11 Oct 1890, Passfield Papers.
20. S. Webb to B. Potter, 17 Oct 1890, Passfield Papers.
21. Ibid, 18 Oct 1890, Passfield Papers.
22. B. Potter to S. Webb, 4 Dec 1890.
23. S. Webb to B. Potter, 5 Dec 1890, Passfield Papers.
24. Ibid, 27 Jan 1891, Passfield Papers.
25. B. Potter to S. Webb, 29 Jan 1891, Passfield Papers.

26. S. Webb to B. Potter, 14 Mar 1891, Passfield Papers.
27. B. Potter to S. Webb, 20 Aug 1891, Passfield Papers.
28. S. Webb to B. Potter, 14 Sept 1891, Passfield Papers.
29. B. Potter to S. Webb, 21 Oct 1891, Passfield Papers.
30. S. Webb to B. Potter, 14 Nov 1891, Passfield Papers.
31. B. Potter to S. Webb, 18 Nov 1891, Passfield Papers.
32. Ibid, 22 Nov 1891, Passfield Papers.
33. Ibid, 8 Dec 1891, Passfield Papers.
34. S. Webb to B. Potter, 9 Dec 1891, Passfield Papers.
35. B. Potter to S. Webb, 25 Dec 1891, Passfield Papers.
36. Ibid, 1 Jan 1892.
37. B. Potter to M. Playne, 8 Jan 1892, Passfield Papers.
38. B. Potter to L. Holt, written Dec 1891 sent Jan 1892, Liverpool Record Office.

4
1892–1897
Marriage, Politics and Writing

'Our Business is to Convert the Whole Community to Socialism.'

On 24 July 1892 the Webbs set off to Dublin for their honeymoon. As so often abroad, their reaction towards the natives was less than charitable: 'the people are charming but we detest them', Sidney wrote to Wallas 'as we should the Hottentots – for their very virtue'. And Beatrice acidly added: 'Home Rule is an absolute necessity – in order to depopulate the country of this detestable race!'[1] It was a busman's holiday: in Dublin they investigated the 'ramshackle' trade societies and in Belfast they interviewed 'hard-fisted employers and groups of closely organised skilled craftsmen'.

They ended their holiday at Glasgow, where Sidney had first declared his love for Beatrice, and attended the Trades Union Congress taking place there. The 1892 Congress, meeting against the background of recession, was less stormy than on previous occasions. Beatrice, never wholly understanding nor in sympathy with the new unionists, noted that 'the sting of the New Unionist has been effectively drawn out by the adhesion of the cotton officials to the eight-hour day' (August 1892). The socialists, she observed, had abandoned their 'scurrilous and aggressive' tactics of the Dundee Conference of 1889 in favour of Fabian permeation.

The first six years (1892–1898) of their married life were amazingly busy. The Webbs were occupied first of all with their monumental enquiry into the British trade union movement which led to two important books: *The History of Trade Unionism*, published in 1894 and *Industrial Democracy*, published in 1897. Both Webbs, and Sidney in particular, were closely involved in Fabian and left-wing politics at a crucial period. At the same time, Sidney played a prominent part (which is described in the next chapter) in London local politics and government. In addition, both were much in demand as lecturers on political, social and trade union issues.

On their return to London from their honeymoon, the Webbs settled in a flat at 10 Netherhall Gardens near Swiss Cottage. Beatrice described the pattern of their day in her diary:

> Each morning we begin work about 9.30 (breakfast, and reading papers and letters take an hour) – Galton joins us about 10 and we three drive through material until 1 or 1.30. Then four days out of six, Sidney hurries off to London and gives the remainder of his day to the London County Council. Meanwhile, Galton goes on steadfastly. I spend a couple of hours either walking on the Heath . . . or shopping.

She and Galton, their faithful secretary (who later they helped appoint as General Secretary of the Fabian Society) then worked for another two hours and at

> 7.30 Sidney returns full of the doings of the LCC or carrying back news of an interview with a Cabinet Minister on some proposed reform. A simple meat supper, cigarettes and then an evening of peaceful happiness – either in reading to me, working at LCC matters, or we entertain workingmen friends, and so forth. (1 December 1892)

In the 'even tenor' of their new happiness, they worked steadily throughout 1892 on the book on trade unions, gathering and sifting material. Beatrice bore the main weight of the research, travelling all over the country to investigate the major trade union branches, sitting in on executive meetings, and having long discussions with local branch officials. She spent some time in Manchester on her own, while Sidney, who disliked interviewing, remained behind to deal with the documentation. Their books were very much a joint effort: Beatrice did most of the research, while Sidney, in his clear handwriting, wrote the books. Beatrice however was more than a talented researcher. Galton recalled that she 'had a very considerable facility for seeing how questions stood towards each other and recognising the common thread of use between things and ideas apparently unrelated to each other'.[2]

As regards the subject of their first joint book, Beatrice had convinced the far from reluctant Sidney of the need for rising young politicians to understand about working class institutions. There had been no mention of trade unions in the *Fabian Essays* and though this was understandable given the authors' background, it was a serious gap. Sidney had been much impressed by the events of 1889 and had become aware of the potential power, industrial rather than political, of the trade union movement. At the same time, their research fitted in with both the Webbs' firm conclusion that the study of social organisations by enlightened specialists would inevitably lead, once the facts had been presented to an educated public, to progress and therefore to socialism. As Sidney declared later of the first of their investigations, 'We learned a lot about . . . social organisation – in short, about Socialism itself.'[3]

Their first six months of marriage drew the couple far closer together than Beatrice had ever imagined. Sidney was enjoying his work at the LCC and the joint writing of the trade union book had begun. Beatrice declared optimistically: 'I look forward with wonderful happiness to the coming year. Creative work is always delightful to me: and the stress and strain of writing a big book will be incalculably lightened by his help and loving kindness.' Even so she was already anxious about the pull of politics on Sidney, 'Who knows how long I may have a large share of his life – how soon he may not belong body and soul to the nation' (1 December 1892). Certainly, despite his marriage, Sidney continued to be closely involved with wider political issues.

The key question in left-wing politics of the 1890s remained whether it was possible to create a radicalised Liberal Party which would implement socialist measures, or whether there was no alternative to pursuing a course of political independence. Sidney's position was ambivalent. His success in the LCC elections and his link with the Progressives brought him closer to the Liberals. He had also been encouraged by Gladstone's adoption of the Newcastle Programme in 1891 with its far-reaching plans for social reform, though this had been due not to the success of Fabian permeation (whatever Shaw's later propaganda might claim) but to the exigencies of the coming General Election in 1892, and a belated response by the Gladstonian leadership to the demands of the radical elements, such as Haldane and Asquith, within the party. Indeed at the Newcastle conference Sidney had neither been allowed to speak nor had his suggestion that fifty parliamentary seats be allocated to Liberal–Labour candidates won acceptance.

But if Sidney preferred to retain his links with the Liberals, he did not want to separate himself irrevocably from those who, like the SDF, Keir Hardie and the New Unionists as well as some Fabians, supported the idea of an independent Socialist Party. At the first Fabian Conference (held in early 1892) Sidney had actually seconded a resolution calling for the working classes to act independently of existing political parties and for the setting up of an independent Labour Party. But in spite of his tactical manoeuvres, Sidney at this stage clearly believed that the kind of reforms which he advocated (such as the demand for an eight-hour Bill, pensions for the aged, municipalisation of major services) could easily be incorporated in radical and progressive programmes.

At the July 1892 election, in which he and the Fabians were closely involved, he gave his support to radical Liberal candidates. Even so, he kept in with those who believed in an independent Socialist Party by working with the SDF candidate at Bradford, Ben Tillett. He explained to Beatrice that the opportunity of using the election campaign to educate the public about socialist issues was more important than the actual result.

The victory of the Liberals, who became the biggest single party, and the poor showing of the independent socialist candidates (only John Burns and Keir Hardie were successful and they both relied heavily on Liberal backing) confirmed Sidney and other leading Fabians in their view that it was best to work within the Liberal Party. But they were over-optimistic about the prospect for social reform because they under-estimated the hold of the Irish parliamentarians over the government. Sidney's own success as a Progressive on the LCC may also have made the Webbs unrealistic about the possibility of Fabian permeation at this time. Beatrice recorded in her diary that Sidney was now 'steadily acquiring influence with the official Liberals: regarded every day more as a man who must be listened to and if possible complied with . . . What he is rapidly becoming is the *chief instigator* of policies; the source of liberal doctrine' (1 December 1892). The *Labour Elector*, mouthpiece of the SDF, made the same point less charitably when it described Sidney as 'a mere Liberal politician with the thin veneer of middle class Socialism put on . . . As a statistician on labour questions, Mr Webb's a jack-daw strutting in peacock's plumes.'[4]

Keir Hardie and other socialists, including Robert Blatchford, Tom Mann, Ben Tillett, Kate Conway and Edward Aveling, drew a different conclusion from Sidney Webb. What was needed (they believed) was not only independent socialist candidates but also an independent political party backed by as many trade unions (some of whom were becoming increasingly politically conscious) as possible. A conference held in Bradford in January 1893, which Shaw attended for the Fabians, established the Independent Labour Party.

The formation of the ILP, which Shaw opposed vigorously as being likely to prove counterproductive, was nevertheless a major challenge to the Fabian Society. The Bradford conference's rejection of a proposal to allow branches to affiliate to other bodies was by implication also a repudiation of the Fabian tactical approach at a time when the disappointing programme of the Liberal government made association with the Liberals seem increasingly unattractive. There was the strong danger that the creation of the ILP would shift the initiative from the Fabians and erode their membership.

Shaw and Webb who, with Wallas, formed the ruling 'junta' of the Society, decided that the Fabians would have to react to the new situation. Sidney wrote to Wallas that there was a need

> for a strong tract showing up the Liberal Party and advocating as many decent Labour candidates as possible. But it ought not to be so difficult to make clear to the members that, with the ILP, various trade union attempts at political action, and the innumerable other Labour Parties in the field, any attempt at SDF sectarian exclusiveness must be fatal.[5]

In November 1892 Webb and Shaw published a devastating attack on the government in the *Fortnightly Review*. 'To Your Tents O Israel' was a detailed exposé of the Liberals. The government, the authors argued, had virtually ignored the Newcastle Programme, failed to bring forward any significant social measures and had not even implemented reforms in those areas where the lack of a parliamentary majority (such as in the administration of Departments) was irrelevant. It was a devastating indictment of a party whose failure, the authors declared, was due to lack of willpower.

Their solution was the formation of a new group of fifty independent working class MPs. Beatrice claimed in her diary that Shaw and Webb had come round to the idea of a need for the setting up of an independent Labour Party backed by trade union money. However a better indication of Sidney's attitude was a letter to Graham Wallas in which he wrote that a third candidate should stand only where 'no advanced radical is in the field'. The fact that they carefully mentioned a number identical to that quoted by Sidney in his earlier negotiations with the Liberals indicates that they saw the fifty members more as a ginger group than a politically independent party, collectivists with Fabian sympathies rather than militant members of the ILP or the SDF.

What is clear is that 'To Your Tents O Israel' shows a new awareness, probably influenced by the Webbs' researches, of the significance of trades unions. There was only

> one organising agency which is so much more effective and advanced than any other, that its superior fitness for the political work in hand is beyond all question; and that is the trade union organisation. There is nothing in the labour world that can compare even distantly with it . . . Neither the Fabian Society nor the Social Democratic Federation, neither the Labour Electoral Association nor the society known as the Independent Labour Party, has the slightest prospect of mustering enough money to carry through three serious candidates, much less fifty. Their part will be to provide the agitation which will enable the trade union leaders to obtain the support of the rank and file in rising to the occasion.[6]

Whatever the underlying implications of the *Fortnightly Review* article, the furore that followed, particularly from Liberals with collectivist sympathies and radicals who were also members of the Fabian Society, was unprecedented. They saw it simply as a Fabian agitation for a new party. Haldane called it 'a stab in the back'. Massingham, editor of *The Star* and a good friend of the Fabian Society, resigned because, as he told Sidney, he disagreed 'with everything in this unhappy and ridiculous document . . . mischievous in the highest degree . . . There is not a serious sentence in it.'[7] Even Michael Davitt, leader of the Irish Parliamentarians, took it upon himself to comment: 'I believe your manifesto *may* do harm to the Home Rule cause but I am certain it will do no good to that of Labour'.[8] For those who believed in an independent political party, it rather looked as if Shaw and Webb were closing the door after the ILP horse had bolted. It was a gesture of defiance which may have had useful publicity value but harmed Sidney's standing with the progressive members of the Liberal party and yet because he was ambivalent about independent politics also failed to strengthen his position with the socialists, the ILP and the more radical elements of the Fabian Society.

Throughout the 1890s the Webbs prevaricated over working class representation in spite of pressure from the ILP. They continued to believe that the Fabian Society had an important role to play in 'permeating' the most powerful and influential groups in the country and that there was hope of converting the Liberals. There was another reason; neither Beatrice nor Sidney, despite their involvement and belief in the importance of trade union organisation, had much faith in the quality of leadership exhibited by the most powerful figures of the movement, particularly as politicians. They were scornful of their failings and irritated by what they thought of as the narrowness of their objectives. They often misunderstood the type of person with whom they were dealing. Beatrice at one moment could say of John Burns that he had a 'fine, strong intelligence, human sympathy, practical capacity' (12 October 1893) and was therefore a potential leader, and yet only a few months later could decide that neither Burns nor Broadhurst (General Secretary of the Stonemasons' Union, Secretary of the Parliamentary Committee of the TUC and Liberal MP from 1894 to 1906) were men of great calibre because they admired 'extravagantly' the middle classes, and that there was 'no sign yet of any real leader either in the Labour Movement or the radical ranks' (2 March 1894).

They also underestimated Keir Hardie's qualities, refusing to accept him as a serious figure, 'he knows little and cares less for any constructive thought or action' (23 January 1895). Indeed, Beatrice even toyed with the idea that Sidney should become a political leader. With devastating clarity, however, she weighed up the pros and cons of such a move and decided that Sidney would not do:

> For a popular leader his personality is not sufficiently striking and attractive for real 'Direction' and 'Mediation'; his intellectual grasp, his resource, ingenuity, quickness and lucidity of expression,

> above all his quite extraordinary freedom from personal vanity or the vulgar form of ambition, render him an admirable instrument. It is my business to see that he has the material to work upon in so far as hospitality, discretion and tact can bring it. It will be discretion that I shall lack most! (12 March 1894)

She was even hostile to the idea of a parliamentary career for Sidney. She wrote in her diary that he was too good for the 'manipulations and intrigues' of Parliament, and she also noted that if Sidney was in Parliament it would 'cut at the root of a good deal of our joint effort . . . it would take so much away from me – personally – would add so many ties and inconveniences' (10 July 1894). Beatrice had a point: clearly they could never have produced the volume of work they did if Sidney had been tied up in Parliamentary politics from the beginning of their married life.

In the autumn of 1893 the Webbs took a long lease on a house, 41 Grosvenor Road (on the Embankment), where they lived until the 1920s. It was near Westminster, near Spring Gardens (then the headquarters of the LCC) and near Whitehall and the major departments of state; an altogether convenient location. The house was also designed to suit their way of life. The dining room, which was on the ground floor, was converted into a workroom and was lined with Government blue books; the drawing-room had no sofa so they could accommodate the largest possible number of guests; and in between, on the half-landing, Galton's room was covered from floor to ceiling with boxes filled with research notes and shelves crammed with pamphlet literature. However, though a determined utilitarian, Beatrice took some trouble over the furniture and the William Morris hangings. 'I do not wish it to be thought that simplicity of daily life means ugliness and lack of order and charm' (17 September 1893). She also recalled that the best thing about the house was the beauty of the view:

> To spring out of bed on a summer morning and see, spread out before you, the sun rising behind Lambeth Palace, on clear days the Dome of St Paul's and the spires of the City churches, its rays lighting up the tiny waves breaking the surface of the swift-flowing tidal river, whilst oar-steered barges, some with red or yellow sails, drifting rafts of timber and steaming colliers passed under the Vauxhall and Lambeth bridges, was a joyful greeting to another day.[9]

Beatrice was now extraordinarily happy in her new life although still occasionally unable to escape those moments of self-doubt and guilt which plagued her all her life. 'Sometimes', she wrote at the end of 1893,

> one feels guilty of this abundance of happiness – as if of a monopoly. Sometimes I feel that the ease and comfort of our lives is stolen from others and that we ought to be more ascetic. We work hard it is true – Sidney especially – but this work is what we like and we deny ourselves nothing that we really desire – we are – at any rate I am, self-indulgent – more self-indulgent than we ought to be. (25 December 1893)

Even so, she could add: 'all said and done, I am triumphantly happy'.

The Webbs' *History of Trade Unionism* (which is discussed with their *Industrial Democracy* later in this chapter) came out in the spring. It was exceptionally well received and their friends were unstinting in their praises. Frederick Harrison the positivist talked about "your great and quite invaluable book. It is a monument of labour, judgement and energy which will long remain the classical textbook of labour.' Even Mary Booth, who still found it difficult to accept Beatrice's marriage, broke her long silence to admire their 'intensity of purpose'. To write a history of trade unionism at a time when high politics alone was considered a suitable study for historians was in itself a breakthrough; to make such a success of it was not only a great personal achievement, but also a significant contribution to a better understanding and therefore acceptance of British trade unions.

As a consequence of their joint work on trade unionism, the Webbs became well known figures at TUC and trade union conferences. Sidney was also much in demand as an expert on labour questions. In November 1892 he was asked to give evidence to the Royal Commission on Labour. In his evidence he emphasised the need to extend public control over all industries. He also suggested that the *ad hoc* approach should be abandoned and that instead there should be an extension of 'public organisation or public services wherever possible'. What was needed, he went on, was decent public housing and the municipalisation of transport and docks. His evidence is important not just as a statement of radical reform but also as an indication of his political beliefs. Socialism, he stated, was 'a principle towards which we are moving'. It did not necessarily imply that it would ever be reached but, he added, 'my view of socialism is not that it is a kind of heaven, a kind of stationary state, but a principle of action which more or less influences our practical action'.[10]

Following this evidence he also helped Tom Mann, the dockers' leader, who was a member of the same Royal Commission on Labour, to produce a Minority Report. It was a well-kept secret which was suddenly sprung on the Commission in early March 1894. Although there was nothing particularly revolutionary about the Minority Report proposals, which included among others such old Fabian demands as Factory Act reforms, enactment of a legal eight-hour day and land nationalisation, the other Commissioners were enraged by the element of surprise and by the publicity which the Report received. When Sidney's involvement in the preparation of the Report became known, his standing in the Labour movement increased. Although many Liberals were less impressed, he continued to put great faith in the power of minority reports, pamphlets and lobbying as a means of turning the reluctant Liberal party in the direction of reform; and it was with this in mind that he wrote his second Minority Report, again at the instigation of trade union members, for the Royal Commission on the Aged Poor.

To celebrate the publication of the *History of Trade Unionism* the Webbs went for a badly-needed (they had had no break for three years) spring holiday in Italy. They went first to Venice where:

> our days were spent on the water with an old gondolier whom we engaged by the day, and in St. Mark's Piazza and in St. Mark's itself – that vision of sumptuous beauty which it is a glory to recall. Very sweet hours of companionship – not thinking, but simply feeling the beauty around us – a true honeymoon of love and common enjoyment. (21 May 1894)

But they only had a short rest from working. They had come to the conclusion that the History had merely been a historical introduction to a scientific study of the trade union movement and that it ought therefore to be considered as a preface to the theoretical work which they realised they had yet to write. So, in early 1894, they began to plan their next book which was to be entitled *Industrial Democracy*.

The Webbs found the writing of this new book much more difficult, partly because they were more at home with facts than with theory. Though, according to the pattern that they had earlier established, they retired from July to October to the countryside, the solitude in that first year of writing for once failed to sooth them. Beatrice was surprised by the difficulty, 'not getting on with the book', she recorded in July. 'It is a horrid grind, this analysis – one sentence is exactly like another – the same words, the same construction – no relief in narrative' (10 July 1894). A fortnight later now writing from a farm in Surrey which the Webbs shared for three months with Shaw and Graham Wallas she wrote, disgusted, that she 'was no good at this analytic deductive work . . .' and even began, unrealistically but characteristically, to hanker after another kind of life, claiming in a curiously revealing passage that she would like to have been a mother, although she and Sidney had agreed not to have children – 'but then I had passed the age when it is easy and natural for a woman to become a childbearer – my physical nature was to some extent dried up at 35 after ten years of stress and strain of a purely brainworking and sexless life.' If she were again a young woman, she noted with sadness, she would have opted for motherhood rather than brainwork, 'as it is, I sometimes wonder whether I had better not have risked it and taken my chance' (28 July 1894).

Consistent with her anti-feminist views, Beatrice attributed her difficulties over conceptual thought to her sex rather than to her own lack of analytical power. As we have seen, she initially refused to support the suffragette movement and genuinely believed that woman's place was in the home – partly for rather romantic reasons. 'Surely' she wrote during this time when her work was going badly,

> it is enough to have half the human race straining every nerve to outrun their fellows in the race for subsistence or power? Surely we need some human beings who will watch and pray, who will observe and aspire, and above all, who will guard and love all who are weak, unfit or distressed? (28 July 1894)

Her anti-feminist stance and her dislike of emancipated women was however tempered by her belief that it was the duty of mothers to be educated for the sake of the future race, a theme that runs through much of Beatrice and Sidney's work. A new educated and healthy race needed to be produced so as to be able to take advantage of the opportunities created by the collectivist state of the future.

If 1894 was the year of the books, the following twelve months was the year of electioneering. The LCC elections were held in March, and the Liberal government, wracked by internal dissension and threatened by defeat over Home Rule, was generally expected to fall, thus precipitating a general election. With the Liberals in disarray, Ramsay MacDonald and Frank Smith, members of both the ILP and the Fabian Society, approached the Webbs to see if there could be better liaison between the ILP and the Fabians. Beatrice and Sidney, following their usual policy of keeping their options open, gave a supper party for the ILP and leading Fabians, inviting among others Keir Hardie and Tom Mann, as well as Shaw and Pease. The ILP hoped to persuade the Fabians to disassociate themselves from the Progressives, believing rightly that their continuing co-operation added political muscle to the Liberal Party. If the Society came out against the Liberals it might not give the ILP extra seats but it would certainly strengthen its standing. But the Webbs would have none of it. Sidney claimed that the Fabians were merely an educational body and not a political organisation. As he told Hardie, the Society's future plans were to

> continue our policy of inoculation – of giving to each class – to each person – that came under our influence the exact dose of collectivism that they were prepared to assimilate . . . Of course, this slow imperceptible change in men's opinions and in the national institutions is not favourable to the growth of a revolutionary party. (23 January 1895)

The evening was not a success. The Webbs found it difficult to accept the truth of Hardie's allegation that they were the worst enemies of the socialist revolution, though they themselves charged the ILP with being a revolutionary party, not apparently understanding that independence was not revolution but the most effective way of holding onto the leadership of the labour movement. The meeting underlined the basic differences of approach between the more realistic and politically motivated ILP and the 'Old Gang' of Webb, Pease and Shaw. Beatrice and Sidney genuinely believed that both Keir Hardie and Tom Mann were guilty of a 'narrow sectarian policy' which would be counter-productive to what the Webbs considered essential – 'no great transformation is possible in a free democratic state . . . unless you alter the opinions of all classes'. The ILPers' demand that the

Fabian Society should instruct its members not to vote in the LCC election for any candidate who was not a declared socialist horrified them, particularly Sidney, who as a Progressive candidate believed that the only way to achieve collectivist aims was to take over the running of the various important committees and swing them over to acceptance of socialist objectives.

In the LCC elections, Sidney, running on his own as well as the Progressives' record, was returned comfortably even though the elections themselves produced deadlock between the Progressives and the Moderates. The Webbs were bitterly disappointed at the overall result the more so as the national political scene was also one of discouragement and confusion. Haldane complained to Sidney about the state of the Liberal Party and Massingham, who had forgiven Sidney for his *Fortnightly Review* article, even went so far as to suggest that he should stand for Parliament and, 'become one of the leaders of the reconstruction party'. But Sidney, without Beatrice's wholehearted backing, did not feel able to accept the offer.

July 1895 saw the expected and little lamented demise of the Liberal government on a snap vote. The Webbs, unhappy with the Liberal performance, were not altogether disappointed with the Conservative success in the subsequent general election which gave them a majority of more than 150 seats. 'It leaves us free indeed,' Beatrice wrote, 'to begin afresh on the old lines – of building up a new Party on the basis of Collectivism' (16 July 1895). They were also not displeased with the failure of the ILP to win any seats. As Beatrice noted, so long as the ILP 'existed as an unknown force of irreconcilibles, the more reasonable policy of permeation and levelling up was utterly check-mated' (16 July 1895).

Joseph Chamberlain became Colonial Secretary in the new Conservative Government at a time when South Africa was in ferment: Cecil Rhodes, Prime Minister of the Cape Colony, had clashed with the President of the Boer Republic of the Transvaal, Paul Kruger. The outcome had ended in the ill-starred failure of the Jameson raid by the Cape Colonists. Beatrice, who usually had little interest in anything outside Britain, was intrigued, partly because she approved of Joseph Chamberlain's repudiation of the raid. 'It is a comfortable thought' she wrote, 'that we have a Government of strong, resolute men – not given either to bluster or vacillation – but prompt in taking every measure to keep us out of a war and to make us successful should we be forced in it' (5 January 1896).

Admiration for Chamberlain encouraged the Webbs to mend their fences with the new Conservative government. They believed that the disarray of the Liberals would ensure that the Conservatives remained in power for some time. Sidney, as Chairman of the Technical Education Board on the LCC, was drawn into discussions on the new Education Bill which the Conservatives were proposing[11] and gradually they found themselves having dinner with both the Government and the Opposition, discovering no difficulty in eating one night with Haldane and Asquith and the next with Sir John Gorst and Lord George Hamilton, as well as meeting as many top civil servants as they could. It was the kind of political wire-pulling they believed would achieve the most satisfactory result. In addition, Beatrice derived some innocent pleasure from their, and particularly Sidney's, social success: 'all this is in a way pleasant. I do not hide from myself that I am pleased and flattered that my boy is recognised as a distinguished man' (Whitsun 1896).

Meanwhile, their exasperation with the infant British socialist movement is well illustrated by Beatrice's comments on the International Socialist Congress held in London in the summer of 1896. She was impressed by the German socialists. ('The party is closely knit together and apparently free of the frothy irresponsibility of our English movement') and the Belgians who, like the Germans, were 'preparing themselves (perhaps prematurely) to become H.M. opposition'. In contrast, most of the socialists, particularly the British, were 'unusually silly folk (for the most part feather-headed failures) and heaped together in one hall with the consciousness that our every word would be reported by the world's press, they approached raving imbecility'. She admired the Fabians sitting silently, 'taking notes as reporters for the "Capitalist Press"' (14 August 1896). Sidney, who described the event in the *Manchester Guardian*, also could find little to approve. If the Congress had been less unwieldy or less caught up in credential issues 'instead of being swamped by faggot votes manufactured in the interests of this or that faction, it might not lead the world but its members would gain a great deal of wisdom'.[12]

It would be giving a mistaken impression of the Webbs to imply that they did nothing but write books and 'permeate'. They much enjoyed the company of their Fabian friends, particularly Wallas and Shaw, with whom they went away for the weekend together, often to the Argoed, the Potter summer home. Beatrice admired

Wallas for his intellect but was often exasperated by his indecision.

> It is all very well not to commit yourself; but if you are not already committed at the age of forty, it is a little late to step out of your trammels! Poor Graham, he is one of those sensitive, self-conscious men who will always be in trouble about his soul. (25 September 1895)

Her first impression of Shaw was somewhat unfavourable – 'a slight personality; agile, graceful and even virile; but lacking in weight (17 September 1893). But she became fond of him. After a holiday at the Argoed she wrote of him 'a perfect "housefriend" – self-sufficient, witty and tolerant, going his own way and yet adapting himself to your ways' (25 September 1895). The Webbs also came to like Bertrand Russell, who stayed with them at the Argoed. Bertrand, a brilliant don at Trinity, Cambridge ('subtle and contentious') was married to Alys Pearsall Smith, 'a pretty, bright American Quakeress, some years older than himself with anarchic views of life'.

A year later the Webbs' houseparty at a rectory near Saxmundham in Suffolk included Charlotte Payne Townshend and Bernard Shaw. Charlotte was 'a large, graceful woman with masses of chocolate-brown hair, pleasant grey eyes (*later*: they are green) "matte" complexion which sometimes looks muddy, at other times forms a picturesquely pale background to her brilliant hair and bright eyes' (16 September 1896). Beatrice had had hopes of marrying her off to Graham Wallas but, as she noted with some amusement of Charlotte and Shaw, 'they have been scouring the country together and sitting up late at night . . . She is in love with the brilliant Philander and he is taken in his cold sort of way, with her . . . ' After a long drawn-out and erratic courtship on Shaw's part, they were married two years later.

A memorable occasion was when the Fabian junta stayed in a hotel at Beachy Head and learned for the first time how to ride a bicycle, then becoming all the rage. Beatrice loved bicycling and, as a friend recalled later, 'I have a little picture in my mind of Mrs Webb, who rode extremely well, scudding on before me down one of the back streets of Pimlico with both hands behind her back, steering by her pedals. She was a graceful and intrepid rider'.[13]

To the outside world the young Mrs Webb was anything but an

arid investigator. The interviewer for the magazine *Young Woman* was evidently captivated by her:

> She speaks in a sweet clear voice with great ease and fluency and her conversation is interspersed with flashes of playful humour. There is nothing dry, prosaic or blue-stocking about her. A careless ease and grace and a delightful portrait of one of whom it was said that she ate government blue books for breakfast.[14]

However in many ways they were an extremely self-sufficient couple working closely together. Their 'heaven-sent union' was a source of great happiness to Beatrice. The companionship over *Industrial Democracy*

> has been delightful – the constant testing of the thought by the two minds – the act of *combined thinking* in which the experience and the hypotheses of the two intellects become inextricably mingled, so that we are both unconscious of what we have each of us contributed, has been extraordinarily stimulating. (1 May 1897)

And she reminded herself that had she not been encouraged by a friend, Alice Green, to believe that Sidney 'was essentially distinguished in character and intelligence', she might not have married him.

> For it was reason and not love that won me – a deliberate judgement of the man's worth and an almost cold blooded calculation of the life I could live with him and he with me . . . To a well-trained commercial mind there is charm in making the ideal bargain – the best possible to both parties. (24 May 1897)

Marriage, she felt, had improved Sidney;

> the perfect happiness of his own life has cured his old defects of manner – he has lost the aggressive, self-assertive tone, slight touch of insolence which was not only another form of shyness . . . his improved manner is due to happiness – to the blessed fact of loving and being loved with a love without flaw and blemish. (Christmas 1895)

Industrial Democracy was published at the end of 1897. Together with the *History of Trade Unionism*, it established the Webbs' credentials as the leading scholars of British trade unions – a reputation which still stands today.

The *History of Trade Unionism* traced the growth of the trade union movement from its origins in the seventeenth and eighteenth centuries as a reaction to capitalism ('in all cases in which trades unions arose, the great bulk of the workers had ceased to be independent producers . . . and had passed into the condition of life-long wage-earners . . .'),[15] through to the Combination Acts and their repeal, the upheavals of Owenism and Chartism, the emergence of 'the new model unions', and the supremacy of the junta, and the coming of the 'new' unionism of the unskilled at the end of the 1880s. The final chapter of the 1894 edition surveyed trade union strength as it was in 1892 when trade unionists numbered about twenty per cent of the adult male manual workers and about four per cent of the total population. The Webbs concluded that

> the trade union world was . . . in the main composed of skilled craftsmen working in densely populated districts, where industry was conducted on a large scale. About one half of the members belonged to the three staple trades of coalmining, cotton manufacturing and engineering, whilst the labourers and the women workers were . . . on the whole non-unionist.

Of course, some of the Webbs' judgements have been challenged by Labour historians. In the light of subsequent research, A. E. Musson has queried the Webbs' over-estimation of the influence of Robert Owen on trade unionism in the 1830s and also suggested that what occurred in the 1850s and 1860s was not the creation of a 'new model' but 'a strengthening of the old'.[16] The Marxist historian E. J. Hobsbawm has criticised the Webbs' misunderstanding of the Luddites, while their treatment of 'new unionism' seriously under-estimated both its novelty and importance.

Even so, the Webbs' pioneering work has never been wholly superseded and rightly remains on academic reading lists. Based on original material and meticulously researched, its clarity and authority make it a model of historical writing. It is hardly surprising that Henry Pelling in his own standard *History of British Trade Unionism*, referred to 'the classic work by Beatrice and Sidney

Webb', and that Hobsbawm described them as 'extraordinary scholars'. Most telling of all is the judgement of Musson who, despite his criticisms, paid tribute to 'their immense research and interpretative insight' and judged their book to be 'a monumental piece of scholarship'.

The Webbs designed *Industrial Democracy* to be the analytical and theoretical sequel to their History. In the preface they accurately described it as 'made up of descriptions of fact, generalisations in to theory, and moral judgements'. The first two parts examined trade union structure and function. Drawing on their comprehensive research the first part showed how in many unions 'primitive' or direct democracy had been succeeded by representative control through elected councils. The second part analysed different trade unions, functions and methods including the provision of benefits, unilateral trade union regulation, collective bargaining and legal enactment. The third, and perhaps most interesting, part attempted to construct a theory of trade unionism to explain the work which they had explored and also to predict how trade unionism might develop in a democratic society and the implication of trade unionism for that society.

The extent of the influence that the theory of trade unionism formulated in *Industrial Democracy* has had on subsequent generations, (particularly of British industrial relations scholars) is indicated by the fact that the recent academic controversy between Allan Flanders and Alan Fox about the nature of collective bargaining took place in the form of a discussion about the Webbs' views, put forward over seventy years before.

In his own definition of trade union objectives, Flanders criticised the Webbian model because it was based on a confusion between individual and collective bargaining and because it overemphasised the economic at the expense of other reasons for trade union involvement in collective bargaining. According to Flanders, the main trade union aim is the establishment of a system of industrial rights through joint regulations.[17]

In his devastating reply, Fox defended the Webbs against Flanders' attack by showing that when they saw collective bargaining as the collective and therefore most advantageous equivalent of individual bargaining ('instead of the employer making a series of separate contracts with isolated individuals, he meets with a collective will, and settles, in a single agreement, the principles upon which, for the time being all workmen of a particular group or class or grade, will be engaged')[18] they were fundamentally right. As Fox pointed out, they correctly identified the significance of the trade union protective function by demonstrating that

> whereas, under purely individual dealings, the agreement which governs the contract is usually the product of a grossly unequal power relationship, the collective situation enables the employee to approach the living process greatly strengthened by a collective agreement which is the product of a significantly smaller disparity of power.[19]

With respect to trade union objectives, Fox convincingly argued that the Webbs were well aware of the broader aspects of trade unionism. Indeed, in their chapter on the assumptions of trade unionism, they had drawn a distinction between one based upon the 'Device of Restriction of Numbers' and one based upon the 'Device of the Common Rule'; the first sought to apply restrictions in the supply of labour, output, mechanical improvements and so on, while the second aimed to establish minimum standards, not just over wage rates but also over leisure, training, health, safety and other basic requirements of working life. The Webbs left readers in little doubt which model they preferred. Long before Flanders, they were urging trade unions to see their objectives in a wider context;

> to obtain . . . not what will be immediately most enjoyed by the 'average, sensual man' but what, in the long run, must conduce to his efficiency as a professional, a parent and a citizen. In all the better-paid crafts of the England of today, shorter more regular hours, greater healthfulness, comfort and refinement in the conditions of work, and the definite provision of periodical holidays for recreation, are, in the interest of industrial and civic efficiency, more urgently required than a rise in the Standard Rate.[20]

Clearly the Webbs were themselves in favour of establishing a system of industrial rights through joint regulation.

In the last forty three pages of *Industrial Democracy* the Webbs turned to the relationship between trade unionism and democracy. One commentator has seen their predictions as milestones in a corporate state.[21] A careful reading of what they wrote reveals the Webbs in a different light. It is certainly true that they believed that, in a fully developed socialist democracy, with its commitment to the community as a whole and equality of opportunity for all, there would have to be some modification in trade union practices. They argued, for example, that 'a vested interest in occupation' and 'restriction of numbers' would have to be abandoned, as well as disruptive industrial disputes. However, although the development of democracy would modify trade unionism, what the Webbs called 'the spontaneous democracy' of trade unionism was incompatible with autocracy. They further held the view that trade unionism was not merely 'an accident of the present phase of capitalist industry but has a permanent function to fulfil in the democratic state'.[22]

Workers as individuals might be seen as relatively passive observers of the democratic process; mass them in trades unions (especially the older, skilled organisations whose effectiveness the Webbs argued, was based on a professional approach to organisation) and they could play a vital part in asserting the interests of producers in industry, as well as taking over some of the administrative functions (particularly in technical education) from the central state and acting as a pressure group at a higher, more political level.

To the Webbs the management of industry was of crucial importance for democracy. Although they argued that the trade unions were not competent to decide what should be produced (this was a question for the consumers) or the methods of production and distribution (this was the prerogative of managerial expertise), they were expected to have the major say in determining the conditions of employment. As we have seen, the Webbs interpreted conditions of employment in the broadest possible sense to include not only wages and working conditions but also education, health and leisure, what they called the National Minimum. 'It is accordingly upon the Trade Unions that the democratic state must mainly rely for the stimulus, expert council, and persistent watchfulness, without which a National Minimum can neither be obtained nor enforced.'[23] So in a socialist state, trade unions had a vital role to play in the protection of employees' interests. In time, with the 'progressive nationalisation or municipalisation of public services, on the one hand, and the spread of the co-operative movement on the other'[24] the Webbs expected the trade unions to become less involved in a conflict with employers over working conditions and more interested in 'raising the standard of competency in its occupation' and 'educating their masters' as to the best way of 'carrying on the craft'[25] – more professional associations than trade unions. They also saw no reason why trade unions should not take over some of the functions of the state in technological education by becoming the local administrative committees of the Technical Education Authority, as well as compiling statistics and disseminating information useful to particular occupations. In other words state power would be decentralised and dispersed through the trade unions.

In the wider political sphere, they expected trade unions to act together as a powerful and well-organised body, speaking-up for the interests of employees. The Webbs criticised, in a side-swipe at New Unionism, trade unions meddling with what they called wider issues of a general political nature, such as the abolition of the House of Lords, secularising education, and nationalising the means of production and the means of exchange. What was required to make trade unions into effective political pressure groups was a clearly conceived and distinctive programme based on the employees' industrial needs, and which would include the defence of freedom of association, the extension of collective bargaining, and the establishment of a National Minimum.

The Webbs concluded by considering what lessons for wider democracy could be learned from the study of trade unionism. First, the development of trade unionism meant the concept of democracy had to be widened to include economic as well as political relations. The uncontrolled powers of the owners of the means of production were incompatible with the democratic ideal. Second, they noted that the growth of trade unionism did not lead to a 'dead level' uniformity – on the contrary, it resulted in the organisation of a whole range of grades and classes including the different groups of management. In other words they saw democracy as likely to lead to a varied and pluralistic rather than a uniform and monolithic society. Thirdly, they commented on the way in which trade unions had begun to combine administrative efficiency with popular control. Trade unions held strongly to the democratic view that one man was as good as another, but with the growth of collective bargaining they had been forced to use professional negotiators. The Webbs believed that the evolution of trade union government (the development of elected representative assemblies which nominated and controlled an executive committee under whose direction a permanent and official staff performed its work) had implications for democracy as a whole; 'trade union experience points clearly to an ever-increasing differentiation between the functions of three indispensable classes of Citizen – Electors, chosen Representatives and expert Civil servants'.[26]

Where did this initial discussion of democracy lead the Webbs? Foreshadowing their later rejection of Syndicalism, they argued that the citizen as producer was ultimately subordinate to the citizen as consumer and elector. However, trade unions as representatives of the producer were expected to have the major say on living conditions in the widest sense and act as a pressure group for employees as well as carrying out the functions devolved to them by the state. In this sense the sectional power of unions could be used against authoritarianism, a clear indication of the fact that the Webbs were very much aware of the need for countervailing power against an overmighty state. The novelty of their approach was to draw lessons from trade union experience and to show how the trade union movement was a vital part of the democratic process rather than the threat to the fabric of society which so many Victorians believed.

NOTES

1. S. Webb to G Wallas, 29 July 1892, Passfield Papers.
2. F. W. Galton, in M. Cole (ed) *The Webbs and their Work*, p. 33.
3. *St. Martin's Review*, Oct 1928.
4. *Labour Elector*, 28 Jan 1893.
5. S. Webb to G. Wallas, 12 Sept 1893, BLPES.
6. *Fortnightly Review*, Nov 1893.
7. H. J. Massingham to S. Webb, 18 Oct 1893, Passfield Papers.
8. M. Davitt to S. Webb, 25 Nov 1893, Passfield Papers.
9. *Our Partnership*, M. Cole (ed).
10. Evidence to the Royal Commission on Labour, 17 Nov 1892.
11. See Chapter 5.
12. *Manchester Guardian*, 30 July 1896.
13. Quoted in N. and J. Mackenzie, *The First Fabians*, p. 220.
14. *The Young Woman*, Feb 1895.
15. *The History of Trade Unionism*, B. and S. Webb, p. 25–26.
16. A. E. Musson, *British Trade Unions*, p. 50.
17. A. Flanders, *Management and Unions*, pp. 220–226.
18. *Industrial Democracy*, B. and S. Webb, p. 173.
19. A. Fox in *British Journal of Industrial Relations*, Vol XIII, No. 2. p. 156.

20. *Industrial Democracy*, p. 816.
21. T. Kennoy, 'From the Webbs to Corporatism' in *Essays in Law and Society*, ed. G. Mungham and Z. Bankowski.
22. *Industrial Democracy*, p. 823.
23. Ibid, p. 817.
24. Ibid, p. 825.
25. Ibid, p. 826.
26. Ibid, p. 844.

5
1892–1897
Local Government, the TEB and the London School of Economics

'Mr Webb is not a candidate for today, he is one for the day after tomorrow.'

In December 1891 Sidney agreed to run as a Progressive candidate for Deptford in the forthcoming LCC elections. The first elections for the LCC had taken place in 1889 and there was a good chance that the Progressives, a new alliance of London Liberals, nonconformist radicals, religious philanthropists and trade unionists, would win the next election. Sidney believed that the Progressive alliance, which was in the market for radical ideas, could be captured for the collectivists.

Just after the 1889 elections, the Fabian Society had published his *Facts for Londoners* a pamphlet which set out detailed proposals for municipal reform and which had attracted Progressive support. Sidney's proposals owed much to two famous municipal reformers, J. F. B. Firth and Joseph Chamberlain. The former believed that local government should be mostly financed and controlled by central government; the latter that local authorities should have as much freedom as possible. Sidney's reform programme skilfully combined overall central control through grants in aid with local autonomy over the pattern of spending, thus accommodating both centralisers and de-centralisers. In the year leading up to the second LCC elections the Fabian Society devoted much of its efforts to the

Progressive cause, producing a series of propaganda leaflets as well as a detailed *London Programme* written by Sidney. This was collectivist in spirit and dealt with all aspects of a Londoner's life. Individual action, Sidney prophesied, was bound to fail:

> the hope of the future for dense urban communities admittedly lies in the wise extension of collectivist action. By himself the typical Londoner is a frail and sickly unit, cradled in the gutter, housed in a slum, slaving in a sweater's den and dying in the workhouse infirmary . . . Collectively he is a member of the greatest and most magnificent city which the world has known, commanding all the latest resources of civilisation and disposing of almost boundless wealth.[1]

What was needed was a radical extension of LCC powers. Instead of dealing only with 'a strange hotch-potch' of lunatic asylums and fire brigades, main drainage and industrial schools, bridges and baby farms, the LCC would become a powerful authority with control over water, gas, transport, housing, hospitals, docks and the police. Sidney Webb's 'gas and water socialism' was accepted by the Progressives and, though good organisation clearly played a major part in the Progressive victory,[2] the Fabian contribution to the electoral appeal of the alliance should not be under-estimated.

Sidney campaigned for three months in Deptford. In his election address he called for trade union wages for all municipal workers, an eight hour day, relief for the rate-payer and municipalisation of major services. He appealed to the electors as a 'Londoner born and bred' who had made London questions the chief study of his life and who now, after thirteen years administrative experience in a government office, had resigned to give his whole time to the service of the capital. Backed by the Joint Committee of Delegates of the Liberal and Radical Association, the Women's Liberal Association, the Workingmen's Clubs and by the leading trade unionists of Deptford, he declared that he wished to lift the contest 'above any narrow partisan lines'. His victory was overwhelming. He polled 4088 against the 2503 of the Moderate (Conservative) candidate. The Progressives gained a big majority, while Labour candidates running alongside the Progressives won nine seats.

He wrote excitedly to Wallas about his triumph.

> The result was not declared until after 1 a.m. I made a little speech, etc. and then was lifted shoulder-high by an excited mob,

carried downstairs to the imminent risk of scraping the ceilings with my nose, and so out into the road amid a fearful uproar . . . I was *delighted* at the general results elsewhere. It is simply a gorgeous justification of Fabian electioneering . . . I felt inclined to go round by Cannon Street in order, like Jack Cade, to smite London Stone with my umbrella, and shout out into the night 'Now is Mortimer lord of London!' But I went by the Central Telegraph Office instead![3]

At thirty three, Sidney Webb was launched on a new career.

The new member for Deptford was already well known. As the *Pall Mall Gazette* commented,

Mr Sidney Webb is a very remarkable man, much more remarkable than anybody thinks, excepting himself. Since Mr Chamberlain arose in Birmingham, there has been no man so like him as Mr Sidney Webb, who aspires to be Mr Chamberlain of London–only more so. For to all the energy and perseverance and municipal spirit of Mr Chamberlain, Mr Sidney Webb has a great literary gift and a philosophical conception of social progress to which Mr Chamberlain can lay no claim. He is a socialist; but he is no utopian dreamer, he is a man crammed with facts; he is no fanatic, but a wily, shrewd, adroit, wire-puller whose hand is felt in a great many quarters where it is not seen . . . Mr Webb is not a candidate for today he is one for the day after tomorrow.

Sidney certainly took his new responsibilities seriously and devoted every afternoon to the LCC. In the first year after his election, he was a member of eight committees, including the Technical Education Committee of which he was chairman from 1892–98, the Local Government and Taxation Committees of which he was vice-chairman and the Public Health, Housing and Parliamentary Committees. While his main work was in education, it is clear from a study of the records that his interests were far-ranging. Between 1892 and 1904 he served on twenty one committees; Beatrice remarked that 'Sidney . . . is one of that little circle of a dozen committees who practically run the LCC – for the simple reason that they do the work, and he is the trusted confidant and helpmate of the great officials of the Council' (1 December 1892). He was a punctilious attender of committee meetings as the records testify. In the 1893–4 session alone, he went to thirty seven out of forty four council meetings and attended 249 others. Such assiduity paid off and he quickly won a reputation as one of London's most effective politicians.

Despite Sidney's preoccupation with the LCC the Webbs understood that fighting local elections could provide an opportunity of getting across the Fabian message. At the end of 1894 Sidney and Beatrice both stood for the Westminster vestry election though, as Beatrice remarked, there was little hope of victory. Their purpose in standing was to put the case against the breaking-up of the LCC into separate boroughs, which, it was rumoured, was the intention of the Conservative government. Even so the Webbs took electoral organisation seriously. Beatrice wrote that they created the organisation and selected the 90 candidates

> with singularly little trouble. The first stage was to create a branch of the London Reform Union – Sidney Chairman, Galton Secretary; the second, to call, in the name of the LRU branch, a conference of all the temperance, Trade Union, and political organisations and to form a Progressive Council – Sidney Chairman, Galton Secretary; the final step, to select our candidates and to form these into one organisation, Sidney chairman, Galton secretary. These three organisations under their respective chairmen and secretaries have worked with wonderful harmony! (1 December 1894)

In spite of support from the leading municipal journal ('When such women as Mrs Webb in Westminster . . . stand for the vestries, it may indeed be hopeful for the future of local government') they were soundly beaten, only five Progressives out of ninety six candidates being returned in their vestry. However, the Conservative government kept the LCC intact which in part justified the Webbs' decision to stand.

The 1895 LCC elections proved to be a great disappointment for the Progressives, who had hoped (on the basis of their record) to increase their majority. Instead they were faced with a deadlock.

In his election address to his Deptford constituents, Sidney had set out the impressive achievements of the Progressive majority: improved sanitation, better fire services, over a thousand acres added to London's open spaces, the Thames purified so that 'whitebait could once more be caught where sewage lately floated up and down with every tide', better housing 'of the slum population', and 'trade union wages' with a 'moral' minimum, established in every council department. He also demonstrated to his electors how Deptford itself had benefited – technical education scholarships for over fifty of Deptford's poorer boys and girls, slums pulled down and replaced by new housing and a new fire station – all this without 'raising the Deptford rate a single penny'. And he concluded, 'you trusted me as an untried stranger. I now appeal to you on the record of the three-years work I have done for Deptford.' Sidney held his seat comfortably, winning the largest vote ever given to a Progressive candidate. Despite his own personal success, Sidney was 'low about the LCC – brooding over the defeat'. His running mate was defeated which added to his disappointment. The Webbs blamed the poor results on 'the lack of employment during a time of fearful cold – with the indifference and even savage hostility to all existing institutions which this state breeds' (5 March 1895).

In spite of the deadlock, Beatrice's firm conviction that wherever the groundwork had already been laid affairs would continue to run smoothly proved to be correct and, although for the next three years no new or extensive plans for municipalisation were encouraged, the Moderates did not reverse Progressive party policies and Sidney remained chairman of the Technical Education Committee.

Sidney was in part responsible for the setting up of the Technical Education Committee. After the ominously poor quality of British exhibits at the Paris Exhibition of 1867 pressure had been applied on successive governments for an extention of technical education. By the Technical Instruction Act of 1889 the LCC found itself in charge of technical education and was allowed to levy a penny rate with which to pay for it. The following year, after further pressure, particularly from the persuasive chairman of the National Association for the Promotion of Technical Education, A. H. D. Acland, revenue from a tax on beer and spirits ('whisky money') was successfully allocated to county councils for the purpose of promoting technical education.

The LCC however had been slow in using its powers and even before the 1892 election, Sidney had attacked the council for their dilatory tactics. His first motion on the council was to propose, in general terms, that a Committee should be appointed to look into the question of the LCC response to the Technical Instruction Act. As Beatrice commented, so cautiously worded a resolution, not taken seriously, was adopted unanimously and the mover was left to choose the committee, subject to the usual exact representation of the party balance on the Council. SW . . . explained how, in his anxiety to put on the ablest members from the various sections, he found he had not provided for a chairman . . . He was therefore driven to preside himself.[4]

In a typically Webbian gesture Sidney, finding himself in a position of power, immediately asked that the committee should appoint an expert, Herbert Llewellyn-Smith, Secretary of the National Association, to look into the state of London education. While the Committee waited for his report, they accepted, on Sidney's suggestion, a new constitution: membership would now be composed of twenty council members and fifteen nominated ones. This meant that Sidney could bring onto the Technical Education Board (as the Committee now came to be called) those outside bodies such as the London School Board, teachers and trade unionists, who might otherwise have been hostile if their voices had not been heard.

As expected, Llewellyn-Smith's report, which was placed in front of the TEB in 1893, confirmed Sidney's worst fears; not only were London children provided with poorer education than their counterparts in Germany, Britain's greatest rival, but they were also worse off than children in cities such as Manchester, Birmingham or Liverpool. Sidney acted immediately. He had already discovered from the Minister of Education that the TEB could teach a wide range of subjects: 'it can now lawfully teach anything under the sun except ancient Greek and theology,' he enthused to Beatrice.[5] He was therefore in a position to put a comprehensive scheme to the TEB:

We want the very poorest child to be able to remain in school until at least thirteen or fourteen. We want him then to have the chance of adequate scholarships for the secondary schools, and so on to the University or Technical College; and the rest we want through evening class instruction brought to their very door and systematically leading on to the same goal.[6]

And he added, 'I want to make it no disadvantage to a boy to be born in London . . . I want the London workman to become once more the skilled craftsman.'[7] As he later told an audience,

> the only hope, the only chance of raising the standard of Life of this degenerate residuum, is to take care that all the forces of the community, all the influence of the State, are wisely, deliberately and persistently used in such a way as always to elevate, and never to depress, the economic conditions of the weakest wage-earners.[8]

What this entailed was the setting up of a 'scholarship ladder', running parallel for day and evening students so that all who wished to succeed could get to the top. These scholarships would not only enable elementary schoolchildren to continue with their education at secondary level (which they could not do before) but also provide a £10 maintenance grant to compensate parents for their children's loss of earnings. Scholarships were also provided for those who wished to go into higher education. By the time that the TEB was reorganised in 1904, well over 2000 scholarships had been made available to London children.

Sidney's method was to work through existing institutions rather than create new ones, both because he felt that this would be cheaper (and therefore more acceptable) and also because he believed it to be the quickest way to reform. The new constitution of the Board meant that it had close links with all the schools within its boundaries and the 'scholarships brought a steady stream of clever boys and girls to the languishing endowed secondary schools, to the expanding technical institutes and to the unfilled classes of the university colleges'.[9] Not only were existing schools, whether under the London School Board or endowed, given aid, but new art schools, technical schools and polytechnics were also created during his tenure of office. There was also better co-ordination between the educational establishments. Sidney's dynamic chiarmanship (he came to be known as the 'Napoleon of the TEB') provided a vital element in the growth of a more efficient and up-to-date education for London. Under Sidney's guidance the TEB not only brought order to the chaotic structure of the capital's education but also made its influence felt in every educational centre in London. The TEB's organising ability and the substantial help of its subsidies brought about great improvements in schools and enormously advanced technical education.

> It has grappled with the problem in a statesmanlike spirit. From the small, struggling, private school up to the leading poly-

> technic, the impetus it has given to education has been felt . . . Instead of chaos there is something like harmony . . . It is to Mr Sidney Webb, above all others, that London owes the TEB and the excellent work it has done . . . If Mr Webb has done nothing else, his work on the TEB would have deserved the eternal gratitude of Londoners.[10]

There is no doubt that Sidney was highly successful as an administrator. He used existing institutions, injected them with funds and encouraged them to grow. Under his chairmanship the opportunities of schooling for London children increased considerably. It has however been argued that Sidney aimed at replacing the old, aristocratic elite with a new meritocratic one and that it was for this purpose that he created the scholarship ladder.[11] It is certainly true that he wanted to be able to detect who might become one of the new breed of 'experts', provide them with a rigorous training, then insure that they played their allotted role in the overall increase of national efficiency. The Webbs *were* meritocrats. What they aimed for was to make certain that those who had the ability should be given the opportunity to exercise their talent. It was, in a way, part and parcel of their interest (as with other Victorians) in eugenics – that is, with the improvement of the British race. All the same, this did not mean that they were unconcerned with the education of working class children. Sidney was once asked who would perform manual tasks if everyone became educated; he turned on his questioner and angrily denied such an assumption of elitist principles. 'I may be a dreamer of dreams', he furiously replied

> but I thought that the doctrine that education was only for a part of the nation was buried a hundred years ago . . . I want no class of hewers of wood and drawers of water: no class destined to remain there and prevented from rising, because we do not provide for it . . . Our convenience! Our comfort! Our comfort is to stand in the way of enabling these people, our fellow citizens, to attain anything better than being mere hewers of wood and drawers of water![12]

The whole point of Sidney's educational reforms was to provide opportunities, for the first time, for all working class children, the less able as well as the able.

Sidney had not long been on the TEB when he became involved in an 'odd adventure' which led to the birth of the 'favourite child' and the 'biggest single enterprise' of the Webb partnership. Henry Hutchinson, who had previously provided money for the Fabian Lancashire campaign, committed suicide in 1894. He left a will in which he bequeathed £10 000 to the Fabian Society, to be administered by Sidney (who was to be the chairman) with three Fabians, (Clarke, Pease and DeMattos) and his own daughter Constance, as the other trustees. The wording of the gift was somewhat obscure in that the Fabian Society was to spend the money within a period of ten years on 'propaganda and other purposes of the said Fabian Society and its Socialism and towards advancing the objects in any other way they deem advisable'. Apart from the ambiguity of the phraseology, the will could also have been contested (on the ground that Henry Hutchinson had been of unsound mind) by the family, who had been left very little.

In spite of these obstacles, the day after Sidney received the letter he and Beatrice informed Graham Wallas and Bernard Shaw (who were staying with them that summer) that they had discussed the matter between themselves and had decided to use some of the money to found a school of economics. Wallas left an amusing vignette of the Webb announcement.

> So many causes go to every effect that it is generally impossible to assign the invention of any important institution to a precise date. There is no such impossibility in the case of the School. It was invented at Borough Farm, a couple of miles south-west of Godalming, early in the morning of a certain day in August 1894 . . . Mr & Mrs Webb, Mr G. B. Shaw, and I were staying at the little farm. The day before, Mr Webb learned that, by the will of Mr Henry Hutchinson, he had been given the duty of directing the expenditure of a sum of money. He and Mrs Webb woke up early, had a long discussion, and at breakfast told us that part of the money would be used to found a school in London, on the lines of the École Libre de Sciences Politiques in Paris.[13]

Beatrice's account is less dramatic:

> the question is how to spend the money. It might be placed to the credit of the Fabian Society and spent in the ordinary work of propaganda. Or a big political splash might be made with it – all

> the Fabian executive might stand for Parliament! And ILP candidates might be subsidised in their constituencies.[14]

Neither appealed. Instead Sidney

> has been planning to persuade the other trustees to devote the greater part of the money to encouraging *research* and economic study. His vision is to found, slowly and quietly, a London School of Economics and Political Science – a centre not only of lectures on special subjects, but an association of students who would be directed and supported in doing original work. Last evening we sat by the fire and jotted down a list of subjects which want elucidating . . . reforming society is no light matter, and must be undertaken by experts specially trained for the purpose. (21 September 1894)

And, as she wrote later, 'For two relatively unknown persons, without academic distinction, holding outrageously heterodox opinions in the very branch of knowledge that they were intent on promoting . . . such an enterprise seemed an impertinence'.[15]

In fact, the decision to set up the LSE was not a sudden flash of inspiration. Sidney had been thinking along these lines for some time. He had been impressed by the Massachusetts Institute of Technology, which he had visited with Pease in 1899, and was also acutely aware that a previous Commission on higher education had particularly stressed the need for the setting up in London of the equivalent of the École Libre de Sciences Politiques. Having decided how to use the money Sidney turned his attention to the Fabian executive which he was certain would want to spend the bequest within the Society. At first he was reluctant to allow them even to discuss the matter, claiming with some justification that the will had put the trustees in charge of the money.

But if he was to get the agreement of the family to the will, he thought he ought to double Mrs Hutchinson's annuity from the bequest and to do that he needed the approval of the executive. The executive met to discuss the bequest towards the end of September and it was clear that Sidney would have a difficult task in persuading them to accept his plans. Shaw saved the day for him by pointing out that a dispute might jeopardise the legacy and by arguing that it would not be desirable to give members the impression that the Society was in funds to the extent that they would relax their own efforts.[16]

Later that day Shaw wrote firmly to Sidney that it was wrong, and in any case impossible, to keep the members of the Society in the dark.

> You cannot treat them as children; and now that several thousand pounds are at stake, the slightest attempt at evasion or concealment would destroy our influence at a blow. Ask yourself what you would think if you were a member of the Society and found that the trustees of a public bequest shuffled when you asked the first inevitable, natural question. How much? We should simply be suspected of wanting to job it or steal it; and we should have to answer after all.[17]

Sidney reluctantly agreed to consult Fabian members. He therefore sent a carefully worded letter which he hoped would influence their response.

> The Hutchinson trustees would be very glad if you would help them with any suggestions as to the best way of using their fund . . . The most pressing needs of the Collectivist movement in England at the moment appear to be (1) a wider diffusion among the people and especially among socialists and ILP members of accurate knowledge as to the economic bearings of public administration; (2) further research into the unsolved problems of municipal and national government, so as to renew and freshen the propaganda; (3) the attraction to these studies of clever and educated recruits.[18]

The Fabians typically refused to be guided and responded with a plethora of proposals on how to use the unexpected windfall, including the founding of a Fabian newspaper, and the setting up of a correspondence school. None appealed to Sidney who claimed that they would not fulfil the function of exercising a 'solid and lasting influence' on the progress of collectivist ideas. During the winter Sidney went ahead with his plans for the School. He needed additional finance and managed to persuade city financiers, academics, as well as the TEB, which was prepared to grant the School £500, to support the project. At a meeting in February 1895 he got the official backing of the Hutchinson trustees for his proposals. As a sweetener for the Fabians, the trustees agreed to donate a small part of the trust money annually to the Society for general overheads, increasing Pease's salary as General Secretary, and underwriting the cost of 'Hutchinson lecturers' who would carry the Fabian message into the provinces.

In April, after Graham Wallas's refusal, the Webbs offered W. A. S. Hewins the post of Director of the School at £300 per year. They had met Hewins, who was a young Oxford economic historian, when they were working at the Bodleian and, although he was not a socialist, they were immediately impressed by their shared dislike of the Manchester School and their common faith in the practicability and urgent necessity of a concrete science of observation and statistical verification. The School found lodgings in three rooms rented at 9 John Street, Adelphi, and by the end of the first academic year had attracted between two and three hundred students.

However, the support from the City and the appointment of Hewins awakened Fabian misgivings. Shaw complained to Beatrice in July 1895 that 'the Hutchinson Trustees are prepared to bribe the Fabians by subsidies for country lectures and the like to allow them to commit an atrocious malversation of the rest of the bequest.' Although Shaw was prepared to back the LSE project, he advised the Webbs that 'the Collectivist flag must be waved and the Marseillaise played' to attract new bequests and to appease Fabian and socialist critics.[19]

Fabian doubts about the LSE were brought to a head in 1896 by Ramsay MacDonald. He had been a member of the Society for some time and in 1894 was elected to the executive. At the time of the discussions over the Trust he had apparently raised no objections to Sidney's proposals as to how the money should be spent and in 1895 was appointed one of the two full-time Hutchinson lecturers. However, by the spring of 1896, MacDonald, probably disappointed by the Webbs' refusal to give him a lectureship at the LSE, began to have second thoughts about the scheme. He sent Pease a memorandum outlining his own proposals for expanding the propaganda side of the Fabian Society and objecting to the Hutchinson bequest being used to set up the LSE, and on 8 April 1896 he accused the Trustees of misappropriating the Hutchinson money and threatened that if it could be shown that they had 'mortgaged the Trust for £150 a year for the Fabians . . . and the rest to the School of Economics, I shall certainly oppose them and carry through the opposition to an appeal to the Society if need be'.[20]

Pease, appalled at this dissension and very much an ally of the Webbs, begged him not to 'cause a rumpus', but MacDonald refused to be pacified and proceeded to move a resolution at the April Fabian executive demanding a statement from the Hutchinson Trustees as to how the money had been spent. The resolution, after a lengthy and acrimonious debate, was passed at the next executive.[21] At the same time MacDonald bombarded Sidney and Beatrice with letters denouncing not only the setting up of the LSE but also the Hutchinson Trustees' decision to spend another £1500 capital to help set up a Library of Political Science. MacDonald's own proposals, which assumed an expenditure by the Society of an extra £500, included the establishment of a permanent travelling scholarship and an extension of the provincial lectures. They were discussed at the June executive and although some extra money (about £200) was given to the Society from the Hutchinson Trust, it was to be used only for educational purposes.

There was some justice in MacDonald's criticisms of the Webbs' behaviour over the LSE. Although in October 1894 Haldane had given counsel's opinion that it was not illegal to spend the Hutchinson bequest on setting up the School, it was certainly arguable that the Webbs' interpretation of the will was morally questionable. In a letter to Pease in June 1895, Sidney wrote that

> the Fabian Society had better be kept *quite* out of it for the moment; hence please be absolutely discreet . . . it is better not even to give the names of the Trustees and certainly not to mention Hutchinson. Above all, show *no one* a copy of the will. It is vital to get started without any compromising suspicions.[22]

This is scarcely the letter of someone certain that others would be persuaded of the rightness of their cause.

It is of course true that the Webbs believed that the kind of systematic research and teaching which was to be undertaken at the LSE would lead in the end to the triumph of collectivist ideas. The Webbs could claim as well that one of the objectives of the Fabian Society was education and research. Certainly, Sidney in a later letter to Dr Archibald Robertson, Vice-Chancellor of the University of London 1902–3, gave this as the reason, for using the Hutchinson money to set up the School.

> I decided that, if possible, I would neither hand it over to the Fabian Society, nor spend it in political propaganda. It has

always been a special feature of the Fabian Society . . . that it has added to its work of propaganda, a great deal of purely educational work in economics. Moreover, it had for many years included among its functions, in its printed prospectuses, the promotion of economic investigation and research, and it has always done its best to foster this. I, therefore, urged upon my co-trustees that it would be far better to devote some of the funds now at their disposal, not to propaganda of any sort, but to education and, above all, to advancing one of the declared functions of the Fabian Society, namely economic investigation and research.[23]

Here was certainly a re-writing of history. As Sidney perfectly well knew, if he wanted to set up a school which would produce ammunition to further the collectivist cause, others in the Society like Bland, Olivier and Shaw, were far more interested in furthering socialism by an increase in propaganda.

It can, however, also be argued that the LSE's triumphant success as a centre for the teaching of economics and social sciences has proved the Webbs right. But the fact that the end eventually justified the means does not exonerate them from criticism.

Behind the controversy about the LSE, lay a deeper issue; how Fabian resources were to be most effectively deployed. MacDonald believed that the most urgent task was to educate working class socialists – to bring the Fabian message to the 'active centres of socialist work', or, as David Marquand puts it, to 'Fabianise' the ILP.[24] In contrast, the Webbs' top priority was to educate intelligent opinion. As Beatrice Webb wrote: 'do we want to organise the *unthinking* persons into socialist societies or to make the *thinking* persons socialistic? We believe in the latter policy' (18 April 1896). Hence their support for the LSE project, rather than, for what they regarded a secondary objective.

To give the LSE additional status Sidney decided that the School ought to become part of a reformed London University. At that time London University was little better than an Examining Board giving external degrees. Sidney Webb lent his support to the ideas of Haldane, who proposed that London University should become, in addition, a collegiate university involved in teaching and research. Sidney's plan was that the LSE would become one of the colleges of the university. He was also conscious that a reformed London University would need a large allocation of funds and proposed that the TEB should donate £10 000 per year of its 'whisky money' to it.

Haldane, with the assistance of Sidney, put forward his plans in the form of a Private Member's Bill, which was twice killed in the Lords. Beatrice described their energetic lobbying: Sidney and Haldane were

> rushing about London trying to get all parties to agree to a Bill for London University. If it goes through, it will be due to Haldane's insistence and his friendship with Balfour – but the form of the Bill – the alterations grafted on the Cowper Commission (set up to examine the proposals) are largely Sidney's. He thinks he has got all he wants with regard to the Technical Education Board and the London School of Economics. The Commission appointed to carry the Act out is largely favourable, or at any rate susceptible to right influence. (16 July 1897)

In 1898 the Government, at Balfour's insistence, backed Haldane's proposal and introduced their own Act, which set up a reformed London University.

By 1898, Sidney had been on the LCC six years. He had transformed the entire pattern of schooling in London, founded the London School of Economics and had been partly instrumental in the setting up of a new University of London. Taken together, these educational reforms were the capital's most far-reaching for over a hundred years. So great was his reputation that it was said of him that 'his hand is seen in every provision made by the Council for the benefit of its employees and for the increasing of the civic efficiency of London'.[25]

NOTES

1. *London Programme*, 1891.
2. A. G. Gardiner, *John Benn and the Progressive Movement.*
3. S. Webb to G. Wallas, 6 Mar 1892, Passfield Papers.
4. *Our Partnership*, p. 78.
5. Ibid, p. 80.
6. *London*, 9 Feb 1893.
7. Ibid.
8. Ibid, 12 Oct 1893.
9. *Our Partnership*, p. 79.
10. *London*, 10 Jan 1895.
11. Among others, E. Brennan, *Education for National Efficiency*, p. 30ff.
12. Speech to Association of Technical Institutes, 1909.

13. *Our Partnership*, p. 86.
14. Ibid.
15. Ibid.
16. Quoted in N. and J. Mackenzie, *The First Fabians*, p. 215.
17. Hutchinson Papers, PPX.
18. Ibid, Letter from S. Webb to Hutchinson Trustees, 27 Nov 1894.
19. G. B. Shaw to S. and B. Webb, 1 July 1895, Passfield Papers.
20. J. R. MacDonald to E. Pease, April 1896, PS archives.
21. Fabian Society Executive Minutes, 17 Apr 1896.
22. S. Webb to E. Pease, 9 June 1895, F. P.
23. S. Webb to Dr Archibald Robertson, 3 Jan 1903, WSC.
24. David Marquand, *Ramsay MacDonald*, p. 43.
25. *The New Age*, 12 Mar 1896.

6
1898
Busman's Holiday

'What taste! Just what one might expect of them!'

In March 1898, after the publication of *Industrial Democracy* and the exertions over London University and the LSE, Beatrice and Sidney Webb decided to take a year's sabbatical in order to visit America, Australia and New Zealand. Delighted with the victory of the Progressives in the March elections, the Webbs felt that they would 'close this portion of our life with considerable complacency and start on our long journey with a light heart' (March 1898). There was, Beatrice felt, much to be thankful for:

> Our book has been extraordinarily well received, our party has recovered a good working majority on the LCC; the London School of Economics is growing silently though surely into a centre of collectivist-tempered research and establishing itself as *the* English School of Economics and Political Sciences.

The journey was to be a busman's holiday. The Webbs had decided to inquire into English local government, and the purpose of the visit to America and the Antipodes was to give them an insight into about forty different governing bodies. In preparation for the trip Beatrice went on a spending spree for the first time in many years, though her natural bent for self-deprecation and general puritanical approach, as so often, spoiled half her enjoyment.

> I am revelling in buying silks and satins, [she enthused] gloves, underclothing, furs and everything that a sober-minded woman

> of forty can want to inspire Americans and Colonials with a due respect for the refinements of attractiveness! . . . For this tour, I harmonise some extravagance with my conscience by making myself believe that I must have everything new and that I must look nice! I *believe* that it is a deliberate expenditure. (11 January 1898)

The journey also provided an opportunity to rearrange their lives: the house was reorganised, Galton found another job and even the cats were given a new home. 'All will have to be new and strange when we return – Work, Secretary, Servants' (March 1898).

Beatrice and Sidney, accompanied by Charles Trevelyan, the future Labour politician, were seen off in royal fashion by Pease, Shaw and the Wallases. They travelled with Sydney Olivier who was sailing for Washington on Colonial Office business. Their accommodation on the *Teutonic* was splendid, 'magnificent upper-deck cabin' which, as Sidney wrote to Shaw they owed to Beatrice's sister Lallie, who had married the rich ship owner Robert Holt, who had pulled strings on their behalf. The sea voyage was uneventful though somewhat marred for Beatrice by her dislike of her fellow passengers. On their arrival in New York on 30 March, they immediately began to tackle their very full programme. They visited Columbia University, of which they were mildly contemptuous, on 1 April. 'The various professors', Beatrice noted scathingly, 'are much more like the professors of a German Real Schule than the tutors of an English university. But,' she went on, 'I rather doubt from the individuals I talked to whether their lack of breeding and culture is compensated for, as in the case of the Germans, by thorough-going specialism' (1 April 1898). Beatrice's foreign diary, to which Sidney also contributed for the duration of the trip, revealed a less attractive side to the Webbs. They tended when investigating abroad to regard the institutions they examined with a prejudiced English eye. They viewed the legislative assemblies and municipal institutions they visited from the standpoint of Westminster, Whitehall and Spring Gardens, so that although in theory the purpose of their journey was to assimilate new facts and draw deductions from them, they often ended up with a tendency to lecture the natives they were investigating. Foreign travel brought out the worst in the partnership.

Early in their stay in New York Beatrice and Sidney, on the basis of a few meetings, came to the conclusion that all New York politicians were corrupt, disinterested and individualist. 'The two great party machines' Beatrice commented soon after they had docked,

> are in collusion against the ordinary citizen: they recognise that they are each the only alternative to the other and so long as they can both consent to any given act of dishonest government, there is not much to fear . . . Private enterprise is permitted to trample on the individual; to shut off the light of his house, to disturb him by noises, or even to kill him by carelessness, without exciting any particular public objection. (1 April 1898)

Clearly, New York was no collectivist paradise.

From there they went to Washington where they found the politicians engrossed in talk of war – it was the height of the crisis of the 1898 war with Spain over Cuba – so that (unhappily for Beatrice and Sidney) they were little inclined to discuss American political institutions. They saw Theodore Roosevelt, whom Beatrice thought a remarkable man, witty and full of courage, although their admiration was slightly tempered by Beatrice's conclusion that he had 'the loudness and hearty egotism of a man who has shouldered his way through life', and that as far as she could tell, he had 'no particular political views except jingoism' (6 April 1898). The Webbs also managed to meet the Speaker of the House, Thomas (Tsar) Reed, with whom they discussed the organisation of Congress. Immediately they put it into a British context and noted the similarities between the committee system of the LCC and that of Congress. Beatrice had little good to say about Reed, dismissing him sharply as 'a rule of thumb man, destitute of any kind of culture, and therefore with little capacity for suggesting alternative and better methods of doing public business' (6 April 1898). She unbent a little to acknowledge, grudgingly, that he was upright and public spirited and 'deliciously unselfconscious and endowed with a fine stock of primitive humour'.

Having discussed the organisation of the House of Representatives with Reed and engaged various Congressmen in interviews, Beatrice and Sidney decided that they were not impressed with what they had seen so far. Unlike the LCC or even Parliament, Beatrice felt that if she were an American

> I should feel utterly despondent about the future of the House of Representatives. With abominable procedure – procedure which

would disgrace an International Socialist Congress! – with no self-respect, with little intellectual leadership, with a predominantly loose moral character – it seems doomed to impotence varied by disorder. (18 April 1898)

It was all a far cry from the orderly proceedings of Spring Gardens and Sidney's punctilious chairmanship of the TEB.

Neither were they impressed by the Senate, 'other than its appearance and manners', concluding that the United States suffered from a lack of responsible government, since there was no one body which was accountable or which could be controlled by the electors. Their verdict was harsh: American government suffered from 'a hidden and irresponsible authority' (6 April 1898).

From Washington the Webbs travelled through to Baltimore and Philadelphia before making the return journey to New York. They admitted their disillusionment with the machinery of government to Shaw. 'This people,' Sidney wrote, 'in all that concerns the *machinery* of government, is infantile. I suspect the St Pancras Vestry is a finished product – a masterpiece – by comparison.'[1]

Disillusioned they may have been but their thirst for knowledge remained unquenched as they relentlessly investigated as many American universities as they could. Three weeks after having set foot on American soil they visited Howard University, which catered for coloured students. It was the first of its kind that they had encountered and their reactions were mixed. A hint of racialism broke through. The University, they decided, was inferior and pitiful. 'It was a pathetic sight to see these young men and women of all degrees of blackness . . . gathered together to take part in a sniffling little religious service' Beatrice recorded (21 April 1898).

The Webbs then continued on to Johns Hopkins where they paused to address the students and then journeyed on again. The indefatigable couple reached Philadelphia at the end of April where they stayed with Talcott Williams, an assistant editor of the main newspaper in the city. Philadelphia turned out to have a more congenial university than any they had previously encountered. Professors there, the Webbs concluded, were superior to Johns Hopkins because they were 'not so common in appearance and manner' and their cultural background was similar to that of English dons.

At Princeton they particularly admired Woodrow Wilson, then Professor of Political Science at the University and later President of the United States. They regarded him as being by far the most intellectual man they had met in America, 'an attractive-minded man – somewhat like a young John Morley – literary in language, but with a peculiarly un-American insight into the actual working of institutions as distinguished from their nominal constitution' (21 April 1898).

By the end of April the Webbs were once more back in New York for a further investigation into municipal institutions. They now had their first glimpse of Tamany Hall, which, even though corrupt, impressed them because it worked; 'government by a firm of contractors, who are given the job of governing the city for so many years by the electors and who quite naturally govern it entirely through their own men' (31 March 1898). They also as administrators themselves felt sympathetic to officials who, they saw, had to deal with the niggardliness and anarchic character of the ratepayers. They were however appalled by the slums of the city, infinitely worse than those of the East End, and once again their impression of the corruption of American politicians was confirmed. There was a type characteristic of all American representative assemblies, Beatrice wrote dismissively, 'Heavy jaw, aquiline nose, eyes bulging, sandy hair, the main features of the face being embedded in unhealthy-looking fat. The type combined the characteristics of a loose-liver, a stump orator and intriguer with the vacant stare of the habitual lounger' (4 May 1898). After a month neither Beatrice nor Sidney were prepared to make allowances either for a different culture or for a different political tradition.

It was not until they reached Boston that they came across the first politician whom they felt they could respect: John Quincy, Mayor of Boston. He reminded them of Arthur Balfour, and they also suspected him of leanings towards Fabian collectivism. The Webbs admired Quincy's success in persuading the old families of Boston, as a disinterested, conscientious elite, to sit on governing boards, and the local political bosses to agree to paid officials. The example of public spirited and 'well-informed' brains running a competent administration, enthused the couple. Having sampled the delights of East Coast intellectual life and city administration, the Webbs now launched themselves into the industrial hinterland. They journeyed to Pittsburg which they thought pushing, squalid and shabby, and then went on to Cincinnati where they were introduced to the famous railway king, Ingalls, President of the Big Four Railway. Beatrice was reminded of her earlier childhood visit with that other railway king, her father, but was more interested in her investigations than youthful memories. Ingalls set up a special electric trolleyride for the Webbs, inviting the major figures of the town to join them as they proceeded through the city in what was undoubtedly a novel experience for the two investigators. But they had no time to sample the delights of the spectacle; Beatrice, pleased to find herself in such close proximity with useful subjects of investigation, immediately concentrated on detailed questioning so that, as she later recorded with pride, she was so 'absorbed in talking shop . . . that I hardly noticed the miles of pretty suburbs through which we passed' (24 May 1898).

But the pace was suddenly too much for them. They arrived in Chicago on 1 June exhausted and feeling unwell. Sidney went down with a sore throat and fever and was prostrate for four days and Beatrice soon followed. Their visit to the great city was therefore, as Beatrice conceded, 'blurred by ill-health and anxiety'. Even so their short glimpse of Chicago confirmed them in their increasing distaste for American municipal administration. They could find little good to say about the city's local government, the inefficiency appalled them, and they hated the 'unswept, unwashed, untended streets'. Suffering from heat and the aftermath of their illness, the Webbs decided to cut short their researches and go to Colorado where they could take a week's holiday in the mountains. The strain of innumerable interviews, the long train journeys and the heat and noise of the cities had considerably undermined their health. Beatrice, in particular, found it difficult to stand up to the rigors of incessant discussions, the lack of exercise (she was a fanatical walker) and over-indulgence in food. She had neuralgia and toothache and 'developed a mania lest all my teeth were about to collapse'.

Once in the peace of the Rockies, Beatrice and Sidney took stock of their investigation. They concluded that so far there was little that they could learn from American institutions. 'The theory of checks and balances,' they argued, 'the refusal to construct one supremely responsible body, leads inevitably either to subterranean government by secret committees or to the creation of an autocrat responsible to no-one during his tenure of office' (June 1898). Their stay outside Denver in Colorado, soothed and recuperated them. By the end of the month Beatrice even felt well enough to deliver a paper on 'How to do away with the Sweating System' to a convention of the Federated Women's Clubs, which she enjoyed even though she had little good to say of her audience, whom she dismissed as having merely a 'good intention toward social reform without the requisite knowledge' (21 June 1898).

Much refreshed, the Webbs now moved further west to Salt Lake City, which Beatrice remembered slightly from her previous visit. Here at last they found something worth admiring: the City Hall, the 'first really self-respecting abode of a municipal authority come across in the United States'. The Mormons were very much the kind of administrators of whom Sidney and Beatrice could approve – level-headed, cautious and apparently free from corruption. Beatrice, fascinated by Mormon polygamy, wondered about the benefits of scientific breeding. What a loss to the world, she mourned that, 'the experiment of polygamy was not continued by a sect exceptionally well-fitted to give it a fair and full trial and to develop the experiment in to other forms of "scientific breeding" if polygamy pure and simple proved unsatisfactory' (29 June 1898).

From Salt Lake City the Webbs journeyed slowly towards the Pacific. They arrived in San Francisco on 4 July and were immediately and with great reluctance caught up in Independence Day celebrations. Scarcely recovered from their experiences, the noise and confusion of the revels depressed them profoundly. They looked at the city with tired, jaundiced eyes, liking it for its cosmopolitan character, but dismissing it for its lack of breeding; 'no standards, no common customs; no common ideals of excellence, of intellect or manners – only one universal anarchy' (7 July 1898).

The Webbs looked back on their three months in the States whilst on board the *Coptic* and bound for Honolulu. On the whole, they concluded, they had been unimpressed by most of what they had seen; Americans, Beatrice allowed, were hospitable, free from snobbishness and well-mannered. They were decisive, although often too impatient to think problems through. Their impatience however encouraged them to invent time-saving devices, of which she approved. All the same this 'most intelligent and least intellectual of White races' dissipated its energies.

Beatrice scathingly remarked that the Americans were under the 'tyranny of the state platitude' so that, in spite of what she called a good social and environmental mix, the country had produced 'a race positively wearisome to the European in the uniformity of its social habits and intellectual assumptions'. The trouble, according to Beatrice, was that the Americans were prisoners of two fallacies. The first that all men were born equal, encouraged each and every American to give his opinion on any topic; the second that the best way to serve the interests of the community was to pursue their own gain, meant that the Americans failed to understand the need for a spirit of community service. Not surprisingly the Webbs, in spite of the hospitality they had received, remained untouched by the warmth and energy of the Americans, recording their distaste for a nation which had failed to understand 'that good government rests not merely on democratic institutions but on the growth of a new motive, that of social service, combined with the selection of men for the work of government according to their capacity for that work' (10 July 1898).

Beatrice and Sidney now set their face towards the Hawaiian capital Honolulu, and New Zealand, in the hope that in the Antipodes they would discover at least some measure of Fabian collectivism. By the time they reached Honolulu the *Coptic* was the bearer of the news of the annexation of Hawaii by the Americans. This was the nearest that the Webbs came to the American-Spanish War. They were enchanted by the island, seeing it as 'the Island of Skye, with Kew Gardens let loose on its beach and the temperature of a hot house' (15 July 1898). Enervated by the climate for once they did no investigating and instead surfed and bathed with the charming Princess Kaiulani, niece of the former Queen.

Their stay however was short, and soon they were on board the 3000 ton *Almaida*, bound for New Zealand. It was an uncomfortable journey, Beatrice felt queasy for most of the time and could only watch with amazement as Sidney sat on the deck, 'reading, reading, reading, in daily dread of the awful tragedy – a book famine'. He managed to work his way through the whole of the ship's library, leaving to last the American Encyclopaedia, 'towards which his eye wanders every time he returns a book to the library' (25 July 1898).

Immediately they docked in Auckland Sidney and Beatrice felt at home. It was, they decided, delightfully British, and they at once plunged into an orgy of investigative visits. Their early euphoria came to be tempered as they began to uncover New Zealanders' apathetic attitude towards local government and the astonishing spectacle of town councils re-elected without a contest. They examined the educational system, found it wanting at all levels and were particularly horrified to find that at University College no political economy or philosophy was taught. Sadly, having had such hopes of Auckland, they packed their bags; 'seedy in appliances, immitative of old English models in method, honourable and gentlemanly in its spirit, but quite without originality, independence, or modern ideas' (3 August 1898), was their verdict. But there were at least compensations. They became very much intrigued with the working of the Compulsory Arbitration Act (between employers and workmen) for which they had hopes for the future, particularly as they had laid stress in *Industrial Democracy* on the need for just such an arbitration process to by-pass the 'tyranny' both of the employers and trade unions.

They also fell in love with the New Zealand countryside (as opposed to the towns which they disliked as much as they had done those of America) and were able at last to indulge themselves in a considerable amount of walking. Even so, Beatrice was not impressed by one of the country's great claims to fame, the Hot Lakes; 'one soon tires of nature's curios if one has no special scientific interest in them', she wrote disparagingly (12 August 1899).

The Webbs then went on to investigate Wellington. There they met the reforming New Zealand Prime Minister, Richard Seddon, as well as leading Conservative statesmen. Seddon, they concluded, was the leader of a collectivist Party enacting 'unscientific Collectivist measures' which nevertheless worked. Beatrice was fascinated by the Prime Minister, a vulgar giant 'courageously and enormously hard-working and running most government departments'. She again noted with approval that there appeared to be little corruption and what there was she deduced was simply the result 'of vulgar favouritism, vulgarly executed on rare occasions' (22 August 1898). They found the same vulgarity and lack of manners in the House of Representatives, where the often-drunk and loud-mouthed Members of Parliament were little to their liking.

After their short visit to New Zealand Beatrice summed it up as a place relatively free from corruption, politically apathetic, with an antiquated franchise and inadequate provision for education, but at least it was clean. She and Sidney disapproved of the bewildering chaos of independent local bodies which they found overlapping each other in total confusion, but there was hope. New Zealand, they decided, was 'the ideal country for a thoroughly equipped statesman. So long as he sympathizes with the general drift of democratic desires, he could pretty well mould legislation according to his personal convictions' (24 August 1898). It looked indeed to be fertile ground for collectivism.

New Zealand was an agreeable place much like England, but better – free of large class divisions, few slums and containing many vigorous, public-spirited men and women. The New Zealanders, Beatrice concluded, were an easy-going though moral race – an excellent and appealing combination. Here was material that could be moulded and she presented their final accolade: 'Taken all in all if I had to bring up a family outside of Great Britain, I would choose New Zealand as its home' (24 August 1898). Writing to her sister, Kate Courtney, she was remarkably enthusiastic.

> All together we are delighted with New Zealand. The climate and country are ideal; and there is a splendidly healthy public spirit with very little corruption. There is any amount to criticise: but unlike America, one feels that there is nothing to prevent it being put right – the people have control of their government and they themselves mean well.[2]

The Webbs were now on the last leg of their journey. Again the sea voyage to Australia proved uncomfortable so that they arrived in Sydney, some seven months after they had set out for England, the worse for wear and in poor temper, ready to stand in judgement on those whom they met. It was not difficult to find the Australians wanting. Sydney, Beatrice noted sourly, was 'seemingly inhabited by a lower middle class population suddenly enriched; aggressive in manners and blatant in dress' (8 September 1898). Everything was in bad taste. Within three days they had met the major politicians, including the Prime Minister and leader of the Opposition, all of whom they disliked, dismissing them as 'heavy, common persons', and wherever they went the Webbs found much to criticise, whether it was the restricted franchise, gross incompetence, the backwardness of the political life or the lack of constructive policies and ideas. Again Beatrice was struck, as she had been in New Zealand, by the apathy of those not involved in politics. She had also little good to say about the politicians she met, whether in government or not. After earnest questioning she found them prejudiced against factory legislation, 'timid about the taxation of wealth', having no conception of collective ownership and 'regard municipal matters as almost exclusively the concern of the property-owners' (8 September 1898). And Sidney, fresh from his triumph on the TEB, was horrified to discover the apparent indifference of the rich towards education.

As with Sydney, so with New South Wales, both were found

inadequate. Beatrice even complained about the Australian countryside, taking a dislike to the ubiquitous gum tree, which she found particularly unattractive. 'Not only from its tired colouring but because it seems to have no organic form' (29 September 1898).

In Brisbane they met members of the recently formed Labour Party, whose leader reminded them of Keir Hardie, and whose members they dismissed condescendingly as they had the early ILPers. They were, Beatrice complained, 'a respectable, well-conducted set of men, attending punctiliously to their parliamentary business but showing no parliamentary capacity as an Opposition, and utterly unfitted to take up the work of government' (29 September 1898).

Arriving in Melbourne, the Webbs again found little they could admire. They criticised the payment of members of the Victoria government (on the grounds that they had little work to do) and even went so far as to doubt, in their gloom, the wisdom of paying British parliamentarians. Unfortunately, Beatrice throughout her stay took an immediate dislike to the Australian ladies she met and would comment adversely on them in her diary whenever she had the opportunity. The men of Melbourne, she recorded, were superior to those of Sydney, but the 'women alas! are equally intolerable, untrained minds, overdressed bodies and lacking in the charm of physical vigour or grace of manner' (26 October 1898). Melbourne was not a success for the choleric Webbs. They again met socialists: 'A nondescript body of no particular class', Beatrice sweepingly asserted, 'and with a strong infusion of foreigners' and condescendingly agreed to give them a lecture on female suffrage. They looked so earnest and wistful, she recalled, that 'I had not the heart to tell them that I was against the suffrage'. Sidney also gave a talk on Fabian permeation, which clearly so confused the audience that the chairman at the end of the meeting recommended the adoption of 'Mr Webb's suggestion of taking the capitalist down a back street and then knocking him on the head!' (26 October 1898). Beatrice and Sidney found Victoria dull and parochial; once more the educational system proved inadequate and the civil service incompetent. Their only praise was for the new legislation which had recently been passed, fixing minimum wages in certain sweated industries.

The last day of their stay in Victoria was spent in the unlikely setting of a race course, watching the Melbourne Cup. Afterwards they were presented with an honorary membership of the Victoria

Racing Club, an accolade which astonished even the local papers. The *Sydney Bulletin* commented: 'Mr and Mrs Webb investigated the working of the crack race course much as though it had been a factory.'

They were now near the end of their visit, which finished on a pleasant note. The last town they visited was Adelaide which they, with some relief, likened to the New Zealand town of Christchurch, which they had much admired. Here they found, at last, comfort, refinement and ease, which gave the city 'far more amenity than is possible to restlessly pretentious Melbourne, crude chaotic Sydney or shadily genteel Brisbane' (12 November 1898).

The Webbs had expected much of democratic Australia but found its society as alien to them as its hot, parched landscape. They were offended by its vulgarity and gross materialism. They also condemned the Australians for their self-indulgence and apparent dislike for regular work. Yet they were disinclined to write off Australia altogether. 'With more careful selection', Beatrice summed up, 'in its civil service, and better trained intelligence in its public men, the Australian government would become a striking instance of successfully democratic institutions. At present, it is at least a most promising experiment' (8 December 1898).

They had gone on their long journey expecting to be able to apply to Britain what they saw abroad. Though they only looked at foreign institutions from the point of view of British Fabianism, they derived little benefit from their experiences. They failed to consider American, Australian or New Zealand politics and institutions in their own context. Instead they judged these from the often impossibly high standards of Fabian principle and usually found them wanting. On this, as on other visits abroad, the Webbs were at their least impressive.

NOTES

1. S. Webb to G. B. Shaw, 26 Apr 1898, British Library.
2. B. Webb to K. Courtney, 24 Aug 1898, Passfield Papers.

7
1899–1904
Permeation and Educational Reform

'The ultimate course of society is decided by the thought of the time and your effectiveness will be determined by your contribution to this thought.'

On their return from their long journey abroad the Webbs picked up the threads of their lives. Beatrice wrote:

> We were back in our little home on the Thames embankment, resuming our work in the triple capacity of investigators into social institutions, promoters of the newly-established London School of Economics and, in the case of the other One, as Chairman of the Technical Education Board, a determined organiser and agitator, intent on unifying all public education . . . under one local government authority – that of the London County Council.[1]

She might have added that they were also involved, sometimes to their regret, in controversial political issues, such as the Boer War, tariff reform and the formation of a Centre Party.

Their new investigation of social institutions was devoted to local government, a task which was to occupy them for the next twenty years and stretch over fourteen volumes. There were three main reasons why the Webbs embarked on their work on local government. The most obvious was Sidney's interest and involvement in the LCC. Secondly, the study of the compulsory association of local government was a natural development of their work on the voluntary associations of consumers and trades unions. Thirdly, they had concluded that the local provision of services according to need was likely to become increasingly important. What was required was an authoritative account of the development of functions and organisations of local administration.

Their researches took them and their research assistants (F. H. Spencer, a former elementary schoolteacher and one of the first part-time students at the LSE, and Amy Harrison, also an LSE student whom Spencer was later to marry) all over the country. They went to Manchester, Leeds, Liverpool, Newcastle, Leicester, Plymouth and other large towns where they met local councillors and officials and meticulously studied and annotated and classified parish, municipality, and county records. Beatrice, who was able to get away without difficulty, was often gone for days at a time, though occasionally she was joined by Sidney. However, they did much of their work in London. They spent two or three mornings a week from 9.15 to 1 o'clock reading records together in the British Museum; Sidney would then go off to his LCC committees while she either walked or occasionally entertained. They continued the habit of staying for long periods in the country so as to have quiet conditions for work. For two years running they shared a house with the Bertrand Russells but occasionally took bicycling trips either in England or Scotland, and once even went cycling in Normandy. For a pair of middle-aged researchers they were physically extraordinarily active. Beatrice thought nothing (for either herself or her guests) of a six-mile tramp, and succeeded in imbuing Sidney with her enthusiasm, so much so that even when away from home he would take a long daily walk – or so at any rate he told her!

Although these were extremely productive years, and although the Webbs were very happily married, Beatrice's diaries show that she continued to be prone to periods of self-doubt and intense anxiety. The early Fabians, including Sidney, found in socialism a faith that resolved some of their inner uncertainties. To Beatrice, who was more complicated than Sidney, socialism was not enough; it might provide a blueprint for a better society but there was nothing mystical in it. On the other hand, no religion could satisfy her firmly held belief that a human being's most important function was service to mankind and not to God. This striving after human perfectability as well as a mystical *deus ex machina* produced a conflict in Beatrice's mind between what she called a 'strictly rational approach' and 'an instinctive longing for some sanction other than scientific reasoning for believing in the eternal worthwhileness of human life'.[2]

Her failure to solve this dilemma caused her great unhappiness and was probably the reason for the various attacks of migraine, neuralgia and eczema with which she was afflicted. For a time, she was drawn towards Roman Catholicism on the grounds that it provided a 'mental hygiene and discipline of the emotions, an authoritative guidance to the *motive* of conduct' (25 September 1900), and one that asked for physical control, humility and disinterested love. At the end of 1900 she turned to medical remedies. In October she came under the influence of a certain doctor, Ragbliatte, whom she met in Bradford while researching for their book on local government. He was the author of several treatises on diet and at their first meeting half convinced Beatrice that her nervous disposition, and what she considered her unstable temperament, was due to her eating habits. Immediately, she turned her formidable intellect to the problem of her nutritional intake. Her zeal was such that she soon worked out a regime which was so excessively strict that it consisted of only 1 lb of food per day. She allowed herself four ounces for breakfast, six at lunch and six in the evening; and as a sop to what she considered the frailty of her character, indulged in a small early-morning cup of tea without milk or sugar, another at teatime, and a cup of black coffee (always one of her favourite drinks) for dinner. She tried to eat no starch, merely lean meat, vegetables and fruit. In this way she hoped to purify what she considered to be her inner malignant humours.

Surprisingly, given the extreme severity of the diet, she initially felt fitter and the indigestion from which she suffered intermittently throughout her life appeared to leave her; but the weight loss was too sudden and she began to feel faint and to sleep badly. Daily she charted her dramatic sliding off of ounces, eccentrically weighing herself at Charing Cross Station, no doubt a useful half-way house between Millbank and St Paul's where she often went to pray in the afternoons. Her weight dropped suddenly from nine stone to nearly five, and although some of her ailments disappeared, one of her most painful, acute eczema in the ears, remained to plague her. It was probably at this time that she began to acquire that look of a beautiful brooding eagle, so characteristic of the older Beatrice.

Inevitably her excessive dieting made her listless and tired 'more health and less strength'. The new discipline also added to her

unsettled feelings. 'I longed for music, I desired to be religious, I allowed my mind to dwell on all sorts of sentimental relations', she recalled at the end of 1901. She gradually evolved a compromise diet (although from this time onwards she always ate sparingly) and accepted that near-starvation was no substitute for a religious faith, particularly for one obsessed by a sense of her own sinfulness, exemplified, as she put it, in a 'desire to magnify, to pose, to mislead'. Her prayers were highly revealing. 'Every morning . . . I will concentrate my desire on physical self-control, intellectual concentration and moral purity. Health, Truth and Love of God' (26 March 1902). Beatrice never discovered a religion which suited her but she found relaxation in theological study which she claimed rested her brain and refreshed her spirit. She now began to pray regularly, went to church on Sunday and sometimes even on weekdays walked the not-inconsiderable distance from 41 Grosvenor Road to St. Paul's. It must be said that she never forced Sidney to join her in her various dietary excursions which he always regarded as light-heartedly as he did her lapses into religious fervour. He remained immune to Beatrice's quest for a faith, firmly calling himself 'a religious-minded agnostic'.

However, despite their disagreement over religion, there is little doubt that marriage to the stable and optimistic Sidney saved Beatrice from complete mental and physical breakdown and perhaps even suicide. Although Beatrice felt that Sidney often regarded her uncharitably as simply neurotic, she had a deep faith in his goodness, admired his character and believed him to be one of the sanest people she had ever met. As she once put it, he had 'a sanity and sense of perspective which keeps him free from all elation at his little successes' (December 1902). He was, she thought, a man totally without pretentions, 'as Graham Wallas once remarked watching him running to catch a train – "what I like about you Webb is that there is no damned nonsense about style"' (1 December 1903). Beatrice always considered it a privilege to live with Sidney who for her was the 'companion who knows neither malice, nor envy, nor desire to excel, nor the remotest tinge of what the world calls snobbishness . . . He is sometimes tired, occasionally bored but never unkindly or anxious to shine or be admired' (17 April 1905).

One facet of Beatrice's character for which critics give her little credit was her kindness and her great sense of duty to both family and friends. There are many examples of her going out of her way to give sustained help either to friends or relatives. Late in 1900 one of her favourite brothers-in-law, Alfred Cripps, barrister and politician, fell gravely ill with influenza. The illness was brought on by failure to be promoted (he had hoped to become Solicitor General) and by the loss of his parliamentary seat. Beatrice, alarmed at his condition, took him to Margate to give support to what she called 'a hypochondriacal wreck' and managed to cure him in a short time. She was also extremely helpful to Alys Russell, sister of Logan Pearsall Smith, the critic and literary essay writer. Beatrice, always the more sensitive of the partnership, began to discern a growing alienation between Bertrand Russell and his American-born wife. She became so concerned that she suggested that she should take her to Switzerland, even though this would cut heavily into her work. The visit consoled and strengthened Bertrand's wife, although the marriage broke up a few years later.

Two important links were severed for Beatrice during these years. Herbert Spencer, old friend and mentor, died on 8 December 1903. Characteristically Beatrice had refused to feel rancour at his dislike of Sidney and continued to visit and cherish him in Bournemouth as often as she could. She mourned for him not only because he was the only person whom, she claimed, 'singled me out as one who was worthy of being trained and looked after', but also because talking to him had stimulated the curiosity which had led her to become a social investigator. She was also saddened by the death of another old friend, Manville Creighton, Bishop of London. She first met him and his wife in 1887 and was much impressed by his sensitivity and toleration. They had grown closer over the discussions of the church's role in education and it was mainly because of his influence that the Webbs were determined to get the church to accept the new Education Act of 1902. His death was a particularly sad loss for Beatrice who had been able to confide her deepest religious anxieties to him.

The Webbs also made new friends. They were introduced to H.G. Wells and his wife: 'An interesting though somewhat unattractive personality except for his agreeable disposition and intellectual vivacity', Beatrice recorded after their first meeting on 28 February 1902. They stayed with the Wellses at their house in Sandgate, Kent. Beatrice, in turn, gave a grand dinner for him, to which she invited among others Balfour, then Prime Minister, the Bishop of Stepney and the Bernard Shaws. The Webbs were impressed by Wells's ability to throw off ideas, 'in one sense he is a romancer spoilt by romancing – but, in the present state of sociology, he is useful to grad grinds like ourselves in supplying us with loose generalisations which we can use as instruments of research' (19 April 1902).

Although the Webbs would have preferred to devote their time to education, there was no way they could avoid becoming involved in political controversy at a time when so many of the foundations of Victorian Britain were under challenge.

The first great question which nearly brought about an irrevocable split in the Fabian Society and which added further confusion to the already fragmented Liberal Party was the Boer War. When war was declared in October 1899 the Liberal Party divided into three groups: the Liberal Imperialist faction, known as the Limps, whose leaders were Rosebery, Haldane, Asquith and Grey, supported the Conservative Government; the pro-Boer faction led by Leonard (Courtney), Beatrice's brother-in-law, opposed any form of aggression; lastly the grouping led by the new leader of the Liberals, Sir Henry Campbell-Bannerman, although against the war accepted the need to pursue it once the fighting had begun.

The Fabian executive was split between the 'Old Gang' including Sidney Webb and Bernard Shaw, who, fearing the disruptive effects of a stand either way, wanted the Society not to take up a position on the war; and a vociferous anti-war group led by Ramsay MacDonald, Sydney Olivier, Peter Curran, George Barnes MP and S. G. Hobson, the famous economist. After a prolonged debate in the Society, it was agreed that the best course was to accept a resolution from MacDonald which called for a ballot of the members. The result was a narrow majority for the Old Gang by 259 to 217. When the outcome was announced, eighteen members, of whom Ramsay MacDonald, Walter Crane and Emmeline Pankhurst were the best known, resigned from the Society: a split had been averted but at some cost.

The Webbs tried to keep out of the controversy over the war but found sitting on the fence increasingly uncomfortable: 'Sidney does not take either side and is therefore suspected by both', Beatrice recorded sadly. 'He is against the policy that led to the war, that issue being past he believes in a policy of thorough in dealing with the Boers' (December 1899). She later noted that 'not one of the contending factions in Britain and South Africa . . . ever mentioned the claims of a native population whose conditions of life were at stake, even to be considered in the matter'.

In the end Sidney found himself forced to take sides. His public avowal of pro-war sympathies was made at a dinner given in July 1900 for Asquith, who had made a strong attack on the leadership and pro-Boer sentiments of Campbell-Bannerman. Beatrice wrote that 'Sidney is pro-Boer in sentiment: he agrees with Asquith and Haldane by reason; but he has not thought out the question, has paid little or no attention to it. It suits him infinitely better to keep out of the whole affair' (9 July 1900). However, he told Beatrice that 'one must be ready occasionally to step forward for our friends if one has no conviction to the contrary'. The Webbs' reluctance to make up their minds unless they were certain of the facts laid them open to the charge by their contemporaries that they were bloodless intellectuals. Today their refusal to be overwhelmed by the hysteria and emotionalism generated by the Boer War appears in a more attractive light.

But, if the Webbs' stance on the Boer War can be justified, their involvement in an attempt to form a centre party and their neglect of the infant Labour Representation Committee, was a serious miscalculation. The success of the Conservatives in the 'Khaki Election' of 1900 and the disarray of the Liberals, encouraged the Webbs to believe that it was possible to persuade the Liberal Imperialists, under Lord Rosebery, to set up a new party based on efficiency and social reform. The Limps, as they were known, were not only at odds with the majority of the Liberal Party over the Boer War (because they believed in the civilising mission of British imperialism) but were also in favour of a more collectivist approach domestically. The Webbs, enouraged by Haldane, hoped to capture the Limps for their ideas. After all, whatever his shortcomings, Rosebery was 'the acknowledged High Priest of the Cult of Efficiency', and was therefore likely to be attracted to the Webbs' objective of a national minimum – or so Beatrice supposed.

In contrast, the Webbs held out little hope for the Labour Representation Committee, although Pease was present at the original Farringdon Street meeting in February 1900 and subsequently represented the Fabians on the LRC. They were unimpressed by the trade union leaders, they quarrelled continuously with Ramsay MacDonald who became Secretary of the LRC, and they did not consider that such a disparate group of trade unionists, ILPers and members of the SDF could combine effectively – mere 'administrative nihilists', as Sidney dismissed them. It was more sensible, the Webbs concluded, to work with experienced politicians who believed in disinterested public service than with a bunch of agitators, many of whom saw politics in terms of class war and class envy.

Sidney announced the Webbs' new political initiative in an article entitled 'Lord Rosebery's Escape from Houndsditch', which appeared in the *Nineteenth Century* in September 1901 and was published two months later by the Fabian Society as Tract No. 108, *Twentieth Century Politics: A Policy of National Efficiency*. The title was a reference to Rosebery's letter to the City Liberal Club in July in which he had given a hint, albeit in a characteristically ambivalent fashion, that he had broken with Gladstonian Liberalism. Webb urged Rosebery to put himself at the head of a group of progressive Liberals, like Asquith, Haldane, Grey and Acland,

> Men of diverse temperaments and varied talents, imbued with a common faith and a common purpose, eager to work out and severally to expound how each department of national life can be raised to its highest possible efficiency. If he does nothing but plough his own furrow, Lord Rosebery will, I fear, have to plough it alone.

Sidney also underlined the need to construct a new alternative programme based on collectivism which would provide solutions to the problems of the twentieth century: poverty, bad working conditions, inadequate housing and sanitation, an out-dated education system and an archaic parliament and civil service. He agreed that

> to think out such a programme is, of course, irksome and, as every political Polonius will advise, to commit yourself to it is inconvenient – if you do not believe in it. But to create a live opposition – still more to construct an alternative government – this new thought and this new propaganda must be undertaken. If even one half of the study and conviction, money and capacity were put into such a Campaign for the next five years that Cobden and Bright put into the Anti-Corn Law, the country could be won for a policy of national efficiency.

The quest for national efficiency was an attractive rallying call. The Darwinian controversy, the Paris Exhibition of 1867, the disasters of the Boer War, the threat from German industry and the discussions over educational reform, had brought out into the open the need to improve national standards. Social reformers like Haldane, educators like Llewellyn Smith, journalists like H. G. Wells, were united in their belief that it was their duty to preach the gospel of national efficiency.

To further the Webbs' plan, Beatrice founded the Coefficients' Club in November 1902. It was to be a small dining club with a membership of around twelve which would meet initially at 41 Grosvenor Road and would be composed of those who were interested in promoting national efficiency at home and encouraging the idea of Britain's civilising mission abroad. Subjects to be discussed were: 'The Aims, Policy and Methods of Imperial Efficiency at Home and Abroad.'[3] The purpose of the club was to bring together as many 'experts' as possible. The membership list included, among others, Haldane, representing law, Hewens economics, Grey foreign policy, H. G. Wells literature, Bertrand Russell philosophy and L. S. Amery, who had become famous as a Times correspondent during the South African war, representing journalism. Shaw and Lord Milner, the South African commissioner, joined later. As the author of the most comprehensive study of the National Efficiency Movement has pointed out, the members formed 'socially and politically a microcosm of that segment of the public which subscribed to ideas of national efficiency'.[4]

The Coefficient Club was not just to be an expert talking club; it was also to provide a possible forum for a Centre Party. Experts, radicals, Liberal Imperialists and the more reforming sections of the Unionist Party would come together, so the Webbs hoped, to form the nucleus of a new political grouping. It was a scheme which was stillborn. The trouble was that the politicians, even the Limps, were not convinced of the need for a new party and were in any case divided by the two most controversial questions of the day, tariff reform and imperialism. In any case, the idea of national efficiency could not by itself provide the underlying ideology or interest group support which was required to sustain a new party. The Coefficients continued to meet until about 1909, though as time went on, less and less frequently. The idea of the Centre Party faded into oblivion.

In May 1903 Joseph Chamberlain electrified the political world and destroyed any idea of an alliance between the Unionists and the Limps by launching a campaign for tariff reform in a speech to his Birmingham constituents. Initially the Webbs were attracted by the idea. Beatrice admired what she considered to be its economically sound scientific basis, though both the Webbs were opposed to taxes on food. However, as with the Boer War, they did not wish to get involved on either side of the issue, which they saw as peripheral to the advance of Socialism. It was also essential, the Webbs believed, to keep both the Fabian Society and the LSE out of the controversy. With respect to the Fabian Society, they enlisted Shaw's help: he wrote such a balanced pamphlet that only Graham Wallas, an out and out free-trader, resigned and once again a major Fabian split was avoided. There were greater difficulties with the LSE. The Director, Hewens, was an ardent supporter of Chamberlain and the Webbs were concerned lest the recently established School became 'indirectly identified with either side' (15 June 1903). To reassure the School's backers Sidney had to make clear that he had not joined the tariff reformers. The problem was solved when Hewens resigned to take up a post as Secretary to Chamberlain's tariff commission and was replaced by a less controversial director, Halford MacKinder.

However, despite their political involvement, the Webbs' main preoccupation during these years lay in the field of education, with their first consideration the consolidation of the position of the LSE within London University. At the same time Sidney became involved in Haldane's scheme for the setting up of Imperial College which both hoped would provide a much-needed technological institute of learning. Beatrice and Sidney's most difficult task was the drafting, in conjunction with the Conservative Party, of an Education Bill, whose main purpose was the overhaul of the educational system, and persuading the unwilling Progressive Party on the LCC to accept it.

It was his LSE commitments which in the first instance appeared the most pressing. As early as March 1899 Beatrice had noted that Sidney was hoping to create a separate faculty of Economics and Political Science, as well as encouraging the TEB to continue to endow the new faculty. 'Everything seems to be going excellently', she recorded on 7 March 1899.

By the end of nine months Sidney's 'engineering' was well on the way to success. First, he had been offered both a site free of charge, in Clare Market just off the Aldwych, by the LCC and the money to start the first building. Secondly, he had persuaded, as Beatrice noted,

> the Commission to recognise Economics as a Science, and not merely as a subject in the Arts Faculty . . . This divorce of Economics from metaphysic and shoddy History is a great gain. We have always claimed that the study of the structure and function of Society was as much a science as the study of any other form of life and ought to be pursued by the scientific methods used in other organic sciences. (20 February 1900)

The following year, the first degree probably of its kind, a BSc (Econ) was introduced, while the new School buildings were formally opened two years later. 'There is the building and equipment, all admirably planned to suit the sort of work and life we have built up,' Beatrice enthused.

> There are the staff of teachers modestly but permanently endowed, there are the formidable list of 'governors' over which Sidney presides and last but not least, the School has attained University status with its own curriculum, its own degrees, and with even a prospect of its own 'gown'. (30 May 1902)

The Webbs' brilliant child had come of age.

If they had created nothing else, the establishment of the LSE would have made their reputation as educational innovators of the first order. Their concentration on the social sciences, their insistence on high academic standards, their determination to get the best experts in the field for the new institution, all these things ensured that the LSE became a unique institution which was able to attract the ablest staff and students.

The Webbs' great achievement was won by continual bullying and manoeuvring which even Sidney found wearying. The most tiring and annoying aspect of the struggle to create the LSE was dealing with the petty-minded antagonism of Ramsay MacDonald with whom they had already quarrelled over the Hutchinson will. Sidney hoped to persuade the TEB to donate an annual grant to the School, a contribution which was vital to its survival. MacDonald, who represented the ILP on the LCC, adamantly opposed such a grant on the curious grounds that the LSE was politically biased. In his previous battle with the Webbs he had opposed the Hutchinson money given to the LSE partly because he claimed that the School would not help socialist propaganda. Now he argued that the LSE had been captured by Fabian ideology and was therefore not a fit institution to be the recipient of state aid. Quite inexcusably,

1a Beatrice, aged 5
by kind permission of the Passfield Trust

1b Mr and Mrs Richard Potter with some of their daughters; Beatrice, wearing a hat, is centre-right
by kind permission of Rachel, Lady Clay

2a Beatrice Potter
The Mansell Collection

2b Joseph Chamberlain, 1880
Photo by Elliot & Fry

2c Sidney Webb, 1885
by kind permission of the Passfield Trust

3a The Young Left, painting by Bertha Newcombe; Mr G. Bernard Shaw, Mrs Sidney Webb, Mr Sidney Webb and Mr Graham Wallis
The Mary Evans Picture Library

3b Beatrice Webb

4a Mr Sidney Webb on his Birthday, 1914, by Max Beerbohm
The Ashmolean Museum, Oxford

4b The Webb of Destiny, by Frank Reynolds
Punch, July 1923

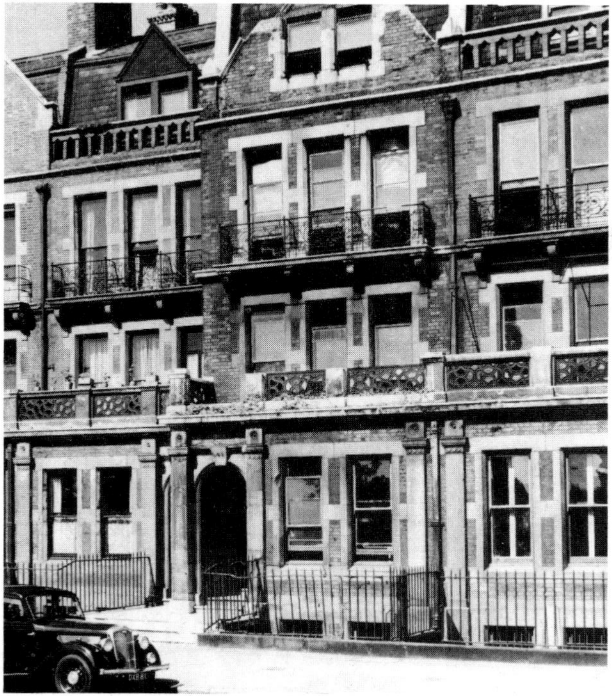

5a 41, Grosvenor Road (Millbank), photo by Godfrey New
reproduced by kind permission of the Greater London Council Photograph Library

5b Passfield Corner, Liphook
The Passfield Papers, by kind permission of the London School of Economics and Political Science

6a At Passfield Corner, 1929; Sidney and Beatrice Webb, painted by William Nicholson, to celebrate their 'joint 70th birthday'
by kind permission of the London School of Economics and Political Science

6b Sidney and Beatrice Webb, *c.* 1900
G. Bernard Shaw papers 'Other People'

6c The First Trip to Russia, May–July 1932
by kind permission of the Passfield Trust

7a The First Meeting of the Labour Cabinet, 10 June 1929
BBC Hulton Picture Library

7b Beatrice and Sidney Webb with Bernard Shaw at a Garden Party at Passfield
Photograph by courtesy of Thomas Ponsonby

8 At Passfield Corner: The Last Photograph
by Allan Chappelow, M.A. F.R.S.A.

MacDonald (as has been mentioned previously) also spread the false rumour that the Webbs were making money out of their LSE lecturing. Sidney was reluctantly forced into battle. He immediately wrote off to the Vice-Chancellor of the University categorically denying the allegations of pecuniary interests as well as vehemently confirming

> that no influence has been attempted or used either by donors of one side or by donors of the other side, of any controversial question of politics or economics to bias or control the work of the School, and none such would be permitted by its governing body.[5]

Webb's intervention was successful and the School obtained the grant from the TEB.

MacDonald continued his vendetta against the Webbs by attempting to block TEB funds for the new Library because he claimed that the British Library of Political Science was a different body to the LSE. It is difficult to understand Ramsay MacDonald's virulent antipathy to the Webbs. His biographer, David Marquand, chronicles the row but does not explain why MacDonald continued to snipe so waspishly at the Webbs. The charitable interpretation is that there was a genuine difference of opinion over the Hutchinson money and that maybe MacDonald had doubts about the Webbs' commitment to socialism. But perhaps the strongest motive was MacDonald's pique at the Webbs' failure to invite him to lecture at the LSE. Nobody is so vindictive as the vain man scorned!

As part of his plans for a reorganised London University (see Chapter 5) Sidney Webb, together with Haldane with whom he worked in close collaboration, insisted that the newly formed University be strengthened by the foundation of the equivalent of the German Charlottenburg, that is an institute of technology which would produce highly qualified engineers and scientists able to compete against their European and American rivals. Strengthened by the success of the LSE they had by 1903 raised sufficient money (mainly from two South African millionaires interested in technical education – Sir Julian Wernher and Alfred Bait – as well as Lord Rothschild) to be able to propose the incorporation of the old Royal Schools of Sciences and Mines into a modern Imperial College of Science and Technology as part of London University. As well as fighting Tory educationalists, once again they had to do battle with Ramsay MacDonald, who encouraged Labour councillors to oppose their proposals, this time on anti-imperialist grounds.

Ramsay MacDonald's antagonism towards Imperial College was also founded on a belief that schemes for national efficiency were irrelevant to working class problems. But again his continued opposition showed a lack of vision and a general pettiness, while his antagonism to the Technical Education Board's involvement in any form of higher education (coupled with his failure to win that particular battle) weakened his position in the LCC. Sidney again had to manoeuvre behind the scenes, a situation which he found as taxing as when he had set up the LSE. 'Fagged with combination of work and entertaining', wrote Beatrice in a fit of gloom. 'Before the [Charlottenburg] scheme was launched we spent ourselves, money and energy, in tuning the press and trying to keep the Progressives straight' (8 July 1903). Their hard work and energetic lobbying paid off: few members of the TEB eventually opposed the donation of a £50 000 grant to the new institute even though 'JRM made a long and virulent attack on Sidney', as Beatrice noted sourly. ' "Mr Haldane and Mr Sidney Webb had presented a pistol at the head of the Council" ', he was reputed to have said (25 July 1903).

As with the LSE, so with Imperial College, Sidney, in his support of what was originally Haldane's scheme, showed an intuitive grasp of the problems facing twentieth-century Britain. He saw clearly that one of the main reasons why Germans far outstripped their British competitors was because their technical colleges attracted the brightest brains. The hold of Oxford and Cambridge on academic life, he believed, ensured not only that the best intellects were drawn into the non-productive fields of the civil service (a chair in engineering was only established in 1907 at Oxford) but also, and more importantly, that industry and technology were despised. Far-sightedly he hoped to remedy this fundamental defect by ensuring that the reputation for excellence at Imperial College would become a counter-attraction of Oxbridge.

Sidney was also successful in a different field of higher education, that of teacher-training. London had few teacher-training colleges and those that existed were associated with religious societies and mostly inadequate. Sidney, prompted by the grumblings of London schools, whose members saw for themselves the poverty of teacher-training in the capital, persuaded the TEB and the newly created Senate of London University to establish a training college for teachers. The London Day Training College was founded in October 1902.

These were extremely rewarding years for Sidney, whose intense preoccupation with higher education, coupled with a determination to succeed, ensured that his goal of the creation of as many centres of advanced learning in London was achieved. In an important article entitled 'London University: A Policy and a Forecast' which he wrote for the *Nineteenth Century* in June 1902 Sidney summed up his views on higher education. London University was to be a place, he wrote, where students would no longer be able to have the leisurely 'curriculum' of Oxford and Cambridge. Instead they would have to be trained as experts and administrators.

> This involves a revival of the old conception of a university course deliberately framed so as to prepare the undergraduate from the outset for the practical pursuit of his profession, but in such a way as to turn him out equipped, not only as a trained professional but also as a cultivated citizen.

But as a good socialist, Sidney was also determined to provide equal opportunities for all and therefore hoped that the teaching of the new university, at any rate at an undergraduate level, would be as fully accessible as possible to every Londoner, and available both during the day and in the evening so that as many students as wished to be enrolled could be accommodated. As he put it:

> If we can show that there is no incompatibility between the widespread instruction of an undergraduate democracy and the most effective provisions for the discovery of new truth; between the most practical professional training and genuine cultivation of mind; between the plain living of hard-working students of limited means and high intellectual achievement, we shall not, I venture to believe, appeal in vain.

It was, however, over the reorganisation of elementary education that the Webbs had their greatest difficulty. They had come to the conclusion that the administrative muddle and the great disparity in resources and standards between the various school boards could only be corrected by a complete reorganisation. What was required was the abolition of all *ad hoc* school boards and the transfer of their powers to newly-created county and county borough councils. In order to widen educational opportunity and ensure uniform minimum standards, all schools, including denominational ones whose educational attainment was generally low, should be rate-supported and under public supervision. In return, denominational schools were to remain free to carry out religious instruction and to choose their own teachers. The result of these reforms would, the Webbs believed, create not only a more centralised but also a more effective educational system, without offending the conscience of parents or teachers. But if their ideas were to be translated into practice they had to win over powerful groups of opinion, including the Nonconformists so strongly represented in both the Liberal Party and the LRC, whose position would be challenged by the new reforms.

Sidney had already begun to fight the centralising battle (which he accepted would be at the cost of state aid to church schools) some time earlier within the Fabian Society. In 1899, soon after the Webbs' return from their journey abroad, he had started to work on a Fabian pamphlet entitled *The Education Muddle and the Way Out*. The central theme was the abolition of school boards and their substitution by one main authority. The idea was greeted with immediate opposition, particularly from those Fabians, like Graham Wallas and the Rev. Stewart Headlam, who had sat on the London School Board and were incensed not only that their own power base would be destroyed but also that the abolition of the school boards, which one authority has called 'the most democratically constituted of all elected bodies of local government' would lead to a diminution of grassroots democracy.[6] Their opposition came to a head at a crowded and heated meeting held on 26 May 1899 at which Sidney, on behalf of the executive (whom he had skillfully managed to convert to his views), put forward six resolutions on education. The core of the argument lay in resolution six which declared 'that it is undesirable to increase the number of separate public authorities; and that whilst it is important not unnecessarily to interfere with existing bodies, any reform should proceed on the lines of concentration and simplification'.[7]

In spite of the opposition Sidney won the day, though the publication of the *Education Muddle and the Way Out* was delayed for two years. He also had to make concessions. In June 1901 at a meeting of the Society held to discuss the Conservative education proposals, he agreed to an important compromise which was suggested by the executive, that in London and possibly in a few large county boroughs, the school boards should retain their powers at least for the time being. On the other hand, the executive accepted the principle of state support for denominational schools – an easy victory compared to the bitter battle that Sidney was to fight with the Progressives. Resolution five on the Education Bill now read:

> No measure dealing with primary education will be satisfactory unless it empowers the local authorities not only to maintain and improve the present Board schools but also to raise the efficiency of those existing public elementary schools which are not under School Boards by bringing them under the management and control of local committees of a public character and by making grants to improve their teaching staff.[8]

It says much of Sidney's powers of persuasion that, in spite of heated opposition within the Society, brilliantly organised by Wallas and Headlam, he still managed to get his main proposals accepted.

The Webbs generally agreed with the outline educational reforms put forward by the Conservatives and their chief educational expert, the highly influential Robert Morant. Sidney and Morant, working closely together, united in pressing the government to put forward an Education Bill based on the former's ideas. According to Robert Morant most of the Cabinet were so little interested in education that it was difficult to anticipate beforehand which of their proposals they would accept or reject. What they did know was that a considerable number of Conservatives were opposed to the idea of handing educational authority over to the LCC (which they saw as a left-wing dominated body) and preferred to give any new power into the keeping of a joint committee of the London Metropolitan Councils which they proposed to create. Both Sidney and Beatrice thought this a definitely retrogressive step, as it would mean that London's particular needs would not be met.

However, they not only had to change Conservative thinking but also to persuade the Church (and here their friend Manville Creighton, Bishop of London, proved a useful and powerful ally) to allow denominational schools to come under the authority of county councils. They had also to face the fierce opposition of the Progressives, who declared themselves totally opposed to the proposals and horrified by the idea of putting 'Rome on the rates'.

The Webbs marshalled their forces with care. Dinners which

increasingly played a key role in Webbian lobbying tactics (even though much disliked by Sidney himself) were carefully arranged to include the Conservative Prime Minister, Arthur Balfour (who had, Beatrice thought, 'the charm of genuine modesty and unself-consciousness' and who was 'a sympathetic and attractive person who easily tunes his conversation to other minds' (15 November 1902), Conservative politicians interested in education, and Liberal Imperialists who supported the Bill on grounds of national efficiency, those Progressives who would come, and every educational reformer friendly to the Webbs. Sidney also spent a considerable amount of time sending letters to influential politicians and churchmen, writing editorials for important journals and giving lectures. The result of his highly successful campaign was that the Education Act of 1902 was based on the Morant-Webb plan and the only cloud as far as Sidney was concerned lay in the Conservative refusal to include London in the Bill; that particular problem was shelved for the time being. Even so the Webbs were delighted with the new legislation, Beatrice going so far as to claim that the *Educational Muddle and the Way Out*, had been one of the main influences on the Conservatives and therefore on the drafting of the Bill. It was true that the proposed Bill contained most of Sidney's suggested reforms and that the Fabian tract had become an instant bestseller. His argument that without government support Anglican and Roman Catholic children would remain permanently ignorant had been particularly persuasive. But they owed their influence not so much to the novelty of their ideas as to the clarity with which they had pinpointed the weaknesses of the educational system and the persuasiveness with which they had set out a programme of reform acceptable to the Conservatives.

No sooner had the 1902 Education Act become law than the Webbs set out to persuade the Conservatives to tackle the problem of London. Here the battle was more intense in that there was opposition from all sides and a school board system which, on the whole, worked. Conservatives disliked the LCC because of the iron grip of the Progressives, and were therefore reluctant to put more power into the hands of a party which might (given the opposition over the 1902 Education Act) refuse to carry out its provisions for the legislation of London. The solution they had put forward was the setting up of joint committees of metropolitan boroughs, a move strongly opposed by Sidney. Apart from Tory antagonism, the Webbs also had to deal with continuing opposition from the Wallas and Stewart Headlam faction within the Society, whose defeat over the 1902 Education Bill had made them even more determined opponents of a similar scheme for London. They again had to convince both the Catholic and the Anglican hierarchy in the capital that their influence over the denominational schools would remain untouched even though the pursestrings would now be held by a party famous for its vociferous Nonconformist criticism. Most difficult of all, they had to persuade the Progressives that unless they accepted the principle of rate support for religious schools, they would find that the LCC would lose the opportunity of becoming an educational authority.

Sidney tried to win over the opposition. He wrote a letter to Wallas in which he attempted to persuade the latter by setting out the reasons behind his support for the London Bill:

> I quite realise that the mass of children, having to go to work at fourteen or fifteen, can get no other day-schooling than what is provided on the 'primary' schools; and I want *all*, whether denominational or not, these to be made as perfect as possible. What the perfect curriculum for them is I don't assume to know – whatever it is decided to be by you and the other educationalists, let us by all means have it. Then to that let us add the best possible evening opportunities and the best teachers.
>
> The children picked out to have both maintenance and 'higher education' paid for must always be a relatively small minority. But if there *is* any other way, by which higher education in day schools can really be made accessible to the children of the wage-earners, than maintenance scholarships, I should be glad to hear of it . . . Surely we want *both*. I can hardly calculate which is the more valuable to the community. What I want is (a) the best possible primary schools available to all. (b) the largest possible scholarship system. (c) the best possible evening instruction. (d) the most efficient secondary schools and University colleges. (e) the most thorough provision for post-graduate study and research.
>
> It is because the Bill *enables* the new authority to pay for all of this, without limit, that I think it a great stride onward.[9]

Wallas, however, refused to be persuaded and his criticism of Sidney's Fabian tract on London education remained uncompromising; 'insidious ecclesiasticism' he called it.

Early in 1903 Beatrice summarised the various problems over the London Bill.

> The Political Conservative is dead against the LCC and London . . . Moreover, the official opposition has declared in favour of an *Ad Hoc* body: the Progressives on the LCC have not liked to claim Education as their province, have only just been frightened by Sidney with the bogey of the Borough Council into holding their official tongue. (16 January 1903)

Sidney's next move was to persuade Alfred Harmsworth, owner of the *Daily Mail*, to come out in favour of making the LCC the education authority of London, by suggesting that if a campaign run by the newspaper changed the Government's mind, the *Daily Mail* could get the credit for it. Harmsworth, who claimed to know nothing about education, was taken by the proposal and agreed to run a vigorous campaign. Sidney for a week came in nightly to correct all the reports and comments published about London education.

Sidney also continued to put pressure on the Church, on London educationalists and on the Progressives. His most formidable opponent was once again Ramsay MacDonald who fought him as bitterly over these proposals as he had over Imperial College and the Hutchinson will, this time with the support of both the ILP and Progressive members. On 15 March 1903 Sidney was defeated in a caucus of Progressives on the TEB and lost his position as chairman. Beatrice, summarising the 'slump in Webbs', thought that the complaint against Sidney

> revolves itself into this: (1) he is 'in' with the Government; (2) he might sacrifice the interests of primary to secondary and university education; (3) he ignores the 'religious difficulty' and is willing to be impartial between Anglican and undenominational Christianity. (14 March 1903)

Initially it looked as if MacDonald's determined preference for the creation of an *ad hoc* body and non-sectarian education would lose the Bill for the Webbs. Even so they refused to be flustered or to change their attitude. 'We are not in favour of ousting religion from the collective life of the State;' Beatrice declared firmly,

> we are not in favour of the cruder form of democracy. And we *do* believe in expenditure on services which will benefit other classes besides the working class and which will open the way to working men to become fit to govern not simply to represent their own class; and we are in favour of economy as well as expenditure. (15 March 1903).

Slowly the mood swung in their favour. Some of the Progressives saw the advantage of the LCC becoming an educational authority; the Conservative cabinet's resolve, which had been vacillating in the face of Progressive opposition, as well as shaken by a series of disastrous by-elections lost to Nonconformists, was strengthened by Sidney's argument that Nonconformists would, in any case, dominate any *ad hoc* authority set up. By the end of April a much-amended London Education Bill was passed 'in almost exactly the shape Sidney would have given to it' (15 June 1903).

The battle had been intense and prolonged, and the Webbs, though victorious, had made many enemies. They antagonised most of the Nonconformist element in the LCC; their relationship with Wallas was seriously strained; and they were regarded as traitors by the Labour movement. The 'slump in Webbs' seemed destined to continue for some time. As far as the Webbs were concerned, they now put the establishment of the legally enforced 'minimum standard of life' before support for any political party. 'We have, in fact,' Beatrice recorded, 'no party political ties. It is open to us to use either or both parties' (25 July 1903). Their fear that a 'wrecking' majority of Progressives would be returned at the 1904 London elections, led Beatrice to hope for a Moderate victory. They even produced a secret list for the Conservatives of those Progressives who would refuse to make the Education Act work and who therefore 'will be best knocked-off' (3 November 1903).

In the March elections of 1904 the rising tide of liberalism returned the Progressives to power in London. To the Webbs' delight, however, they seemed 'literally *chastened* by their prosperity'. There was even a suggestion that Sidney could chair the new Education Committee, set up by the 1903 Act – an honour he declined, 'it would be adding insult to injury to appoint the executioner as executor or trustee of the dead man's property', Beatrice recorded placidly (11 March 1904). Instead he accepted the post as Chairman of the Higher Education Sub-Committee.

By the end of 1904 the Webbs could congratulate themselves at least on their success in the educational field. Two Education Acts had been passed which bore their imprint, the London School of Economics was flourishing, Imperial College had been founded. The future began to look even brighter when in the November of the following year, Beatrice was asked to serve as a member of a proposed Royal Commission on the Poor Law.

NOTES

1. *Our Partnership*, p. 147.
2. Ibid, p. 256.
3. S. Webb to H. G. Wells, 12 Sept 1902, University of Illinois.
4. G. R. Searle, *The Quest for National Efficiency*, p. 150.
5. S. Webb to Dr A. Robertson, 3 Jan 1903, in S. Caine, *Foundations of the London School of Economics*, Appendix to ch. 1, p. 9.
6. J. S. Hurt, *Elementary Schooling and the Working Classes 1860–1918*.
7. *Fabian News*, June 1899.
8. Ibid, June 1901.
9. S. Webb to G. Wallas, 4 Dec 1902, Passfield Papers.

8

1905–1911

Royal Commission on the Poor Law

'It will need all my self-command to keep myself from developing a foolish hostility, or becoming self-conscious in my desire to get sound investigation.'

The next four years were crucial for the Webbs. Beatrice's role as Royal Commissioner had far-reaching results. As a consequence of her research into the workings of the 1834 Poor Law the Webbs formulated a radical scheme for the provision of a comprehensive system of welfare services. The subsequent rejection of their Minority Report persuaded them to launch a campaign in favour of their proposals. The failure of this campaign forced Beatrice and Sidney to reappraise their political allegiances and to conclude that their future lay in the Labour Party.

Beatrice was asked by the Conservative Government to be a member of the Royal Commission in November 1905. The Commission was set up to enquire:

> into the working of the laws relating to the relief of poor persons in the United Kingdom, into the various means which have been adopted outside of the Poor Laws for meeting distress arising through want of employment, particularly during periods of severe industrial depression; and to consider and report whether

> any, and if so what, modification of the Poor Law, or changes in the administration or fresh legislation for dealing with distress is advisable.

Such a broad based enquiry indicated the government's acceptance that the Poor Law of 1834 had failed and urgently needed to be reformed.

The Poor Law of 1834 had been based on three major principles; confining relief to the destitute, applying this formula uniformally throughout the country, and ending outdoor 'relief' by setting up residential workhouses under such strict conditions that it was hoped only the most desperate would enter. Judged by these criteria, the Act was not a success. In some areas it was not applied; in others it was applied only in a piecemeal way. There was also the growth, outside the Poor Law, of new health and education services. The result was a confused, haphazard and frequently inhumane system which totally failed to solve the problem of 'pauperism'. In addition, there was the impact of the economic depression and high unemployment of the last quarter of the nineteenth century which not only put an unbearable strain on the Poor Law authorities but also showed conclusively that poverty was deep-seated.

There was, however, no consensus on what was to be done. Some demanded that the 1834 Act should be more stringently applied, while others more realistically, as well as more humanely, wanted a complete break-up of the Poor Law. In these circumstances the Conservative government, in one of its last decisions, appointed a Royal Commission staffed by experts to enquire into the problem. The Commission included nine Poor Law administrators; six members of the Charity Organisation Society, including its founder, Octavia Hill, and Helen Bosanquet; two orthodox political economists; members of the Anglican and Roman Catholic churches; Charles Booth; and three representatives of the labour movement, George Lansbury, Francis Chandler (General Secretary of the Amalgamated Society of Carpenters) and Beatrice Webb. The Chairman was Lord George Hamilton, a Conservative ex-Cabinet Minister and Chairman of the London School Board in 1894.

Beatrice, delighted at the first public acknowledgement of her standing as a social investigator and expert, immediately set out her objectives:

> What I shall aim at is to concentrate my attention on three aspects of the Poor Law – leaving the remainder to the other Commissioners. At present these departments seem to be (i) the interaction of Poor Law relief and the sweated industries, (ii) the exact working constitution of the Board of Guardians; (iii) the policy of the Central Authority. I shall exclude altogether the provision of relief for the sick, the children and the aged – subjects about which others are keen. (23 November 1905)

The Webbs' first move was to discover what conclusions the Local Government Board, which had had overall supervision of the 1834 Act, required from the Commission. Beatrice, adept at dealing with government departments since the Webbs' experience over the Education Act, found no difficulty in extracting the information. It was, she discovered, a radical reform of the structure of Poor Relief which she was inclined to favour and a return to the principles of 1834 'to stem the tide of philanthropic impulse' which she vehemently opposed. 'It is just this vital question of what and which forms are right that I want to discover by this Commission to investigate,' she wrote soon after the Commission had begun to sit, remarking at the same time that she was determined not to be 'spoonfed by any civil servant' (2 December 1905).

At the first meeting of the Commission, Beatrice put forward the sensible suggestion that all the inspectors of the Local Government Board should be called to give evidence, so as to get as comprehensive a view as possible. To her surprise she met with no support; 'It will need all my self-command to keep myself from developing a foolish hostility, and becoming self-conscious in my desire to get sound investigation. Certainly the work of the Commission will be an education in manners as well as in Poor Law', she wrote in her diary. She added self-critically: 'I was not over-pleased with my tone this afternoon . . . Beware of "showing off" superior knowledge on irrelevant detail.'

The chairman, Lord George Hamilton, had also made it known that he disliked agendas, concrete resolutions or 'any formal appointment and authorisation of the Committee', announcing at the same time that Commissioners who wished to dissent should do so by post. This was too much for Beatrice who was shocked by both Lord Hamilton's style of chairmanship and the Commission's apparent disinclination to approach the enquiry in a professional manner. She complained to the secretary of the Commission and, through him, asked for and obtained a more formal procedure. Meanwhile the formation on 5 December 1905 of a Liberal Government under Campbell-Bannerman, following the resignation of Balfour, had raised the Webbs' hopes. Their old friend John Burns became President of the Local Government Board and thus directly responsible for the Commission, while Haldane was in the War Office, (a post, however, which isolated him from the mainstream of political events). A general election followed in the new year which was won by the Liberals by an overwhelming majority. The election of a strong Liberal government, with many of their friends in it, seemed to offer a good opportunity for the advancement of the Webbs' ideas.

However, unlike Sidney, Beatrice found it difficult to work effectively in a committee. She bombarded the chairman with memoranda on how to run the Commission – and antagonised other members of the committee by sending suggestions and proposals only to those two or three she thought she could influence. When she did send a memorandum to all her colleagues, the effect was often to irritate them into producing retaliatory documents of their own. Nevertheless Beatrice won the first round. Her memorandum on investigative procedure was finally accepted and on 5 February 1906 a sub-committee was set up, of which she was a member, to look into the methods of inquiry. She herself had already begun to be clear as to what she wanted the Commission to undertake.

> (1) Survey of all English Unions, with regard to diversity of constitution and methods of administration of Union. (2) Analysis of the whence and wither of pauperism in some among them. (3) Clear vision of course of legislation. (4) Analysis of developments of policy of central authority. (5 February 1906)

The Webbs swung into their by now customary lobbying. Lord George Hamilton was invited to dinner, others came to lunch or tea and, partly because she was the only commissioner with a detailed plan, Beatrice managed to persuade her reluctant colleagues to agree to the setting up of three more committees – on statistics, local administration and central policy. However, in attempting to 'guide' the committees on which she sat into accepting an analytical framework, she usually found herself in a minority. This would so infuriate her that she tended to forget her own recognition that her colleagues were, after all, 'after public objects however much we may disagree what these objects are and how to arrive at them' (12 February 1906), and antagonised many of her fellow commissioners who believed, with considerable justification, that their lifetime interest and work in dealing with the Poor Law gave them a better grasp of essentials than one who had come lately to the subject. She often had to be reprimanded by Lord George for her hastiness, impatience and arrogance towards the commissioners. She was usually contrite after an outburst, 'Ah, how hard it is for a quick-witted and somewhat vain woman to be discreet and accurate', she wrote sadly. 'One can manage to be both in the written word – but the "clash of tongues" drives both discretion and accuracy away' (15 May 1906). But the damage had been done.

As the investigation proceeded, so the rift began to grow wider. In May 1906 after only six months of sitting, Beatrice attempted to steer her cross-examination of witnesses into a discussion of the causes of destitution rather than sticking to the narrower question of 'granted destitution is inevitable, how can we prevent pauperism?' This was too much for those like C. F. Locke, one of the founders of the Charity Organisation Society, who were determined to avoid this kind of general issue. Her gambit in bringing about a discussion on economic doctrines and then opening up the question of the causes of poverty was not only firmly resisted, but also lost her influence among her fellow commissioners.

In June, however, Beatrice became more optimistic. The commissioners now agreed to enquire into the connection between sweating and pauperism – one of her own special interests since the Booth enquiry. At the same time, Charles Booth had 'scampered off with the Statistics of Today, I have seized upon the Historical Survey', she recorded exultantly. 'Mrs Bosanquet has captured her own little corner of outdoor relief as a rate-in-aid of wages to women' (15 June 1906). Each commissioner would therefore be investigating his or her own field of interest which Beatrice hoped would at least lead to a more professional inquiry – even if they failed to arrive at the same destination.

The History of Local Government which the Webbs were working on had to be put aside as Beatrice's investigations for her own side of the Royal Commission were now more important. Her research assistant was switched accordingly. As she had 'seized upon the historical survey', her first task was to trace the policy of the central authority from 1834 to 1906. Her second, quite different, was to see if there was any connection between bad conditions of employment, insanitary overcrowded houses, and pauperism. To supplement the work of her assistant, Beatrice asked for, and received, help from the Fabian Society. Charlotte Shaw also helped her out by funding some of the research. Sidney remained ready to write reports, to criticise, and to produce the final draft of the Minority Report.

Beatrice proved not only to be a brilliant but also an intuitively imaginative cross-examiner. There is an interesting account of her technique by A. G. Gardiner, the well-known journalist.

> There is no cross-examiner at the Bar more sure, suave or subtle than Mrs Webb. When I was called to give evidence before the Poor Law Commission, I entered the room in the midst of her examination of Mr. Walter Long . . . step by step she led him unconscious to his doom with gentle, innocent-seeming questions. Suddenly he saw that he was being made to admit that voluntary effort was a failure and that the rates must be used, but it was too late to retreat. With the quiet 'Thank you, that is all', she snapped the bracelet on her wrist, folded her hands and sat back in her chair, the picture of demure, unexultant charm.[1]

She also had unexpected flashes of inspiration; in the middle of a cross-examination she would suddenly see problems in a totally different way. Once she recorded

> listening to the evidence brought by the COS members in favour of restricting medical relief to the technically destitute, it suddenly flashed across my mind that what we had to do was to adopt the exactly contrary attitude and make medical inspection and medical treatment compulsory on all sick persons – to treat illness, in fact, as a Public Nuisance, to be suppressed in the interests of the community. (17 July 1906)

Gradually she came to accept the need for more regulation and more public provision as of right. By July she was envisaging a scheme for reform whose scope was far wider than the Commission's original remit. She had come to the conclusion that the state ought to be responsible for establishing certain minimum standards of life.

Such a comprehensive reorganisation, which would entail both the complete break up of the Poor Law and a wide measure of state intervention, was not surprisingly opposed by most of Beatrice's colleagues, particularly those from the Charity Organisation

Society whose existence would be threatened if the state took over. If Beatrice's intention was the publication of an agreed report, the most fruitful approach would have been to try and win over the commissioners. Instead she went her own way. 'I just take my own line', she stated complacently, 'attending for just as long as it suits me, cross-examining witnesses to bring out my points and conducting the enquiries that I think important independent of the Commission's work' (17 July 1906). By the summer recess, she and her staff were well on their way to producing independent memoranda on central policy, the relation of Poor Law medical relief to Public Health, and the relationship between bad conditions of employment and pauperism, and had begun an investigation into the administration of the Boards of Guardians.

She continued to be bitterly and, no doubt, noticeably critical of the way in which the Commission was organised. 'We slide and slide along', she complained to her sister Mary,

> Massing up bulky blue books, always evading difficult points, sprawling all over the place, beginning multitudinous and often irrelevant enquiries and completing and perfecting none . . . no-one knows what the others are doing – the result being that we shall all be proceeding on different evidence.[2]

In the end such an attitude proved counter-productive; those commissioners who might have been persuaded by the logic of her arguments were put off by her behaviour.

The Commission returned to its work after the summer recess (used by the Webbs to carry out their own independent investigations) on 1 October. Lord George now suggested the setting up of two more committees – to consider indoor and outdoor relief, and proposals on them. Beatrice declined to sit on either on the grounds that she did not feel sufficiently at one with her colleagues to co-operate usefully in the discussions. She preferred, in fact, to see which way the deliberation went, and then to decide whether to throw in her 'lot with all the Commission or any section of it' (6 October 1906). The Commission, she recorded, was still divided between those who were determined to retain the stigma of destitution and those who accepted the view that every citizen had a right to state aid.

Beatrice continued with her own private investigations. By the New Year of 1907 it had become evident to the Royal

Commissioners that they would have to investigate not only pauperism but destitution, adding another facet to their enquiry. Beatrice now hoped that they might at least back the idea of the 'transference of Poor Law medical relief to the Public Health Authorities', a major step forward which could well lead to the break-up of the Poor Law. However, it was just at this moment that Beatrice's high-handed behaviour again infuriated her fellow commissioners; this time they discovered that she had been questioning the Medical Officers of Health behind the Commission's back. Beatrice smoothed the situation over and even got them to accept her independent investigation but the effort and ensuing nervous exhaustion of preparing her defence took its toll. She suddenly collapsed in early February 1907 and had to retreat to the Beachy Head Hotel where she took to her bed. It was in moments like this that she became conscious of how much she relied on Sidney's support. 'I tremble to think how utterly dependent I am on him', she recorded from her sick bed. 'Both on his love and on his unrivalled capacity for "putting things through". When he is late I get into a panic of fear lest some mishap has befallen him. This fear of losing each other is always present – more with me, I think, than with him' (16 February 1907).

She was not ill for long. By April she and Sidney had drafted a memorandum on the employed ready for discussion by the Commission. This was followed by a further memorandum on the policy of central authority over poor relief and they envisaged a third on medical relief and public health. Beatrice felt that the evidence was going her way and that the majority of the commissioners would have to accept at least the idea of the transference of Poor Law medical relief to public authorities. She was also encouraged by the commissioners' appointment of a number of her investigators to look into the plight of widows with children on outdoor relief, and their decision to launch an enquiry, to be carried out by Beatrice's friend, Dr Ethel Williams, into the Poor Law and its treatment of children.

It was in that year that Beatrice began to see her way more clearly. She now came to the conclusion that the way to reform the Poor Law was to take away from the boards of guardians various categories of the destitute and hand them over to the relevant departments. The destitute sick, as well as the aged and infirm would come under the Public Health Authority, while the education authorities would be responsible for pauper children. The

Webbs' argument was that as each department had to deal with only one specific problem (unlike the Poor Law authorities who had to administer the entire field) the singling out of particular cases would ensure a professional and competent appraisal. The result would be the gradual elimination of pauperism, as well as the stigma attached to it.

One major problem still unresolved was how to deal with the able-bodied poor. 'The crux of the Able-bodied question', she wrote to Sidney from Scotland where the Commission had gone to investigate the Poor Law,

> seems to be the 'marginal man' – the man not young enough or not skilled enough, or not well-conducted enough for employment in normal times. He is not vicious, he is not ill, he wants to work: you cannot reform him, you cannot detail him as a nuisance, he has not sufficient pluck or initiative to wish to emigrate.[3]

'What I have got to discover in the next year' she noted in July, 'resolves itself in two questions: one, must we have a national authority in dealing with the able-bodied? Two, if national or mainly national, what must be the constitution of the body?' (31 July 1907).

In October Beatrice became more optimistic. Lord George Hamilton circulated an 'astonishing' memorandum which proposed a weakening of the Poor Law 'by taking out the sick, aged and the vagrant, but proposes to set up a new *ad hoc* elected Poor Law authority and county borough'. Beatrice thought the scheme impracticable – the Webbs were adamantly opposed to *ad hoc* bodies. 'But it is all in the right direction and, incidentally, sweeps on one side the "principles of 1834"' (8 October 1907). Given the memorandum, Beatrice began to hope that the majority, even the members of the COS, might come round to the idea of taking medical relief out of the Poor Law and transferring it to the Public Health Authority, which would mean a step towards the break-up of the 1834 Act.

But by 29 October after only a few weeks she again quarrelled with her colleagues, this time over the question of her previous investigations into medical relief. Mrs Bosanquet of the COS demanded to see Beatrice's correspondence with the Medical

Officers of Health (to prove, so Beatrice suspected, that the MOHs had in fact been against the transference of the pauper sick to the Public Health Authorities). She decided to make a suitable selection of the letters in spite of 'qualms of conscience' as to what should be sent. At the same time, when Mrs Bosanquet demanded they be printed, Beatrice refused on the grounds that 'I had no authority from my correspondents to circulate their letters in a printed form' (29 October 1907). It worried her that she had been less than honest in not sending all the correspondence, so much so that she again collapsed in a state of exhaustion and high fever. Her nervous breakdown, helped along by another row over her personal investigations, was probably further exacerbated by a talk she had with the President of the Local Government Board, that 'monstrosity John Burns', who refused to back her. The Webbs believed that he was wholly in the hands of his civil servants: 'an enormous personal vanity', she wrote of him bitterly. 'Feeding on the deference and flattery yielded to patronage and power' (30 October 1907). She again fled to Beachy Head where she recuperated slowly.

On her return, Beatrice asked to be excused from any more writing of reports to the Commission because of her breakdown. All the same, she refused to put an end to her private investigation into the problem of the able-bodied unemployed.

In spite of the heated controversy which she continued to generate, Beatrice was the only member of the Royal Commission who had worked out wide-ranging proposals and who had the support of a number of colleagues. The others had now been looking into the Poor Law for nearly two years and had come to no conclusions. It therefore seemed easier to ask her to put her proposals formally to the Commission. It was a breakthrough which she had never anticipated. Delighted, she agreed to submit 'a fully formed scheme of reform – the *Break up of the Poor Law* – in all its detail' (26 November 1907). It was a bold move on her part, she felt, but on the whole a wise one. 'The majority of the Commission are tired of wandering about the subject without a leader . . .' However she had little hope that she could ever persuade the Commission to agree to her 'more revolutionary scheme of dealing with unemployment' which the Webbs had recently evolved, even though her colleagues had come to accept a good deal already with 'the transference of medical relief to public health authorities and the County and County Borough as the authority for the treatment of all destitute persons'.

Beatrice presented her scheme on 9 December 1907, nearly two years to the day that the Royal Commission had begun its sitting. It was received with hostility, partly because, as a fellow commissioner once told her, any proposal she might make would always get a negative reaction; the problem was that she was 'so clever, and that however harmless my proposal *looked*, it meant socialism'.[4] She also forced her colleagues to vote on the crucial question of whether a statutory committee of the county council should be set up to oversee the working of the Poor Law or whether the various elements should be merged with the appropriate departments, as the Webbs felt more appropriate. Inevitably Beatrice was defeated and immediately, probably to the detriment of her cause, announced that she, Lansbury and Chandler considered the Webbian formula to be the only acceptable one. They would be forced to issue a minority report. She was undaunted by her setback; 'the activity of the Majority would be on the Commission', she noted smugly. 'My activity will be outside it – investigating, inventing, making an atmosphere favourable to my inventions and where possible, getting the persons with right opinions into high places, and persons in high places in the right state of mind' (9 December 1907). In other words, Beatrice intended to use her remaining time on the Commission for her own ends.

The Webbs spent most of the following year working on the final draft of the Minority Report. Beatrice still kept a tenuous link with the Royal Commission when it suited her. She went with her colleagues to labour colonies which had been set up for the unemployed and was particularly impressed by one run by the Salvation Army, though with its staff, 'a true Samurai class', rather than with the colony. On the whole, her energies were directed elsewhere: lobbying the Labour Party, sending her scheme to Balfour, discussing details with Haldane and Asquith, creating a suitable climate of opinion.

In the middle of February 1908 in the third year of the Commission, the outline of the Majority Report had also begun to take shape. 'The majority have definitely decided to abolish the Board of Guardians and set up the County Council and County Borough Council as the supreme authority', Beatrice wrote with delight. 'But this authority is to be exercised by a Poor Law Statutory Committee of the Council itself, as regards institutions, and by local committees, nominated by the Council, as regards outdoor relief' (17 February 1908), a move to which the Webbs were fundamentally opposed because it failed to remove the stigma of pauperism. The Commission still continued to meet (they and Beatrice spent some weeks in Ireland in April and May) and the Webbs, Sidney now more than Beatrice (who was again on the verge of a nervous breakdown caused by overwork and tensions generated by the Commission) drafted and redrafted their largest undertaking – an enquiry into the problems of unemployment.

By May, the Commission had more or less come to the end of its investigation and the Webbs worked through the summer months preparing their final report, 'the great collectivist document' in a cottage in the grounds of the home of the South African millionaire Sir Julius Wernher. They decided to circulate privately a hundred copies of their scheme for breaking up the Poor Law to, among others, Asquith, Lloyd George, Haldane, Winston Churchill, Burns, the two Balfours and McKinnen. Beatrice was particularly anxious to persuade John Burns and the Local Government Board to back her, but again it was impossible to move him. He refused to accept the need to abolish the workhouse test for the able-bodied, to which the Webbs were passionately committed, and continued to remain sceptical of the need to set up a 'great national authority' for the unemployed.

If they had failed with Burns, they still hoped to persuade his Cabinet colleagues, particularly Lloyd George, the new Chancellor of the Exchequer and Winston Churchill, who had recently been appointed by Asquith to the Board of Trade. These two were very much in the market for new ideas on how to tackle the problem of the unemployed: Lloyd George was interested in social insurance, whilst Churchill was taken up with the idea of labour exchanges to improve the working of the labour market.

In early October they had a working breakfast at 11 Downing Street with Lloyd George and his officials, Haldane, and Churchill. The Webbs had 'a heated discussion' with the Chancellor, during which they tried to persuade him that 'any insurance scheme would leave over all the real problems of Public Assistance.' Beatrice also argued that

> any grant from the community to the individual beyond what it does for all, ought to be conditional on better conduct and that any Insurance scheme had the fatal defect that the State got nothing for its money – that the persons felt they had a right to the allowance whatever their conduct. (16 October 1908)

Haldane attempted to act as a mediator suggesting that 'insurance had to be part of a big scheme with conditional relief for those at the bottom, and insurance for those struggling up', but the Webbs would have none of it. As Professor Mackenzie points out, their insistence on their own scheme meant that they missed the opportunity of influencing the Liberals.[5]

In September, Beatrice had finally broken with her colleagues on the Commission. The Webbs had given L. S. Amery, then still working on *The Times*, a copy of their Poor Law proposals on the promise that he did not mention the Commission or their names. This indiscretion swiftly came to light when a series of articles began to appear on the break-up of the Poor Law. Lord George Hamilton, furious at the suspected breach of confidence, denounced the Webbs in all but name. 'The net result', noted Beatrice complacently though unwisely, 'of our indiscreet or, as some would say, unscrupulous activity, has been to damage the Webbs but to promote their ideas' (15 September 1908). She and Sidney hoped the publicity would provide a formidable back up for their cause. What it certainly did accomplish however, was a final break between Beatrice and her colleagues. Deciding that there was no point in staying on, she suggested to Lansbury and Chandler that they should use delaying tactics in order to enable the Minority Report to be published at the same time as that of the Majority Report. As the year drew to a close, so Beatrice began to become more agitated and nervously exhausted and to regard herself at times with a sense of loathing, a sure sign of an impending breakdown. She and Sidney had to work at high pressure around the clock in order that the Minority Report would be presented alongside that of the Majority.

The Royal Commission met for the last time in the first week of January 1909, to be photographed and to sign a blank piece of paper as the Report was still unfinished. Beatrice was quite certain that the Minority Report would be the one to be finally accepted by the Government, even though she became more or less incapacitated, sinking into one of her deep melancholic moods.

On 17 February both Reports of the Poor Law Commission were published. To the Webbs' great astonishment the Majority got 'a magnificent reception . . . we secured . . . belligerent rights but not more than that. The Majority held the platform' (18 February 1908). Five days later, still depressed at their rivals' success, Beatrice attempted to sum up the reasons why the Webb Report, despite constant previous publicity, had failed to catch the public eye. 'In our depreciation of the Majority Report', she wrote honestly just before she and Sidney took themselves off for a much-needed holiday in Italy for six weeks,

> and our false expectation of its failure to 'catch on', we overlooked the immense step made by the sweeping away of the deterrent Poor Law – *in name, at any rate*, and, to some extent, in substance, by municipalising its control . . . However, I am inclined to think the distinction between the two reports – the fact that only by distribution of the services can you obtain 'curative and restorative' treatment – will become gradually apparent to the nation. (22 February 1909)

It is certainly true that the Majority and Minority Reports had much in common partly as a result of Beatrice's own pressure.[6] Like the Minority Report, the Majority Report recommended the abolition of the general workhouse and the transfer of the administration of the Poor Law to the local authorities. It was also in favour of a substantial extension of social services for the sick, the aged, children and the mentally defective. It proposed a national system of labour exchanges and state subsidies for the unemployed. Looked at from the perspective of the early 1900s, the Webbs can be criticised for their wholesale rejection of the Majority Report. But whatever the tactical shortcomings of the Webbs, the imaginative grasp and comprehensive sweep of the Minority Report make it a much more impressive document than the Majority Report. The first part of the Minority Report proposed the abolition of the Poor Law authority and the transfer of its functions to specialist committees of local councils. The Board of Education, through the local education authorities, was to be responsible for both the education and welfare of all children; the Local Health Authority was to be in charge of maternity and infant welfare, for domiciliary medical services, for hospitals and for homes for the aged; local pension committees, already operating under the 1908 Act, were to have power to recommend local pensions for those not entitled to national pensions; while a local committee for the mentally defective was to be responsible for all those certified as being of unsound mind.

The Webbs' welfare plan was based on three assumptions. First, that poverty was not the fault of individuals but 'a disease of society itself'. It followed not only that destitution would lose its stigma, but also that the community would have to assume the responsibility for dealing with it. Their second assumption, derived from their investigations and research, was that there was no one single reason but a number of reasons for poverty. It was therefore far more logical to break up the Poor Law functions and allocate them to specialist committees. Thirdly, these committees, backed up by the special skills and knowledge of officials, would be able not just to relieve poverty but actually to prevent it; 'the problem of destitution has, in fact, now become manageable; we have both the knowledge and power to cope with it, as we have coped with cholera and typhus, highway robbery and the slave trade, if only we have the will.'[7]

The second part of the Report dealt with unemployment which they had shown to be one of the main causes of poverty. Here the Webbs proposed the setting up of a Ministry of Labour to prevent or minimise unemployment, with responsibility for a national system of labour exchanges for planning the labour market and for running training centres. The idea of labour exchanges (already established in Germany) had figured prominently in evidence to the Royal Commission, including the influential memorandum presented by Beveridge. It was accepted by the Majority, and implemented by Winston Churchill as President of the Board of Trade in the Liberal government. The original feature of the Minority Report, apart from its proposal for a Ministry of Labour, was its advocacy of deliberate government action to keep up the demand for labour in times of recession. The Webbs argued that 'the government can do a great deal to regularise the aggregate demand for labour as between one year and another by a more deliberate arrangement of its orders for work of a capital nature',[8] and recommended counter-cyclical public spending to be financed by borrowing which, as the Webbs pointed out, was far cheaper in a depression. The Minority Report concluded; 'we have to report that, in our judgement, it is now administratively possible, if it is sincerely wished to do so, to remedy most of the evils of unemployment.'

The Minority Report can be criticised from a number of directions. First it ignored social insurance which was supported by the Liberals. Instead it advocated a combination between grants-in-aid from the Exchequer and cash payments where individuals could afford to pay (though arrangements for payments were to be separate from the provision of services). The Webbs believed that social insurance was both an unfair weekly poll tax on the manual workers and would not 'ensure either the medical treatment or the personal conduct likely to lead to the earliest possible restoration to productivity, or even to the adequate maintenance of the patient, his wife or his child, in which the community has the greatest interest'.[9] The Webbs did not foresee that the Labour government of the 1940s would introduce a new insurance scheme as one of the means of financing the welfare state which they had advocated.

The second criticism was that the Webbs' scheme was too bureaucratic and inflexible. It is certainly true that, in contrast to the Majority Report, they envisaged very much a secondary role for voluntary relief. They also were in favour of the provision of services by function rather than treating the family as a whole. But the Webbs believed that if the Majority Report's approach was accepted there would be discrimination between those cases dealt with by voluntary organisations and those dealt with by the state and also between those under the care of public assistance authorities (proposed in the Majority Report) and those looked after by the functional departments. In their view, the only way to secure the national minimum standard of civilised life 'open to all alike of both sexes and classes',[10] which was their main objective, was to give specialist civil servants the responsibility for the provision of services and assistance.

Thirdly, it can be argued that the Minority Report was utopian. Certainly their proposals involved far-reaching administrative changes which, in the absence of an agreed report and without the support of radical Liberals, were unlikely to be implemented in the near future. More fundamentally, was it realistic for the Webbs to suppose that their objectives – the eradication of poverty and the abolition of unemployment – could be achieved in the context of a fully fledged capitalist society? When Beatrice Webb looked back on the Minority Report in the early thirties, she was sceptical, especially about the abolition of unemployment. 'Confronted with this dismal tragedy of mass unemployment', she wrote, 'it is futile to suggest that the recommendations of the Minority Report . . . even if fully implemented, would or could prevent mass destitution of the able-bodied'.[11] Certainly, it needed the more favourable economic climate of the 1940s, the application of Keynesian policies, and the introduction of a 'mixed' economy, before the Webbs' ideas could be put into practice.

But whatever the criticisms, the importance of the Minority Report should not be underestimated. Margaret Cole has rightly called it 'one of the greatest State papers of the century',[12] while Joan Clark, who was Beveridge's research assistant, claimed with justice that its imaginative realism and its administrative vision derives, undoubtedly, from genius.[13] The verdict of social historians has also been favourable: T. H. Marshall has pointed out that the Webb's plan was 'a brilliant anticipation of the eventual results of a movement which had just begun and of which they sensed the nature', and R. C. Birch has concluded that 'in the story of the Welfare State, the place of the Webbs is secure'.[14]

However, despite the merits of Majority and Minority Reports, it soon became clear to the astonished Webbs that neither was to be implemented. Refusing to believe that their lack of success could be anything but temporary, they decided to push forward with a public campaign backing their proposals. In May 1909 they set up the National Committee for the Promotion of the Break-up of the Poor Law, a 'cumbrous and equivocal title', as Beatrice noted, which was changed the following year to the National Committee for the Prevention of Destitution.

The Webbs' switch to propaganda was an admission that the round of illustrious little dinner parties with Balfour, Haldane, Churchill, Lloyd George, and famous civil servants such as Morant and Newsholme, had not succeeded in persuading the 'right people' – that permeation had failed. The Minority Report was not taken up either by the Conservative Party (who were still in the midst of their own turmoil over tariff reform) nor by the Liberals, who were bent on their own plan of social insurance. The Webbs were not prepared either to throw in their lot with the supporters of the Majority Report or to try and exert some influence on the social insurance plans of Lloyd George and Churchill. They believed that the Minority Report represented the most effective solution to the problems of poverty and unemployment and that, given that they already had the support of a number of Poor Law administrators, they would be able to convert public opinion to their cause and so force either a Liberal or a Tory government to implement their proposals.

The Webbs quickly came to the conclusion that the most practical way of mounting a national campaign was working with and through the Fabians. Over the previous three years, the Society had been going through a period of turmoil and change which it is necessary to consider briefly. The 1906 election, which had returned some 30 Labour MPs as well as a Liberal Government, had stimulated a mood of excitement through the Labour movement, not least among the Fabians. Many young intellectuals joined the Society and were anxious to rejuvenate it. Three new members (Clifford Sharp, later to be editor of the *New Statesman*, the journalist and historian Robert Ensor, and the future Labour politician, Leslie Haden Guest) united together to set up a reforming 'Ginger Group'. They found a leader in H. G. Wells.

Wells, who had been a member of the Society since 1903, was by now a famous and prolific writer whom the Webbs still admired. Wells, flattered by the attention he was receiving, particularly after the publication of *A Modern Utopia* in 1905, which portrayed a selfless oligarchy of Samurai running a socialistic state, began to have political pretensions. In the summer of that year he told a friend that he was 'going to turn the Fabian Society inside out and throw it in the dustbin'.[15] He and his friends were encouraged to put forward reforms by Shaw, who could see no harm in a reappraisal of the Society's aims. In February 1906 Wells delivered a lecture entitled 'The Thoughts of the Fabians' in which he singled out the Webbs and the rest of the 'Old Gang' for attack and criticised the Society for its loss of political momentum and its inward-looking and dull character. The 'Old Gang', unruffled, agreed to set up a special 'Reform' committee, including Wells. Wells, however, went off to the United States and it was not until his return in the summer that he completed his proposals for a 'New Model' Society which would put up candidates for Parliament. The Webbs, now alarmed by his activities, went to see him at his home at Sandgate and Beatrice returned depressed by his attitude. 'I inclined to the prophecy that five years will see H. G. Wells out of the Society', she wrote. 'He has neither the patience nor the good manners needed for co-operative effort – and just at present his conceit is positively disabling' (15 July 1906); which is more or less what Shaw told Wells to his face.

In October, Wells returned to the attack in another lecture entitled 'Socialism and the Middle Classes', in which he mixed a passionate plea for free love and liberated women with yet another renunciation of the 'Old Gang'. The Webbs remained calm in the face of his onslaught: Beatrice thought it important not to write him off as 'he is going through an ugly time and we must stand by him for his own sake and the good of the cause of collectivism' (18 October 1906). She rejected his philosophy of free love (though noting that 'if you could have been the beloved of the dozen ablest men you have known it would have greatly extended your knowledge of human nature and human affairs') but it was partly as a result of Wells's lecture that she re-examined her attitude towards women's suffrage. On 2 November she wrote to the suffragette, Millicent Fawcett explaining that she now accepted that women's 'social obligations compel them to claim a share in the conduct of political affairs'[16].

With two different proposals circulating, one from Wells and one from the executive, it was agreed to hold two special meetings to discuss the two reports. It was clear from the outset that Wells was determined to get rid of the Old Gang. Sidney pointed out to fellow members that what Wells and his acolytes on the special committee wanted was 'a complete reversal of the principles which made the Society what it was. Intellectual persuasion and argument, that is to say permeation, was still the vital and only possible policy for such a body as the Fabian Society.'[17] That particular meeting was adjourned to the following week on 14 December. With seven days to brood over the possibility of a split, the Fabians' mood changed. The consensus now stood for no recriminations and a desire for unity. After a brilliant attack on him by Shaw, on behalf of the executive, Wells was defeated.

The battle between the two factions, however, rumbled on. In the March 1907 elections for the Fabian executive, Wells's followers won nine out of the twenty one seats. In the summer, mostly in response to Wells's demands for reform, special groups (catering for women, etc.) were started as well as a new political committee whose aim was to promote local socialist societies based on Fabian membership, with the object of increasing socialist representation in Parliament. These societies were to be independent yet closely linked to the Labour Party. Sidney was asked to be chairman, a move which was denounced by Wells. Even the mild Sidney was now stirred by Wells's continuing invective and sent the irate novelist a sharp little letter in which he explained how the committee had been set up, adding acidly, 'do you *really* believe that *I* have packed this Committee with a strong bias in favour of this new middle class, Socialist Party project? What an extraordinary and total misconception of my bias!'[18]

But Wells, encouraged by the continuing influx of new members (over one thousand by 1907), continued to scheme against the Old Gang. He now insisted that the Society's constitution should be changed, although it was not exactly clear what changes he actually envisaged. Sidney, angered by the continuous sniping, wrote clarifying his position.

> As a matter of fact, what moves me is a desire to *get things done*. I want to diminish the sum of human suffering, I am not concerned about this party or that but about getting things done, no matter who does them. Elections and parties are quite subordinate, *even trivial* – parts of political action. More is done in England in politics whilst ignoring elections and parties than by or with them. Nevertheless, they, too, form part of life which the Socialist cannot ignore.[19]

However, after his latest burst of activity, Wells quietened down. Shaw had sent him a draft of a newly reformed constitution to which he did not bother to reply and it was not until March 1908, a whole year later, that he bestirred himself once more. He re-wrote Shaw's draft and suddenly demanded that his own version be discussed. Sidney was particularly busy working at the Royal Commission evidence and had no time to spare. As he brusquely told Wells: 'We can't all be disengaged at a particular moment when you are.'[20] In any case, it was unlikely that Wells would bother himself in further schemes of reorganisation. He had other interests by then.

There was to be one final showdown: Wells had suggested in the *Daily News* on 21 April 1908 that Churchill, standing as a Liberal in a by-election in West Manchester, should be supported in preference to the Socialist Dan Irvine. The apparent change of heart was due simply to the fact that the Conservative, Joynson Hicks (a previous Home Secretary) had publicly denounced Wells's attitude towards free love and Wells thought Churchill more likely to beat the Conservative. Although Sidney accepted that Wells had a right to express his opinion, he felt it necessary to point out at the Fabian annual general meeting that it would at least have been more polite to have informed the executive. Wells, furious, stalked out, and resigned six months later. That particular 'storm in a Fabian teacup' (as Wells later called it) was over.

The battle over reform left the Society, particularly the younger members, restless and dissatisfied. As Wells had rightly observed, they needed a cause. Paradoxically, the Webbs' new campaign in support of their Minority Report gave them one. In their turn, the Fabians provided the Webbs with the committed manpower they required to spread the message. Both the Webbs and the Fabians became 'political'.

The campaign was in effect publicly launched by Beatrice on 19 May 1909 at a testimonial dinner given in honour of the Webbs and the Minority Report, by the Fabian Society. She placed herself at the head of 'a "secretariat" of young men and young women' (15 May 1909) whom she hoped would 'do the work'. A headquarters was set up between the Fabian Society and the London School of Economics, a 'sort of middle turn between avowed Socialism and non-partisan research and administrative technique'. Meetings and conferences were organised and a newspaper, the *Crusade*, with Clifford Sharp as editor, was started; soon money and members were pouring in: by December 1909 there were 16 000 subscribers, a colossal number by Fabian standards. Beatrice and Sidney, with two pauses for Fabian summer schools which they had recently introduced with great success, toured up and down the country, making speeches in support of their campaign. Beatrice particularly revelled in it. It was her first experience of a whistle-stop tour. 'I enjoy it', she wrote congratulating herself after some six months hard campaigning

> Because I have the gift of personal intercourse and it is a gift I have never, until now, made full use of. I genuinely *like* my fellow mortals, whether as individuals or as crowds – I like to interest them, and inspire them, and even to order them, in a motherly sort of way.

Also, she added honestly, 'I enjoy leadership' (31 December 1909).

She absorbed herself completely in the campaign. Even during the Fabian summer school at Harlech, she practised 'voice presentation between 6.30 and 8.00 a.m. every morning on the beach – orating to the Waves! I want', she wrote to her sister, Georgina Meinertzhagen, 'to be able to speak without effort which is really a question of proper tone of the voice'.[21] But in spite of the public acclaim, she often yearned for the even rhythm of her previous existence. 'All this office organisation', she wrote sadly, 'writing ephemeral tracts, preparing speeches and talking to all sorts of different persons, is soul-destroying; excites but does not satisfy. There is none of that happy alternation of strenuous work and complete rest which made such a pleasant life' (18 June 1909).

At first, the Webbs had no competition and the campaign

appeared to be gathering momentum. On 8 April 1910, they managed to persuade the Liberal MP, Sir Robert Price Jones, to introduce a Private Members' Bill based on the Minority Report. Asquith, Burns and Balfour all contributed to the debate. But the 'forces of reaction' were beginning to reorganise. Lord George Hamilton, supported by the Charity Organisation Society, joined Burns and the Local Government Board, and the boards of guardians, and formed the 'National Poor Law Reform Association' in direct opposition to the Webbs. The latter, aware of the powerful groups arraigned against them, cleverly realised that 'we must change the direction of propaganda from a destructive to a constructive policy; from "the break up of the Poor Law" to "the prevention of destitution" '.[22] Hence their new title – The National Committee for the Prevention of Destitution.

But in spite of the new name, and in spite of the fact that in early 1910 Sidney decided to leave the LCC so as to devote his whole time to the campaign, in spite of good organisation and growing membership, the Webbs made no perceptible progress in converting those that mattered. Through no fault of their own they had chosen a bad year in which to fight. 1910 was not only the year of two elections but the great struggle between the Lords and the Commons which ensured that the 'political class' was preoccupied with the excitement of the constitutional crisis. By the end of December 1910 Beatrice began to have doubts:

> Sidney and I are both feeling weary and somewhat dispirited. In spite of all our work the National Committee does not seem to be gaining many new members and our friends are beginning to melt away. One wonders whether we have not exhausted the interest in the subject. (10 December 1910)

The failure of the Webbs' campaign was not just because the government and the opposition had other matters to concern them. More fundamentally, their conclusions were too ambitious and far-reaching for either the Liberals or Conservatives. The Webbs always stressed not only the non-party but even the non-socialist character of the Minority Report. In the February 1910 issue of the *Crusade* under the heading 'Is the Minority Report Socialist', Sidney (in an unsigned contribution) pointed out that if by socialism was meant nationalisation of the means of production, then clearly the Report had no 'Socialist tendency'.

> But if you mean State action generally, then all these proposals are Socialism. But so is the present Poor Law . . . it does not prejudge the real issue between Socialists and Individualists but it (or something like it) is indispensible if you wish to have a healthy foundation on which to build your superstructure, whether you tend it to be along Individualist lines or Socialist.[23]

But Sidney's argument was somewhat disingenuous. The proposals to transfer Poor Law functions to government departments and to set up a Ministry of Labour to deal with unemployment, amounted to a comprehensive welfare programme well in advance of its time. The Conservative attitude is best summed up by Austin Chamberlain's comment that it would 'establish an intolerable bureaucratic tyrrany'.[24] But even the Liberal Radicals like Lloyd George and Churchill were sceptical about the practicality of the Webbs' proposals and were far more concerned with their own more limited (though extremely important) measures of improvement. If permeation had failed, so had non-party political campaigning. The way was clear for a more direct involvement in the only party that consistently supported the Webbs' solutions – the Labour Party. As Beatrice put it on the eve of their journey abroad,

> The whole attitude of the government about the destitution question, together with the leaderless state of the democratic movement, makes me feel more strongly every day that our duty, when we return, *may be* to throw ourselves into the democratic movement. (12 March 1911)

As to the nature of their duty, Beatrice remarked

> I am not sure that the time may not have arrived for a genuine socialist party with a completely worked-out philosophy and a very detailed programme . . . We will see how the land lies . . . I am not sure whether we had better not throw ourselves into constructing a party with a religion and an applied science. (7 March 1911)

In March 1911, they let their house for a year and went to Eastbourne and Luton Hoo where they completed *The Prevention of Destitution* which set out the Minority Report proposals in a more positive form. Then in June they sailed for Canada.

NOTES

1. Quoted in *Our Partnership*, p. 390 from A. G. Gardiner, *Pillars of Society*, pp. 204–206.
2. B. Webb to M. Playne, 29 July 1906, Passfield Papers.
3. B. Webb to S. Webb, mid June 1907, Passfield Papers.
4. Ibid, 25 Apr 1908, Passfield Papers.
5. See N. and J. Mackenzie, *The First Fabians*, pp. 358–359.
6. There is a considerable amount of literature on this subject. See (Bibl.) Searle, Emery, Mackenzie, Una Cormack, A. MacBriar, B. Gilbert.
7. S. and B. Webb, *The Prevention of Destitution*, p. 5.
8. Ibid, p. 281.
9. Ibid, p. 213.
10. *Our Partnership*, p. 481–482.
11. Ibid.
12. M. Cole (ed.), *The Webbs and Their Work*, p. 138.
13. Ibid, p. 111.
14. R. C. Birch, *The Shaping of the Welfare State*, p. 25.
15. Quoted in N. and J. Mackenzie, *The First Fabians*, p. 326.
16. *Our Partnership*, p. 363.
17. *Fabian News*, Jan 1907.
18. S. Webb to H. G. Wells, 12 June 1907, Wells Archives.
19. Ibid, 15 June 1907, Wells Archives.
20. Ibid, 10 Mar 1908.
21. B. Webb to G. Meinertzhagen, 8 Aug 1909.
22. *Our Partnership*, p. 441.
23. *The Crusade*, Feb 1910.
24. *Our Partnership*, p. 450.

9
1911
Far Eastern Travels

'We believe that it is still the Land of the Rising Sun.'

Although (or perhaps because) the Campaign against Destitution had reached a stalemate, the Webbs decided that they could no longer put off their tour of Canada and the Far East which they saw as a complement to their previous journeys of 1898. In any case, two years hard crusading on top of the years on the Royal Commission had left their mark. Beatrice was prone to nervous exhaustion and the pressure of the campaign had eaten into her reserves of strength. She now felt that she could no longer continue without a lengthy break. Had she not had one it is quite possible that she would have had another breakdown.

On the 1898 trip the Webbs had set out anxious to learn what they could from American and Antipodean institutions. They had hoped that their journey would provide them with ideas for their work on local government. The outcome, as we have seen, was not entirely successful. The Webbs had enjoyed themselves but their inability to detach themselves from British assumptions marred their research. This time they would be visiting mainly Asiatic countries (Japan, Korea, China, Malaya and Burma) and they believed that there was little in the experience of these societies which was of relevance to British administration and government. The voyage was to be a break from the ceaseless and exhausting campaigning of the last two years. The Webbs on this occasion were going not as academic investigators but as intelligent visitors, prepared to comment freely on what they saw.

But once more they failed to leave their prejudices and preconceptions behind.[1] For the most part they judged the countries they visited from the standpoint of efficiency and democratic accountability, imposing an alien framework which took little account of the historical background of these societies. Nor were they deterred by language barriers, trusting perhaps too easily in the official interpreters they were allocated. Again, the Webbs (and particularly Beatrice whose diary sometimes reflects an unthinking racial superiority) revealed their limitations abroad-especially in their judgements on the Chinese and Koreans.

Before going on to the Far East they first went to Canada where they arrived in June 1911. They found a booming, ebullient, opportunist society whose unshaken optimism in its future delighted the Webbs. 'Capitalism—', Beatrice told readers of *The Crusade* is 'on its good behaviour and is quite sincerely seeking its gain in efficient direction of the national enterprises.'[2] They warmed to the Canadians whom they considered, in spite of their rampant individualism and their unabashed materialism, among the most amiable people they had encountered. 'I like the native born Canadians – they are so tall and straight and resourceful – full of "anticipation",'[3] Beatrice wrote to her sister Kate.

They travelled all over Canada. They went to Quebec, where they admired the French Canadians who 'had a metaphysic' of their own, and Montreal whose captains of industry endeared themselves to the Webbs by their lack of 'conspicuous lavishness of expenditure' and considerateness. Escaping from the heat of eastern Canada, they took a steamer travelling across Lakes Huron and Superior, reaching Port Arthur some three days later, and then finally went on to Winnipeg where they stayed on a wheat farm on the prairies. Beatrice was enchanted not only by the 'delightful, mystic distances' but also more particularly by the 'comradeship of perpetual co-operation between settler and settler'.

It was this feeling of social solidarity and moral purpose which the Webbs found so attractive about Canada. It was the kind of attribute which they expected from civil servants but which they now discovered existed among the majority of Canadians, even to some extent, among the upper echelons of the country's big businessmen. They were also impressed that they found so little evidence of destitution. They explained this by the 'opening up' of the continent in the previous twenty years: 'What is just now happening . . . is the individual appropriation and reduction to effective use of the natural resources of a vast Continent.' Another reason was that only the able-bodied were allowed to come into the country. 'Canada is still a nation of healthy adults, self-selected for energy, enterprise, ambition and endurance.'[4]

Their final judgement on Canada was relatively favourable. Although the 'get rich quick' philosophy produced a 'monotonous society, singularly devoid either of depth of feeling or brilliancy of intellect', and with 'practically no consciousness of art, music or literature,' their last impression was 'that of a hopeful, happy, virile and well-conducted people, grappling energetically and successfully with the conquering of a new country for wealth production.'[5]

Beatrice and Sidney came to Japan predisposed to like Japanese society. They were intensely curious about this new nation which had defeated the Russians in the 1904–5 war and was in the process of modernising itself, guided by a centralised bureaucracy. They were not disappointed.

In the two months in which they were in Japan, they saw a great deal, both of the countryside and the towns.

> We have found travelling in Japan unexpectedly easy, pleasant and . . . cheap. It is so civilised a country that one goes everywhere, even in the most lonely forests and the slums of its great cities, without the slightest fear of molestation by man or beast.[6]

They visited the temples of Kyoto and the slums of Osaka and Nagoya. They walked from Nikko to Nagano, a ten days' hike over mountain passes, through forests, by rivers, lakes and waterfalls past 'countless shrines, tombs and temples of century-old piety' and from village to village – all this in the tropical heat of a Japanese August, 'very much like the atmosphere of the great Palm House at Kew'.[7] They spoke to statesmen, civil servants, bankers, professors, priests, businessmen, villagers and workers. Beatrice took part in the tea ceremony but wrote it off as a 'silly business' with its 'partly arbitrary conventions and elaborate formalities leading to nothing but a sip of tea' (14 September 1911); and then she and Sidney took time off to talk to a prostitute (he paid her two shillings for her time) in a whorehouse which they described 'as a gruesome sight . . . the coarse, weary, apathetic faces of the girls, the crude animalism of the business . . . though, of course, the analagous evils of the

English system could be painted in as dark a light' (5 September 1911).

They summed up their impression of Japanese society in a lively article in *The Crusade.* They were charmed by the independent peasantry and 'petty handicraftsmen' of rural Japan: it represented 'the perfection of *la petite culture* and *la petite industrie*'. However, it was a 'community of superstitions of all sorts', was incapable of the wider political interests essential for a modern democratic state and created a surplus population that had to leave the land.

Industrial Japan they found 'reproducing, with minute accuracy, all the features of the industrial England of 1790 to 1840': wage slavery, exploitation of young children and girls, appalling slums and sanitation and abject povery. They were particularly horrified by the treatment of women:

> what is remarkable . . . is that a very large proportion of its women are also passed into bondage for a term of years. There is the annual recruitment under contract of the million of factory operatives. There is the not-inconsiderable annual recruitment – virtually sale by the parents – of girls to be trained as geishas. And there is the still darker shadow of the passing into the almost hopeless bondage of the 'licenced quarter' . . . of literally thousands of young girls every year.[8]

If they found the ruthless Japanese capitalism disturbing, they were impressed by the civil servants. 'They appeared to be taking the keenest interest in their work and eager for public welfare; to be full of intellectual curiosity about it, open-minded and curiously unprejudiced'. But, contrary to the impression given by J. M. Winter in his *Socialism and the Challenge of War*, the Webbs were concerned by the lack of accountability and democracy in Japan. Civil servants were 'beyond all effective check or criticism' and the Webbs noted with anxiety that 'the Japanese Cabinet has adopted a bureaucratically controlled and minutely supervised system of local administration . . . and has failed, as yet, to learn . . . how to create real independent centres of local initiative and local administration.' Their final judgement was, however, optimistic.

> Japan has the advantage . . . of facing its problems with an instructed and highly intelligent civil service, and with the mass of the common people . . . essentially civilised. It has the further advantage . . . of being open-minded, eager to learn, and intel-

lectually modest . . . In short it is a land full of hopefullness. We believe it is still the Land of the Rising Sun.[9]

From Japan the Webbs went north to Korea where they spent six days mainly as guests of the Japanese administration. They saw palaces, tombs, schools and hospitals but were not much impressed by the Koreans. Either they were tired from their strenuous tour of Japan or were very much under the influence of the efficient Japanese. Whatever the case their attitude to the Koreans was curiously antagonistic. They disliked the inhabitants on sight: 'Unsavoury mortals', Beatrice decided. 'Horrid little race'. Their clothing 'from their absurd little black hats to their equally absurd baggy trousers, is the most perfect example of hideousness of unfitness . . . The hair of both sexes is dirty and unkempt and the expression unintelligent and sulky' (22 October 1911). They even lacked a religion.

Whether it was racial prejudice, Japanese influence or a misunderstanding of the internal situation, the Webbs saw Korea in the most naïve terms. Their criticism of the institutions in fact failed to take into account that the Koreans had been a subject race for a long time, nor did they understand that their poverty and lack of organisation might have been due to the failure of the ruling Japanese to provide an adequate system of government. Their attitude towards the Japanese colonisation of Korea was similar to their views on the British Empire. They believed that it was Japan's mission to civilise the barbarian people and that the Japanese were doing their best to achieve that mission. The shortness of the visit and the heavy load of official engagements probably added to the hasty and ill-conceived exasperation with which the Webbs viewed the Korean people: 'Twelve millions of dirty, degraded, sullen, lazy and religionless savages', as Sidney wrote dismissively to Shaw.[10]

It was with relief therefore, that they crossed to China, only to be met with the news that the country was in the midst of a revolution. The Webbs were not put out; their only concern was that the revolution would interfere with their travel arrangements, particularly on railways and trams (which were now crammed to overflowing with refugees) and cut back on their investigations. They were curiously untouched by the events unfolding around them – the beginning of an epic struggle which was to change the course of Chinese history by bringing down the Manchu Dynasty and plunging China into a civil war which was to lead eventually to a communist state. Again the language barrier could have made them misjudge the situation. More probably it was a reflection of their distaste for the Chinese. Whatever the cause, the Webbs refused to consider the revolution with any seriousness and insisted on making the rounds of the government departments as if nothing were amiss. As with the Koreans, the Chinese too were found wanting. Chinese officials, Beatrice acidly noted at the beginning of their visit were, of course, immeasurably inferior to the Japanese officials – a self-indulgent, indolent looking lot, 'who seem to be perpetually smoking and drinking tea, and who are only too ready to leave their offices at any excuse . . . Chinese administration seems that of an uncivilised race' (25 October 1911). Beatrice was both repulsed and made uneasy by the Chinese she met, who gave the impression, she wrote critically, of glib superficiality; servile acceptance of their nation's inferiority to the white man and of an insincere politeness. 'One does not feel in the least sure what they may be saying behind our backs' (5 November 1911). The Chinese, she convinced herself, were 'an essentially unclean race'.

In spite of the revolution and its hazards, Beatrice and Sidney managed to cover much of the country, visiting Peking, Shanghai and Canton, where they witnessed a historic event: the cutting off of pigtails to mark the end of the three hundred year subjugation by the Manchus. Finally they reached Tiensin in the south and from there were to continue on their way to Calcutta. Tiensin provided a particularly endearing Webbian encounter. Pushing their way onto a crowded platform they were eased onto the train

> by favour of the English guard who turned out to be an enthusiastic member of the ILP and subscriber to the *Labour Leader*; and whose fraternal intervention proved of more practical use in the terrified mob than all the efforts of a high Chinese dignitary from the Ministry of Railways who had come down to the station to befriend us.[11]

The guards' efficiency merely highlighted their own dislike of the Chinese, whom they dismissed as inefficient, obstinate individualists, 'idle and apparently incapable even of understanding any conception of the common weal' (8 November 1911). The Webbs concluded, in an article in the March edition of *The Crusade* that 'this so-called "great" race, whose capacity is so much extolled by those who profess to admire them and whose reputed achievements in the distant past claim our respect, is, today, by all the available evidence, capable of nothing.' The 'yellow peril' which Europeans talked about was not the millions of Chinese who might one day infiltrate European society; it was more invidious – 'the real Yellow Peril is the moral and intellectual decadence into which this vast empire has fallen . . . the helpless incapacity of its people to create even a decent social organism; the failure to develop the vast material resources of their country.'[12] A weakened and feeble China, such as this, they believed, could have disastrous consequences on the rest of the world. It would inevitably lead to rapacious colonization, colonizing wars bringing with them untold misery for both victor and vanquished.

On the steamer which was to take them to Hong Kong, Singapore and Rangoon (where they stayed for a very short time) and their final destination, Calcutta, Beatrice reflected on their experiences in both China and Japan and summed up her impressions. She saw the Chinese as a thriftless, drifting, idle race who, in spite of glaring defects, suffered from an intellectual arrogance, wholly at variance with their present status. Their past achievements, far more subtle than anything Europe had produced, meant little to the Webbs and their dismissal of everything Chinese, again showed them at their most blinkered. As to the Japanese, Beatrice had nothing but praise.

> They have shown themselves capable, first of the momentous decision to emerge completely from (that) isolation and to take on all the civilization of Europe, and secondly, in the short space of fifty years, of constructing a social organisation able to claim equality (and to make good that claim) with first class Western powers . . . What has made these wonderful achievements possible is the character of the Japanese people; its extraordinary idealism or mysticism, which manifests itself in its all-pervading reverence . . . which is seen in the amazing patriotism and self-sacrifice for Japan; and which is accompanied by a remarkable capacity for deliberate plan, persistent effort and subordination of the present to the future. (18 November 1911)

If the Webbs persistently under-rated the Chinese, they seemed blithely unaware of the dangers of Japanese imperialism.

However, they began to change their attitude towards colonialism once they reached India. In a sense India took them by surprise.

They had expected to be presented with clear-cut evidence that the civilising role of the British empire was a vital element in the education of the Indian people. This, after all, was a conviction which had lain behind their acceptance of the South African war, and to a certain extent they felt that their expectations had been justified. What they did not foresee was that they would be caught up in a great wave of nationalism and that their response to the movement would be so positive, so much so that they now questioned the whole purpose of the British Raj.

As the Webbs journeyed from Calcutta to Benares, on to Lucknow and Agra, and then to Delhi, their preconceptions began to be undermined. At first they found Indian society and individual Indians difficult to understand. 'India is a desperately baffling place', wrote Beatrice to Clifford Sharp soon after their arrival, 'which leads you gasping at the questions it presents, confused with multitudionous impressions – squalor and picturesque beauty, piety and vice, starvation and magnificence.'[13] The Webbs were determined to see as many aspects of Indian life as they could and organised their journey with this in mind. They ended with a mixture of impressions and a variety of experiences which included a visit to the Ghats of Benares, an inspection of a Raj state and a stay with two British Collectors (as local administrators were known). With one of the two John Hope Simpson, whom Sidney, when he became Colonial Secretary, appointed to look into the problems of Palestine, they went on a long expedition so as to see for themselves how a population of three and a half million was administered. This part of their visit was particularly pleasant. They were given a free hand to inspect schools, police stations, roads and were allowed to sit in' on an appeals board and conferences with village headmen.

The Collector lived up to the Webbian ideal of selfless, dedicated, public service, a 'patriarchial head of his district' and obviously incorruptible. In Benares they looked up their old Fabian friend and theosophist, Annie Besant, who had founded a successful Hindu Central college in the city and who was later to become involved in the Indian National Congress. They also spent some time talking to leading Mohammedans who ran the All-India Moslem League, as well as to their rivals the Hindu Nationalists. After one such meeting Beatrice decided,

> I don't much believe in the loyalty of Mohammedans further than as the only practical alternative to Hindu domination.

Personally, I would rather play for the general education of the Hindus in self-government and their retention in the Empire of their own free will, than for the artificial safety of putting the Mohammedans against them, relying on the hatred of the Mohammedan to keep the Hindu in permanent subjugation.[14]

In spite of the Collector, Beatrice and Sidney found that they could see less and less justification for British rule. They perceived the problem of British subjugation as 'a stupid people finding themselves governing an intellectual aristocracy' (10 April 1912). As Beatrice wrote a fortnight later 'three months' acquaintance has greatly increased our estimate of the Indians and greatly lessened our admiration for and our trust in this government of officials' (5 April 1912). The Indian visit brought out the more admirable qualities of the Webbs, for it made them examine their own preconceptions – and finally to disregard them. Here was a problem they could understand and a task they could tackle, and if the evidence pointed to a different conclusion than they had anticipated, then they were broad-minded and scholarly enough to accept that they had to change their view. The journey brought into sharp focus some of the policy issues with which Sidney, as a future Colonial Secretary, would have to deal. India had proved a fascinating and extraordinary venture, full of magical moments, picturesque confusion, something of a turning point in their lives.

Beatrice summed up their journey in her diary:

The Japanese are a race of Idealists, but these Ideals are fixed and amazingly homogeneous and are always capable of being translated into immediate and persistent action . . . What revolts us in the Chinese is, on the one hand, the absence of the idealism of the Japanese and Indian races, and on the other, their present lack of capacity for the scientific method, and for disciplined effort of the Japanese . . . the Hindu [is] a delightful and refined intellectual companion – whom one instinctively feels to be one's superior. What strikes us as serious in the present state of feeling between the British Ruler and the Indian Ruled, is the complete and almost fatuous ignorance of the bulk of British officials of their essential inferiority in culture, charm, and depth of intellectual and spiritual experience, to the Indian aristocracy of intellect . . . if . . . the English would realise this new governing class – and would gradually take them into his confidence,

> with a view to making them pair to the Government of India, then the British race might pride themselves on having been the finest race of school-masters, as well as the most perfect builders of an Empire. (25 April 1912)

The Webbs got back to England by May 1912 having missed the months of industrial unrest which had divided the country and brought the Syndicalist movement into prominence. A new phase, their wholehearted involvement in the socialist movement, was about to begin. The new mood of Labour militancy suited their purpose, the time seemed right for the socialists to move into action. Newly created agitators as they were, the Webbs prepared for battle.

NOTES

1. See George Feaver, 'The Webbs in Canada. Fabian Pilgrims on the Canadian Frontier', *Canadian Historical Review* vol. LVIII No. 3 Sept 1977.
2. *The Crusade*, Sept 1911.
3. B. Webb to K. Courtney, 27 July 1911, Passfield Papers.
4. *The Crusade*, Sept 1911.
5. Ibid.
6. Ibid, Jan 1912.
7. Ibid.
8. Ibid.
9. Ibid.
10. S. Webb to G. B. Shaw, 29 Oct 1911, British Library.
11. *The Crusade*, Mar 1912.
12. Ibid.
13. B. Webb to Clifford Sharp, 15 Jan 1912, Passfield Papers.
14. B. Webb to Lady Betty Balfour, 28 Jan 1912, Passfield Papers.

10
1912–1918
Labour and War

'The Labour Party exists and we have to work with it. A poor thing but our own.'

Before they left for the Far East, the Webbs had already decided to commit themselves to the Labour movement, which unlike the Liberal Party, had backed the Minority Report, and the Prevention of Destitution Campaign. The strategy of 'permeating' all the political parties had been finally abandoned. From 1912 onwards they were set on a new course of close involvement with Labour.

The Webbs were now both in their fifties. One side of Beatrice was tempted by less public life, devoted to research and study of local government. She often felt that their closeness was such that writing books in the country would be the best way to spend the rest of their lives. Leonard Woolf, who became friendly with them during this period, recalled the deep mutual affection and devotion of their partnership:

> When they stayed with us they brought all the paraphernalia for making tea, including kettle and spirit lamp. Very early in the morning – six o'clock I think it was – Sidney made tea in his room and carried it along to Beatrice and he then read aloud to her until it was time to get up.[1]

But they were too caught up in their new role as mentors to the Labour movement to be content with a life of rural retirement. In

1912 that movement was in considerable turmoil. Although ably led by MacDonald, the Parliamentary Labour Party had been subjected to much criticism for its too intimate relationship with the Liberal government, particularly over its insurance legislation. Outside Parliament two explosive forces gathered strength: the suffragettes, whose hopes had been dashed by the defeat of the Conciliation Bill, turned increasingly to direct action; while the new wave of industrial unrest led to strikes in the docks and the coalfields.

The Webbs, impressed by the opportunities opened up by these new movements, believed that they could provide a popular base for an effective socialist party.[2] Though they were unhappy about its militant excesses, they believed that the suffrage campaign was 'one of three simultaneous world-movements towards a more equal partnership among human beings in human affairs', and was changing women's attitudes towards the Labour Party and towards socialism.[3] They also saw that labour unrest, by creating a new class consciousness amongst wage-earners, could assist the growth of a socialist Labour Party.

Yet they firmly rejected the fashionable syndicalist doctrine of using the strike as a political weapon to overthrow Parliamentary government and replacing it by a council of industrial unions. In an article published in *The Crusade* in August 1912, they pointed out that, as the manual workers actually constituted the majority of the electorate, the 'ballot box had made obsolete the barricade'. Socialism could be achieved by parliamentary means. At the same time, they argued forcibly that government by the National Unions, which the syndicalists intended to set up to replace Parliamentary government, would result in a new authoritarianism. If trade unions became part of the structure of government they would no longer be able to represent the employees within industry. So syndicalism would rob workers of their trade union rights. In addition, whole groups, such as women, professional people, pensioners and the unemployed were not producers and would therefore lose their political rights. Their most fundamental objection, however, was to the lop-sided nature of syndicalism, founded as it was on the narrow and often conflicting interests of producers. The Webbs argued that 'we must reconstruct society, on a basis not of interests, but of community of service, of that "neighbourly" feeling on which local life is made up, and of that willingness to subordinate oneself to the welfare of the whole.'[4]

Nevertheless they accepted that there was some underlying truth in the syndicalist argument. Workers needed control over their working lives so that they could become equal partners in industrial enterprises. At the same time they emphasised the need for decentralisation and dispersal of power which, in the socialist state, would be achieved by the setting up of consumer associations, self-governing workshops and the encouragement of the individual craftsman; for, as they wrote, if their 'co-operative Commonwealth' was

> not to be the 'horridest tyranny' over the individual, we must, as far as possible, avoid the centralisation, either of power or knowledge or authority and give as much as possible to local organisations from any of which we can easily escape, if we choose, and which will, at any rate, not be all alike.[5]

If the Webbs saw the importance of the suffrage movement and labour unrest for the Labour Party, they were not at all satisfied by the leadership provided by the Parliamentary Labour Party. Sidney had been particularly upset by the acceptance by the Parliamentary leadership of the insurance principle. He commented that 'the working class is being in this matter abandoned by those on whom it ought to rely for advice.'[6] On 11 October 1912, Beatrice wrote in her diary that

> what annoys me is the absence of any relation, good or bad, between the Labour MPs and the labour movement in the country. The Labour MPs seem to me to be drifting into futility – a futility that will be presently recognised by all whom it may concern. J. R. MacDonald has ceased to be a socialist, the Trade Union MPs were never socialists, Snowden is embittered and Lansbury is wild. At present there is no co-operation between the Labour members themselves, nor between them and the trade union leaders.

She then went on to consider the Webbs' own rather isolated position:

> We personally have no relations either with the Parliamentary Party or with the trade union or co-operative movements: our only connections are with the ILP branches and individual

> Fabians throughout the country . . . All one can do is to go steadily forward without considering the likelihood of results. (11 October 1912)

As part of their new approach, Beatrice joined the ILP. Though the Webbs had been unimpressed by the ILP's evangelical socialism, they now had little alternative. As Norman and Jeanne Mackenzie pointed out, they had broken with their Liberal and Tory friends and their antagonism to MacDonald made it hard for them to see any useful role for themselves in the Labour Party.[7] In any case, at this stage the Labour Party did not have individual members. They also saw the ILP as a useful campaigning body. Indeed, by the end of 1912, Beatrice had persuaded the ILP to launch a joint campaign with the Fabians over the national minimum.

The Webbs also decided to galvanise the Fabian Society. Beatrice had been elected to the executive in their absence abroad and together the Webbs set about attempting to make the Society once again the centre for new ideas in the labour movement. The destitution campaign had brought a large number of professional men and women into the Fabian fold who could be used as researchers. The Webbs therefore proposed the setting up of two research committees, one on rural problems, the other on the control of industry.

The control of industry inquiry, which Beatrice chaired, was clearly designed to provide a Fabian answer to the challenge of the syndicalists. In a memorandum she wrote that

> the object of our enquiry is to work out . . . the main lines on which in the control and management of the industry and commerce by which the nation lives, we can combine the widest measure of personal freedom and initiative with the maximum democratic control: the largest national product with an equalised distribution of services and commodities among the whole people.[8]

She went on to argue that socialists were in considerable confusion; some believed in nationalisation, others in local control, and others in syndicalism. She warned that

> the existing chaos and disorder among Socialists, whenever we are asked for constructive proposals, together with our inability to

> state, with any degree of unanimity or precision, what we are asking for with regard to the future organisation of industry and commerce, will lose us our hold on the younger intellectuals . . . the Socialist Party has aroused great expectations as to the construction of a New Socialist Order . . . unless we can meet these expectations by carefully drafted and tested specifications, we shall be adjudged by the rising generation of thinkers and workers, intellectually bankrupt.[9]

Unfortunately, the control of industry inquiry became the battleground between the Webbs and a new younger element within the Fabian Society, the Guild Socialists. Inspired by A. R. Orage and S. G. Hobson, the guild socialists attempted to marry syndicalism with collectivism – they believed that industry should be taken into public ownership but should also be managed by guilds of producers which were, in effect, industrial unions. There was also a difference of style and generation: the guild socialists made waspish attacks on the Webbs and what remained of the 'Old Gang':

> Oh that Beatrice and Sidney
> Would get in their kidney
> A loathsome disease –
> Also Pease

was one guild socialist sally.

From the beginning, the Control of Industry Committee separated itself from the Society and in 1913 changed its name to the Fabian Research Committee. It had its own secretary (the first secretary Julius West soon moved to the *New Statesman* and was succeeded by William Mellor, a guild socialist and later editor of the *Daily Herald*) and a large committee which had as many as eighty five members, as well as numerous consultants and four subcommittees: the wage-earners, the producers, the consumers, and public services.

The Webbs had assumed that the Committee's findings would take about a year to produce and that the result would be a sensible and constructive amalgam of collectivism with the maximum possible industrial democracy. But the Wage-earners Committee was dominated by guild socialists, including Mellor and G. D. H. Cole who became the Webbs' chief antagonists. Of the latter, Beatrice wrote: 'He has a clear-cutting and somewhat subtle intellect. But he lacks humour and the bonhomie which springs from it, and he has an absurd habit of ruling out everybody or everything that he does not happen to like or find convenient' (14 February 1915).

In April 1913 H. J. Gillespie, the Honorary Secretary of the Research Department and G. D. H. Cole moved that the Fabian Society should disassociate itself from the Labour Party on the grounds that 'it had ceased to be capable of formulating a policy', that the Society should be in a position to influence all parties and that, in any case, research was the main Fabian business. The resolution, after intervention by Sidney, was lost by a two to one majority. Cole tried again at a members' meeting in March 1914; but a resolution declaring that the Society's function was 'primarily to conduct research' was amended by Sidney to make research 'one of the primary functions' and carried by one vote. The quarrel continued into 1915 and was only resolved at a members' meeting in June where Cole and the guild socialists were decisively defeated. Cole resigned from the executive and from the Society. Beatrice commented

> it is the old story of H. G. Wells and J. R. MacDonald. It is all the more annoying to us as we are honestly anxious to find successors and if these rebellious youths and maidens had only refrained from asking for a public execution of the old people we would have gladly stepped down from our position directly they had secured some sort of respect from the members at large. (15 May 1915)

On the question of research she wryly recorded that

> the situation is certainly humorous. The Webbs have not been behind in the work of Research, indeed we have been up to now the only Fabians who have been noted for Research. Of course, what the little knot of Rebels are after is not Research at all, but a new form of propaganda and a new doctrine which they believe themselves to be elaborating with regard to the Control of Industry. (8 March 1914)

Apart from the Webbs' direct involvement with the Fabians, they also supported the attempt of the Second International to weld together the various British socialist organisations. They encouraged the setting-up of a joint ILP and Fabian campaign against poverty in the hope that some form of integration of the two would come about, and that this would lead to a further merger with the Marxist British Socialist Party (BSP). Things looked promising in 1913 when Emile Vandervelde, Chairman of the International Bureau, persuaded the three factions (ILP, FS and BSP) to set up a United Socialist Council chaired by Beatrice. The *quid pro quo* was acceptance of the BSP back into the Labour fold.

Their expectations proved abortive. Despite Beatrice's efforts the delicate negotiations foundered on the outbreak of war. It was the first serious attempt to unite the disparate socialist organisations and was very much in keeping with the Webbs' aim of providing firm leadership to what they considered a weak and demoralised socialist movement: 'If it were not for the Fabian Society, the proposed reconciliation would have broken down' (8 March 1914). The Webbs had also hoped to widen the expertise of the Fabians by extending the Society's links with socialist authorities on the continent. As Beatrice recorded:

> My purpose is to connect the Research Department with the International Socialist Movement and thus bring to bear, on all the problems that confront Socialists the finer intellects of our German, Belgian and Dutch comrades. We ought to have an International programme and International literature and the Fabian Research Department ought to be the centre. (8 March 1914)

In 1913 the Webbs founded the *New Statesman*. When abroad in 1911 they had already decided that it was important to launch a serious socialist weekly journal which could influence the broad spectrum of radical and left-wing opinion to which they had appealed in their Destitution Campaign. Initially they had hoped to use *The Crusade* but the editor, Clifford Sharp, persuaded them that a new paper was required. Shaw gave them little encouragement; he wrote that the Webbs were too old and too quarrelsome. But they refused to be put off: 'Though we are wholly inexperienced on the business side, we have initiative, persistency and audacity which more conventially experienced persons lack' (January 1913).

They first collected together a modest £5000 (to which Shaw was a contributor). They then appealed to all Fabian members by offering a reduced rate for an annual subscription, taken out in advance. They pointed out that the paper was to be written by Fabians and that

> the distinctive object of the new journal will be to give an opportunity for the continued expansion of Collectivist opinion on all the topics of the day and for the steady development of Collectivist theory and policy in the light of experience afforded by the changing economic circumstances of the different nations of the civilized world.

Their appeal was astonishingly successful. Over 2000 Fabians subscribed, thus establishing a reasonable financial basis. Clifford Sharp became editor, with Julius West as company secretary. Desmond McCarthy was appointed drama critic, while a Fabian stockbroker, Emile Davies, wrote a city column. Bernard Shaw agreed to write but refused to sign his articles. The first issue came out on 13 May 1913 as the *Statesman*: for its second issue it was renamed the *New Statesman* to avoid confusion with the Calcutta daily newspaper.

The paper quickly established a reputation as a serious journal of the left and by 1918 had a circulation of over 6000. Though the Webbs left its running to Clifford Sharp, they were on the editorial board and often contributed to the *New Statesman*. To help the launch they wrote twenty articles on their approach to Socialism. The purpose of these articles was not only to provide a definition of what they meant by socialism but also to defend their position against critics from both left and right who argued that their socialism was coercive and bureaucratic.

According to the Webbs, socialism was about equality. Socialists believed in equality as 'an essential element in any real civilization' and also that unrestrained private ownership was incompatible with the need to 'choose equality'. The Webbs understood the necessity for redistributive taxation but argued that it was 'a clumsy and essentially temporary method of approaching equality.' 'Why,' they asked, 'permit Paul to abstract more than his share, why give Peter less than his share, when, in the end, they are driven to redress the balance by government action?' What was required was public provision of services and an incomes structures related to the requirements of the community.

They recognised that a more socialist society would have to be underpinned by a new social awareness – an acceptance of mutual obligation and dependence. Socialism would therefore require a transformation not only of property and power relationships but also of social values. There had to be 'a radical change of heart' which would permit 'gradual reconstruction of society on the basis of public service instead of on the basis of the desire for riches.'[10]

Another test of socialism was the degree of participation, 'in the formulation and execution of [the] general will by every member of the community'. Only by such participation could 'either the greatest possible individual freedom or the highest possible development of personal character and capacity' be ensured. The Webbs argued not only for female emancipation but also for the extension of democracy, 'from the political into the economic or industrial sphere.'[11]

The socialist state was collectivist certainly but it was in no sense 'servile' (as Hilaire Belloc had charged). For the Webbs drew a distinction between the coercive function of the state and the modern one (which they expected to increase) of providing services. 'The State has become a sort of extended Co-operative Society, performing for the great public of consumers the services that they require, and supplying these, not necessarily compulsorily, or even universally, but often only by definite individual request.'[12] Whereas previously the state had concerned itself solely with the maintenance of existing order, now it devoted its energies to securing progress or, as they called it, 'National House-Keeping'. This could be most successfully brought about, they claimed, through a free and democratically organised system of local self-government, overseen by an efficient central executive whose aim was to achieve national minimum standards through supervision and through 'securing the general application of the common policy decided upon by the Legislature – without either unduly burdening the localities on the one hand or, on the other, impairing their sense of independence or freedom.'[13] This was best implemented by Grants in Aid, one of Sidney's favourite methods of government, a device whereby the distribution of central government money ensured a minimum standard but left a large measure of freedom in its detailed spending to local government authorities.

But the 'National Housekeeping' role extended further. The material resources of the country had to be run for public rather than private profit. And the Webbs argued for the nationalisation of the mines, railways, iron and steel industries not just on ideological grounds but because, as so many regulations already existed which caused friction between government and capital, nationalisation would eliminate dissension. They were however cautious in setting a time-scale for their reforms: the progress of Socialism resembled 'the approach of the hyperbola to its asymptote: it was always going on, always getting nearer completion, yet only at infinity can we conceive of it as completed.'[14] Public ownership was proposed not only as part of a socialist creed but as a pragmatic and necessary tool of government.

The Webbian state was to be neither monolithic nor centralised but with a strong in-built democratic element. They pointed out that 'it is a curious misconception which associates Socialism with a gigantic centralised, bureaucratic, coercive and all-pervading government, administered from the State capital. As a matter of fact, the theorists of Socialism have talked far more of "free, democratic communes" than of state government.' And if local government had a major role to play, so too did the trade union movement. Significantly the Webbs called their article on trade unions 'organisation from below as a safeguard of liberty.'

The main importance of trade unionism was that it gave employees 'an effective participation in power and a real consciousness of consent.' They were well aware that it was not enough to put industrial control in the hands of even the most democratically-run state. Only the producers organised in trade unions were competent to judge on conditions and standards of work. But they rejected the syndicalist argument that the trade unions should run the state:

> What they demand is a complete ousting from the organisation of the community, both of the inhabitant elector and of the citizen-consumer, and the arresting of all power and control in the producers organised as producers. To this the Socialist objects that he cannot entrust power to a minority of the community still less to a minority of which each member will have interests and conflicts with that of the majority.[15]

The Webbs, influenced by Beatrice's study, believed that co-operative ownership of production and distribution was 'destined to progressively widening influence'. They saw their county groupings of consumers as valuable for the expansion of individual personalities as for safeguarding liberty.

They summed up the socialist state as 'a highly diversified and numerous set of social groupings' and

> a complex hierarchy, in which the citizen consumers organised on a geographical basis will have, in their local or national governments, the ownership of the instruments of production, and the supreme control; but in which the producers, organised in vocational associations, will also have their admitted place, the decisions with regard to each industry being arrived at by agreement between them; whilst it will be open to any persons to co-operate voluntarily for the production of any commodity or the promotion of any social end that they prefer.[16]

What were the chances for socialism? Because they did not believe in predicting the future, the Webbs provided the *New Statesman* reader with two alternatives. One was optimistic: social and economic developments were leading inexorably towards socialism. They concluded that the 'advance in knowledge and public spirit . . . coupled with democracy . . . means, in our judgement, a continuously developing Socialism.'[17] The other was more pessimistic: if the working classes were unable to organise themselves or proved themselves 'intellectually incapable of the complicated Democracy required by a highly involved Industrial State' then

> the increased productivity of industry might well result in nothing more seriously useful than the growing luxury of British, German or American millionaires, and the steadily increasing number of their demoralised, personalised retainers and dependents.

Echoing Hobson, the Webbs gave a sombre warning.

> The political ambitions of the Great Powers, sharpened by their industrial and commercial rivalry will, unless there is a change of heart . . . inevitably lead to constantly increasing armaments and to periodical wars of a destructiveness that the world has never yet witnessed. In this atmosphere of international aggression the military spirit becomes more and more dominant.[18]

However, when war came in August 1914, the Webbs were taken completely by surprise. According to Beatrice, Sidney had dismissed the possibility of war as 'too insane'. She wrote later that 'we had never interested ourselves in European Politics and had known nothing of the diplomatic world' (August 1918). Her initial reaction was to support the government ('We had to stand by Belgium') but she also noted that 'there never has been a war in which the issues have been so blurred and indistinct – we English, at any rate, are quite uncertain who ought to win . . . The best result would be that every nation should be soundly beaten and no-one victorious. That might bring us all to reason' (5 August 1914). Three months later, in a reply to Professor Gilbert Murray's request to add their names to a manifesto supporting the British declaration of war on Germany, Beatrice replied: 'We have both of us a rooted disinclination to signed statements on questions about which we have no special information or enlightenment.'[19]

The Labour Party was deeply split over the war. On 5 August Ramsay MacDonald resigned the leadership of the Parliamentary Labour Party when the majority voted for war credits, and was succeeded by Arthur Henderson. MacDonald argued that Britain ought to remain neutral in a contest which had been brought by 'the policy of the balance of power through alliance.'[20] He was supported by the ILP but not by the majority of the Labour movement who were outraged by the violation of Belgian neutrality: both the PLP and the trade unions backed the government. Sidney gave his support to the majority position because he believed that German aggression had to be resisted and that war was inevitable.

One result of the war was to bring Sidney into the centre of Labour Party affairs. He became a member of the executive of the powerful War Emergency Committee. Henderson had originally called a meeting of all major trades unions and socialist bodies for 5 August to support a peace offensive. But once the National Executive Committee of the Labour Party had come out in support of British entry into the war, the conference changed its character and set itself up as the 'War Emergency: Workers' National Committee', 'to consider the industrial and social position of the working classes as affected by the war'. It appointed an executive of fifteen, comprising three members each from the Parliamentary Labour Party, the Parliamentary Committee of the TUC and the General Federation of Trades Unions, and six others, including Robert Smillie, President of the Miners' Federation, and Sidney Webb representing the Fabian Society.

The importance of the War Emergency Committee (WEC) was that it united almost the whole of the labour movement under its umbrella. J. S. Middleton, who was Assistant Secretary of the

Labour Party and became Secretary of WEC, saw the committee as a force for unity. Close to MacDonald, Middleton was determined that those who were against the war should not leave the Labour Party; the role of the WEC was 'to hold the forces of Labour together'.[21] Primarily an organiser, he encouraged Sidney to formulate policies first on the impact of the war on the workers and then later on post-war reconstruction. As Winter rightly points out, Sidney was ideally suited for this role:

> His unparalleled knowledge of social administration and his persistent dedication to the minutiae of labour problems, were indispensible. His organisational ability, procedural tact and draughtsmanship, made him the complete committee man. And most importantly, his unselfishness and lack of personal ambition, disarmed those who would mistake the advocacy of policy for the pursuit of political power.[22]

The most immediate issue was employment. Sidney was convinced that private industry would not be able to switch over to a war economy without major dislocation. What was required was the kind of government intervention which the Webbs had envisaged in the Minority Report. On 6 August 1914, the WEC passed a resolution calling on the government to instruct government departments, local councils and other employers 'to maintain the aggregate volume of employment by keeping their staffs at the fullest possible strength and if circumstances allow, to undertake additional enterprises in order to prevent the occurrence of as much unemployment as possible'.[23] In October Sidney presented the Committee's view to the Chancellor of the Exchequer, Lloyd George, and complained of the Chancellor's speech on the necessity of 'economising'. Webb pointed out that unless something was done 'to reassure municipalities and disabuse them of the impression that it was not the wish of the Government that they should start works, it will be very bad'.

Sidney believed that the war could bring with it a different attitude towards poverty and destitution. As Beatrice wrote, 'it is useless for Lord Kitchener to think that he can repel the invader if the working class is starving behind his line of troops'.[24] The Prime Minister had given a commitment that there should be no recourse to the Poor Law as a result of the war and the Prince of Wales' Relief Fund was set up, which the WEC insisted should be used to provide hardship relief for the civilian population. Sidney also presented a strongly-worded protest on the inadequacy of the level of relief: 'The needs of the poor are not to be measured by the sums the rich choose to spare; the relief of the suffering caused by the war is a national concern and has to be met by the nation as a whole out of national resources.'[25]

With Sidney Webb's guidance, the WEC acted as a labour movement pressure group on such important issues as food prices, the supply and cost of coal and rents. Sidney persuaded representatives of building societies, ratepayers' organisations and small property companies to agree to the restriction on rents and mortgage interest. The Committee also pressed for increased old age pensions, disablement allowances, separation allowances for the family of servicemen, and free milk for children under five. In September 1915 Beatrice recorded that the Committee

> has laid down the policy for Labour and Socialist Movement during the war. Sidney . . . has been able to make himself useful by drafting the resolutions, pamphlets and leaflets that the Committee has issued . . . One result of its existence is that we personally have never been more intimate with all sections of the Labour Movement. All they ask is that Sidney's name should not appear. It is interesting that in the new *Labour and Socialist Year-Book*, though Sidney has written more than anyone else, his name is nowhere mentioned . . . We can still be useful as the 'clerks' of the Labour Movement if we are content to take a back seat. (9 September 1915)

However, if the war years were intensely rewarding for Sidney, they were less so for Beatrice. She continued to be heavily involved with the Fabian Research Department, chairing the numerous sub-committees which it spawned, and took over Sidney's role on the Fabian executive. She also sat on a Statutory Pensions Committee (set up by the government). But as the war went into its second year she began to feel more and more depressed about the horror of the endless slaughter. 'I cannot bear to look at the fresh, young faces in each week's Roll of Honour' she admitted on 16 April 1915, and by the end of the year she was on the verge of a nervous breakdown.

'I am haunted with the fear that all my struggles may be in vain' she wrote despairingly.

> That disease and death are the Ends towards which the individual, the race and the whole conceivable Universe, are moving with relentless certainty. If so my own life is not happy enough to justify human existence . . . The certainty that an abstract Being – an intellect inspired by Love – was active in the Universe and that Human Beings were among his agents on this Earth would transform even the life of material misery into a pilgrimage to Heaven. (14 November 1915)

Her early hypochondria returned. She was afraid that she had a cancerous growth (one of her sisters had died from cancer). 'I feel humiliated', she wrote sadly. 'Humiliated alike by my absurd obsession and by the absence of courage, even if it had been justified in meeting physical pain and death' (24 June 1916). She brooded over her weaknesses.

> I have always been a prey to fear. As a child I would suffer mental agony over some trifling incident: fear of physical pain, fear of the exposure of some wretched little delinquency, or a state of emotional misery arising out of the presumed dislike of someone I cared for . . . Sidney is an ideal companion for me: *he is always sane*.[26]

It was, she later recorded, the opening phase of a breakdown which lasted in acute form for six months 'and from which I did not recover for over two years. Partly war neurosis, partly too persistent work to keep myself from brooding over the horrors of the war, partly I think from general discouragement arising out of our unpopularity with all sections of the political and official world' (June 1919). It proved, she believed, the turning point from middle to old age.

Beatrice's diary entries towards the end of 1916 show a slow mental recovery, although she was depressed and pessimistic about the post-war future. Unlike Sidney, she remained ambivalent about the war – particularly as it was clear that the end was nowhere in sight. 'I want a peace', she wrote,

> in which no one of the great belligerents gain anything whatsoever. I want all of them to see that the war has been a hideous calamity without any compensating advantages – the gigantic and wicked folly from which no good can come . . . I should like the propertied classes of all the belligerents to be mulcted and the working classes to suffer sufficiently to make them wise

> revolutionaries . . . on this basis of universal loss and humiliation, I will build a new League of Nations with the USA as one of the guarantors.

The war was the main reason for her depression, another difficulty was that during this period, the Webbs changed places. Beatrice, who had been the activist and propagandist behind the destitution campaign assumed a background role (although she served on a number of prestigious government committees) while Sidney became more and more influential in the Labour Party.

As the war continued into its second and third years, the labour movement began to assume greater importance. In the famous 'Treasury Agreement' of March 1915, Lloyd George negotiated a deal with trade union leaders by which, in return for compulsory arbitration and the 'dilution' of skilled labour, the government agreed to control profits of munition firms. In May 1915 Henderson accepted a post in Asquith's Coalition Government and, when Lloyd George became Prime Minister at the end of 1916, he brought Henderson into his War Cabinet.

Sidney realised that Labour's wartime bargaining power, enhanced by the government's conscription, gave the Labour Party a new political opportunity. Although, like most members of WEC, Sidney was not in principle opposed to conscription, he persauded the Committee to adopt a campaign for the Concription of Riches, as a *quid pro quo*.[27] Webb argued for increases in taxes on higher incomes, a capital tax and sequestering unearned incomes – proposals which Winter has called 'the first independent Labour programme during the First World War'. The WEC, under Sidney's inspiration, also turned its attention to post-war problems. In a report published in February 1916, the committee warned that demobilisation would lead to 'several millions of men and women simultaneously running about seeking employment' and that government policy was totally inadequate; the labour movement should unite together to press the government at all levels to expand employment through public work and relief measures.

In November 1915 Sidney took the Fabian place on the NEC of the Labour Party. As Middleton pointed out, 'this was a position of immense advantage to Webb.'[28] It brought him into contact with Arthur Henderson who, with the resignation of MacDonald, had become the leading figure in the Party, being a Cabinet Minister, Chairman of the PLP and Party Secretary. The Webbs were impressed by Henderson: Beatrice noted: 'I rather like Henderson, he has sterling qualities, a veritable rock of bourgeois respectability and self-control' (23 June 1918). Henderson, as aware as Sidney of the prospects opening up for Labour, was obviously appreciative of Sidney's ability to formulate policy, draft reports and to manage committees. According to Margaret Cole, their relationship became so close that Henderson took something of Shaw's place in Sidney's life.[29]

In February 1916 Sidney was appointed to serve on the subcommittee which the NEC had set up to deal with the problems of post-war reconstruction.[30] From then, according to Winter, he shifted his allegiance from the WEC to the Labour Party because it gave him 'the opportunity to translate his work on the WEC into the basis of a much wider political programme.'[31]

A new Joint Committee on Post-War Reconstruction, including the WEC but under the control of the NEC, was established, with Sidney as the WEC representative. To assist the Joint Committee's work, sub-committees were set up to deal with various areas to include unemployment, taxation, education, trades unions and demobilisation. The Webbs arranged to have the research for the specialist sub-committees carried out by the Fabian Research Department. Given that the other members of the policy committee included such important but overworked trade union leaders as Smillie, Thorne and Clynes, it is not surprising that their reports should have had the stamp of the one member who could devote himself fully to the problems of reconstruction and who had clear ideas in which direction it should lie.

1917 – the year of the two Russian Revolutions – was critical for the development of the Labour Party. Henderson, who was sent to Russia in May by the War Cabinet, came back convinced that if the Kerensky Government was to continue, there must be a negotiated peace. Accordingly, he favoured the attendance of the British Labour Party at a socialist and labour conference to be held at Stockholm and at which representatives of the German and Austrian labour movements would be present, and persuaded a special Labour Conference in August to agree to send delegates. Whereupon Lloyd George, at the request of Conservative members of the War Cabinet, reprimanded Henderson, who immediately resigned from the Cabinet.

Though the Labour Party remained in the coalition, the resignation of Henderson was the key to the emergence of Labour as a truly independent party committed to a socialist programme. Beatrice wrote: 'From that day Henderson determined to create an independent political party, capable of becoming HM Government – and he turned to Sidney to help him' (May 1918). Henderson wanted to construct a party open to individual members and with a programme able to attract wide support among the newly enfranchised. Sidney was the obvious person to assist him. 'Sidney has become the intellectual leader of the Labour Party', noted Beatrice proudly (11 December 1917). In January 1918 Beatrice spelled out Labour's new opportunities.

> The Labour Party is bounding forward into public notice and Henderson becomes every day more audacious in his programme. How far this new reputation is ficticious, I do not know. We do all we can to stimulate both Henderson's audacity and to advertise the reality of the movement. The Party itself is tumultuous in its cross-currents. Its apparent unanimity arose from its being, for the first time, in open opposition to the Government on all economic issues and insisting on independence in the statement of war aims. It is the 'new thing' round which all who are discontented with the old order foregather. (10 January 1918)

Henderson's first move was to reunite the party around a statement of war aims. Henderson, MacDonald (whom Henderson wished to bring back into the leadership) and Webb collaborated with Camille Huysmans, Secretary of the 2nd International, in drawing up a document which was approved by a special Labour Party and Trade Union Conference held on 28 December 1917. Labour's war aims emphasised the need for a secure and lasting peace, a world safe for democracy, and an effective means of preventing war. It preceeded President Wilson's 'Fourteen Points' in its demands for an end to secret diplomacy, the limitation of armaments, collective security, an international court and the establishment of the League of Nations. The League of Nations idea owed much to the Fabians. In 1915 Sidney, on behalf of the Fabian Society, had asked Leonard Woolf to look into the possibility of a supra-national authority: 'Why should not Council of all the Powers *impose* the Treaty of Peace on the world as a law, constitute a permanent tribunal to try all the issues between nations with power to fine heavily and pledge all the signatories to contribute their share towards the sanction of forcing the tribunal's decision?[32] Leonard Woolf's study was published in two *New Stateman* supplements during 1915, and later, in 1916 as a book entitled *International Government*. There is little doubt that the publication of Labour's war aims, particularly the support for the League of Nations, influenced Lloyd George and Woodrow Wilson. As to Sidney's contribution, Middleton wrote that 'it would be too much to claim that Sidney Webb was the sole author of this historic party document . . . but it is right that his great contribution to its production should be placed on record.'[33]

In February 1918 Henderson and Webb gave the Labour Party a new constitution and structure. Until 1918 the Labour Party was a federation of trade unions and socialist societies without individual membership. The Henderson–Webb structure was a compromise, opening up the Party to individual membership by creating local Labour Parties, while retaining the support of the trade unions by giving them the block vote at Party Conference and a dominant place on the NEC. Beatrice wrote that 'the new constitution aims at combining the mass vote and financial support of the big battalions incorporated in the National Unions with the initiative and enthusiasm of the brainworking individual members of the local Labour Parties' (21 January 1918).

The new constitution of 1918 also contained the famous Clause Four formulation of socialist objectives. Two versions were originally put forward to the NEC: the first one was to 'secure for the producers by hand or brain the full fruits of their industry by the common ownership of all Monopolies and Essential Raw Materials'. The second was wider in scope:

> to secure for the producers by hand or brain the full fruits of their industry and the most equitable distribution thereof that may be possible upon the basis of common ownership of the Means of Production and the best obtainable system of popular administration and control of each industry or service.

McGibbin has argued that the first draft was written by Henderson (on the grounds that the specific mention of monopolies reflected his well-known hatred of cartels) while the second was by Sidney.[34] Winter, however, suggested that the first draft was Sidney's (because it bore a close resemblance to the Constription of Riches programme) while the second 'incorporated some of the spirit of the Guild Socialist critique of Webbian ideas'.[35] It is far more likely that the broader, second alternative came from Sidney – an interpretation that is supported by Middleton.[36] Unlike the first draft, it contains the essential elements of the Webbian approach to socialism: there is the inclusion of the brainworkers; there is the argument for fair shares and social justice; there is the general statement in favour of collectivism, 'upon the basis of the common ownership of the means of production'; and in the phrase, 'the best obtainable system of popular administration and control', there is a Webbian compromise between parliamentary and local government control on the one hand and industrial democracy and union control on the other.

The purpose of Clause Four was to give the Labour Party a distinctive and socialist character which would attract, so Sidney hoped, the radical middle classes. In an article in the *Observer* of 21 October 1917, he wrote that 'the Labour Party of the future . . . is to be a Party of the producers, whether manual workers or brain workers, associated against the private owners of land and capital as such. Its policy of "common ownership" brings it . . . decidedly under the designation of Socialist.'

He went on to explain, however, the undoctrinaire and pragmatic nature of that socialism:

> It is a Socialism which is no more specific than a definite repudiation of the individualism that characterised all the political parties of the past generations and that still dominates the House of Commons. This declaration of the Labour Party leaves it open to choose from time to time whatever forms of common ownership from the co-operative store to the nationalised railway and whatever forms of popular administration and control of industry, from national guilds to ministries of employment, and municipal management may, *in particular cases*, [Sidney's italics] commend themselves.[37]

In June 1918 the Labour Party endorsed the statement of policy *Labour and the New Social Order* which was drafted by Sidney. As Middleton rightly pointed out, it was 'ostensibly the Report of a special committee of the National Executive, but, with the exception of one or two paragraphs it is . . . unmistakeably the work of Webb.'[38] *Labour and the New Social Order* was a powerful argument for a new social order,

> based not on fighting but on fraternity – not on the competitive struggle for the means of bare life, but on a deliberately planned cooperation in production and distribution for the benefit of all who participate by hand or brain – not on the utmost possible inequality of riches, but on a systematic approach towards a healthy equality of material circumstances for every person born in the world – not on an enforced dominion over subject nations, subject races, subject colonies, subject classes, or a subject sex, but in industry as well as in government, on the equal freedom, that general consciousness of consent, and that widest possible participation in power, both economic and political, which is characteristic of Democracy.

Labour's programme rested on four solid Webbian pillars – the 'National Minimum', the democratic control of industry, redistributive taxation and public expenditure. Under the heading of the 'National Minimum', the programme set up policies for securing full employment by public works (on the lines of the Minority Report) adequate minimum wages and conditions for those in work and income maintenance for those out of work. The 'democratic control of industry' heading contained Labour's immediate plan for public ownership, including the railways, the canals, the mines, the insurance companies and the land (though the last was only to be introduced 'as suitable opportunities occur'), as well as the adoption 'in particular services and occupations, of those systems and methods of administration and control, it may be found, in practice, to promote, not profiteering, but the public interest'. It also included commitments to complete adult suffrage and the abolition of the House of Lords. Under the heading of 'a revolution in national finance' a number of redistributative tax measures were proposed, including a capital levy, stiffer death duties, and a progressive income tax. Under the heading 'the surplus for the common good' there were proposals for public spending on social services, education and leisure. Finally, the document repudiated imperialism and colonialism, and gave its support for the establishment of the League of Nations.

Labour and the New Social Order may have been, particularly in its economic sections somewhat imprecise. But whatever its shortcomings, Sidney had provided Labour with a distinctive and attractive programme. For the first time Labour was equipped to challenge for power. In the words of the American ambassador, 'The Labour Party is already playing for supremacy.'[39]

Sidney, encouraged by Henderson, had reluctantly decided to stand at the coming general election. He put himself forward as the Labour candidate for the London University seat and during the last months of the war became engrossed in the campaign: 'Oddly enough he confesses that in spite of all appearances to the contrary, he believes that he will win. "A superstitious feeling" he suggests. "J. S. Mill was just my age when he got into Parliament and I have always felt that I am his successor in British political life"' (8 September 1918).

On 7 November, the Labour Party executive voted by twelve to four to leave the Coalition and bid for power at the forthcoming election. The Labour ministers in the government were opposed to leaving the Coalition. Beatrice, depressed by the future ('no citizen knows what is going to happen to himself or his children . . . all that he does know is that the old order is seriously threatened with dissolution without any new order being in sight' (4 November 1918)), had little confidence in the Labour Party which she claimed was going into the election as a 'distracted, divided and depressed rabble of some 300 nondescript candidates' (7 November 1918).

The armistice was signed on 11 November: 'The people are everywhere rejoicing. Thrones are everywhere crashing and the men of property are everywhere secretly trembling . . . How soon will the tide of revolution catch up with the tide of victory?' (11 November 1918). An emergency Labour Conference supported the executive and voted to withdraw representation from the Coalition government. Lloyd George's 'Khaki' Election of 14 December, a crude appeal to the electors to support the victorious Coalition government, proved tactically successful. A considerable number of Labour leaders, including Henderson, MacDonald and Snowden, were defeated. Labour won only fifty seven seats, though its 316 candidates polled nearly a quarter of the greatly expanded total vote.

Sidney did quite well, coming second with 2141 to the Unionist vote of 2810. Although Beatrice never disguised her relief at his defeat, she was honest enough to accept that Sidney was disappointed that he had not won. 'I think he had been looking forward to a spell in Parliament' she acknowledged, and

> wanted to test his powers as a Parliamentarian. And yet he does not want it sufficiently to get himself adopted for a constituency

which he could win, he wants to be put into Parliament, he does not want to push himself in. Once he is engaged in a fight he fights hard and leaves nothing undone. But he hates taking the plunge from the dignified and detached position of a disinterested helper into rivalry with colleagues for prized positions. He fought the University seat because no other member of the Labour Party would dream of doing it. He cannot bring himself, even to hint that he has a claim to a winable constituency. (22 December 1918)

The war years had been a period of great achievement for the Webbs. Through Sidney's work on the WEC and the NEC and his relationship with Henderson, they had captured the Labour Party for their ideas, and in so doing, helped to prepare Labour for power. With Labour now in opposition and Sidney outside Parliament, Beatrice hoped for quieter times. She decided to refuse to serve on any more government committees, 'I am tired of investigating new subjects', she reflected 'I want to brood over the past and reflect on men and their affairs . . . I want to summarise my life and see what it all amounts to' (22 December 1918). Perhaps the time had arrived for the Webbs to bow gracefully out of politics. Their young colleagues in the new Labour Research Department could now be expected to take their place. The quiet country house of Beatrice's dreams, 'a comfortable small country house, noiseless except for birds and the rustling of water and wind – with my diaries to type' (18 March 1917), could become a reality.

NOTES

1. L. Woolf, *Beginning Again*, p. 118.
2. J. M. Winter, *Socialism and the Challenge of War*, p. 52.
3. Ibid, p. 53.
4. *The Crusade*, August 1912.
5. Ibid.
6. J. M. Winter, *Socialism and the Challenge of War*, p. 54.
7. N. and J. Mackenzie, *The First Fabians*, p. 383.
8. Cole Collection, Barrow House Papers, B3/5/E Box 3.
9. Ibid.
10. The *New Statesman*, 26 Apr 1913.
11. Ibid, 3 May 1913.
12. Ibid, 31 May 1913.

13. Ibid.
14. Ibid.
15. Ibid, 14 June 1913.
16. Ibid.
17. Ibid, 6 Sept. 1913.
18. Ibid, 30 Aug 1913.
19. B. Webb to Gilbert Murray, 14 Oct 1914.
20. D. Marquand, *Ramsay MacDonald*, p. 169.
21. J. M. Winter, *Socialism and the Challenge of War*, p. 189.
22. Ibid, p. 193.
23. Ibid, p. 192.
24. *Labour Leader*, 25 Aug 1914.
25. Workers Emergency Committee papers, Box 14.
26. J. M. Winter, *Socialism and the Challenge of War*, p. 207.
27. J. R. Middleton in *The Webbs and their Work*, ed., M. Cole, p. 171.
28. Ibid.
29. M. Cole, *The Story of Fabian Socialism*, p. 169.
30. Labour Party Executive Committee, 14 Feb 1916. See also Winter, *Socialism and the Challenge of War*, pp. 216–217.
31. J. M. Winter, *Socialism and the Challenge of War*, p. 219.
32. S. Webb to L. Woolf, 21 Jan 1915, Passfield Papers.
33. J. R. Middleton, in *The Webbs and their Work*, ed. M. Cole, p. 175.
34. Ross McGibbin, *The Evolution of the Labour Party*.
35. J. M. Winter, *Socialism and the Challenge of War*, p. 259.
36. J. R. Middleton, in *The Webbs and their Work*, ed. M. Cole, p. 172.
37. The *Observer*, 21 Oct 1917. The New Constitution of the Labour Party, reprinted on behalf of the Labour Party.
38. J. R. Middleton, in *The Webbs and their Work*, ed. M. Cole, p. 175.
39. H. Pelling, *A Short History of the Labour Party*, p. 42.

11

1918–1924

From Opposition to Office

'The hectic days of victory.'

If the Webbs hoped to retire completely from public life after the war, the demand for Sidney's abilities and services made it impossible to do so. Almost inevitably, although somewhat to Beatrice's regret, he was drawn into active politics, Parliament and then government office.

In February 1919, Sidney was appointed to a Royal Commission on the mining industry. By the end of 1918 only the mines and the railways remained in public hands. The Miners' Federation had hoped that, given the bad management and poor wages in the industry, the government would come down in favour of some form of nationalisation. They demanded a six hour day, a 30 per cent increase in wages and nationalisation of the industry. Lloyd George, anxious to avoid a confrontation either with the miners or the Conservative supporters of his coalition, who were strongly against public ownership, proposed the setting up of a Royal Commission to look into both wages and conditions and the ownership issue. The Commission was chaired by Lord Sankey, a judge and future chancellor, and its membership comprised not only three miners, including Smillie, the miners' leader, but three experts chosen by the union, as well as three colliery owners and three other employers. The experts were Sidney, the socialist thinker and historian R. H. Tawney, and Leo Chiozza-Money, a Liberal who had recently joined the Labour Party.

The Webbs were delighted at Sidney's appointment. It was not only that he was a superb committee man who loved committees;

they also approved of the way the Commission was run. Beatrice noted that 'in its proceedings (it) is far more like a revolutionary tribunal sitting in judgement on the capitalist owners and organisers of the nation's industries' (12 March 1919). The business of the Commission was to examine the report of the miners' claim for a rise in wages and a reduction in hours, but 'owing to the superior skill of the miners' representatives, it has become a state trial of the coal owners and royalty owners conducted on behalf of the producers and consumers of the product, culminating in the question, Why not nationalise the industry?' Beatrice wrote that

> Mr Justice Sankey is an urbane lawyer, who treats every commissioner, in turn, as the most distinguished of the lot and gives almost unlimited licence to questions and answers, interruptions and retorts. On his right sit the representatives of capital: three inferior businessmen who are coal owners and three superior businessmen representing other interests. On his left sit Smillie, Hodges and Smith, three miners' officials, then Sidney, Tawney and Chiozza-Money – typical intellectuals of the Labour Party. Smillie is the protagonist of the miners' cause, Chiozza-Money is the most aggressive and self-assertive of the miners' advocates, Sidney draws out damaging admissions and claps on the right conclusion to every line of argument, whilst Tawney raises the whole discussion to the highest planes of moral rectitude and sweet reasonableness. The other side are absurdly out-classed. (12 March 1919)

No wonder that Sidney was enjoying himself hugely: 'I have never seen him so keen on any task since the halcyon days of the LCC'. He was determined to prove that only nationalisation could end the chaos of the industry, and that what the Royal Commission had to accept was that the 'object of the nationalised industry is not to make or lose money, the object of a nationalised industry is to supply coal and supply it as it is required in the best possible way and at as little cost as possible'. Reorganisation, unless it were in the form of nationalisation, would be ineffective. 'If you were going to make a gigantic coal trust in capitalists' hands', he argued persuasively, 'would it not be like rather arranging for the full-sized tiger and then having safeguards? Is it not a tiger in electing to have a capitalistic trust and then cutting its claws?' (12 March 1919)

On 20 March 1919 the Sankey Commission produced an interim report on wages and conditions which was accepted by the Miners'

Federation. Though there was no unanimity about the second report which came out at the end of June, the Federation's six nominees all recommended public ownership and control of the industry by a National Mining Council. The coal owners and employers opposed nationalisation but Sankey, who put in his own report, recommended the acceptance of the principle of public ownership. The majority of the Commission thus came down in favour of nationalisation but this recommendation was turned down by Lloyd George who, despite a miners' strike, returned the mines to their owners. Sidney, however, believed that 'the Coal Commission would be the beginning of a landslide into the communal control of industries and services' (23 June 1921).

While Sidney had been serving on the Sankey Commission, the Webbs had also been writing a *Constitution for the Socialist Commonwealth of Great Britain* – 'designed to be a summary of the wisdom of the Webbs – a sort of last will and testament' (12 March 1919). They prepared the book in response to a request by the secretary of the Socialist International but in fact it was both a counter to the guild socialists (in 1919 Sidney had also written an article, 'A Stratified Democracy' in which he had criticised some of the arguments of G. D. H. Cole) and an ambitious attempt to sort out the framework for a democratic socialist state. As it is one of their most important books, it is worth examining in some detail.

The Webbs were among the first to see the dangers of a modern centralised state. They noticed that

> under the guise of government by a majority of the people acting through its elected representatives, we have now the dictatorship of one man, or of a small group of men, exercised through a subservient party majority of more or less tied members, and an obedient official hierarchy of unparalleled magnitude – a dictatorship tempered, on the one hand, by a continual watchfulness against explosions of popular feelings, and on the other by the necessity of privately securing the acquiescence or, at least, preventing the revolt, of powerful capitalists and other interests.[1]

Their blueprint for democratic change was not, however, 'a model constitution for a utopian community', but one which took account of the actual trend of 'development towards a fully democratised community', including the rise of consumer organisations, local government, trades unions, professional associations and the Labour movement. Given the complexity of modern developments, there could be no single democratic solution. As the Webbs put it:

> Any fully developed democratic community must take account of the fact that 'government of the people, for the people, by the people' is not and cannot be made simple, homogeneous and indivisible but must adapt itself to the interests and purposes which are simultaneously diverse and varied, not only as among different sections of the people, but actually within each man or woman.[2]

They based their democratic theory on three major factors: man as producer, man as consumer and man as citizen 'in a two-fold aspect: on the one hand concerned with national defence and internal order . . . on the other concerned with the promotion of the type of civilization that he desires'.[3] What the Webbs hoped to achieve, despite industrialisation, despite a 'closely integrated economic life and densely crowded communities', was a democracy in which no one stratum would hold the monopoly of power and where the individual enjoyed the maximum amount of liberty as was compatible in his place in a complex inter-dependent community. Democracy, they postulated, cannot afford to

> dispense with complication in administrative machinery, because only by an extensive variety of parts, and a deliberately adjusted relation among those parts, can there be any security for the personal freedom and independence in initiative of the great mass of individuals, whether as producers, as consumers or as citizens.[4]

A novel feature of their new system was the creation of a political parliament which would deal with law and order, foreign relations and be based on a cabinet system of government, and a social parliament to deal with social and economic problems, administration, social welfare, the Treasury and to be run on LCC lines, by a series of standing committees. Their arguments for two parliaments rested on the assumption that 'no one elected assembly can possibly express the General Will of the inhabitants in all subjects whatsoever'.[5] The Webbs recognised that there were difficulties involved in such a separation of power; either conflict between the two parliaments would lead to deadlock or supremacy would go to the parliament with the power of the purse. But they failed to propose any credible solution for these glaring weaknesses in their schemes.

As to the organisation of industry the Webbs proposed two main principles: first that citizen consumers should own the main instruments of production (though they accepted that there was a place for private ownership) and second that producers should control working conditions. Their definition of industrial democracy fell short of workers' control, although their interpretation of working conditions was an extensive one. They emphasised that it would be wrong for producers to elect their own managers because they would be likely to choose not on grounds of efficiency but on grounds of acceptability. Instead managerial appointments should be made by a selection committee of experts in the 'art of selection'.

The Webbs envisaged a system of industrial organisation in which control of policy was divorced from administration. As far as policy was concerned, the standing committees of the social parliament had a vital role. They were to be assisted by control units (bodies which foreshadowed some of the ideas contained in the Fulton Report) in each government department which could provide the basic information of how industry or the services were being run. Administration of these would be carried out by national boards approved by the social parliament and composed of representatives of management, trade unions and consumers in equal proportion. Working under the national boards would be district councils constituted on similar lines whilst works committees would represent the producer groups directly at grass roots level. The function of the works committees was primarily to discuss grievances and make suggestions but the Webbs also envisaged a wider role for them, including a right to be consulted 'about any industrial change'. They summed up the works councils as providing the opportunity for 'taking council together' for which 'the removal from industrial administration of capitalist autocracy ought to open a wide field of usefulness'.[6]

The new democratic structure would be underpinned by 'the disinterested professional expert' who would produce reports for the various bodies although (contrary to prevailing mythology about the Webbs) he would have 'no power of command and no right to insist on his suggestions being adopted'.[7] The Webbs believed that a combination of 'measurement with publicity' was vital to democracy. As they stated, 'the deliberate intensification of the *search-*

light of published knowledge, we regard as the cornerstone of successful Democracy'. The old capitalist autocracy would now cease to be necessary and a 'steadily increasing sphere will, except in matters of emergency, be found for consultation among all grades and sections concerned, out of which will emerge judgements and decisions arrived at, very largely, by common consent'[8] – a common consent reached partly by the authority of 'reported facts' and partly by 'the silent persuasiveness' of public opinion. At the same time, in answer to the charge that they were introducing government by committee, they pointed out that, under capitalism, industry was already run by committees. What they suggested was a more co-ordinated system – 'what we propose to end is not simplicity but secrecy'.[9]

The Webbs then turned to local government. They believed that the

> sense of solidarity amongst neighbours, living in the same environment, and using the same complex of local services, is a valuable social asset which socialism aims at preserving and intensifying . . . The very differences among localities, with the different local administrations, that they involve, provide an increase in the scope for individual choice, a widening of personal freedom, and a safeguard against a monotonous uniformity and a centralised tyranny over the individual.[10]

Beatrice and Sidney attached so much importance to local democracy that they considered that as much as half of industries and services should come under the authority of local government – a direct refutation of the view that they were blind supporters of the centralising state.

To complete their pluralistic design, the Webbs envisaged an important role for a strengthened system of consumer co-operatives and for reorganised vocational groups who would develop into almost self-governing professional bodies, responsible for overseeing training and efficiency. They summed up their system of democracy as not that of a drab uniformity 'either of faculties and desires or of education and qualification, but one of an infinite divergence of line and colour.'[11] Their concern was not to diminish liberty but through a more democratic system to widen individual opportunities. They concluded,

> What we visualise is a community so variously organised, and so highly differentiated in function as to be not only invigorated by

> a sense of personal freedom, but also constantly swept by the fresh air of experiment, observation and verification . . . a free Democracy inspired by the spirit of social service, and illumined by ever increasing knowledge.[12]

Finally, we should note that the Webbs believed that the development of socialism would strengthen democracy by the introduction of a morality based on service rather than gain. Somewhat naively perhaps, they thought that the substitution of the motive of public service for the motive of self-enrichment would be brought about mainly by the social approval given 'not to success in a man's riches but to disinterested and public service'.

In his highly stimulating study of G. D. H. Cole, A. W. Wright accuses the Webbs of largely dispensing with democracy, of imposing democracy from above, of ignoring individual rights and a contempt for the ordinary people.[13] Even a cursory reading of *Socialist Commonwealth* reveals that these charges have little substance.

Wright's criticism that the Webbs dispensed with democracy is based on their concept of vocational self-determination. It is true that they were not prepared to go as far as Cole in giving democratic rights to the workers, for example, in choosing their managers, but the extent of worker participation in the Webb model should not be underestimated. In any case, any limitation in their concept of industrial democracy hardly justifies the charge that they dispensed with democracy. Their support for a more powerful system of local democracy in consumer co-operatives and their emphasis on decentralisation and dispersal of power also makes nonsense of the claim that they were merely imposing democracy from above.

As far as the Webbs' view of the relationship of the individual and the state is concerned, it is certainly the case that they considered that nineteenth century individualism was outdated by the development of modern society. They were aware that the community had to be protected against the selfishness and power of individuals and groups, but they strongly believed that their new democratic system would protect liberty and increase individual rights and opportunities.

As to their alleged contempt for the ordinary man, the *Socialist Commonwealth* is far more optimistic about the possibilities of individual participation than *Industrial Democracy*, written twenty years earlier. The citizen was not only involved in electing a government but also in working in his vocational and consumer co-operative group as well as concerning himself with local issues. The Webbs also laid stress on the educative success of democracy and in particular on the impact on authority of the wide dissemination of knowledge:

> the real authority will more and more be exercised by the public opinion of the successively enlarging circles of persons concerned – a public opinion which the practice of wide and gratuitous publication of the reports will make both well-informed and all-persuasive.[14]

Whatever criticism can be made of the *Socialist Commonwealth* it is most certainly an argument for a democratic structure based on a system of countervailing checks and balances, a considerable dispersal of power and a meaningful level of participation – a case which still has its relevance today.

Sidney's membership of the Sankey Commission gained him considerable status not only within the Labour Movement (he topped the poll for the Labour Party executive that year) but among the miners. It was not therefore surprising that he was approached in the latter half of 1919 by miners' lodges in the newly formed Seaham Harbour constituency to stand as their candidate at the next general election. The local Durham Miners' Association put pressure on the party to nominate a local miner. The local party, however, decided to secure a candidate who was already a national figure ('a real politician'),[15] hence the choice of Sidney, whose initial reaction was to refuse. It was the conscientious Beatrice who 'begged him to pause because I thought he ought to respond to any request by organised labour to have him as their Parliamentary candidate in the coming crucial contest' (18 February 1920).

Sidney, however, had no desire to fall foul of the Durham Miners' Association and cautiously asked for a ruling from them. After a five month period of silence he provisionally accepted the nomination, only to be immediately informed by the Durham miners' executive that they wanted a miner. Sidney decided to withdraw but was finally persuaded, through local pressure, to accept the nomination in July 1920. There 'is a strange irony' Beatrice wrote,

> in these simple-minded miners, living in a remote backwater, seeking out and persistently pressing into their service the most astute and subtle – and, be it added – the least popular leader of the Labour and Socialist Movement. The explanation is that these leading men in these isolated villages are readers of books and not hearers of revivalist speeches and propagandist lectures. (11 July 1920)

The Webbs went up to the constituency in May, mainly in order to be vetted by the miners' lodges and Labour Party branches. They found the north east bleak and uninviting. 'There is no centre of intellectual or spiritual life', Beatrice noted with a singular lack of understanding. 'A mechanically black-proof union as the only corporative life, a dingy and commercialised co-operation, a vigorous Club movement for purposes of drinking . . . little or no social life' (8 June 1920).

But whatever the drawbacks, Sidney's age, the travelling, the election expenses (which Sidney had promised to meet) the Webbs decided Sidney should accept the nomination. They were, as Beatrice recorded, 'quite pleased with this adventure'.

In his letter of acceptance to the secretary of the Seaham Harbour Labour Party, Sidney gave his reasons for agreeing to become prospective Parliamentary candidate.

> As you know, this position was not of my seeking. It is now just upon a year ago that I began to receive requests from organisations in the Seaham Division that I would permit my name to be put forward. I held off for a long time, and suggested the choice of someone connected with the local industry. When the requests were renewed, actually from the Miners' Lodges themselves, as well as from Trade Union Branches and other bodies representing different sections of the community, I preferred to visit the constituency and address more than a dozen meetings in the various districts, in order that everyone might have an opportunity of judging whether my candidature would be the one most generally acceptable. The evidence then afforded to me, together with the decision now given, leaves me no excuse for doubt. To an invitation emanating from the Lodges of the Durham Miners' Association, and very nearly every other Trade Union and Labour organisation in the Division; joined in by leading members of the Co-operative and Friendly Societies; supported by Ministers of Religion of various denominations and by electors of all classes – by shopkeepers, professional men, officials and

> teachers as well as by wage-earners and by women as well as men; and conveyed to me as the unanimous decision of the Divisional Labour Party – I have no right to oppose my own reluctance to assume a new responsibility. In accepting the position I thank all concerned for the honour of their confidence.[16]

It was, of course, more than an 'adventure' for Sidney. 'Last night', he wrote to Beatrice from the north soon after he was selected,

> It blew so hard that I could do nothing but think of my dear wife and my great happiness, and good fortune in life, and perhaps also the obligation that it put me under, more than ever, to remember the millions less fortunate and deprived unnecessarily of the opportunities and happiness that might be much more evenly shared, and thereby actually increased for all. My own particular way is not to be always thinking of that obligation, but to make it the base of life and work, so that merely in doing what is habitual we may be fulfilling it, perhaps even more effectively than by always having it in mind as a motive – I am amused to think that this, too, is a sort of 'Economy' and 'Efficiency' for which we are reproached: but all the same it is my way.[17]

Seaham Harbour had not yet been won for Labour and, despite the miners' union, was at that time still poorly organised. Sidney was well aware of the problems of his new constituency. 'It is difficult to stir these people up to interest in public affairs', he wrote disconsolately to Beatrice in December 1920.

> Everywhere there are a few enthusiasts but they are depressed with the difficulty of getting anyone to take part. The women are nearly untouched and unaware that anything is going on . . . I feel pretty confident that the miners' vote will go fairly solid for me when the time comes; I am not at all confident either of the women or any other section of the population.[18]

It is clear that, apart from the devoted assistance of his honorary agent, J. R. Herron, a congregationalist minister, and a few trade union officials, mostly from the Durham miners, Sidney had little help. Undeterred, the Webbs made themselves experts on the mining industry (Sidney wrote *The Story of the Durham Miners*) and instituted 'a most exacting programme of lectures, meetings and organisation of propaganda'. They spoke in every village hall on a wide range of subjects; Beatrice was told that 'We learn so much at your meetings it is better than a tutorial.'[19] She herself encouraged the formation of Labour women's sections in the mining villages.

Meanwhile, back in London, Sidney was still leading an active life. In 1919 he forced Pember Reeves to resign from the directorship of the LSE and chose Beveridge to take his place: 'a good administrator – an initiator of both ideas and plans and a man who will concentrate his energies on the School' Beatrice wrote presciently (23 June 1919). He also remained on the NEC, drafting major policy papers for its various sub-committees. It was work he disliked as he often felt no interest in the subjects he was asked to write about, but, as Beatrice noted approvingly, 'he is "the man of all work" of Eccleston Square and accepts his position with almost excessive good nature. When no-one else likes doing a necessary job, he brings it home and sits down resignedly to do it until it is done. Very naturally he is much beloved at the Office' (28 August 1921). As she reflected at the end of the year:

> Sidney has been in fine health and spirits, keenly enjoying his daily task, and on the best of terms with his colleagues at the Labour Party, and I think, on the whole, looking forward to his probable parliamentary career. 'No doubt I am old', he constantly says, 'but I don't feel it in body or mind' . . . His immense knowledge and great skill in handling facts and proposals, his unpretentious helpfulness, makes him the best of mates for men like Henderson and Clynes; whilst the fact that he is not a popular speaker or a magnetic personality, saves him from the envy and jealousy of the leading personalities of the democratic world . . . And the very fact that Sidney, though he feels young, *knows that he is old*, prevents his consciousness of successful work turning into the illusion of personal power. (24 December 1921)

The following year went less smoothly. Sidney had a serious breakdown in the summer whose cause remained unknown. It may have been a long delayed reaction from the blackout he had experienced the previous winter or, more likely, the strain of nursing a distant and unfamiliar constituency. It was his first serious illness of their marriage and a great shock to Beatrice. She had also been suffering from a severe colitis and wrote in her diary,

> Living the life of invalids anxious about each other and unpleasantly doubtful about the future of 'the Webbs' . . . what would Sidney do without me if he became an invalid? I have always contemplated leaving him still vigorous with Parliament as a new career to interest and absorb him. There is no one to look after him and he is so absurdly dependent on me. (9 August 1922)

However, Sidney was soon thrown into the hurly-burly of a general election. With the break-up of the Coalition, the new Conservative Prime Minister, Bonar Law called an election in October. Sidney campaigned vigorously on his record of work in the constituency and the failure of the Coalition, and on Labour's alternative programme which he had helped to prepare. Beatrice wrote,

> Sidney is thoroughly enjoying himself in this election: six meetings he is taking today, morning, afternoon and four 'appearances' in the evening. He is remarkably fit – all his giddiness has ceased; he sleeps well and eats sufficiently. In the intervals between the meetings he writes letters and articles. (9 November 1922)

In a letter to women electors she confessed that she grudged him 'to the House of Commons' but promised if the electors at Seaham wished to have him as their member, 'We will work together for them, even if the writing of more books has to be stopped'.

The Seaham result was a personal triumph for Sidney who won with a big majority of over 11 000 in a three-cornered contest. Beatrice wrote: 'The ballot papers were counted in lots of fives and twenties, looked almost as if they had been marked by a machine with here and there a fault in the working of it'. (17 November 1922) Labour, with 142 seats, became the largest opposition party, polling more than four million votes. In the new parliament, the balance of the PLP moved away from the trade unionists. MacDonald, Jowett (founder of the Bradford ILP) and Snowden were returned, as were a considerable number of ILPers and well-known former Liberals such as Arthur Ponsonby, son of Queen Victoria's secretary; Sir Charles Trevelyan, son of Sir George Trevelyan, biographer of Macaulay; and the Buxton brothers. MacDonald, with the support of the ILP members, was narrowly elected chairman of the Parliamentary Labour Party.

The Webbs, never friendly with MacDonald, nor he with them, welcomed the new appointment with a certain restraint. 'Mac-

Donald's chairmanship', wrote Beatrice,

> has much to recommend it. He is abler than Clynes; he is free to devote his whole energy to being Parliamentary leader; he has a greater hold over the Scottish contingent and his Chairmanship prevents him from deprecating the Parliamentary Party in the country which he would have done if he had been passed over. If he is not the best man for the post, he is at any rate, the worst and most dangerous man out of it! (23 November 1922)

MacDonald, in turn, accepted that Sidney should be offered a place on the Opposition front bench to speak on unemployment and social affairs.

The Webbs were conscious that they were beginning a new phase of their life:

> To enter Parliament for the first time at sixty three years of age is a risky adventure from the standpoint alike of health and reputation. It would be a foolhardy risk if the need within the Parliamentary Labour Party for steady-going intellectuals were not so great and Sidney's training in Government Departments, LCC administration and sociological research did not fit him in a peculiar way for the task. (23 November 1922)

For Beatrice, Sidney's election to parliament was in reality a mixed blessing. Since the end of the war, she had almost retired from public life. Already in her sixties she had become increasingly conscious of the short time left for the partnership. At the beginning of 1920 she wrote, 'I am . . . on one of the watersheds of life. Behind me is the long record of each stage of my journey . . . in front of me, the last stage, of our working comradeship – and probably a short stage – completing as far as strength permits all our unfinished work' (25 February 1920).

In July 1921 she was contemplating her death:

> Our personal life flows smoothly to its end with a settled conviction, on my part, that for me the end is not far off. Every night when I embrace my boy and give him my blessing before I retire to my room there is sadness in my heart at the thought that some day – and a day that cannot be far off – it will be our last embrace.

She admitted to herself that she had no evidence that she was about to die though she suffered

> now and again from insomnia and indigestion and aches and pains here and there and occasionally have a panic about a mortal complaint – usually cancer – which turns out to be wholly imaginery. I enjoy good health, if health be measured by capacity to walk eight or ten miles. (16 July 1921)

With these intimations of mortality, it is not surprising that she began to take stock of her life and their joint work.

> As I near the end of life, I become more contemptuous of cynicism, more convinced that what we know as 'goodness' is in accordance with 'the nature of things'. Looking back on my own failures and humilitations, they nearly all arose from a strain of worldliness or cynicism, a lack of scrupulousness in my manner of life, a giving way to personal vanity and vulgar egotism and all the petty lying that this vanity and egotism entails. The great sources of my happiness, my work and my marriage to Sidney, sprang straight out of a religious purpose, an ideal end, not for myself, but for the world of men . . . deep down in one's heart is a realisation that the discovery of the laws of nature in order that men may become creators of a better world, is an act of piety, one of the ways that we can bring about the Kingdom of God. (17 September 1920)

As part of her new mood, in 1922 she began to arrange her diary into autobiographical work, although the first volume, the brilliant *My Apprenticeship* took six years to produce. So she was not exactly the right age or in the right frame of mind to be an MP's wife.

However, whatever her inclinations and her long-held misgivings about a parliamentary career for Sidney, she believed that it was her duty to assist her husband in his political activities. She took an active role in the constituency. Immediately after the election, Beatrice wrote, 'Now we are in, we must do something to rouse the miners and their wives to be interested in public affairs . . . I am haunted by the vision of those pit villages and those strained faces' (23 November 1922). Together the Webbs usually spent two weeks during Easter and two further fortnights during the summer recess addressing meetings, giving lectures and, in Beatrice's case, setting up new women's sections. Although they lived in London, they packed more into those three fortnights than most other far younger MPs who lived in their constituencies. Writing a year after Sidney was elected, Beatrice summed up their relationship with Seaham:

> So far as we ourselves are concerned, we are on velvet in this ideal constituency. There is far more enthusiasm than a year ago – far more voluntary work. The miners have become genuinely attached to their member; they are proud of him; they trust him and they feel that he is 'their man' . . . that he has proved himself to be . . . the best member Seaham has ever had for local purposes. And the miners' wives are fond of me; I have raised their status with their husbands and neighbours; they regard me as *their representative* and they are delighted with the monthly letter giving them special news from London. (3 December 1923)

By the election of 1924 Beatrice felt that she had 'the sense of belonging' to the miners' community. 'Especially gratifying to us has been the growing affection of these men and women for the Webbs: they and we are co-religionists, we have the same faith but we hold the faith in a different and complementary way' (29 October 1924). The impact made on the north by the Webbs and by the north on the Webbs was confirmed by Jack Lawson, the Labour MP for Chester-le-Street, and Minister for War in the Attlee administration, in a memorial essay:

> It is a fact that in time Webb 'got' his audiences in his own quiet way, but it is also true that his audiences in time also 'got' him . . . But there was one thing certain and it was that Mrs Webb gripped the women much more than ever did he. There was the real stuff of the north when she addressed meetings and she left a memory which will never be forgotten by those now living.[20]

Beatrice's monthly Newsletter which was circulated to all the women members was a clever and successful innovation which served as propaganda and a means of keeping the Webbs in touch with the local party. The letters, which often had a photo of Beatrice, were read aloud at the meetings and then passed round the constituency. The following letter, her first, gives their flavour.

Dear Friends, My husband has already discovered that one of the difficulties of being a Member of Parliament is that you see very little of your electors . . . the Member is compelled to live in London in order to attend Parliament . . . He has to be perpetually thinking about all sorts of subjects from foreign treaties to the sugar tax, from the problem of unemployment to that of housing . . . I think it may interest you to know exactly where we live and how we live, before I begin to talk to you about public questions . . .

My husband and I live a very regular life. Every morning at 8 o'clock punctually we have each one cup of coffee and bread and butter on a tray in our workroom; we read our letters . . . and then we get to work, and work steadily until our mid-day meal at 1 o'clock. When Parliament is sitting my husband has to be in the House of Commons at 2.30 to late at night . . .

Now I want to tell you something about public affairs. The two questions that have most interested us during the last month and which are being most talked about in London, are unemployment, on the one hand, and on the other the determination of France to invade Germany and take possession of some of her coalfields and forests. Unfortunately these two questions are closely connected one with the other . . . My husband and I are coming up to Seaham for Easter week, when Parliament will not be sitting. If possible I should like to meet the members of the Dawdon Women's Section some afternoon in that week. Yours very sincerely, BW.[21]

The letters may now seem *de haut en bas* but Durham constituents, for the first time ever, were kept in close contact with their Member of Parliament.

In London Beatrice introduced a second, though far more controversial innovation – the Half Circle Club. She first decided to form a club for wives of Labour politicians and trades unionists in 1920, while attending the International Socialist Conference in Geneva. After talking to the wives of the delegates she became conscious of the solitary nature of their existence. Generously, she thought she could help by providing a place where Labour wives could meet regularly; hence the setting up of the Half Circle Club. As she said of it: 'If it has done nothing else, it has led to something like personal friendship between the little group of women who form the Executive and to friendliness to some hundreds others' (19 June 1922). Those mistrustful of the Webbs (MacDonald was actively hostile towards the venture) criticised her on the grounds that her only aim was to provide the members with a veneer of society manners. But the evidence seems to point to the Club being a successful and friendly meeting place. As a member of the Labour Party once told her, it completely revolutionised the life of some of the wives who now felt for the first time that they were 'part and parcel of the Labour movement' (16 July 1921). It was a kindly gesture towards those who had been uprooted from their normal surroundings and now had to suffer the strains and loneliness of parliamentary politics.

These years of added political involvement put an extra burden on Beatrice. She would have preferred to have lived a quiet life in the country, writing and researching. Instead she conscientiously visited the constituency and entertained politicians and their wives. She rarely complained, particularly as she saw Sidney's evident delight in his new political life-style. Her only demand after his election was to persuade him to buy a country retreat so that he could come down for quiet recuperatory weekends and she draw strength for her political excursions to London.

They had often talked of living peacefully in the country, in a house which they would turn over to the London School of Economics after their deaths. Beatrice saw no reason to postpone that pleasure just because Sidney had become an active politician. Initially they had thought of building a cottage and in the summer of 1923 they had inserted a characteristically precise advertisement in the *New Statesman* for a country house;

> Mr and Mrs Sidney Webb require a building site of an acre or more within a radius of 50 (or 75 miles) of London in any direction south (south preferred); preferably with a habitable cottage which could be developed. It must be relatively high with a pretty view; and above all completely isolated from houses harbouring cocks or dogs. Anyone knowing of such a site for sale is begged to inform Mr Webb, 41 Grosvenor Road, Westminster.

In fact the advertisement yielded nothing but soon after they found a suitable place near Liphook in Hampshire which could be converted. It had 8 acres of ground with 'a delightful corner of woodland. Happy hours Sidney and I spend', recorded a joyful

Beatrice, 'in discussing alterations and possible extensions and if we keep our health and strength we can hope for a happy old age under our own oak tree'. (31 August 1923) She named it Passfield Corner and, as Sidney became more and more absorbed in political life and she in her autobiography, Beatrice came to spend the major part of her time in the country. Their lifestyle changed considerably; she retreated to the seclusion and simplicity of Passfield Corner (a very modest house), whilst Sidney, forced by chance and circumstance to continue in politics until 1931, remained in London during the week, only coming down at the weekend. In spite of the enforced separation they either wrote to each other daily or telephoned. Beatrice found a new contentment. 'The cottage', she wrote a year after she had moved in,

> with its comfortable study and delightful loggia, its woods, and views and walks, is almost too good to be true! To make a new home when one is nearing seventy seems, in some moods, a melancholy task; one is haunted by a vision of the funeral procession wending its way down the new drive. (28 June 1924)

Despite some loneliness she felt the need to lead her own life,

> Now, when he returns, we love each other; but he has interests about which I know little and I am absorbed in creative writing in which he has no part, but that of a kindly and helpful critic of style. Still it would be purposeless for me to waste my strength and such wits as I have, in doing odd jobs which are not needed. . . . He is happy and contented in his new task and so am I in mine.

Parliamentary life gave Sidney a new lease of life. 'Sidney is like a boy going for his first term to a public school!' Beatrice noted with some amazement. 'This lightheartedness, odd for a man of sixty three, is due to the youthfulness of the party; as individuals and as an organisation: and to being elected on the Executive Committee of the Parliamentary Party and also to being asked by JRM to sit on the Front Bench'. (13 February 1923)

Sidney made his maiden speech on 20 February 1923 during a debate on pensions. According to Beatrice, who sat in the gallery, it was a success but one of the very few that he was to have. Sidney was not a natural House of Commons debater; his delivery was pedantic, he tended to mumble and he was easily put off by opposition heckling. His first speech as a front bench opposition spokesman came a month later when he was asked to wind up the debate on unemployment insurance. Parts of the speech whose tone was learned and educational read very much like his previous statements on the national minimum and on the prevention of destitution. The theme was the wastefulness of unemployment on the nation's resources, included a brief historical aside on the problems of unemployment in 1841 and ended on a stern note (typical of many of his speeches) which particularly aroused the wrath of the government.

> The psychological reaction among the people against what, I venture to think is the dark shadow of profit-making capitalism, which is not so much the danger of low wages, or even long hours, but is the haunting sense of insecurity, the perpetual fear of unemployment and the consequent risk of ruin that dogs the life of the wage-earner today. I venture to say that it is that and not the proletarian Sunday School which is the seedbed of what honourable members opposite might call sedition and which I might call divine discontent.[22]

The speech did not go down well. Sidney was nervous and the jeers of the Tory backbenches confused him. 'He repeated himself', Beatrice observed critically 'and failed to make all his points and sat down without making his last words intelligible'. (6 March 1923) Altogether Sidney spoke fourteen times in the 1923 Parliament on those subjects such as housing, education and unemployment on which he was considered to be an expert.

How did the Webbs see that year of Labour opposition? The Parliamentary Labour Party was now more effective: the membership reflected a wider cross-section of the population, and MacDonald provided a vivid and commanding leadership, and perhaps, most important, there was the greater sense of purpose. The Labour Party had come of age. 'It is,' wrote Beatrice,

> a closely knit organisation with a vivid internal life of its own. The leaders do not dominate; and in so far as they lead, they lead by perpetual consultation with the rank and file members . . . The Whips are distinctly the servants and not the bosses of the party. (11 May 1923)

A month later she admitted that Sidney's new found delight in his work was due to 'the attitude of the Party to him – they are not suspicious or resentful as the Progressives on the LCC were: they are affectionate – call him "Sidney", push him to the front in spite of his protests'. (8 June 1923) The Webbs saw the Parliamentary Labour Party

> in fact very much a Family Party living on terms of frank intimacy – some of the members are young and disorderly, tho' the majority are austere in their habits; . . . Undisciplined in appearance, they are, but in effect the most highly disciplined political party that have ever existed in England. [All the same] the growth of the Labour Party and its present position as the alternative government does not represent a movement of thought among the whole population: it is largely if not mainly, the result of the striking capacity for organisation of the British working man inspired by the fervent non-conformist spirit, which no longer finds an outlet in religion and has found it in social reconstruction. (8 June 1923)

Half way through the year Beatrice had to admit that parliamentary life suited Sidney. He was 'very happy . . . and they all say he looks more vigorous and younger than he has done for years. "Getting quite combative", one of the ILP members said'. (11 May 1923) His most successful speech as a front bench spokesman was made on the Labour Party amendment for the rejection of the Rent Restrictions Bill.

> He has caught the right tone and has got command of his audience. His work becomes everyday more exciting as the Parliamentary Party is making full use of his services. He is enjoying the life; enjoying it far more than either he or I could have expected. And his relations with JRM are certainly unexpectedly cordial. (30 May 1923)

The Webbs now began to meet the new and rising stars of the Labour movement. Oswald Mosley fascinated them, 'The most brilliant man in the House of Commons.' He had originally sat in Parliament on the Conservative benches and had joined the Labour Party in 1923. 'Here is the perfect politician who is also a perfect gentleman . . . If there were a word for the direct opposite of a caricature – for something which is almost absurdly a *perfect type* – I should apply it to him,' Beatrice enthused. Even so, though clearly captivated, she had some reservations. Was there, she wrote with foresight, 'some weak spot which will be revealed in a time of stress – exactly at the very time when you need support – by letting you or your cause down or sweeping it out of the way?' (8 June 1923)

During that first year of opposition, the partnership supported Ramsay MacDonald's style of leadership. Nevertheless he was, Beatrice felt, (after listening to a crucial debate in which MacDonald replied to Baldwin's sudden adoption of protection as a cure for unemployment) a politician who made clever and eloquent speeches but who lacked intellectual and emotional sincerity. But as she generously summed up,

> JRM is certainly more than a passable leader; he is an extremely *accomplished* leader – nothing ragged or obviously defective in him – but he is not more than that except perhaps in the tenacity of his purpose, and it is certainly marvellous how the achievement of his ambition has improved his manners and swept away his rancours. (5 November 1923)

That year Sidney was chairman of the Labour Party Conference. In his presidential address he described the major themes which, he argued, now characterised the post-war Labour Party – realism, responsibility, internationalism. Sidney began by stressing that the Party had to convince the majority of the electors not that the Conservatives had failed to deal successfully with major problems 'but that these problems can be satisfactorily solved on the principles that we preach'. In other words, the Labour Party had to demonstrate its ability to provide a viable alternative programme.

He then launched into a fierce attack on the Versailles Peace Treaty which, he claimed, was the basic reason for the international unrest. 'We can all see now that Europe could no more be rebuilt upon the passion of hate, the passion of greed, and the passion of fear than upon anger and violence. And neither hate nor greed, neither fear nor violence is brought more into accord with the requirements of economics or of ethics merely by being national instead of individual.' Sidney maintained that the answer was a foreign policy based on morality and not on what

> we presume to think our rights, but on what we can discern to be in the common interests of the world; not on national hatred, national greed, or even national fear, but on a sense of brotherhood with all men; not on what we may hope to make out of other nations to our own profit, but on how, with our peculiar gifts and special opportunities we can best serve humanity as a whole.

Rising prices, unemployment, attested to the bankruptcy of the governing classes, a weakness which played into the hands of the Labour Party because it 'has not only principles but also a practical programme worked out in considerable detail; and a programme which flows out of its principles, and is consistent with these'. He was, of course, referring to *Labour and the New Social Order*.

Sidney went on to describe, in a phrase later to become famous, what he called 'the inevitability of gradualness'. The common interpretation of his meaning has been that he was reasserting the old Fabian belief in the eventual triumph of permeation. Professor Mackenzie, however, has put forward the alternative view that Sidney simply meant that the Labour Party would inevitably come to power. There is perhaps a third interpretation. Sidney was also anxious that the Labour Party should not (particularly at a time of industrial unrest) be seen as the party of revolution. Its socialism had to be both respectable and responsible, otherwise it would never become the party of government. His message therefore, was that the Labour Party would achieve power democratically and that the means it would employ to change the structure of society would be both democratic and gradual.

The statement is worth quoting in full:

> First let me insist on what our opponents habitually ignore, and indeed what they seem intellectually incapable of understanding, namely the inevitable gradualness of our scheme of change . . . for the Labour Party, it must be plain, Socialism is rooted in political Democracy; which necessarily compels us to recognise that every step towards our goal is dependent on gaining the assent and support of at least a numerical majority of the whole people . . . That, indeed, is the supremely valuable safeguard of an effective democracy. But the Labour Party when in due course it comes to be entrusted with power, will naturally not even want to do everything at once . . . Once we face the necessity of putting our principles first into bills, to be fought

> through Committee, clause by clause; and then into the appropriate administrative machinery for carrying them into execution from one end of the Kingdom to the other – and this is what the Labour Party has done with its Socialism – the inevitability of gradualness cannot fail to be appreciated. This translation of Socialism into practical projects to be adopted one after another, is just the task in which we have been engaged for a whole generation.

Sidney's concluding remarks rang with moral fervour. The success of the Labour Party, he insisted, depended

> more than on anything else, upon the spirit in which we hold our faith . . . the spirit in which we fulfil our obligations, the spirit in which with inevitable backslidings we live our lives. We shall not achieve much, whatever changes we can bring about, unless what we do is done in the spirit of fellowship. For we must always remember that the founder of British Socialism was not Karl Marx but Robert Owen and that Robert Owen preached not 'class war' but the ancient doctrine of human brotherhood – the hope, the faith, the living fact of human fellowship.[23]

At the end of 1923 Baldwin's sudden conversion to protection changed the political situation dramatically. He believed that he needed a mandate for his new policy and called an election. Polling day was 6 December. Sidney had an overwhelming victory at Seaham, gaining 71.3 per cent of the vote in a straight fight with the Tories. Overall the result was far from clear cut. Although the Conservatives remained the largest party in parliament, with 258 seats, they were outnumbered by the two opposition parties, as the Liberals (recently united under Asquith) had 158 seats and the Labour Party, benefiting from its new position as the largest opposition party in most constituencies, 191. The initiative now lay with the Liberals. It was clear that, although the Tories decided to continue in office until Parliament met, Baldwin had failed to gain a clear mandate for protection. On the other hand, there were obvious dangers for the Liberals in voting in a minority Labour government. On 18 December, however, Asquith told the Parliamentary Liberal Party that the Liberals would not keep the Conservatives in office. If a Labour government was ever to be tried, he declared, 'it could hardly be tried under safer conditions'. The Liberals also hoped that a spell in office would demonstrate Labour's inability to govern.

In a memorandum on the first Labour government, Sidney Webb explained that initially Labour leaders did not believe they would be called to form a government. But once they saw the possibility, they quickly realised that they had to accept office. Sidney wrote that by 'refusing office . . . the Labour Party would, in fact, have lost the enormous advance it had made at the 1922 election in becoming definitely HM Opposition'.[24] On 10 December there was a lunch of the most important Labour leaders, (MacDonald, Henderson, Clynes, Snowden, Thomas and Webb) at the Webbs' house in Grosvenor Road. MacDonald noted in his diary, 'All agreed that we should take office . . . unanimous that moderation and honesty are our safety. Agreed to stand together.'[25] According to Beatrice, Sidney was in favour of taking office, 'with the probability of being beaten on the Budget or before', while she saw the logic but was concerned that Labour had 'no mandate for carrying out its distinctive policy' (12th December). The position of the leadership was supported by both the NEC of the Labour Party and the General Council of the TUC.

It was not until 21 January 1924 that the Labour and Liberal Parties combined to vote Baldwin out of office. However, by the end of December, it was clear that Labour would form the next government and that, as leader of the Labour Party, MacDonald would become Prime Minister. MacDonald's task in choosing a government was made easier by Sidney persuading his colleagues to leave the job entirely to their leader, who retired over Christmas to Lossiemouth to construct the first Labour administration. As Sidney wrote, 'I had very vividly in my mind the possibility of an attempt to get all appointments made by vote at the Party meeting.' Although the Liberals had expected Labour to ask for their help, MacDonald was able to form a government without any Liberals. He acted as his own Foreign Secretary, Snowden was given the Exchequer while Clynes became Lord Privy Seal and Leader of the House of Commons. Of the ILPers, John Wheatley was given the Ministry of Health but MacDonald refused to have George Lansbury in the Cabinet. (Sidney felt his exclusion 'to be a mistake'.) He brought in three non-Labour peers, Haldane as Lord Chancellor, Parmoor as Lord President, and Chelmsford, a former Conservative Viceroy of India, as First Lord of the Admiralty.

There was some controversy over the position of Henderson who had lost his seat in the election. His claim to a major cabinet post was outstanding. He had not only been a cabinet minister under Asquith and Lloyd George, but, as secretary of the Party, was one of the architects of Labour's advance. But MacDonald, realising that his government could not last many months, wanted Henderson to look after the Labour Party machine with a view to strengthening it for the next general election. Henderson, however, wished to be a cabinet minister as well and MacDonald was forced to offer him the Home Office.[26]

Sidney Webb's judgement was that 'there was friction with Henderson, to whom I thought that MacDonald behaved with extreme gaucherie; as well as with fundamental ingratitude, unfriendliness and discourteousy.'[27] Sidney's view of MacDonald's handling of the Henderson problem was based on his belief that MacDonald had failed to consult Henderson and was proposing that Henderson should become chairman of Ways and Means, a post which was obviously unsuitable. Marquand argues that Sidney Webb's charges were misplaced. However it is clear from his letter of 23 December to Henderson that MacDonald did mention the chairmanship of Ways and Means and there was no real dialogue over cabinet positions between the two men. Henderson, who wanted to be Lord President or Lord Privy Seal, because these posts could be easily combined with the secretaryship of the Labour Party had in the end to force MacDonald's hand to be given a senior Cabinet position – something which, given Henderson's importance and seniority, should not have been necessary.

Sidney was initially offered the Ministry of Labour with particular reference to the 'unemployment difficulties' and Ramsay MacDonald suggested that Margaret Bondfield, the well-known organiser of the General Workers' Union, should be his Parliamentary secretary. MacDonald was already playing a cautious line, 'As little legislation as you can do with, please, although you will need some', he wrote anxiously to Sidney, while at the same time assuring him that the Ministry of Labour was not second best; 'I should in the ordinary way be inclined to offer you another office but Labour and the Foreign Office are the two arduous and important jobs we have to face. I pray you to consent.'[28] Sidney was delighted to do so. 'It is an unpretentious office with a low salary and no social duties . . . What a joke – what an unexpected and slightly ludicrous adventure . . . for a man of sixty four to become first a Member of Parliament, and within a year, a Cabinet Minister'. (3 January 1924) His letter of acceptance demonstrated his usual foresight and ability to grasp essential problems. In it he pointed out four areas which needed immediate attention, and suggested that far-reaching plans based on a ten year period should be drawn up and published by the government. He also foresaw the difficulties:

> Housing, for instance, . . . and with it dilution and training of building operatives, by agreement with the building trade unions . . . But this means cordial co-operation by the Ministry of Health who ought to work out a plan with the Minister of Health, who ought to work out the plan with the Minister of Labour and President of the Board of Trade . . . I am very much concerned with the possibility of finding *some* indispensible Minister obstinate, not against this or that colleague only, but against the Cabinet itself![29]

However, MacDonald sent for Sidney on 17 January 1924 to inform him that his colleagues felt (Haldane mostly it turned out) that the Ministry of Labour was the 'Cinderella of the government office'. He therefore offered Sidney the more prestigious Presidency of the Board of Trade. Sidney, at the age of sixty four, was not interested in self-advancement and would have preferred the Ministry of Labour and told MacDonald so. 'If they were all as considerate as you have been,' MacDonald told him, 'there would not be any difficulty in making a Cabinet'. (18 January 1924) In the end he reluctantly accepted the new post which covered unemployment. Apart from the Board of Trade, he was also given the chairmanship of the Housing and Unemployment Committees which split into two sub-committees: one under Wheatley, the other under Tom Shaw who became Minister of Labour.

To his surprise, Sidney enjoyed himself enormously at the Board of Trade. As an old civil servant with thirteen years experience, he got on extremely well with his department. As Beatrice put it: 'Every professional man likes his vocation to be appreciated by laymen . . . The Socialists – at any rate the type represented by the present Government – idealise the salaried public servant: they look to him to save the world!' (15 February 1924). It has been said of Sidney that he was too much in the hands of his civil servants – a charge that was particularly levelled at him as Colonial Secretary in the second Labour administration. The truer picture is that he accepted his civil servants' decisions because they often reflected his own.

Sidney did not make a great impact either at the Board of Trade or as chairman of the key cabinet committee on Unemployment and Housing. At the Board of Trade, he piloted through the London Traffic Bill and gave 'an impression of calmness and quiet competence'.[30] Webb was quite honest about his lack of success as Cabinet Committee chairman. 'I certainly failed to do any lasting good in this field. The Committee at once divided into two sub-committees on Unemployment and Housing respectively . . . these then "ran away" with their respective subjects and would not, in practice, be either helped, usefully criticised or controlled.'[31] In fact, Wheatley ran his own housing policy, while the Unemployment sub-committee, having failed to make much progress, was replaced by another committee, chaired by Snowden.

The Labour government was very much a caretaker administration; indeed, given its lack of majority, it could be little else. On the other hand, for MacDonald who was both Prime Minister and Foreign Secretary, the first seven months were a triumph. Not only did he play a major part in solving the difficult problem of German reparations through the Dawes' Plan, but he also managed to persuade the French (who had occupied the Ruhr because of German non-payment of reparations) to evacuate German territory. MacDonald's diplomacy immediately ensured him a front rank among the statesmen of Europe. Sidney was also impressed by the way MacDonald handled the Cabinet. 'The Prime Minister's behaviour in Cabinet was perfect', he wrote,

> he was never discourteous, never overbearing, never unduly dogmatic, patient to everyone, watchful to give everyone a chance to speak and nevertheless quick to close the debate as soon as it was proper to do so with his own summary of the 'sense of the meeting.'[32]

But, although accepting that MacDonald was a success as Prime Minister, the Webbs, particularly Beatrice, had reservations about him. In March, after two months in office, Beatrice observed that MacDonald, 'deep down in his heart . . . prefers the company of Tory aristocrats and Liberal capitalists to that of the Trade Union Official and the ILP agitators. It may be human nature but it is not good comradeship; it is not even successful politics' (3 March 1924).

In April, Beatrice recorded that 'MacDonald remains the "mystery man" to all his colleagues – who know little or nothing of his thinking or doing . . . Altogether personal relations within the Cabinet are not happy'. (7 April 1924) She was also worried about MacDonald's long-term political strategy:

> It is clear that the Prime Minister is playing up – without any kind of consultation with the majority of his colleagues, or scruple, or squeamishness about first pronouncements – towards the formation of a Centre Party – far less definitely socialist in home affairs, far less distinctly pacifist in foreign affairs, say than Sidney would be if he were Prime Minister. MacDonald wants eight million voters behind him and means to get them even if this entails shedding the ILP, the idealistically revolutionary section who pushed him into Power. That ladder will be kicked down! MacDonald is, in fact, returning to his policy of 1910–14, as we always foresaw he would; but with a different facet. In those years he was willing to merge the Labour Party in the Liberal Party: today he realises that the Liberal Party is dead; so he is attracting, by his newly-won prestige and personal magnetism, the Conservative Collectivist element – but insists that his collectivists shall dub themselves 'Labour' and accept him as their Leader. I do not accuse him of treachery; for he was never a socialist, either revolutionary like Lansbury or administrative like the Webbs; he was always a believer in individualist political democracy tempered in its expression by Utopian Socialism. Where he has lacked integrity is in *posing* as a socialist and occasionally using revolutionary jargon. (15 March 1924)

After five months in office, the Webbs reflected on Sidney's contribution to Parliament. Sidney, Beatrice recorded, was

> still enjoying his work, and as far as his own department is concerned he succeeds in and out of Parliament. In *general* debate on a *general* question – he is not so good – he does not always seize the operative points or wind up triumphantly. But he has the satisfaction of feeling that Fabianism is justified – that slowly attained incomplete and mixed communal control is all that is either practicable or desirable, and that the rival policies of revolutionary action or 'workers' control', or anti-socialism or fiscal 'protection' are all on the down-grade and cannot be put in force. (25 May 1924)

Beatrice was totally honest as to the reason why Sidney was not considered a successful parliamentarian. 'Sidney', she wrote in August, 'does his level best for his country and his party; he works up to the limit of his strength during the working months. But in his heart of hearts he remains essentially a detached observer without any keennees for one way over another, or to his own continued participation in the exercise of power' (30 August 1924).

According to Sidney's account, it became clear during the summer recess that the Liberals would try and engineer a Labour defeat in the House of Commons. The pretext which they seized on was the Campbell case. On July 25 J. R. Campbell, the acting editor of the Communist newspaper, the *Workers' Weekly*, published an article calling on troops not to obey orders to intervene in industrial disputes. The Director of Public Prosecutions, on the advice of the politically inexperienced Attorney General, Sir Patrick Hastings, decided to bring a case against Campbell under the Mutiny Act and a warrant was issued for his arrest. After MacDonald and the Cabinet had explained the political implications of such a trial to Sir Patrick, and it had become clear that Campbell, who was in any case only the acting editor, would be prepared to write a letter of apology, the Attorney General instructed the DPP to withdraw the case.

However, the mishandling of the case enabled the government's critics to claim that the DPP had been put under left-wing pressure. After a private notice question on 30 September, to which MacDonald gave a somewhat misleading answer by implying that he had not been consulted over the withdrawal, the Conservatives put down a motion of censure to which the Liberals tabled an amendment calling for the setting up of a Select Committee. In the debate on 8 October, Sir Patrick Hastings defended himself with great skill but 'the Prime Minister produced a bad impression by a strange but characteristic quibbling manner, a lack of frankness in explanation, with withdrawals and corrections of previous statements'.[33] The government was heavily defeated on the Liberal amendment and MacDonald, who had announced that he would regard a defeat as a question of confidence, decided to ask for a dissolution. Webb commented that

> Lloyd George with Asquith's tardy concurrence definitely meant to defeat us dramatically on the Russian treaties, which must come up on the first week of November; and as they chose to subject us to a premature defeat, MacDonald rightly decided to

> avoid a month's further 'hammering' by the entire newspaper press and the combined party platform.[34]

In the ensuing general election, the Labour Party, fighting on a manifesto written by Sidney, was subjected to vitriolic abuse and 'scare tactics'. Labour was not only accused of extremism and pro-Soviet sympathies, but four days before polling day the Zinoviev Letter was published in the *Daily Mail*. Zinoviev, who was President of the Communist International, was said to have written a letter to the British Communist Party ordering its members both to support the Russian Treaty and, at the same time, be prepared for revolutionary action. The letter was dated 15 September and the *Daily Mail* claimed that MacDonald had known about it for some time. What had in fact occurred was that the Foreign Office had already made a formal protest to the Soviet Embassy on behalf of the government – but the newspapers now claimed that the government had only objected because they feared exposure in the press. In any case, MacDonald had claimed that the letter was a forgery which, in fact, it turned out to be. Because he believed that this was the case he hesitated to commit himself and was silent when he should have spoken out.

In the event, the Tories won a massive superiority in seats, with an overall majority of 240. The Labour Party, although increasing its total vote from 4.4 to 5.4 million, lost forty seats. Sidney's majority was down by 7000 votes though, as Beatrice commented, 'still a majority of 10 700 is not contemptible' (Diary, *Fall of the Labour Government*, 1924). The silver lining for Labour was that the Liberals were decimated, being reduced to a rump of forty. Beatrice acutely noted that

> a more careful consideration of the response of the huge electorate to the virulent anti-communist propaganda carried on by Liberals and Conservatives alike makes us almost content with the verdict. Sidney in a speech a week before the day . . . prophesied that, whatever else happened, this General Election would be noted by future historians as 'the funeral of a great political party' – the last act in the story of Liberalism. And so has it proved to be.

She concluded: 'Here ends the episode of a Labour government and also of a Minority government – an episode which Sidney thinks, on the whole, good for the education of the Party – and as far as he is concerned, a good joke which, like most good jokes, ought not to be repeated.'

NOTES

1. S. and B. Webb, *A Constitution for the Socialist Commonwealth of Great Britain*, p. 72.
2. Ibid, p. 102.
3. Ibid, p. xvii.
4. Ibid, p. 201.
5. Ibid, p. 126.
6. Ibid, p. 181.
7. Ibid, p. 198.
8. Ibid, p. 196.
9. Ibid, p. 200.
10. Ibid, p. 214.
11. Ibid, p. 291.
12. Ibid, p. 355.
13. A. W. Wright, *G. D. H. Cole and Socialist Democracy*.
14. S. and B. Webb, *A Constitution for the Socialist Commonwealth of Great Britain*, p. 199.
15. Maureen Callcott: 'Sidney Webb, Ramsay MacDonald, Emanuel Shinwell and the Durham constituency of Seaham', The Study of Labour History, North East Group, *Bulletin* 11, 1977.
16. S. Webb to R. J. Herron, 20 July 1920, Passfield Papers.
17. S. Webb to B. Webb, 28 Oct 1923, Passfield Papers.
18. Ibid, 2 Dec 1920, Passfield Papers.
19. Callcott, op. cit.
20. J. Lawson, *The Webbs and their Work*, p. 197.
21. B. Webb to Friends of Seaham, Dec 1922, Passfield Papers.
22. *Hansard*, 5 Mar 1923, Col 173.
23. Labour Party Conference 1923, Presidential Address.
24. Note by S. Webb, *The First Labour Government*, Passfield Papers.
25. D. Marquand, *Ramsay MacDonald*, p. 298.
26. Ibid, p. 303.
27. S. Webb, *The First Labour Government*, Passfield Papers.
28. J. R. MacDonald to S. Webb, 31 Dec 1923, Passfield Papers.
29. S. Webb to J. R. MacDonald, 31 Dec 1923, Republic Records Office.
30. *The Webbs and their Work*, p. 201.
31. S. Webb, *The First Labour Government*.
32. Ibid.
33. Ibid.
34. Ibid.

12

1924–1929
Opposition Again

'The labour movement is in the melting pot.'

The landslide Tory victory, following on the viciousness of the 1924 campaign, inevitably led to recriminations within the Labour movement. MacDonald's leadership was subjected to intense criticism and it was only because no credible successor could be found that he succeeded in being re-elected leader. As Beatrice recorded there was 'great bitterness among the left . . . Henderson and Clynes and, I think, all the older and saner members of the Party are determined to keep JRM as leader, feeling that once the Party has acquired the habit of casting out leaders, when they displease the left, rot has set in' (21 November 1924). To add to the sense of betrayal, some ex-ministers, in particular Snowden, attempted to disclaim responsibility for the past actions of their own government.

The Webbs had mixed feelings about MacDonald. They questioned his motives and socialist commitment:

> If JRM had been a man of fine character and a convinced socialist, he might have guided a powerful socialist party; he had the necessary artistic gifts, the personal charm, the sonorous voice, the untiring energy, and the sympathic manners with those he liked. But he is an egotist, a poseur and snob, and worst of all, he does not believe in the creed we have always preached – he is not a socialist and has not been one for twenty years; he is a mild radical with individualist leanings and aristocratic tastes. (22 June 1925)

On the other hand, they had to accept the MacDonald made an impressive leader – and that there was no real alternative.

Following the defeat they retreated to the country, supervised the builders at Passfield Corner and again looked forward to their retirement, salving their conscience, as Beatrice admitted,

> by assuring each other that we are preparing a country residence for the staff and students of the London School of Economics, but in our heart of hearts we see pictures of two old folk living in comfort, and amid some charm, writing endless works, and receiving the respectful attention of an ever larger public. (2 December 1924)

To Beatrice defeat was obviously a blessing – she hoped it would mean uninterrupted work in the country on her autobiography and only occasional visits to 41 Grosvenor Road, which the Webbs now shared with Susan Lawrence, MP, and with whom Beatrice had a somewhat spiky relationship.

For Sidney the fall of the Labour government was more of a blow and his surprising depression (given his usual equanimity) even affected Beatrice. He found it difficult to settle down after his nine months ministerial activity. He was not a natural House of Commons man, as Beatrice admitted, 'He has not been well treated by the Tories – the more vulgar of the young bloods jeer at him. He has never got complete control of the House of Commons – he is too modest and feels his own limitations, without having the personal ambition to put himself right'. Also, as she confessed, 'the ruck-up within the Parliamentary Labour Party against the ex-Cabinet and the old Junta of MacDonald–Henderson–Clynes–Thomas–Snowden and Sidney has affected him at least as much, perhaps more, than it has the others as he is a comparatively newcomer in the Parliamentary arena and has never quite got his footing in the Party' (20 February 1925). The life of the Labour Party in opposition, with its doctrinal disputes and faction fights, did not suit Sidney. He began to talk more and more of giving up his seat. As he told Beatrice, he felt that at sixty six it was a waste of his remaining energies, 'to walk through the lobbies and at best lead standing committees – the younger men can do that' (8 August 1925).

Beatrice was by now totally involved in her work on her autobiography. She was disturbed that she felt

> rather morbid about the book – far too anxious for its success and counting too much *on it being a success*. I don't think Sidney quite likes it: he does his best to approve, still more to help me; but there is something about it that he – not exactly resents – but which is unsympathetic. In his heart he fears I am overvaluing it, especially the extracts from the diaries – the whole thing is far too subjective and all that part which deals with 'my creed' as distinguished from 'my craft' seems to him the sentimental scribbling of a woman, only interesting because they are feminine. However, I have enjoyed writing it and the book as a whole will have *some* value as a description of *Victorianism* . . . Old people ought to be *less* anxious for applause. Poor dears, I am afraid they are more affected by personal vanity than the young. It is now or never with them! (19 March 1925)

However, in spite of her anxiety, she enjoyed writing *My Apprenticeship* more than any other book she had ever undertaken. It appealed to the romantic in her and it allowed her to come to some understanding of her complex nature. Here, at last, she was free from the drudgery of research and analysis and able to use her considerable imaginative powers to the full. Although she had firmly decided to deny herself the pleasures of novel writing for the more arid world of academic investigation, she could now, under the pretext of the autobiographical form, let her imagination soar. The effect was so exhilarating that, although she deeply disliked and resented her enforced separation from Sidney once the House of Commons was sitting, she had to admit to herself that there was some compensation; she could now write undisturbed throughout the day. Sidney, on the other hand, missed her constantly: 'I find it *very* lonely without you today', he wrote to Beatrice,

> and I shall be glad when this week is over. We must try to keep together, except when duty actually compels separation. One day one of us will be alone; but we need not multiply separations before then. We might hope for another ten years – this is the 'expectation of life' of each of us from the printed tables.[1]

Looking back at the end of the year, Beatrice reflected that they had come to 'a sort of watershed in our career. During the last three years Sidney and I have both been living a new kind of life – he in Parliament and I in literature – in a sense a separate life – though I have been helping him in his politics and he me with my book' (5 December 1925). She was honest enough to accept that political life did not suit her, nor was she enamoured of politicians. 'I have not exactly enjoyed my associations with the Parliamentary Labour Party;' she wrote.

> I have done my level best, but there remains the fact that I dislike MacDonald, and do not really respect him and it is disagreeable to try to help a person you find neither agreeable nor think admirable. Sidney's other colleagues are, some of them – Henderson and Clynes for instance – men one admires and is interested in – but their companionship is not exciting! . . . I do not, and have never liked political life – there is too big an element of intrigue – too continuous a conflict of personality – too little essential comradeship . . . My relations with the miners and miners' wives in Seaham, in so far as friendly feeling is concerned, has been the best part of the business. (5 December 1925)

1925 had been a year of achievement for her. In October she had finished her book: '*Done it!*' she recorded exuberantly 'And never before have I been so relieved to see the last words of a book; for never before have I been so utterly and painfully uncertain as to its value . . . Added to this uncertainty is the unpleasantness of selling your personality as well as your professional skill – you lose your privacy' (29 October 1925). 'I am downcast!' she wrote on the eve of publication. 'Courage old woman, courage: be game to the end! And don't give way to the egotism of old age: Live up to what old age *ought to be* – the impersonal beneficence of the Ancient, unmoved by the opinion of a world he or she is about to leave' (18 February 1926). She need not have worried; *My Apprenticeship* was an immediate success being widely acclaimed as an autobiographical masterpiece.

It is a fascinating biography, written with Beatrice's customary sharp and critical eye. She spared neither herself nor anybody else and what emerged was one of the most sensitive of autobiographical studies. The book is not only the story of the growth of a remarkable personality, it also provides a vivid picture of the different environments and experiences which shaped the young Beatrice Potter. Prime Ministers and east-end sweaters, philosophers and Lancashire cooperators, west-end drawing rooms and tenement slums are described with a brilliant eye for detail. But it was more than just an original and distinguished account of the lives of Victorians, both eminent and lowly, it was also a description of how under the pressure of this stimulating social background Beatrice served her 'apprenticeship', and began to understand where her vocation in life lay. She accepted that she had to become a social investigator so that, as she put it, she would be able 'to present some clear and helpful idea of the forces we must subdue and the forces we must liberate in order to bring about reformation' (26 November 1889). The book is also a personal odyssey, which explores the conflict between what Beatrice called 'the ego that affirms and the ego that denies', the battle between the good and evil in her nature. And it is this account of her duality of motive, a classic preoccupation of many Victorians, that gives the book an intellectual distinction which sets it apart from other autobiographies of this era.

Finally there is the moving account of how she became a socialist – through her studies in the East End, her experiences of the co-operative movement and through her meeting with 'the Other One'. Socialism, with its scientific approach and firmly-held beliefs answered her need for a purpose in life. For Beatrice the 'science of society' had to be based on an ethical ideal. *My Apprenticeship* remains one of the most outstanding autobiographical studies of the twentieth century.

1925 was also the year in which Winston Churchill, the Conservative Chancellor of the Exchequer, returned the pound to the gold standard. The consequence of this decision was to damage severely the export industries, including coal, and lead not only to unemployment but also to industrial unrest and the General Strike. Sidney, as a representative of a mining constituency and leading member of the Sankey Commission, was obviously closely involved.

The response of employers to the increase in the price of their exported goods was to demand a reduction in wages. The clamour for reduction was particularly strong in the mining industry where about 60 per cent of collieries were unprofitable. Wage reductions therefore began to look inevitable unless the government agreed to a form of subsidy to the industry as a whole. However both the Conservative government and the mine owners found the idea of state intervention unpalatable, the former on ideological grounds, the latter because they believed it could only lead to nationalisation.

By the end of July 1925 the battle lines were drawn. The owners had given notice of coming wage reductions and a restoration of the eight-hour day, the Miners' Federation (whose members' wages had fallen to slightly more than half what they had been four years previously) had rejected the offered terms. In 1921 the Miners' Federation had been deserted by their colleagues on 'Black Friday'. Now the TUC made it clear that they would back the miners and it looked as if confrontation between the two sides was inevitable.

Faced by such obvious solidarity, Baldwin decided to intervene. The Conservative Prime Minister let it be known that the owners' notices would be withdrawn and that he proposed to set up another Royal Commission to look into the mining industry. At the same time he announced that the government was prepared to subsidise the mines until May 1926, by which time the Royal Commission chaired by Sir Herbert Samuel would have reported. It seemed a victory for united trade union action – a 'Red Friday'. Sidney supported MacDonald in his efforts during this period to assert the supremacy of parliamentary means and to oppose those in the movement who advocated direct action. Beatrice commented that 'Red Friday' meant

> the tremendous succession of popularity and apparent power to the left wing of the Labour Party. The ILP and their middle class friends, fearing to be superceded, as the *left wing*, by the communistic-trade union leaders (Cook, Purcell and Co) are plunging head-over-ears into grandiose schemes of immediate and revolutionary changes . . . Most of their proposals . . . are as improbable as they would be mischievious if carried out.
>
> Maxton's notion that if it came to a stand-up fight by *direct action*, against the continuance of Capital enterprise *as an institution*, the workers would win is pathetically absurd . . . But if the General Council of the TUC were really to put into execution their threat of a general strike there would be a repetition of 1848 on a more imposing scale. If I had to prophesy I should forecast some such catastrophe to the Labour Movement as the price of a return ticket to sanity. (17 August 1925)

For the time being, the Parliamentary leaders held their own. After a successful party conference, MacDonald was not challenged as leader, while Sidney regained his seat on the Parliamentary Committee. Even so, the credibility of the leadership ultimately depended on the Royal Commission producing a solution to the crisis. Sidney optimistically continued to hope that it would support nationalisation (16 September 1925).

The Samuel Commission reported on 10 March 1926. It did not support nationalisation but recommended a reorganisation of the mining industry; it opposed an increase in hours but proposed that wages be cut. The miners refused to accept wage reduction as part of a deal for the future reorganisation of the industry. 'Not a penny off the pay; not a second on the day!' became the rallying cry. The owners for their part refused to give into the demands of the miners, and the government, once more caught between the two, this time decided to support the former and announced that the subsidy would end. Although negotiations did in fact continue until early April, there was so little common ground between the parties that they were soon broken off. On 1 May, the miners found themselves locked out. Even so the TUC still hoped to be able to persuade the government to keep the negotiations going, but they were too late. The majority view that prevailed in the Cabinet was that the time had come to take a firm stand against the unions.

The General Council, outmanoeuvred by the government, reluctantly and without having thought through the implications called out all types of transport workers, printers, some building workers and employees in the iron and steel, chemical and power industries in support of the miners. But after nine days, during which the government kept essential supplies going, the General Council called off the strike, on the somewhat nebulous understanding that a memorandum agreed – not with the government but with Herbert Samuel – would provide the basis for a settlement. Trade union leaders had no wish to undermine the authority of a democratically elected government – even a Conservative one – and were only too anxious to get back to the negotiating table.

Sidney remained in London throughout the strike but despite his constituency obligations remained curiously detached from the crisis, spending most of the nine days working in the Public Record Office and the Ministry of Health for their volume on the history of the Poor Law – 'It is difficult to do anything else amidst this excitement!'[2]

On 7 May Beatrice noted that Sidney (who had probably been in communication with her) was far more apprehensive about the possibility of a long strike than she was, in part because he knew that the miners would not accept even a temporary wage reduction.

'Sidney', Beatrice wrote, 'was impressed with the powerlessness of the PLP and the self-will of the trade unionists'. Writing privately to Shaw on 13 May, Sidney was at pains to point out that

> the Labour Party and its Parliamentary leaders or representatives *had nothing* to do with it . . . one cause is that they [the trade union leaders] and the General Council generally, and Citrine the new Secretary thereof, are *anti-political*, jealous of the Labour Party, which has outstripped the General Council and old-fashioned trade unionism, specially as regards 'getting the limelight'.
>
> Of course, once the thing was done, we had all to make the best of it and we started individually to contrive some way of resuming negotiations . . . we know that the general strike was showing signs of collapse; men were beginning to go back; in another day or two there might easily have been a debacle; and hardly anyone doubts that the General Council did the right thing in calling the General Strike off, whilst *there was still something to call off*.
>
> Anyhow I am entirely convinced that we have done the right thing. MacDonald and Henderson (with Thomas) who have been all the week almost continuously at work from early morn to past midnight trying one proposal after another, wrestling with stupidity and obstinacy and jealousy, seeking fresh avenues of negotiation and bringing to bear all possible influences, deserve the greatest possible credit – of course, they will be denounced by the firebrands but they have saved the whole Labour Movement from the most disastrous smash and the most fatal set-back of all our life time.[3]

Beatrice remained in the country for the first week of the strike. On its first night she stayed up late to write her diary:

> The General Strike will fail; the General Council may funk it and may withdraw their instructions on some apparent concession by the Government, or the men may slink back to work in a few days. We have always been against a General Strike. But the problem of the collapse of Capitalism in the coal industry will remain and woe to the governing class that refuses to solve it by taking control, in one form or another, of the organisation of the industry.

On the other hand, she admired the way in which the trade union leaders initially handled the situation: 'The General Council of the TUC has certainly succeeded in giving an epic quality to their slow and reserved, but decisive attitude toward the Miners' dispute' (3 May 1926).

The following day she accurately analysed the weaknesses of a general strike.

> A General Strike aims at coercing the whole community and is only successful *if it does so* and in so far as it does so. Further if it succeeded in coercing the community it would mean that a militant minority were starving the majority into submission to their will and would be the end of democracy, industrial as well as political.

But she had some sympathy with the miners;

> There arise emergencies when it is better to fight even if you cannot win than to take oppression lying down. And this is especially so when the struggle is within a good-natured community who will recognise that men who fight and lose must be generously treated by the victorious party; that a willingness to fight, with the certainty that you will lose, implies a big grievance. (4 May 1926)

However, although she believed that the miners had a strong case, she still suspected that the General Strike

> will turn out not to be a revolution of any sort or kind but a batch of compulsory Bank holidays without any opportunities for recreation and a lot of dreary walking to and fro. When the million or so workers have spent their money they will drift back to work and no one will be any the better and many will be a great deal poorer and everybody will be cross. It is a monstrous irrelevance in the sphere of social reform . . . For the British Trade Union Movement, I see a day of terrible disillusionment. The failure of the general strike of 1926 will be one of the most significant landmarks in the history of the British working class. Future historians will, I think, regard it as the death gasp of that pernicious doctrine of 'workers' control' of public affairs through the Trade Unions and by the method of direct action.[4]

Looking back on the events of the crisis, Beatrice noted,

> A strike which opens with a football match between the police and the strikers and ends in unconditional surrender after nine days with densely packed reconciliation services at all the chapels and churches of Great Britain attended by the strikers and their families, will make the Continental Socialists blaspheme . . . Let me add that the failure of the General Strike shows what a *sane* people the British are. (18 May 1926)

Although the General Strike ended, the Miners' Federation held out until November. The Webbs were asked to give money to the Miners' Relief Fund which they did; although Beatrice truthfully recorded

> neither Sidney nor I would have given a penny to it if no-one had been the wiser . . . Sidney thinks that by holding out they are *diminishing* the amount of reorganisation which will actually be accomplished . . . the probable outcome . . . will be to worsen conditions of employment throughout the industry. (12 June 1926)

However, Sidney's attitude to the strike did not go unchallenged in the Seaham constituency, 'though the audiences were respectful even affectionate . . . it was clear that they were disappointed with his guarded and deprecatory attitude towards the strike and some of them said so. The Shotton branch passed a resolution complaining of his lack of sympathy and understanding' (24 October 1926). Beatrice commented, 'it never seems to occur to them (the miners) that *they* are withdrawing maintenance from the families of shipbuilders and ironworkers by remaining idle . . . The Great Strike, like the Great War, will bring more anger and more misery. It will not bring reconstruction.'

Beatrice summed up the events in her December Constituency letter. She had carefully refrained from commenting during the strike in her belief that her letters might get distorted, or be misquoted to the disadvantage of the miners. To those who suffered the six-month lock-out which followed the collapse of the strike, her arguments, however reasoned, must have appeared insensitive.

> Now that we have practically universal suffrage, a General Strike is out of date . . . my conclusion is that the General Strike of May

> 1926 was a calamitous mistake; among many other bad results it cost the trade unions nearly the whole of their reserve funds, and what is more, considerable indebtedness; and it has led to wholesale victimisation and unemployment, and incidentally hardened the heart of many fellow citizens who were in favour of the miners' cause . . . Now what is the alternative policy to direct action on a huge scale? The answer is, that we must convert a majority of the men and women of Great Britain to the workers' cause. The road to victory is by the roundabout way of the ballot box.[5]

Beatrice had foreseen the disillusionment after the collapse of the Strike. Its failure naturally confirmed the miners in their view that they had been betrayed by the rest of the movement. Among trade unionists as a whole, it bitterly divided shopfloor from the leadership: the activists felt let down, while the leaders resolved to avoid militant action in the future. However, despite its shortcomings, the TUC General Council had shown that it was capable of co-ordinating the trade union movement; the more intelligent employers could see that the trade unions were a force to be reckoned with. In the near future, the defeat of the General Strike, as Beatrice had hoped, encouraged the unions to turn back to Parliamentary politics and to support the Labour Party. The increasingly aggressive approach of the Conservative government, which, quite apart from turning a blind eye to the victimisation of the miners, also introduced the anti-union 1927 Trade Disputes Act (which declared sympathetic strikes illegal, limited picketing, and attacked Labour Party funds by forcing the trade unions to 'contract in') acted as an additional incentive.

However, from 1926, the Webbs began to distance themselves from politics. As far as Beatrice was concerned she was increasingly disillusioned by the Labour Party. 'With the present state of mind of the Labour Party,' she wrote gloomily in the early spring of 1927.

> Sidney and I feel singularly indifferent to their coming into power . . . the Labour Party as at present constituted is not fit to govern. JRM is a fine facade, a platform performance; Snowden is no longer a socialist; Thomas has never been one and is a social climber . . . Henderson is a first-rate general manager, but he is not a first class statesman with a policy of his own to carry out.

> Wheatley and Maxton – in many ways the most attractive figures in the Labour Party – and their ILP followers – are Utopians and pseudo-revolutionaries – pedalling phrases without understanding what is involved or without constructive capacity. (5 April 1927)

In February 1928 she wondered

> without superior brains, money or a Press, it is a marvel that Labour continues slowly to increase its membership . . . MacDonald, Sidney says, looks a broken man; and his heart is no longer in his job . . . Poor MacDonald: it must be mighty uncomfortable to be a facade to such an ugly building. And the worst of it is that he is the best that we have got to put in our shabby shop window! (14 February 1928)

She was little more impressed by the trade union movement. After the Webbs attended the TUC conference at Bournemouth following the General Strike, she recorded:

> The dominant impression left in my mind by the TUC of 1926 was chaos along the rank and file – disheartened chaos and the absence of leadership. We ourselves felt like Ghosts – 'Ancients' coming back from the backwoods of historical research to our old haunts – there to discover other ghosts wandering among a gathering of bewildered and frightened children . . . the British Labour Movement seemed passive and indeterminate . . . G. D. H. Cole, A. J. Cook, JRM, the intellectual fanatic, the inspired idiot and the accomplished substitute for a leader are singularly antagonistic to each other. These three men taken neither apart nor together yield no workable policy for the Labour Movement. (10 September 1926)

While Beatrice criticised, Sidney had decided at the beginning of 1926 not to stand at the next election. 'It is now clear to [Sidney] as it is to me, that he will not stand for Seaham again and that prospect makes him more indifferent than ever in taking a leading part – the episode of a political career has become a cul-de-sac' (30 March 1926).

As to who would replace Sidney in the plum seat of Seaham, she wondered if 'the ambitious . . . little Shinwell the late Labour Minister of Mines – a . . . clever little Jew – will manage to scrape it up' (1 October 1927). However, Sidney, who wrote officially to the Seaham party announcing his retirement at the beginning of 1928, discussed with Ramsay MacDonald the possibility of the Labour leader succeeding him there. MacDonald had found his own constituency of Aberavon a difficult one and was attracted by the sympathetic attitude of the Seaham Party.[6] On 28 May Beatrice noted that 'Henderson and Sidney are conspiring to hand over the safe and cheap seat of Seaham Harbour to "our leader". Who would have thought that the embittered vendetta of former years would terminate in such a model manner?' (28 May 1928). And during the summer the Seaham Party invited MacDonald to be their candidate, an invitation which MacDonald accepted on condition that he did not have to pay any constituency expenses.

The Webbs believed Sidney had done his duty to the Labour Party. What was less certain was that the Party would be willing to let him go. There was now talk of his going to the Lords as a front bench spokesman. Beatrice was horrified, 'I should very decidedly prefer *not* – it would involve the troublesome task of taking the office and refusing the title – this could be done but it would be unpleasant doing it.' All the same she suspected that Sidney would quite like the 'continued political activity under pleasant conditions – it would be an agreeable reason for going to London and a good club to go to. So the simplest way out of the difficulty of deciding is to do what the Party wants' (Whit Sunday 1928).

In spite of persistent rumours that Sidney would be given a peerage, the Webbs began to prepare for complete retirement. Sidney made what Beatrice hoped would be his last major speech, appropriately on the Poor Law. She felt that he was leaving Parliament with a good reputation, in spite of never having felt 'quite at home' in the House of Commons. 'Now that he is known to be retiring', she commented in a brisk epitaph on Sidney's parliamentary career,

> he is beginning to be appreciated as an odd but potent personality equally peculiar in his defects and his qualities, singularly unpretentious and obviously disinterested but without style or parliamentary gift. He is one of the 'characters' of the House and is always being caricatured as the enigmatic learned person, at once absurd and impressive, but, somehow or other, is trusted and followed by the Party of the Proletariat and who does not

hide his boredom, and contempt for the ignorance and indolence of the representatives of property and privilege. (29 November 1928)

As they neared retirement, it was noticeable that Sidney and Beatrice placed a greater store on their friendships. Sidney moved in a political world which was increasingly remote to him and was delighted to see his friends at weekends. Beatrice, alone at Passfield Corner during the week, needed intellectual stimulation and companionship. The Shaws, Herbert Samuel, Haldane, the Hendersons, the Woolfs, Ellen Wilkinson, and others all came to stay. At the same time they sought the friendship of younger, left wing intellectuals such as the Coles, Hugh Dalton and Kingsley Martin from whose ideas they could benefit. From 1926 Beatrice's diary entries centre as much on weekend house guests as on political analysis. Weekends in Hampshire became even more important in their lives than the intimate dinners of Grosvenor Road had been, so much so that Beatrice complained, 'if you happen to combine a hospitable temperament with old age or any other form of delicacy, you find yourself continually overtaxing your strength' (3 June 1927).

The Webbs remained on excellent terms with the Shaws, though Beatrice respected rather than liked Charlotte. For Shaw Beatrice always felt an irritated affection;

He never changes; he never grows old; he has the same delightful personality; he is less vain than he used to be – indeed he is not vain at all; he has lost the old bitterness and capacity for invective but that is perhaps due to his outstanding success. The wonder is not that he has lost the spirit of revolt, but that he has retained the demand for equality and consideration for the under dog . . . GBS and Sidney have both retained their power of work whilst I seem to have lost mine – I am sauntering through the days – doing little – except sketch out work for Sidney to do. (23 June 1926)

Their old friend Herbert Samuel also came to stay. They had known each other for many years and Beatrice happily noticed that

he has changed little, either in appearance or manners, or in outlook from the rich young man, conscientiously and energetically entering public life, whom we first knew nearly forty years ago. He is just a trifle stouter and more debonair; he is even *more* economical in personal expenditure, circumspect in behaviour and discreet in speech . . . Considering his marked success . . . he is in fact singularly modest . . . He is not exciting; his words have no pictures either of events or persons; his arguments are restricted in scope and his conclusions, though sensible, are commonplace . . . the recommendations of the Coal Commission are typical of Samuel's state of mind – sound but ineffectual – sound in doctrine but ineffectual in practice . . . Our long-standing relations with Herbert Samuel, like the man himself, have worn well. Three pedestrian minds enjoyed a weekend together and we parted with the kindliest feelings of mutual respect and friendship. (28 June 1926)

Beatrice was nothing if not clear-sighted about their friends.

They had begun to see more of another intimate friend, Haldane, who they feared was about to die. He was, Beatrice recorded,

a dear soul . . . his conduct has been well-nigh irreproachable. There are few friends who have been so continually friendly to us as R. B. Haldane; there are few men who have been more absorbed in the public good, and more beneficent to other human beings, to all and sundry according to their need . . . His one mental fault is a childish liking, mingled with a personal vanity, in being 'in the know' with, I will not say a finger, but whole hand in the pie! (19 November 1925)

Dispassionately dissecting their friendship, she wrote of Haldane that where he and the Webbs differed was, as she put it,

the difference between his scale of values and ours – the difference between the aristocrat caring for the free development of the select few and the democrat eager to raise the standard of the mass of men. In many ways these two aims can be pursued together . . . whenever and wherever this has been the case, Haldane and we have worked together . . . when you think of him relative to other men of talent, he stands out in a singular way. And this personality has attractive as well as salient factors; a genuine beneficence to his fellow men and amazing loyalty and kindness to his friends, especially when they are aged or

> unfortunate; an untiring public spirit and desire to serve the community, humour and wit, a massive power of mental work, and an increasing curiosity about men and affairs. (30 March 1926)

Haldane lingered on for another two years and, after a long illness, their 'most constant friend . . . passed away', Beatrice wrote in sorrow. It was Haldane, she admitted,

> who created and fostered the flattering 'Webb myth' that flowered so agreeably and advantageously for us and our schemes . . . Even when the idealised myth withered and was replaced by a caricature, Haldane was one of the few who, in spite of a certain disillusionment, remained faithful to an old friendship.

'What bound us together', Beatrice concluded

> was our common faith in a deliberately organised society – our belief in the application of science to human relations, with a view of betterment. Where we clashed was that *he* believed more than we did in the existing governing class . . . whilst we held by the common people, served by an elite of unassuming experts, who would appear no different in status from the common men. (21 August 1928)

They also grew closer to Arthur Henderson. Sidney, who had come to know and admire 'Uncle Arthur' during the war years kept up his friendship during the years of opposition. 'A first-rate *manager of men*', Beatrice rated him. 'The only one in the front rank of the Labour Movement. Without Arthur Henderson, Heaven help the Labour Party!' (10 September 1926). 'Was there ever a more sterling character than his?', she asked after a weekend spent with the Hendersons at Passfield,

> Conduct more uniformly guided by public spirit and personal devotion and good comradeship? He is thick-headed – intellectually clumsy instrument – but there is shrewdness in his judgement; the sort of realisation of the facts which arises from long experience of men and affairs and an absence of self-deception. Further, he is never elated and never gloomy – he just plods on

> along the chosen way towards some dimly perceived social betterment. (5 April 1927)

Rising young intellectuals, politicians and journalists were also encouraged to come down at weekends. As she grew older and more mellow, Beatrice began to feel more kindly towards the Coles, even though their earlier friendship had been marred by rows. She now thought of them as 'always attractive because they are at once disinterested and brilliantly intellectual . . . Middle age finds them saner and more charitable in their outlook' (5 September 1926). GDH, as she finally concluded, 'was an excellent citizen,' indefatigable in his work for the public good. Only lacking

> in humanity and sympathy – I think he is not interested in men; he is not interested in the working of their minds or in the drama of their relationships – he is curiously abstract in his ideas about society; he neither admires nor pities human nature; he is contemptuous of his fellow men – at best he tolerates and uses them . . . Despite desire to be rebels against all conventions the Coles are the last of the Puritans.

A year later Beatrice, in assessing the quality of the new young politicians coming through the Labour ranks, concluded that

> Hugh Dalton is probably the ablest of the younger men but he is obviously playing the political game; some of the Old Hands discount his capacity, whilst his contemporaries distrust his sincerity; Mosley, brilliant but without weight, deemed to be a political adventurer by as many Left as well as Right wing; CPT (Trevelyan) worthy but dull; W. Graham, weighty as well as worthy but if anything duller; Noel Buxton, a charming gentleman, but mediocre in intellectual calibre and physical strength. (5 April 1927)

Not all their friends were politicians, many were academics and a few like Leonard and Virginia Woolf provided an uneasy bridge between the literary and the political world. We know from Virginia Woolf's diaries that she was out of sympathy with the Webbs. Beatrice, however, felt more kindly towards the Woolfs. They were, she thought,

> wholly unconventional in their outlook on life and manners, belonging to a rather decadent set . . . but themselves puritanical – they are singularly attractive to talk to . . . (Leonard) is an anti-Imperialist fanatic, but otherwise a moderate in Labour politics . . . She is uninterested in politics – wholly literary – an accomplished critic of style and a clever artist in personal psychology. (5 February 1927)

All the same, Beatrice found it difficult both to like and understand Virginia's work. 'I do not find her work interesting,' she complained after reading a passage.

> Outside its craftsmanship which is excellent but *précieuse* her men and women do not interest me – they don't seem worth describing in such detail. The mental climate in which they live seems strangely lacking in light, heat, visibility and variety – it is a dank mist of insignificant and monotonous thoughts and feelings – no predominent aims, no powerful reactions from their mental environment – a curious impression of automatic existence when one state of mind follows another without any particular reason. To the aged Victorian this soullessness is depressing – doubtless our insistence on a Purpose whether for the individual or the Universe, appears to them a delusion and a pernicious delusion.

During these years, 'the aged Victorian' became fascinated by the new invention of the radio. She loved listening to music and on 28 February 1928 she made her first ever broadcast on Herbert Spencer in a series of personal reminiscences. Initially nervous, she recovered herself once she was in front of the microphone. 'Indeed, I rather enjoyed myself', she wrote. 'It was like rehearsing in one's bedroom. I had hardly any consciousness of being listened to, so private and quiet was the place one was in' (29 February 1928). Shaw sent her a congratulatory postcard: 'Immense success on the microphone, MUCH the best broadcast so far.'

In January 1929, their long association with the London School of Economics was celebrated by a reception to 'see the Webb portrait hung over the mantlepiece' (16 January 1929). The Webbs had reluctantly agreed to sit for a portrait which was to be hung in the Founder's Room. A pleasant waste of Sidney's time and my strength and other people's money . . . If it be desirable that the LSE should have a Webb seal – this particular seal will do as any other. What I think I have secured . . . is that Creighton and Haldane should hang on either side of us. Social revolutions, backed up by Law and Religion . . . are very Fabian because Fabianism respects and makes use of tradition. (5 May 1928)

'Altogether', Beatrice noted, amused after the reception, 'our stock is up – or rather we have, through old age, ceased to have detractors – no one troubles about aged folk, except those who respect and like them. Which adds to the pleasantries of life, though possibly also to its illusions' (16 January 1929).

At the beginning of May 1929 Parliament was dissolved. The general election was to be held on 30 May. The Webbs were on holiday in Greece and Turkey. Although Beatrice admired the Bay of Corinth and Delphi, she commented sharply on the Greeks and the Turks: 'The modern Greeks are not an attractive race, the Turks are horrid – alike in expression and form' (7 May 1929). Their visit to Turkey was made memorable by a meeting with the exiled Trotsky who was staying on the island of Prinkipo. Beatrice was favourably impressed:

He is a charming and accomplished man; looks more like an intellectual musician than an organiser of war and revolution. Opened in polished French with a suave and deferential claim to being one of our disciples who had strayed from our teaching! . . . I don't think we impressed each other with our respective arguments . . . I think beneath all his polished intellectualism, he has the closed mind of a fanatic who refuses to face the fact of Western democratic organisation. (7 May 1929)

The Webbs returned in time to hear the election results.

Sidney and I sat up with the Laskys until 2.30, listening to the flowing tide of Labour victories – almost hysterical at the prospect of Labour being a majority in the House . . . What has been accomplished is the final collapse of the Liberal Party . . . Considering their money, their press, their brilliant demogogic leader with his pledge 'to cure unemployment in one year', the failure to add even a score to their numbers is decisive. (1 June 1929)

Though the Conservatives had more votes than Labour (8 664 000 to 8 360 000), Labour won 287 seats to the Conservatives' 261: the Liberals polled 5 300 000 votes but only won fifty nine seats. It was clear that there would be another Labour minority government.

NOTES

1. S. Webb to B. Webb, 21 Feb 1925, Passfield Papers.
2. Ibid, 5 May 1926, Passfield Papers.
3. S. Webb to G. B. Shaw, 13 May 1926, Passfield Papers.
4. Ibid.
5. B. Webb to Friends of Seaham, Dec 1926, Passfield Papers.
6. D. Marquand, *Ramsay MacDonald*, p. 481.

13
1929–1931
Lords and Colonies

'It is agreeable to be treated with deference by a long procession of persons of importance.'

The minority Labour Government formed in 1929 only lasted two years. Although no longer at the centre of affairs, as a Cabinet minister Sidney played a part not only in the life of the government but also in the controversial events which led to its collapse and the formation of a National Government under Ramsay MacDonald.

Sidney and Beatrice had discussed Sidney's position in the event of a Labour victory. Both agreed that he should refuse a peerage unless it meant joining the government, although Beatrice was on the whole against the idea of Sidney, at the age of seventy, taking office again. However she accepted that he would like to be in the cabinet and that, despite her doubts, 'there is the all pervading *amour propre* . . . If he were *not* asked he would feel, and I should feel for him, slightly humiliated and depressed' (4 June 1929).

However, at midnight on 4 June, Sidney received a telegram from MacDonald which simply said 'phone me tonight'. Beatrice woke Sidney

> who came near swearing, trying to discover – still dazed with sleep – JRM's telephone number. He is to be up at Hampstead by nine. 'Wants to persuade you to accept a peerage without office', said I. 'I shall not do it' said he, and returned to his bed. I have asked him to telephone to Passfield, wither I go tomorrow at nine

o'clock, what exactly is the meaning of the midnight call. I begged him to assure JRM that he does not *want* office – that he will help in any way that is useful *except* going to the Lords without office. However, it is a nine hours' wonder and will soon be over. (5 June 1929)

The following day Sidney was offered and accepted a place in the Cabinet as Secretary for the Colonies and Dominions with a seat in the House of Lords as Lord Passfield. Beatrice gave the following account of the interview:

The interview ended in Sidney accepting a peerage in order to take over the Colonial Office. The immediate reason for this very handsome offer was that JRM, anxious to complete his Cabinet at once, had not complied with the constitutional requirements that there must be two Secretaries of State in the Lords. He immediately thought of Sidney for the job. Sidney was delighted with the C.O.: it is his old office as a civil servant, and one about which he knows a good deal more than about some others. Meanwhile I was at Passfield awaiting the news by telephone amply disguised by code. An odd compound of satisfaction for him, of tiredness, on my own part, and a rather morbid awareness of old age in both of us, came over me for the rest of the day. (6 June 1929)

So, almost by accident and at the advanced age of seventy, Sidney was back in the Cabinet.

Beatrice may have been happy for Sidney but she had grave reservations about using the title herself. It was partly a dislike of titles but more important was the question of whether the wife of a peer should be forced to adopt what was, after all, only a courtesy title. She considered that it was

a good thing to set the example of not considering a title as honourable to the person legally entitled to use it. And it is exactly this fact that by refusing to use a title you discredit it, but may cause a good deal of resentment on the part of the 'Powers that be' and may lead to a certain amount of disagreeableness. Owing to our peculiar position of acknowledged veterans in the Movement, our example will carry weight. Hence it seems worthwhile to break the convention . . . an Honour ignored is an honour deflated. (20 June 1929)

Ignoring the title was more difficult than she had anticipated, as the following letter from Ramsay MacDonald to Sidney testifies. 'You're getting me into hot water', he wrote,

> Stamfordham [Private Secretary to Queen Victoria and George V] drew my attention this evening to an H. M. Government invitation to Dominion teachers with the Royal Arms upon it, which says that Lord Passfield and Mrs Webb will receive. They object most strongly to this and have referred the matter to me. It is rather awkward as it does set a precedent which needs the consent of the King . . . Cannot you meet us on the matter?'

The Webbs agreed on a compromise; Beatrice's name was left out of official invitations (in any case she only rarely attended any functions), but she still insisted that her name was Mrs Webb as the following letter to the *Daily Mail* indicates:

> Sir – In reply to your courteous enquiry whether I wish to be called Mrs Sidney Webb or Lady Passfield, the answer is that I prefer to be named by my long-accustomed name, Mrs Sidney Webb, and I am so called by all my friends and associates. But I have no right to claim acquiescence from those who have no desire and are under no obligation to meet my wishes, Beatrice Webb (4 December 1930)

During the life of the Labour government, Beatrice continued to live mostly at Passfield, with Sidney coming down to the country at weekends. They changed their London home twice, moving from their old house in Grosvenor Road first to a flat in Whitehall Court which they found too costly ('an expensive slum') and then to a cheaper *pied-à-terre* in Albert Mansions, Victoria which was an easy distance from the House of Lords. On leaving Grosvenor Road, Beatrice wrote:

> Our last twenty four hours in the little house overlooking the Thames, where Sidney and I have spent, off and on, near forty years of married life – an amazingly happy and full life. I, certainly, feel relieved to be rid of it – or rather of the small part of the house which was still our possession. The untidy dingy dining room, the long tramp up three flights of stairs – fifty nine in all – to

> the two little garret bedrooms, and the dreadful noise, back and front, made the old home an unpleasant lodging for me on my occasional visits to London. For Sidney, with his preference for the habitual – it has served well. Incidentally we part company with Susan Lawrence: on the best of friendly terms, but without intimacy, given or taken. I respect and admire her – but I do not like her – a mixed reaction which I recognise that not a few persons have towards me! (29 September 1929)

Beatrice had sometimes to be in London. She did not accompany Sidney on many of his numerous official engagements, although she recorded sitting next to the Prince of Wales at a dinner at York House. She thought him neurotic and a near alcoholic with 'a horrid dissipated look as if he had no settled home either for his intellect or his emotions . . . if I were his mother or his grandmother, I should be very nervous about his future' (13 July 1930). However, she still took her duties as the doyenne of Labour Party hostesses seriously enough to invite over 200 MPs to lunch during the life of the Labour administration – a remarkable feat for a women in her seventies.

But there was no doubt that she much preferred her life in the country, as this extract from her diary shows:

> I love this little house in sunshine and rain; the absolute quietude during the night; the distant sounds now and again in the day; the long rambles in Woolmer Forest and Ludshott Common – honeymooning with my beloved or brooding alone with Sandy as my companion. And I enjoy the visits of friends; listening to the music and talks on the wireless. On the other hand social functions in London weary one past endurance in body and in mind – and if, by chance the people I meet excite and interest me – they excite and interest the wrong part of me and I feel the worse for it. The one pleasure of this episode is watching Sidney enjoying himself in his C.O. office work. He is conscious of doing it well. What troubles me is the off chance that my recalcitrancy might make matters less easy for him – might prejudice the smooth working of his official life. So I press him to accept invitations to dine with Colonial magnates and to be conciliatory towards the Court in the matter of uniform, etc. 'Let me be considered your morganatic wife living in a country cottage', I suggested. (4 August 1929)

Even so, she acknowledged that there were times when their separate lives depressed her:

> I shall be glad when Sidney retires as the lonely life down here, with the alternative of days and nights in London equally lonely, during the whole day, and with the discomforts of the little flat and the noise and bustle of the streets, are beginning to prey on my nerves – and might end in a bad breakdown. I am beginning to feel the *helplessness* of old age, which with me is masked by will power and physical activity; to other people I seem in full possession of my faculties – but in my own consciousness I am depressed and dazed – memory fails me – and I worry about this thing and that. (27 March 1931)

As Beatrice grew older she found it increasingly difficult to work for long stretches on any one project. She divided her time between preparing the next instalment of her autobiography (edited after her death by her niece Barbara Drake and Margaret Cole and published as *Our Partnership*), the occasional lecture, broadcast or pamphlet and reading Russian history and politics.

Beatrice's interest in Russia was stimulated by her friendship with the Soviet Ambassador, Gregor Sokolnikov, and his wife. In February 1930, Beatrice invited them down to stay at Passfield Corner. 'The Ambassador,' she noted, gave

> an impression of sincerity and honesty. His attractive little wife is an author – was correspondent of the *Izvestia* in China and has published a book on Women of the French Revolution. They spend most of their leisure in the British Museum reading room. Certainly they are strange members of the diplomatic circle. The Ambassador would be more at home as tutor in the W.E.A . . . in their simplicity and unpretentiousness the two were an attractive couple and we shall see more of them. (25 February 1930)

By June she was immersed in her Russian studies and as the situation deteriorated in her own country, she increasingly turned for inspiration to the Soviet Union.

On 30 July 1930, Beatrice gave a radio talk on 'Taking the Strain off Parliament', which she later turned into a *Political Quarterly* article and a Fabian pamphlet, called '*A New Reform Bill*'. Although its main themes are developments of ideas contained in the *Constitution for a Socialist Commonwealth*, it is clear from her diary that she was also influenced by her growing disillusionment with the performance of the Labour government and its failure to deal with unemployment. She began with a warning:

> There are many who think . . . that unless we can rationalise the constitution and activities of British Parliamentary institutions, so as to render them an efficient organ for continuous social adjustment and progress, there will ensue a slow decay of our standards of civilization; accompanied, it may be, by a dictatorship, either a Fascist dictatorship, in the interests of men of property and men of rank, or a Communist dictatorship in the assumed interest of the manual workers.[2]

Beatrice argued that though Parliament was overloaded 'The primary evil is an over-taxed Cabinet; over-taxed beyond human capacity for thinking and taking decisive action.' This over-taxing of the Cabinet both magnified the responsibilities of the bureaucracy and disabled and demoralised the House of Commons. Her main proposal for reform was to create a new devolved assembly, either split into separate Scottish, Welsh and English bodies, or combined together to be responsible for mainly social affairs, including employment, education, health, transport and agriculture. This assembly would be run as in local government by committee. She envisaged the House of Commons retaining its financial powers with monies being distributed to the devolved assembly through the grants-in-aid system used for local government. However, she did not rule out additional revenue being raised by the devolved authority.

It is perhaps significant that Beatrice should have sought to remedy the deficiencies of the Labour government not by new policies to bring down unemployment but by reforming the machinery of government. Even so, it can be seen from her proposals that the Webbs' commitment to democratic accountability and dispersal of power was confirmed rather than weakened by Sidney's experience of Cabinet government.

Sidney was delighted with his new position – it amused him to end his career as head of the department in which he had begun it. Others, such as Arthur Ponsonby were pleased to work with him: 'Webb is delightful to deal with . . . He is quick, ingenious, voluble; sees the point quickly but sometimes sees more points than is strictly necessary.'[3] Sidney admitted to Beatrice that it was 'agreeable to be treated with deference by a long procession of persons of importance' (21 June 1929). Beatrice was struck by the curious parallel between Sidney's and Joseph Chamberlain's careers; the latter

> first entered the Cabinet in 1880 as President of the Board of Trade; he finally retired from Cabinet rank in 1903 as Secretary of State for the Colonies. Sidney Webb first entered the Cabinet in 1924 as President of the Board of Trade; he is again a member of the Cabinet in 1929 as Secretary of State for the Dominions and Colonies.

But, unlike Chamberlain, Sidney can hardly be called a radical, innovative Colonial Secretary. He was already in his seventies, in any case, and his skills were never those of a political leader. On the other hand, he tried to deal with a number of intractable problems, particularly in East Africa and Palestine, with honesty and common sense.

The main issue facing Sidney in East Africa was the attempt by the white settlers of Kenya, led by Lord Delamere, and their allies in the Conservative Party to create a self-governing, settler-dominated, Kenyan state on the South African model, and to establish an East African Federation, including Tanganyika and Uganda, which, in the words of Lord Delamere, would lead to 'the solidification of the white ideal'. The settlers' demands centred on obtaining a 'settler' majority in the Kenyan Legislative Council. The previous Conservative Colonial Secretary, Leopold Amery, who was sympathetic to the 'white ideal' and in favour of federation, had set up the Hilton Young Commission to consider how 'closer union and co-operation between the territories may be most effectively secured'.

However, the Hilton Young Report, which was published in January 1929, endorsed the Devonshire White Paper of 1923 which had accepted the doctrine of native paramountcy and the importance of Britain's role as trustee of African interests – a role that the white settlers disputed.[4] It also underlined the need to create a partnership between all races in Kenya rather than the control aimed for by the whites. It even went so far as to support the principle of 'a common roll on an equal franchise with no discrimination between the races'. Closer union should be pursued by the appointment of a Higher Commission for East Africa. The

Report's recommendations, which amounted to an almost complete rejection of their position, infuriated the white settlers and disappointed Amery, who attempted to retrieve the situation by sending out to Kenya his Permanent Under-Secretary, Sir Samuel Wilson, to report on reactions in East Africa. Wilson came out in favour of federation and also backed the idea of a settler majority in the Kenyan Legislative Council, which angered the non-white population, particularly the Indians. Sidney was thus presented with two conflicting reports.

Even though Labour was a minority government, he had also to take into account the approach developed by Labour Party colonial experts like Charles Buxton, Leonard Woolf, Sydney Olivier, and Drummond Shields who became Sidney's Under-Secretary. The Labour Party's Advisory Committee on international questions had produced an important statement, *The Empire and Africa: Labour's Policy*, which put forward policies designed to lead to African self-government. Through increased aid for education, land reform, and development, the conditions would be created for native representation on legislative councils, followed by the gradual transfer of responsible government to the councils. It was extremely critical of the sale of vast areas of land to the whites in Kenya and argued that the right policy, as on the West Coast, was to treat land as the property of native communities. Labour's experts also believed that the white settlers' demands for a dominating voice on the Kenyan Legislative Council should be strongly resisted.

On taking office, Sidney's first reaction to the problem of 'paramountcy', was to discover 'what is practicable in the direction of racial equality – in the prevention of oppressive policy on the part of the White Settlers' (21 June 1929). He was under no illusion as to the aims of the Europeans; their policy, he told Beatrice, was 'to deprive the natives of land ownership and subject them to taxation in order that they should be at their mercy as wage-earners. The wrong turn was taken when the white settlers were given self-government and freed from the controls of Whitehall' (13 August 1929). His aim was to find his way 'to some compromise which would safeguard native interests as far as they can be safeguarded with the white settlers in possession of land and capital', although, according to Beatrice, he was aware that his gradualist approach 'will be denounced by idealists and no-one will be satisfied' (20 October 1929).

The Governor, Sir Edward Grigg, apparently chose to believe

that Sidney intended to implement the Wilson Report.[5] However, by November 1929, Sidney was reporting to the Cabinet about

> what he believed to be a wise compromise between the Hilton Young and Wilson Reports – a report which he suggested should be submitted to a Joint Committee of both Houses as the Cabinet proposals. But the left wing is in revolt – determined to have the blood of the settlers — to make them *feel* they are beaten. So the Cabinet decided that the document submitted to the Joint Committee should not be a scheme of reform but a memorandum *discussing* different proposals and that the Joint Committee is to be left to decided which proposals it would agree to. (28 November 1929)

In June 1930 Sidney published a White Paper on closer union, coupled with a Memorandum on Native Policy in East Africa.[6] The White Paper supported the idea of a High Commissioner for East Africa but the Memorandum came down decisively against the white settlers. The Memorandum accepted the goal of responsible government and argued that this could not be achieved in Kenya until the government represented 'an electorate in which every section of the population finds an effective and adequate voice'. It also proposed action in setting up a common roll and local native councils. Meanwhile, the trusteeship was to rest solely in the hands of the British government and, echoing the 1923 Devonshire Report, it reaffirmed that 'the interests of the African natives must be paramount and that if, and when, these interests and the interests of the immigrant races should conflict, the former should prevail.'[7]

Meanwhile, the Colonial Office under Sidney had been asserting itself in Kenya in other areas. It cut the budget of the Kenyan Defence Force which was a settler corps, slashed £20 000 from the road-building programme (roads affording greater benefit to the white man than to the native community) and attempted to end white obstruction of educational facilities for Africans. Sidney had also insisted that the Native Lands Trust Bill balanced any land taken over by the state with additions to native lands.

Not surprisingly given Sidney's support of native rights, the reaction of the Kenyan settlers to the two government papers – quickly dubbed 'the Black Papers' – was extremely hostile. Huge protest meetings were held in Nairobi, angry cables were despatched to Sidney in the Colonial Office, and large sections of the British press, as well as the Tory Party, gave vociferous support to the white settlers. Even the outgoing Governor General, Edward Grigg, in one of his final speeches before leaving Kenya, expressed his misgivings. Sidney hoped to diffuse the public outcry by the device of a joint committee of both Houses to consider the Hilton Young Report, the Wilson Report and the government's White Paper on closer union, although his intention was, with a new Governor in Kenya, to proceed to implement his Memorandum on Native Policy. In his speech to the House of Lords on 3 July 1930 he made the best of the government's minority position by stating that it was better 'especially in matters connected with native policy and constitutions, that we should go forward in any change with the united support . . . of all Parties, as far as possible'.[8]

The Report of the Joint Committee, published in October 1931 after the Labour government's fall, represented a step back from Sidney's policy. It watered down the principle of native paramountcy by declaring that it meant 'no more than that the interests of the overwhelming majority of the indigenous population should not be subordinated to those of a minority'; it argued that a common role was at present unobtainable; and it advised against closer union as being 'inopportune'.[9] However, for the future, it was perhaps more significant that a body, dominated by Conservatives, should have come down so decisively against a settler majority on the Legislative Council.

Clearly Sidney failed to implement any major advances in East Africa. In that sense critics, like Leonard Woolf (who called Sidney 'a common or garden imperialist Conservative' and claimed that he was in the hands of his civil servants) had justice on their side.[10] But on the other hand Sidney's determined and in the end successful opposition to white settler attempts to make Kenya into another South Africa was in itself no mean achievement.

The major problem in Palestine, which Britain ruled under a League of Nations Mandate, was the British commitment under the Balfour Declaration of 1917 to establish a Jewish national home – a promise which was not only considered inadequate by the Jews who wished to create a Jewish state, but was vehemently opposed by the Arab inhabitants of Palestine because they believed, with considerable justice, that any scheme designed to strengthen the Jewish presence would inevitably be at their expense.

In 1929 the Sixteenth Zionist Congress met at Zurich and, under the influence of Chaim Weizmann, approved the setting up of a

Jewish agency to promote Jewish settlements in Palestine. Not surprisingly the Arabs saw this new initiative as a direct threat to their land, particularly as a number of violently anti-Arab speeches were also delivered at the Congress. In August in the so-called 'Wailing Wall Incident', violence broke out in Jerusalem between Arabs and Jews, in which people lost their lives on both sides; and the British police, in attempting to quell the rioting, killed over a hundred Arabs. The High Commissioner of Palestine, Sir John Chancellor, immediately set up a Comission of Inquiry under the chairmanship of Sir Walter Shaw, a former Colonial Chief Justice, to enquire into the causes of the incident and 'to make recommendations as to the steps necessary to avoid a recurrence'. Sidney, as the incoming Secretary of State, had immediately to deal with this crisis.

Webb's handling of the Palestine issue has been strongly criticised, particularly by Weizmann, who charged him with being anti-Zionist, if not anti-Semitic.[11] It is true that in odd places in her diary and other writings Beatrice made comments with racialist undertones. But in her article for Charles Booth on the tailoring trade in the East End she had also showed that the Jewish middlemen were the victims and not the exploiters of popular imagination. There is no evidence at all that Sidney was anti-Semitic. On the other hand, though he was prepared to honour the commitment under the Mandate for some kind of Jewish national home, he was strongly against the idea of a Jewish state and believed in an even-handed approach towards Jew and Arab. On 2 September, Beatrice noted,

> Sidney annoys the agitated ones, by remaining . . . rather cold. Obviously order must be maintained in Judea; and the responsibility for the looting and murdering must be fixed and proper action taken to prevent recurrence. But the case for the Arab has not yet been heard; the case for the Jew has been vehemently and powerfully pressed on the government. The Zionist movement and the mandate for a National Home for the Jews in Palestine seems to have originated in some such unequal pressure exercised by the wealthy and ubiquitous Jew on the one hand and the poor and absent Arab on the other. (2 September 1929)

He was extremely uneasy about a big increase in Jewish immigration and land settlement because he felt that it would lead to Arab landlessness and unrest. However, his correspondence shows that he went out of his way to keep communications open with Weizmann and was scrupulous at dealing with any queries which Weizmann might put to him.

The Shaw Commission confirmed his misgivings.[12] It found that the underlying cause of unrest was Arab hostility towards the Jews, arising from the fear that Jewish immigrants would eventually deprive Arabs of their land and livelihood. As to the future, it recommended that the British government should issue a clear statement of policy defining its attitude 'concerning the safeguarding of the rights of non-Jewish communities and laying down more explicit directions as to the conduct of policy on such vital issues as land tenure and immigration'. The Commission also proposed more control over Jewish immigration and that the eviction of peasant cultivators from the land should be checked.

The Prime Minister, concerned about Jewish reaction, at once saw that the report would be criticised as being pro-Arab. Beatrice commented that the Palestine Commission

> after adjudicating on the immediate occasion of disorder in August, deliver *obiter dicta* on the impracticability of a national home for the Jews without asking the Arabs – which course they deprecate as inconsistent with the pledges under the Mandate – the Mandate is, they imply, self-contradictory and ought to be revised. The Prime Minister was much perturbed. (30 March 1930)

MacDonald proposed that General Smuts should be asked to carry out an inquiry into the Mandate but as Smuts' pro-Zionist sympathies ruled him out, Sidney suggested the name of John Hope Simpson, who was an authority on the resettlement of populations and whom the Webbs had met as a civil servant on their visit to India in 1911, to enquire into the problems of Palestinian land settlement, immigration and development.

The Hope Simpson Report, published simultaneously with a White Paper accepting its proposals, recommended a large scale investment programme to resettle and educate landless Arabs.[13] Piecemeal buying of land by individual Jewish settlers was to be discouraged. Another feature of the Report was its strong criticism of the Jewish refusal to employ Arab labour, although it accepted that Jewish capital, which increased possibilities of employment, ought to be encouraged. It also proposed that a maximum of about 20000 further Jewish families should be allowed to enter the country.

Although the Report and the White Paper could justly be considered as 'fair and balanced'[14] the Jewish lobby immediately reacted to the British government's attempt at even-handedness.

Sidney had no trouble getting the White Paper through Cabinet. 'I got my great draft declaration policy on Palestine through Cabinet Committee today, easily enough', he wrote to Beatrice early in September. 'Snowden, Thompson and Thomas expressed admiration for it. It is really the work of the office in consultation with Sir John Campbell, Sir John Chancellor and Sir John Hope Simpson, on my instructions.'[15] Sidney, hoping also to neutralise Weizmann, saw him a number of times before publication, as the following letter indicates:

> I hasten, as promised, to send you proof of Hope Simpson's Report . . . together with proof of the Statement of Policy, which will be published next week. I am sure I need not assure you that very great consideration has been given by the government to this statement – latterly in the light of the representations that you have made, which have all been carefully weighed, and certain adjustments have been made in consequence of those representations. I do not hide from myself that the position is grave in some respects: but I am not without hope that you may find, on careful reading, that I have in my talks with you concentrated rather unduly on what seems the adverse elements. We can, at least, try to make the best of the situation.[16]

However, despite Sidney's hopes, Zionist reaction was fierce and worldwide. Eminent Jews such as Lord Melchett and Felix Warburg resigned from the chairmanships of various Zionist bodies and Weizmann himself resigned as secretary of the World Zionist organisation. Sidney did not seem able to comprehend the strength of Zionist feeling. On 22 October he wrote to Beatrice,

> The Jewish hurricane continues . . . They seem to go wild with excitment and rage on mere partisan telegraphic summaries and interpretations of a lengthy document. We are (1) putting *no* limitations on continued colonisation, (2), making no changes as regards the previous limit on non-rural immigration and (3), expressly and defiantly declaring that we will carry out the Mandate whatever the Arabs say or do. The Jews have therefore no *ground* of complaint against us. But we *do* negative the idea of a

> Jewish state which the British government has consistently done – and this (rather than a National Home *in* Palestine) is what so many of them want.[17]

If Sidney was detached, Ramsay MacDonald, under attack not only from Baldwin, Chamberlain and Amery who accused the government of abandoning the principle embodied in the mandate in a letter to *The Times* on 30 October, but also from sections of the Labour Party, decided to give way. The Prime Minister took Palestine affairs temporarily away from Sidney and put them under the control of a Cabinet Committee, in which the Foreign Office was strongly represented. And on 14 February 1931, he repudiated the White Paper in a letter to Weizmann.

How far was MacDonald's repudiation a fair comment on the merits of Sidney's policy? It is possible to argue that his strategy of 'even-handedness' was, as the Cabinet itself agreed, a reasonable attempt to make sense of Britain's conflicting commitments under the mandate. Its weakness – that it could only work if the Jews were prepared to accept a minority status in Palestine – was, after all, only a reflection of the underlying ambiguity of the mandate. Where Sidney was more open to criticism was his failure to carry his colleagues, and particularly his Prime Minister, with him at the crucial time. Sir Drummond Shiels commented that Sidney 'did not carry the weight in the Cabinet that he should have done and, in some of his best efforts, he did not get the backing he should have got'.[18] The trouble was that, at the moment when the Labour government was already under increasing pressure, particularly on unemployment, Sidney's approach to the Palestine issue, however intelligently and rationally conceived, was bound to be criticised by an extremely vocal Jewish community – a reaction which MacDonald was obviously anxious to deflect.

It is also legitimate to ask, as did a number of his friends and colleagues at the time, why Sidney did not resign. In June 1930, his Dominion secretaryship had been taken away from him and given to J. H. Thomas. Now his Palestine responsibilities had been removed and his policy overturned by the Prime Minister. Apparently Webb believed that resignation would harm the Labour Government. In February 1931, he wrote to his colleague, Lord Amulree, giving his reasons for staying on.

> Some Ministers would have resigned rather than stand what I have had to stand since last October. But my resignation would

have aggravated the Government's troubles: and I don't do that sort of thing. So I have put up with everything, and allowed the direction to be taken out of my hands . . . It has been a bad three months: and all the more vexatious because there was really nothing in the White Paper of October (which the Cabinet itself passed) to which the Jews can honestly object.[19]

He was also concerned about the question of government representation in the House of Lords. In any case, Beatrice's diary entries for the 14 December 1930 and 18 April 1931 make it quite clear that Sidney had decided to retire as soon as he possibly could.

Meanwhile, as Sidney wrestled with the problems of Kenya and Palestine, the pressures on the government mounted. The Labour Party had owed its advance at the 1929 election partly to its promise to reduce unemployment. However, the Wall Street crash of October 1929 had a disastrous impact on business confidence, American lending to Europe, and world trade generally. The economies of the industrialised countries were plunged into a deep recession. In Britain, unemployment soared and by December 1930 had reached 2 725 000 or 20 per cent of the insured population. In May 1931 the failure of the Vienna Bank, the Credit Anstalt, immediately affected confidence in German banking, which spread to other European countries. The Labour government now had to deal not only with trade recession and unemployment, but also with a crisis in the international banking system and a run on British gold reserves.

Beatrice's diary showed that the Webbs were concerned about the government's failure to organise itself to deal with the unemployment issue. As early as July 1929 Beatrice was critical of J. H. Thomas, the Lord Privy Seal, and Chairman of the Cabinet Committee on Unemployment.

Oswald Mosley and Lansbury, his lieutenants, report that Thomas does not see them; that he is in the hands of that arch-reactionary, Horace Wilson – my old enemy – whom he calls 'Orace' and obeys implicitly; that he refuses to sit down and study the plans proposed and therefore cannot champion them in the House. That he gets 'rattled' and when not under the influence of drink or flattery, is in an abject state of panic about his job. (28 July 1929)

In November she pointed out that 'all the more courageous and gifted men in the Cabinet – are absorbed in Foreign Affairs and government of the British Empire' (9 November 1929). In December she reported that Henderson was

> most concerned about the collapse of Thomas – who was completely rattled and in such a state of panic that he is bordering on lunacy . . . Henderson is now suggesting to the Prime Minister that he himself must take the subject in hand; but there must be a committee of Home defence against poverty, that Cole must be engaged if possible and a proper department started . . . and that Jimmy, who is drinking heavily, must be sent away for a rest and Oswald Mosley installed and the Council to carry out agreed plans . . . What worries Henderson is the lack of any real organisation of Cabinet business, especially with regard to finance. Ministers come, one by one, with demands for money to successive Cabinet meetings – There is no kind of survey of their respective demands with a view to discovering which of the proposals are most important. (2 December 1929)

But as the unemployment crisis grew in intensity, there is no evidence that Sidney made any significant contribution to Cabinet debates or, indeed, had any contribution to make. In May 1930, Mosley, after the Cabinet's refusal to adopt the expansionist policies contained in his famous memorandum, resigned. Beatrice noted that the Mosleys, who dined with the Webbs the night before his resignation, were 'sincere and assiduous in their public aims', but Sidney doubted whether Oswald had sufficient judgement and knowledge to lead the Labour Party in home affairs (19 May 1930). In the argument over protection (advocated by Keynes, a member of the newly set up Economic Advisory Council, and Herbert Henderson, its assistant secretary, and given some support by the Prime Minister) Webb was on the side of the free traders led by Snowden. Again, in the crisis of August 1931, Sidney broadly supported the Prime Minister and Snowden in their acceptance of the May Committee's proposals for bringing the budget into balance by cuts in public spending, including cuts in unemployment benefits. After meeting TUC representatives on 20 August, Beatrice reported Sidney as saying

> the General Council are pigs . . . they won't agree to any 'cuts' of unemployment insurance benefits and salaries or wages . . . He thinks JRM has behaved in all good faith over the whole business . . .What with the sabotage by the Capitalists of the Labour Cabinet administration and the sabotage of British industry by trade union pig-headedness, the prospect is extremely disturbing to public spirited citizens. (22 August 1931)

The most telling comment was Sidney's own observation that

> he would have resented being excluded from the consultations of the inner Cabinet about the financial position if it were not that he feels that he knows no more than other people about the real situation of the British people in the world welter, and he has no clear idea of the way out.

Why did the leading intellectual in the Cabinet have so little to contribute? After all, the second section of the Minority Report had contained specific recommendations to deal with unemployment. In periods of depression, the Webbs had suggested a counter-cyclical programme of government projects to be financed by borrowing. Why did Sidney not put forward proposals on these lines or at least give his support to Mosley?

It is, of course, true that Sidney was immersed in his duties as Colonial Secretary. As Beatrice recorded some months after the Wall Street crash: 'Sidney goes plodding on at the Colonial Office far too absorbed in his problems . . . to think about unemployment or any other home questions and not inclined to criticise his colleagues' (7 August 1930). He was also, as we have seen, waiting to retire. But there is perhaps a more fundamental reason. The Webbs had envisaged their Minority Report proposals being put into operation in a context of relative prosperity. As Beatrice made clear in the closing paragraph of *Our Partnership*, they had not foreseen such a sudden and catastrophic collapse. It is ironic that, only a year after the fall of the government, the Swedish Social Democrats, partly drawing on the ideas of the Webbs, should have successfully introduced a counter-cyclical, public spending programme which helped reduce unemployment substantially.[20]

Although the chief lesson the Webbs drew from the economic crisis was the need for a fully socialist economy on the Soviet model, Beatrice also had the feeling that they might have been able to think through the problems more effectively if they had been younger. In her diary entry at the height of the 1931 crisis, she remarked that in 1930

> the Labour Government was being urged by the Liberal Party and Keynes and other economists – and even by the Conservative opposition – to *prevent* Unemployment, by setting to work the unemployed . . . Today they are being advised on every side, *to dismiss men and women* engaged in Government work of proved usefulness. It all seems idiotic, this senseless swaying to and from the slogan of 'spend more', to that of 'save more', without having the remotest notion of what the country is 'spending' or what the country is 'saving', and how and why either the 'spending' or the 'saving' is being done, by whom and for whose benefit. . . . If we were 30 years younger, I would throw our whole energies into clearing up this mass of uncertainties so that we could build a sound foundation. (22 August 1931)

The fall of the Labour government and the formation of the National government under MacDonald has been the subject of acute controversy, not only within the Labour Party but also amongst historians.[21] Sidney himself wrote two full accounts, one a private memorandum written in September 1931, the other an article published in the *Political Quarterly* in January 1932. There is also a letter from Sidney to Beatrice, written on 24 August, the day of the last Labour Cabinet meeting, as well as Beatrice's diary entries for the crisis. In addition, there is a letter (both in draft and final form) from Sidney to Malcolm MacDonald, the Prime Minister's son, dated 9 January 1932.

The Webb version, as put forward in the *Political Quarterly* and the September memorandum, was that MacDonald was seduced by the embrace of 'the British governing class' and had been determined for some time to bring about a National government. It was 'a single drama, in all its development foreseen in advance, it is safe to say, only by the statesman who was at once its author, its producer, and its principal actor'.[22] Basset and Marquand, however, argue that MacDonald was only pursuaded at the last moment by the King that it was his duty to form a National government, and that the Webb account was a *post-ipso facto* rationalisation.

It is certainly true that both the September 1931 memorandum and the *Political Quarterly* article were written soon after the event.

The *Political Quarterly* article was in part an exercise in political propaganda following on Labour's disastrous defeat in the 1931 election. But the idea that MacDonald was involved in a plot stemmed from 24 August 1931 – the day of the last Labour Cabinet meeting. Beatrice described how, following the Cabinet meeting at which MacDonald announced that he had been asked to form a National government, Sidney, Henderson, Lansbury and six other Labour cabinet ministers lunched together: 'There was a certain relief that their association with MacDonald was at an end, and a very distinct opinion that he had meant to come out as Premier of a National government, all through these latter days of panic and confusion' (25 August 1931).

The weakness of the 'plot' theory is not so much when it was formulated but the lack of evidence for it. In the September memorandum, Sidney referred to 'various cryptic utterances, by various persons which the subsequent events have both elucidated and recalled to memory'. Beatrice also noted that 'Arnold reports that Lansbury told him that JRM spoke to him casually at the end of July after the issue of the May report as to the desirability of a National government' (27 August 1931). There is also MacDonald's July letter to Sidney, after Sidney had asked to be relieved of his office, 'As you know, I am in the most awful difficulty about the House of Lords . . . We have not the material in our Party that we ought to have. The solution will have to come, I am afraid, by moves which will surprise all of you' (14 July 1931). But none of these substantiate the 'plot' theory. 'Cryptic utterances to various persons' is hardly convincing, while Lansbury, who often crossed swords with MacDonald, is not the most trustworthy of witnesses. As Basset points out, the July letter is open to a very different and much more likely interpretation.[23] MacDonald was clearly referring to the imminent Cabinet reshuffle of which Sidney's retirement would have been a part.

However, a stronger case can be made for a less 'conspiratorial' version of MacDonald's actions to which, at different times, Beatrice and Sidney also subscribed. In the conclusion to the draft reply to a letter from Malcolm MacDonald, complaining about the *Political Quarterly* article, Sidney wrote

> Psychologically it is a case of a complicated mind, habitually running together all possible alternative courses . . . tentatively following out one, and then another; and not coming to any

decision between them, as to what to do when the actual crisis comes – meanwhile taking wholeheartedly the action necessary from day to day – so as to have ready at the final moment, with rival courses still open, fairly well informed and mature decisions, according to the hypothesis ultimately chosen.[24]

Beatrice put the same point in a less complimentary but more succinct way:

> I don't believe that Mac deliberately led the Cabinet into a trap: tried to get them into agreeing to economies in process of bargaining with the USA financiers, all the time intending to throw his colleagues over and form a National Government – *but he drifted into doing it* . . .

What is undoubtedly true is that MacDonald had thought himself into a frame of mind which made it possible for him to become head of a 'National' government, even if it meant cutting himself off from the Labour Party. All through the summer of 1931, admittedly usually with the support of Cabinet, he had been seeing the opposition leaders. The idea of a National government was very much in the air. In the year before the crisis, Garvin, editor of *The Observer*, Lloyd George and Churchill had all discussed it publicly. In September 1930 MacDonald himself wrote to John Buchan in a non-committal but generally favourable terms about a National government.

> I have done everything I possibly can to make such a thing possible. If there is any desire for it, I think that an election within the next two years would be a very bad thing for the country and I shall be no party to forcing it. If others will come to any other reasonable agreement to prevent it, I shall not stand in its way and will be very glad to go into the background if that will make it easy.[25]

When Macdonald first told the Labour Cabinet on 22 August that the King favoured a Coalition with Labour participation as a way out of the crisis, it is significant that Sidney felt that, though Henderson and other members of the Cabinet strongly objected, 'JRM, Snowden and Jimmy [Thomas] might *consider it*' (23 August). Clearly, even before the King's direct appeal to

MacDonald on 23 August to stay in office, Sidney believed that MacDonald's inclinations were in that direction.

As to MacDonald's relations with the Labour Party, the Webbs believed with some justice that he had gradually distanced himself from it. At the 1926 TUC Conference, Beatrice wrote that MacDonald's thoughts and emotions 'are concentrated in his agreeable relations with the men and women – especially the women – of the enemy's camp . . . he is becoming impatient with the troublesomeness of the working class' (1926 TUC Conference). In 1929 she wrote that

> what is only too clear is that the inner circle of the Cabinet – the PM, Henderson, Snowden, Thomas and Clynes – are not working together with any mutual confidence or personal sympathy. The PM invites none of these colleagues to Chequers – but he does invite smart society dames whom he meets casually. Again the disastrous consequences of radically wrong social environment for a Labour Cabinet – it throttles the brain of the Labour Movement. The leaders ought to live with each other and among their own people – They ought to remain a tight bundle of sticks. As it is, the bundle is dispersed and each stick broken on the lap of luxury and social prestige. (23 September 1929)

In his September memorandum, Sidney claimed that since the beginning of the Labour government 'The Prime Minister became steadily more and more out of sympathy with every section of his Party . . . with the intelligentsia of the party, equally with the workmen and with the pacifist and utopian element among which he had originally ranged himself. He has completely changed his *milieu*.'

There is also the further point made by Marquand: MacDonald 'had always believed that party loyalty could conflict with higher or international loyalties, and that it should come second if it did. That was why he had gone against his party in 1914: as he saw it, 1931 was 1914 all over again'.[26] Webb himself wrote that he did not wish to suggest that in accepting the leadership of a National government MacDonald had done wrong in his assumptions of what the country required (September memorandum). Certainly the King was able to appeal to a highly developed sense of what admirers called duty. Others, less charitably, saw MacDonald's acceptance as the vanity of one who believed himself to be the 'saviour' of his country. The country would not necessarily have suffered more if he had taken the advice of his colleagues and stood down, in favour of a Conservative/Liberal Coalition: nor would the Labour Party have been so disastrously defeated at the ensuing election.

However, whatever the motives for MacDonald's actions, the fact remains that, in the crisis, he was prepared to 'ditch' the Labour Party. MacDonald believed it right to form a National government to keep the parity (although on 21 September the National government left the gold standard) even though he knew that such a government would be rejected, not only by his Cabinet colleagues, but by the Parliamentary Labour Party. It is instructive to contrast Sidney's approach. Sidney had backed the Prime Minister's proposal for a 10 per cent cut in unemployment benefit in the crucial eleven to nine Cabinet vote of 23 August. But, though Sidney might agree with MacDonald that cuts were necessary, once the minority, led by Henderson, had said that they would resign, the issue became different. A Baldwin-led government could easily implement the cuts. The priority for Sidney was to help preserve the Labour Party. So after the final Cabinet meeting on 25 August, Sidney immediately joined the dissident ministers who were meeting at the Office of Works to discuss Labour's future.

The Webbs, who had been so noncommittal about the infant Labour Party in the early 1900s, in the end put Labour first, because they clearly understood that, with all its faults and weaknesses, it was the only possible vehicle in Britain for their socialist beliefs.

NOTES

1. J. R. MacDonald to S. Webb, 31 July 1929, Passfield Papers.
2. *Political Quarterly*, vol. I, Jan 1930.
3. Private diaries of Lord Arthur Ponsonby of Shulbrede, 15 and 18 July 1929. Printed by kind permission of the present Lord Ponsonby.
4. Hilton Young Report, CMD 3234.
5. G. Bennett, *A Political History of Kenya*, p. 69.
6. Report of the Commission on Closer Union of the Dependencies in Eastern and Central Africa, CMD 3234. Memorandum on Native Policy, CMD 3573.
7. CMD 3573.
8. *Hansard*, House of Lords, 3 July 1930, col. 289.
9. Report of the Joint Committee. Published Oct 1931.
10. L. Woolf, *Downhill all the Way*, pp. 236–237.

11. See Chaim Weizmann: 'Trial and Error' in Christopher Sykes, *Cross Roads to Israel From Balfour to Bevin*.
12. Shaw Commission Report, Published Mar 1930, CMD 3530.
13. Hope Simpson Report, Aug 1930, White Paper in Palestine, CMD 3692.
14. Drummond Shiels in *The Webbs and their Work*, ed. M. Cole, p. 214.
15. S. Webb to B. Webb, 10 Sept 1930, Passfield Papers.
16. S. Webb to Chaim Weizmann, 17 Oct 1930, WI.
17. S. Webb to B. Webb 22 Oct 1930, Passfield Papers.
18. Drummond Shiels in *The Webbs and their Work*, ed. M. Cole, p. 218.
19. S. Webb to Lord Amulree 10 Feb 1931, Bodleian.
20. See F. Castles, *The Social Democratic Image of Society*.
21. See D. Marquand, *Ramsay MacDonald*, R. J. Skidelsky, *Politicians & the Slump*, R. Basset, *Nineteen Thirty One*.
22. *Political Quarterly*, Jan–Mar 1932.
23. Basset, *Nineteen Thirty One*.
24. S. Webb to Malcolm MacDonald, draft reply, Jan 1932, Passfield Papers.
25. Quoted in D. Marquand, *Ramsay MacDonald*, p. 575.
26. Ibid, p. 641.

14
1931–1933
The Webbs in Russia

'A new civilisation with a new metaphysic.'

With the formation of the National government and its subsequent crushing victory in the October election, Sidney's active involvement in politics ended. It would have been entirely understandable if the Webbs, now both in their mid-seventies, had accepted a life of quiet retirement at Passfield Corner. Instead, following their visit to Russia in 1932, they wrote their long and highly controversial study of the Soviet system, *Soviet Communism: a New Civilisation?*, published in 1935.

How could the authors of the *Socialist Commonwealth*, which proposed a strong democratic structure based on a system of countervailing checks and balances, a considerable dispersal of power and a meaningful level of participation, support one of the most oppressive of totalitarian regimes, even to the extent of removing the question mark from the title in the second edition published in 1937? For the explanation of this apparent volte-face, we need to examine the reasons why the Webbs went to Russia and their account of the Soviet system.

The moving force behind the Webbs' Russian trip was undoubtedly Beatrice. She had not always been enthusiastic about the Soviet Union. In 1924, writing to Dr Sarolea, Professor of French at Edinburgh University, who had sent the Webbs his book on the Soviet regime, Beatrice replied that she had been very much interested in his experiences of 'that very doubtful paradise', but she went on to say that

> my husband and I have always been against the Soviet system, and have regarded it as a repetition of Russian autocracy based on a creed – a very Eastern conception. But some interesting experiments may be the result, though I am afraid the conclusion will be more negative than positive . . . By the way, my husband and I have never been state socialists as you seem to imply in some passage of your book – we have always advocated municipal and co-operative organisation as preferable to nationalisation for any but one or two industries.[1]

It was her disillusionment with Western capitalism that turned her thoughts towards Russia. She honestly admitted that 'all this new structure and function in Soviet Russia would not be exciting attention among intellectuals and social reformers of all countries . . . if it were not for the material and moral collapse of capitalism' (14 May 1932).

While Sidney had been immersed in his ministerial duties, she had had the time to reflect on the crisis of Western society. If it was true, as the daily news bulletins from her wireless seemed to suggest, that capitalism was in a state of terminal decay, then Fabian socialism, instead of gradually supplanting capitalism, was likely to be carried away with it. What might have been an appropriate solution in the 1900s or immediately after the war did not seem relevant in the 1930s. 'What I am beginning to doubt is the inevitability of gradualness or even the practicability of gradualness in the transition from a capitalist to an equalitarian civilisation' (4 February 1931).

In the closing months of the Labour government, she embarked on a study of the literature on the new Russian regime, assisted by the Russian ambassador and his wife. Her growing sense of excitement and discovery was reflected in her diaries. On 22 June, 1930, she noted that

> the Russian Communist Government may still fail to attain its end in Russia as it will certainly fail to conquer the world with a Russian brand of communism, but its exploit exemplifies the Mendelian view of sudden jumps in biological evolution as against the Spencerian vision of slow adjustment . . . The Russian ruling class seems superior to the Anglo Saxon, a humiliating thought for the two English-speaking races.

On 30 June she summarised a report from the British ambassador in Moscow which Sidney had shown her:

> The gist is that Soviet communism is firmly established and increasing its hold day by day in the medley of peoples making up the Russian empire. Communism he holds is analagous to Mohammedanism of mediaeval times, it is a potent religion which is sweeping through continents – and like Mohammedanism and all other religions will sweep on until it finds its margin of cultivation. And he believes the Communist Party will succeed in destroying the Capitalist system within its territories and will bring into practice a way of life based on common property, equality of income and the supremacy of the workers' interests. Autocracy is indigenous in Russia and will survive in the Soviet Republic as a political constitution. What has been revolutionised is the *purpose* of Government, which is, under Communism, to bring about a millenium through the transformation of the motives of man – only in *this* world and not in a mystical after-life. (30 June 1931)

On 28 December 1930 she commented on two books they had read during the Christmas holidays. Adams *Searchlight on America* and H. G. Harben's *Diary of His Russian Tour*.

> The two reports are of unequal value; Harben's is a mere traveller's tale cleverly told; but its hopefulness is catching and then its conclusions about the success of the five Years [Plan] are borne out by the reports of Americans who have been contractors and technicians over there. Adams summarises the experience of a lifetime, spent in business and study. Though he is clearly no socialist his book is a startling indictment of Capitalism as practised in the USA – a terrible indictment – not from the standpoint of the toiling masses whose high wages he grudges! but from that of the professional middle class. Whether this preoccupation with the interests of the intellectual aristocracy be justified or not, the indictment itself leaves the reader under the impression that the USA will crash into some sort of civil war or forcible dictatorship through sheer incapacity of its democracy to maintain law and order and to check corruption, and blackmail in public services and private enterprise. On the other hand

> Russia may succeed in building up a disciplined and purposeful equalitarian state at the cost of a period of terrorism with the loss of intellectual freedom. Certainly the daily life – whether of work or recreation – of the Russian Communist has become intensely serious and public spirited, whilst that of the USA citizen is becoming increasingly dominated by pecuniary gain and frivolous pleasure. (28 December 1930)

As the economic crisis in the West deepened, she deplored the failure of Western economists to consider 'the facts' and regretted that their age prevented the Webbs from undertaking a reassessment of economic theory. In Soviet Russia, things were apparently very different: 'That is why the Russian experiment is so fascinating. They are daring to test their assumptions by observation and experiment – their very ruthlessness may spell failure – but the endurance and subserviency of the Russian people may enable them to pull through' (25 March 1931). By June 1931 she was making confident generalisations about the character of the Soviet citizen and drawing distinctions between the Russians and the West. 'The distinction between Soviet citizens on the one hand and on the other of American or German, British or French citizens', she wrote,

> lies in their respective outlook on the Mediaeval sin of *Covetuousness* – on the desire for personal property or profit in hand – a sin which was turned into a virtue by the Economists of the Industrial Revolution. It is *greed*, pecuniary self-interest, that is the Soviet Devil – the source of all wickedness and this bears on *honesty* and honour in public affairs. (30 June 1931)

During August Shaw, recently returned from a visit to Russia, extolled the regime in such glowing terms that even Beatrice was sceptical.

> He was tired and excited by his visit to Russia: carried away by the newness and the violence of the changes wrought. Here is tragedy, comedy, melodrama, all magnificently staged on a huge scale. It *must* be right! The paradox of the speech: Russian revolution with pure Fabianism – Lenin and Stalin had recognised the '*Inevitability of gradualness*'! Also they had given up 'workers' control' for the Webbs' conception of the three-fold

> state – citizens, consumers and producers' organisation. What is not Webbism or Western, is the welding together of all three by a *Creed* oligarchy of two million faithful, dominating a population of 120 million indifferent, luke-warm, or actively hostile. That is the crux of the controversy between those who approve or disapprove of Soviet Russia. It is odd that it is this domination by a creed that seems so attractive to GBS; he being that great destroyer of existing codes, creeds and conventions, seems in his old age, to hanker for some credo to be *enforced* from birth onwards on the whole population.

But even if Shaw's antics amused her, his support for the Soviet Union was bound to add to Beatrice's fascination and eagerness to visit Russia.

Once the Labour government had fallen there was nothing to hold back the Webbs from their journey. On 10 September 1931, Beatrice wrote,

> In the course of a decade, we shall know whether American Capitalism or Russian Communism yields the better life for the bulk of the people . . . In view of this conclusion, how shall we spend our old age? Am I strong enough to go to Russia to give vividness to any line we take? Can we master the intricacies of capitalist finance sufficiently to be able to expose its futility? For without doubt, we are on the side of Russia. (10 September 1931)

There was also little doubt that the Webbs would go to Russia. Sidney and she settled down to an intensive course of reading in preparation for their trip.

As they worked happily and industriously together they began to build up a picture of the Soviet system – a system which they believed to be an irresistible amalgam of the democratic constitution they had put forward in their *Socialist Commonwealth* and of a powerful secular faith. On 4 January 1932, Beatrice noted;

> The Soviet constitution – the secular side of it – almost exactly corresponds to our constitution – there is the same tripod of political democracy, vocational organisation and the consumers' co-operative movement. And the vocational or trade union is placed in exactly the same position of subordination as we suggested. Also the position of the separately organised

consumers' co-operative societies is similar to ours. There is no d . . . ' nonsense about Guild Socialism! But the spotlight of intriguing difference between the live creation of Soviet Russia, and the dead body of the Webb constitution, is the presence, as the dominant and decisive force, of a religious order: the Communist Party, with its strict discipline, its vows of obedience and poverty. Though not requiring chastity, Communists are expected to be puritan in their personal conduct, not to waste energy, time or health, on sex, food or drink. The exact opposite of the D. H. Lawrence cult of sex which I happen to detest. It is the invention of the religious order, as the determing factor in the life of a great nation, which is the magnet that attracts me to Russia. Practically that religion is Comteism – the religion of Humanity. Auguste Comte comes in to his own. Whether he would recognise this strange resurrection of his idea I very much doubt. Of course the stop in my mind is: how can we reconcile this dominance of a religious order, imposing on all citizens a new orthodoxy, with the freedom of the soul of man, without which science – that sublime manifestation of the curiosity of man – would wither and decay? How can we combine religious zeal in action with freedom of thought? That is the question we want to solve by studying Russia.

If Sidney was more interested in the Russian constitution, the belief that they might discover a new secular creed in operation was of particular importance to Beatrice. 'Personally, being a mystic and a moralist, I always hankered after a spiritual path: always felt instinctively that there *must* be some such a force, if salvation were to be found' (4 June 1932). Though Sidney was cautious enough to warn her not to 'become a monomaniac about Russia' (14 May 1932), the journey for her was a kind of pilgrimage in search of a new faith. 'The experiment is so stupendous, alike in area, in numbers involved, in variety, in speed, in intensity – in technological change and necessary alteration in human behaviour and human motive, that one's mood alternates between the wildest hopes and the gloomiest fears' she wrote.

All I know is that I *wish* Russian Communism to succeed – a wish which tends to distort one's judgement. When one becomes aware of this distortion, one has 'cold feet'. To be for or against Soviet Communism is, today, a big gamble of the intellect. Will our pilgrimage to Moscow bring enlightenment or rightly measured judgement: are events ripe for such an evaluation? (5 April 1932)

The Russia which the Webbs visited with such high hopes in 1932 was in the grips of the first Five Year Plan which Stalin had introduced in 1929 in order to bring about rapid industrialisation and rural collectivisation. Rural collectivisation had particularly severe repercussions. It led to the virtual extermination of a million Kulaks, mass deportations and famine. It extended the hold of the secret police, the OGPU, who were given the task of eliminating the Kulaks, and it increased the scope and numbers of forced labour camps. To reduce the bargaining power of the workers, internal passports were introduced and the trade unions emasculated. As the Communist Party increased its hold over the Soviet Union, so Stalin increased his hold over the Party. There were, of course, some considerable achievements, including the expansion of educational and welfare services and, as a consequence of manpower needs, an improvement in opportunities for women. But, as one authority has concluded, the first Five Year Plan, 'stripped of its propaganda verbiage . . . foreshadowed a profound extension of the scope of totalitarian power'.[2]

But the Webbs experienced little of the reality of Russian life. Treated as important foreign guests, they only saw what the Soviet regime wanted them to see. They were impressed by the Russian ship in which they travelled to Leningrad: 'The crew is a family party; the ship is their home', wrote Beatrice (May 25 1932). They were met by representatives of the Soviet Foreign Office, the Trade Union Council, the Consumer Co-operative Movement and the Leningrad Soviet and driven off to the Hotel Astoria where a suite was placed at their disposal. 'We seem to be a new type of royalty', commented Beatrice. In Moscow, they went one better; they stayed in the guest house of the Foreign Office – the former palace of a millionaire.

From Moscow, where they met government and party officials and labour, consumer and youth representatives, and visited schools, theatres, factories and prisons, they set out on the standard foreigners' tour. Accompanied by Rakov, a leading foreign affairs expert, they took a boat trip down the Volga which they both found uncomfortable. At Stalingrad they were impressed by the tractor plant and by a youth (Komsomol) conference: Beatrice commented that the appearance and behaviour of the Komsomol was 'very striking in its dignity, steadiness and comradeship'. Then, using Rostov as a centre, they spent three days visiting collective farms. The pace was too much for Beatrice, who fell ill from colitis and had to recuperate in the Caucasus. Sidney went on with Rakov to the Ukraine, where he saw more collective farms. The Webbs met up again in Moscow in July and sailed back to Britain from Leningrad later in the month.

It is quite clear that the Webbs only visited the showcases of the regime – the model schools, prisons, collective farms, and factories. There are few notes of criticism in Beatrice's diary entries; one motor plant was admitted to be a 'big failure' and, according to Rakov, there was a grave shortage of collective farm managers of proven ability. The Webbs relied on interviews in which they were dependent on their interpreters, and on government material and statistics which they had no means of checking. They, like many other foreign visitors, accepted at face value what they were told. They believed that Bolchevo was a model prison, instead of the harsh institution it was in reality. They quoted as truth the glowing Gorki description of the Soviet labour force under the command of the OGPU building the White Sea canal, remaining in complete ignorance of the appalling decimation of its numbers.[3] Although they were clearly uneasy about the human consequences of enforced collectivisation, they seemed unaware of the mass murder of the Kulaks. Travelling in hope, they allowed nothing they saw or heard to disappoint them.

On their return, Beatrice summed up their impressions of the Soviet Union in the most glowing terms. 'The Soviet government', she wrote on 20 July 1932,

> is perhaps the most firmly established government in the world and the least likely to be radically altered in the next few decades. It represents a new civilisation and a new culture with a new outlook on life – involving a new pattern of behaviour in the individual and his relation to the community – all of which I believe is destined to spread to many other countries in the course of the next hundred years.

She admitted that the plan was superior to the execution and that some features of Soviet Russia (including the fanatical repression of heresy and its 'behind the scenes' killings of unwanted persons') would 'remain repulsive to more developed races'. She also accepted that the Soviet Union was a long way behind in material progress. For both reasons she doubted whether Soviet Russia would be chosen as a model by the West. She concluded by asking the question

> how far can you disentangle what is good in Russian Communism from what is bad, how far can you single out the expedients which can be usefully applied in other countries and reject those which are either wholly evil or which, at any rate, are only needful in Russia and among other primitive races? Can you take the economic organisation of Russia and reject her metaphysics; can you have the fervour of the CP without its fanaticism, the free and active service of young people, without the repression of 'heresy' among adult citizens? These are the sort of problems we hope to discuss in the last chapter of our book which we promise each other to write during the next twelve months. (20 July 1932)

In another account written a few weeks later entitled 'Some of our Conclusions about Soviet Russia', Beatrice was already beginning to answer the question which she had posed. Significantly she laid stress on what she believed to be the widespread participation in Russia as displayed by its constitution. The strength of the Soviet Union, she argued, was due

> to what might be metaphorically described as the reinforced concrete of its constitution: great blocks of mass organisation in which *all men and women are encouraged to participate* [author's italics]. These four blocks of organisation, sharply differentiated in structure and function, are: (1) the hierarchy of Soviet Democracy from the village soviets to the Congress of the USSR; (2) the hierarchy of the Trade Union Movement; (3) the hierarchy of the Consumers' Co-operative Movement, together with a widespread network of self-governing Associations of Producers, of agricultural and industrial workers, of fishermen and hunters of wild game. All these four distinct types of mass organisation are firmly held together in the powerful framework of the Communist Party – a body of about one and a half million strong, distinguished by its exclusive membership, doctrinal tests and stern discipline, in respect to the personal and public conduct of its members. This variegated constitution, which has never been formally enacted or proclaimed, is being gradually

> extended, in all, or some of its parts, to the remotest corners of the Eurasian continent; and is even being insinuated over the frontiers of the USSR and some parts of China.

She was particularly impressed by the dedication of the Komsomols, the Communist Party Youth Organisation. 'The combination . . .' she wrote with approval,

> of the passion for self-improvement and self-discipline, with the passion for social service and the consequent growth in the young generation of personal initiative and personal responsibility, is one of the finest disciplines the world has ever seen . . . Communist discipline is, in fact, an almost terrifying puritanism in its subordination of man's appetite to his reason and moral purpose; a puritanism which may bring with it among the baser sort, hypocrisy and the hiving up of furtive vice; and which certainly leads to a lack of humour and a self-assertive prejudice. But as a method of lifting the people of Russia out of dirt, disease, apathy, superstition, illiteracy, thieving and brutishness, of the pre-revolutionary days, the self-governing democracy of two and a half million Communist youth appears to be magnificently effective.

In addition, Beatrice also believed that Soviet Communism had 'solved the economic problem' by organising production exclusively from the standpoint of the consumer:

> Under this planned organisation of industry, it seems to me that consumption will always outreach production–as it certainly does today – and that the greater output due to scientific invention and extended control over nature will be continuously absorbed by the increased purchasing power of the workers in our equalitarian state. Thus there will be neither over production nor under-consumption: human faculty and human desire will be automatically adjusted in a steadily swelling flow of commodities and services checked only by a rising demand for increased leisure on the part of all sections of the community. (August 1932)

It was already clear that the Webbs' account of the Soviet regime was going to be overwhelmingly favourable.

The next two and a half years were spent in researching and

writing *Soviet Communism*. It was a formidable task for two septuagenarians. During the first six months they amassed and arranged their material – Sidney's interview notes, the Soviet publications, and secondary work. They were assisted by S. P. Turin, a lecturer at the School of Slavonic Studies. On 27 March 1933 they began writing:

> Sidney begins the book today, and I shall strain and stumble after him – picking up the bits and opening out new aspects . . . Regarded from the standpoint of research, it is an illegitimate venture – neither our equipment nor our opportunities suffice. But like a provisional examination of a new invention by an experienced mechanician [sic] or a preliminary survey of a new island by a knowledgeable geologist . . . it may prove useful to better equipped observers. (27 March 1933)

As they wrote, they had moments of doubt. Malcolm Muggeridge, who was married to Beatrice's niece, was the *Manchester Guardian* correspondent in Moscow and had become highly critical of the Soviet regime: 'That there is some *fire* behind this smoke of Malcolm's clearly malicious but sincerely felt denunciation of Soviet Communism, is clear from the Soviet press itself . . . the USSR has not yet solved the problem of production' (29 March 1933). However, Sidney comforted her. 'Sidney is not daunted . . . the thought that there may be famine in some districts of the USSR does not disturb his faith in the eventual triumph of the Soviet economic principle of planned production' (30 March 1933). And Maisky, the Russian ambassador, assured them that the reports of famine in the Western press were grossly exaggerated. Turin, who helped them with the book, was critical of the use they made of his information: 'Turin says we have *invented* a constitution for the USSR. "Are you going to *invent* the meaning of their activities?" with a stress on the word *invent*. "Telling the truth about things which you cannot tell until you have discovered it, is always invention" I retort' (29 November 1933). Beatrice was also worried about the Soviet government's control of passports; 'other things being equal, personal freedom is in itself desirable – and to refuse it – causes unhappiness to the individual concerned, and scandal among foreigners' (4 June 1935).

However, their disillusion with the alternatives – Western capitalism or Fascist dictatorship – strengthened their commitment to Soviet Russia.

> In Western Europe, in Africa and Asia, and so far as I know in the USA, there is no sign of any new movement, only signs of disintegration of thought and conduct in the existing social order. Fascism and Hitlerism are attempts to get back to a disciplined society; but such creed as they have is no creed at all, there is no intellect in the driving force, mere emotion and that of a debased character. (24 August 1933)

At the end of the summer of 1934, Sidney went back to Russia for a few weeks and was made an honorary member of the Soviet Praesidium. He returned home to Beatrice 'completely reassured as to the eventual success of the new social order' (10 October 1934). True, there was a dark spot, the lack of freedom of expression for dissident intellectuals: 'but this freedom for adverse propaganda can hardly be accorded – or rather would not be permitted in a government of any country – so long as they do not feel secure against active revolt and deliberate sabotage – so long as there is open or underground civil war'. Their faith in the Soviet Union was well summed up by Beatrice:

> The longer we study the USSR, the more sure we are that it is a new civilisation – crude and cruel and definitely inefficient in some of its manifestations – but nevertheless, an immense step forward in the development of a better human nature, alike in physical health and intellectual advancement, personal ethics and social relationships. (8 June 1933)

In December 1935 *Soviet Communism* was published. It had a mixed reception. Beatrice wrote that 'this intense irritation at any acceptance of the reality and success of the Soviet Union will be a big factor in the reception of the book – it will deter many well-to-do intellectuals from reading, still more from buying, the book . . .' (15 December 1935). Maisky gave a dinner for them at the Russian Embassy. Beatrice commented:

> Who would have foreseen this proletarian gathering – in sympathy not in class – at the Russian Embassy with eminent Fabians as the central figures – in those pre war days, when the Tsarist diplomats were the wealthiest, the most sophisticated and the most accomplished aristocrats in London society? (20 December 1935)

The Webbs' book on the Soviet Union was monumental in conception, in scope, and in error of judgement. It was divided into two parts: the first dealt with the Soviet constitution, the second with social trends. The first volume examined the constitution under four headings – man as citizen, man as producer, man as consumer and the so-called 'vocation of leadership'. The Webbs' conclusion was that the USSR had evolved 'a complex and multi-form representative system of complete originality, based upon a principle of universal participation in public affairs, under the guidance of a highly organised leadership of a unique kind'.[4]

The Webbs believed that the key to understanding the Soviet constitution was the extent to which Soviet citizens participated in decision-making. They argued that it was impossible 'to enumerate all the channels and it would be difficult to exaggerate the extent, of the participation in the public affairs of the Soviet electorate of over ninety millions of men and women.'[5] They constructed an ideal model in which at every level from the village up to the highest assembly, the Soviet citizen could discuss, debate and decide.

They supposed that the village Soviet had considerable freedom of action: 'The principle may be summed up as freedom to err, subject always to veto and reversal by superior authority', they blandly declared, though they noted that 'party guidance will not long be wanting if any village Soviet shows signs of going astray'.[6] They had the same misconception about the freedom of debate and independent powers of each tier of the Soviet pyramid – the city Soviet, the rayon, the oblast, the republic up to the all-Union Congress which they quite erroneously judged to be 'a gathering of real political importance.'[7]

The Webbs also completely misunderstood the role of the Soviet trade unions which they saw not as the organs of the state which they had become, but as genuine democratic and independent organisations of unions, albeit with greatly extended functions.

> The Soviet trade union, like the British, is emphatically the organ of the wage-earners as such; it is based on optional individual membership and subscription; it appoints and pays its own officials and manages its business by its own elected committees; it conducts, through its highest committees and its national officials, the collective bargaining with the employing organisations by which the general scheme and standard rates of wages are fixed; piece-work rates are settled in each factory job-by-job after

> discussion with the union's local officials and not without their consent . . . finally the essential function is that of maintaining and improving the workers' conditions of life, taking . . . the broadest view of these and thinking of their advancement only in common with those of the whole community of workers.[8]

When it came to discussing collective farms, the Webbs knew that they were on weaker ground. Given the almost universal peasant hostility to collectivisation, they could hardly praise the level of voluntary participation here. Instead they allowed themselves to be used as apologists for the regime. They accepted that there had been food shortages, deportations and even rough treatment but they refused to believe the accounts which revealed that the 'liquidation' of the Kulaks actually meant just that. Unforgiveably, they wrote 'without such cost in suffering, it is argued the rapid reorganisation of peasant agriculture, which seemed the only practicable means of solving the problem of the national food supply, could not have been effected.'[9]

The Webbs' version of the role of the Communist Party – 'the so-called vocation of leadership' was also totally misconceived. They believed that they had discovered a highly effective and dedicated elite, pledged 'to two out of three characteristic obligations of the religious orders of Christianity, namely to poverty . . . and to obedience' and whose only concern was the well-being of their fellow citizens.[10] 'The party members', they declared enthusiastically

> enjoy no statutory privileges . . . if the party influences or directs the policy of individuals or public authority, it does so only by persuasion. If it exercises power it does so by 'keeping the conscience' of its own members and getting them elected to office by the popular vote. Even when not holding public office, the party members act as missionaries among the non-Party citizens in the organisations of every kind throughout the USSR. It is in this way that the Party secures the popular consent to, or at least the popular acquiescence in, the policy that it promotes.[11]

They also completely misjudged the position of Stalin. 'We do not think', they categorically stated

> the party is governed by the will of a single person; or that Stalin is the sort of person to claim or desire such a position. He has himself

> very explicitly denied any such personal dictatorship in terms which, whether or not he is credited with sincerity, certainly accord with our own impression of the facts.[12]

To the Webbs, Stalin was not a dictator but the secretary of a 'series of committees' and 'a shrewd and definitely skilful manager, facing a succession of stupendous problems'. They admitted that he was virtually irremovable from office, but justified this by his success in overcoming the very real difficulties of 1925, then in surmounting the obstacle of the peasant recalcitrance of 1930–33, and, finally, the successive triumphs of the Five Year Plan. According to the Webbs, the people would not understand his dismissal.

Summing up, they rejected the view that the Soviet regime was in any way a dictatorship:

> Nowhere . . . do we discover anything involving or implying government by the will of a single person. On the contrary, there is everywhere elaborate provision, not only for collegiate decision, but also, whether by popular election or by appointment for a given term, or by the universal right to recall, for collective control of each individual executant.[13]

They believed that they had seen something new:

> Have we perhaps here a case – to use a barbarous term – of a 'creedocracy' of a novel kind, inspiring a multi-form democracy in which Soviets and trade unions, co-operative societies and voluntary associations, provide for the personal participation in public affairs of an unprecedented proportion of the entire adult population?[14]

Answering their own question, they concluded:

> The Union of Soviet Socialist Republics does not consist of a government and a people confronting each other as all other great societies have hitherto been. It is a highly integrated social organisation in which over a vast area, each individual man, woman or child is expected to participate in three capacities: as a citizen, as a producer and as the consumer . . . Meanwhile, leadership is carried on by new professions organised like other professions as a voluntary, enlisted and self-governing unit.[15]

Universal participation and a selfless, dedicated elite, committed to a secular faith – did these two priceless ingredients not add up to a new civilization?

There is no doubt that the Webbs genuinely believed that they were witnessing a society in which the different aspects of human life, man as citizen, man as consumer and man as producer were organised in such a way that the Soviet Union had become a government 'instrumented by all the adult inhabitants, organised in a varied array of collectives, having their several distinct functions'.[16] They argued that democracy was immeasurably strengthened by the large part that participation played in Russian life: 'Universal participation in public business in the midst of incessant oral discussion' was how they termed it.[17] The Webbs insisted that the multiplicity of elections over what they called the separation of issues into common citizenship, distribution of household supplies, and wealth production, meant not only that the Soviets understood the need to differentiate between the different functions of citizen/producer/consumer, but they had evolved a new and more effective means of ensuring that public opinion was heard and consent obtained.

However, in their enthusiastic support for participation, they failed to see that a main component of their *Socialist Commonwealth* – the system of checks and balances – was missing. They grossly exaggerated the influence and independence of the trade union and local government bodies. In their admiration of the dedication of the Communist Party, they refused to acknowledge the dangers of a one-party state. They mistakenly believed that the Party acted only through persuasion and that the people themselves had the final say through their participation at meetings and through elections. Above all, they minimised totalitarian power which Stalin had built up through his control of the party and state apparatus, and through the secret police or OGPU (whom the Webbs amazingly considered were performing 'constructive work').

The second section of the book discussed the development of Soviet society. They described in glowing terms the abolition of private profit, the introduction of state planning, and the growth of social and education services. Their underlying argument was that a new civilization, based on a new social ethic, was coming into being in Russia:

> The characteristics of Soviet Communism . . . exhibit . . . a distinct unity, itself in striking contrast with the disunity of

> Western civilisation. The code of conduct based on service to the community and social equality, and on the maximum development of health and capacity in every individual, is in harmony with the exclusion of exploitation and the profit-making motive, and with the deliberate planning of production for community consumption; whilst both are in full accord with that universal participation . . . which characterises the Soviet system. The economic and political organisations, and with them the ethical code, are alike staked on a wholehearted reliance on the beneficial effort of making known to every citizen all that is known on the facts of the universe, including human nature itself . . . the Worship of God is replaced by the Service of Man.[18]

In their discussion of individual freedom in the 'new civilization', the Webbs claimed that the Soviet system put the emphasis rather on widening opportunity than on absence of restraint. In the West the social environment produced unemployment and an unequal class system in which the freedom of the few was enjoyed at the expense of the many. In the Soviet Union, the government so shaped the environment through economic planning that it was possible to achieve equal rights in employment, health, social benefits, education and in housing. Liberty, they argued, quoting Lenin with approval, 'is so valuable that it must be rationed'. They went on to say that 'so long as the available quantum of liberty is not unlimited, the aggregate amount enjoyed within the community is, by appropriate rationing on an equalitarian basis, actually increased'.[19] They accepted that freedom was linked with economic expansion but believed, however, that planned production in the Soviet Union was increasing very rapidly, so much so, that in a few years, 'the USSR will have become the wealthiest country in the world, and at the same time, the community enjoying the greatest aggregate of individual freedom'.[20] They concluded that the *New Civilization*, reflected the diversity which they had aimed for in the *Socialist Commonwealth*. It was

> a new Society unlike any other; made up of a highly elaborate and extremely varied texture of many kinds of collective organisations by the universal membership of which the *interests and desires of all the different sections of the population will be fulfilled in a manner and to a degree never yet attained in any other community.*[21]

In the postscript to the second edition published in 1937, the Webbs felt they had to comment on a number of events and changes, including the new Constitution of 1936, the treason trials and the Stakhanovite movement. Sadly, in spite of the growing evidence that Soviet reality was vastly different from the ideal model which they had constructed in the first edition, they underlined their faith in the regime by withdrawing the question mark in their title. According to the Webbs, the 1936 constitution was not a sham but 'enormously extended the rights of man.' The treason trials were not a miscarriage of justice but either 'the inevitable aftermath of any long, drawn out revolutionary struggle that ends in a successful seizure of power', or the necessary uncovering of 'administrative corruption'.[22] The Stakhanovite movement was not a systematic exploitation of the workers but a spontaneous exercise in increasing productivity. The Webbs admitted that there was a danger that the repression of independent thinking could lead to stagnation but argued that 'as the imminent danger of counter-revolution and foreign aggression fades away, the repression and discouragement of independent thinking, even on the most fundamental issues, will be silently discontinued'.[23]

Why were the Webbs so mistaken about the Soviet Union? As we have already seen, one reason was that they only visited the places which the regime wanted them to visit. Another reason was that they were totally dependent on Soviet material and sources for information. In addition, they took for granted the good faith of the Soviet authorities. In part this was because they thought that Communist officials, like all good civil servants in the Webbian model, had no particular axe to grind. If high-up administrators, let alone Stalin himself, insisted on the democratic nature of Soviet government, they were easily persuaded that it was the regime and not its biased critics who were right. More fundamentally, the Webbs wanted to believe that Soviet Communism could provide an alternative for those disillusioned by the failure of socialism in the capitalist West. So the partnership, who as eminent Fabians had always emphasised respect for the truth, were prepared to jettison their reputation as careful researchers, for the sake of their socialist faith.

But if the Webbs were careless with the facts, it is quite wrong to suppose that they had suddenly become totalitarian. They genuinely believed that the combination of mass participation and a selfless communist vanguard would lead to a new democratic system. They failed to see that Soviet grassroots democracy was only as meaningful as the Party allowed it to be and that, in addition to participation, democracy required competing political parties, independent sources of power, and limits to authority. If they were mistaken in their analysis of the Soviet system, it was not because they had abandoned their life-long support for pluralist democracy, expressed most forcefully and convincingly in the *Socialist Commonwealth*: it was because they saw in the Soviet regime a democracy which only existed in their imagination. *Soviet Communism* is the work not of two ruthless totalitarians but of two gullible septuagenerians.

NOTES

1. S. Webb to Dr Sarolea 1924, Quoted in Mackenzie, p. 207.
2. Merle Fainsod, *How Russia is Ruled*, p.107.
3. See D. Caute, *The Fellow-Travellers*; P. Hollander, *Political Pilgrims: travels of Western intellectuals to the Soviet Union.*
4. *Soviet Communism–A New Civilization?*, p. 1128.
5. Ibid.
6. Ibid, p. 31.
7. Ibid, p. 84.
8. Ibid, p. 218.
9. Ibid, p. 270.
10. Ibid, p. 93.
11. Ibid, pp. 340–341.
12. Ibid, p. 432.
13. Ibid, p. 429.
14. Ibid, p. 450.
15. Ibid.
16. Ibid.
17. 'Is Soviet Russia a Democracy?', *Current History*, Feb 1933.
18. *Soviet Communism – A New Civilisation?*, p. 1138.
19. Ibid, p. 1036.
20. Ibid, p. 1037.
21. Ibid, p. 1072.
22. Ibid, p. 1157.
23. Ibid, p. 1213.

15
1933–1947
Retreat

'A longing for the eternal sleep of death.'

The last ten years of the partnership were marred by ill health. In October 1933 Beatrice had a severe kidney infection and had to have an operation. A further operation was required in the new year. Even though the second was more successful, Beatrice found it difficult to regain both her strength and spirits. 'It is' she wrote wearily, 'as if my personality were separate from my bodily organs, as if my will and purpose and my knowledge were as strong as ever but my physical organs were weak and brittle instruments breaking down directly I try to use them' (13 February 1934). Her kidneys continued to cause her considerable pain throughout the remainder of her life.

Sidney appeared much sounder in health until 1938 when he had a stroke from which he never fully recovered. 'The inevitable has come', wrote Beatrice in January 1938. 'One of the partners has fallen on the way, the youngest and strongest – he may lie there for a while – but we shall never march together again in work and recreation. I cannot march alone' (5 January 1938). He now became more or less a complete invalid, unable to leave the house, to write or even to think coherently for long stretches of time. He took to reading novels for the first time and became so obsessed by his new infatuation that Beatrice had to order fortnightly batches of fifteen from the London Library to keep up with his pace. He described his new life-style with wry amusement to their old friend Pease.

> My fate has been a somewhat serious one. A year ago I was attacked by what was called a seizure. It has destroyed all my capacity for inventing anything and also my power of writing. My life is now a happy contentment reading books of every kind and in remembering other things, but without any capacity for using either invention or discovery in any new enterprise. My wife, who is fully seized with a desire to enable the husband to live, takes it out in innumerable letters and memoranda which she proposes to transform into books.[1]

Sidney now resigned himself to his 'useless life, reading his endless books'; while Beatrice, growing increasingly frail, struggled on looking after Sidney in Passfield Corner with the assistance of two aged servants and intermittently working on *Our Partnership*. Worn out, enfeebled, with Sidney half paralysed, the Webbs waited for death. 'I am tired of living', wrote Beatrice in 1939,

> I should welcome a painless death if I could take my beloved with me. He would think it hysterical, certainly unreasonable to desire it; but I doubt whether he would resent it. He feels, as I do, that our living life is finished; we are merely waiting for the end. (8 April 1939)

But, despite the physical difficulties of their last years, Beatrice continued to write her diary and reflect on personalities and events. She kept a sharp, critical eye on the Labour Party. Writing about George Lansbury who became leader after the debacle of 1931, she noted,

> everyone loves George Lansbury, no-one speaks ill of him, but no-one takes him seriously, that is, no-one alters by one iota, either his personal conduct or his public action, after hearing him speak or talking to him, or living with him. He serves as a sort of ethical school, his words puff out people with good intentions; but the good intentions subside into the old lassitude when the drug has passed out of the system – perhaps even to a deeper carelessness than before? (11 September 1936)

She was not, however, greatly impressed by his successor Clement Attlee: 'though gifted with intellect, character and also with good will (he has alas! *no personality*!). He is neither feared, disliked nor admired: he is merely respected by Labour men and approved by the government bench' (28 September 1935). Or, as she put it on hearing of his election as leader of the Parliamentary Labour Party, he was 'somewhat diminutive and a meaningless figure to represent the British Labour Movement in the House of Commons!' (27 November 1935). It was as much an error of judgement as had been their faith in Lord Rosebery.

Beatrice and Sidney believed for a considerable number of years that her nephew, Stafford Cripps, would emerge as the new leader. As the founder of the Socialist League, a radical ginger group within the Labour Party, it seemed natural that his brilliant intellectual achievements would be rewarded. On the other hand, in spite of his abilities, they were never quite convinced that he was the right kind of leader for the Party. 'Stafford's personality interests me', Beatrice recorded discerningly in early 1934.

> It changes swiftly from the naivete of a petted child, to the exasperated sternness of the religious fanatic and then relapses into that of an accomplished lawyer expounding his brief . . . he is still an amateur – and a clumsy one – at the political game; and I doubt his judgement of men and policies. (3 May 1934)

'What is against Stafford's success', Beatrice reminded herself some three years later,

> is that he is so obviously the wealthy intellectual and recent convert . . . His opportunity lies in the spinelessness of the Labour front bench, the evil reputation of Citrine . . . and of Dalton, as a time-serving manipulator of the National Executive of the Labour Party at Transport House. (16 April 1937)

As the war approached, her doubts increased. Stafford Cripps' faults, in spite of his good intentions were, she felt, too damaging for a successful leader. He was, she correctly surmised,

> autocratic and aloof in his ways and means; he apparently never consults his colleagues. The act which is needfull to unravel the tangled schemes of the British Labour Movement . . . is not one of Stafford's characteristics . . . moreover, [he] never sticks to one policy or programme; he takes up a cause and then drops it. (21 January 1939)

Another aspirant for the leadership was Hugh Dalton. The Webbs were never fond of him. Beatrice thought, when judging his chances, that Dalton, though less personally attractive than Ramsay MacDonald, had the better brain. She considered him a turncoat and felt uneasy about him, and, though admitting that he was able and public-spirited, described him as having 'one of the most unpleasant personalities I have met with . . . I doubt whether he will be a successful administrator' (9 June 1940).

Beatrice had rarely felt optimistic with regard to any member of the leadership of the Labour Party and in her seventies was unlikely to change her opinion. Even Herbert Morrison ('Mr. London') she dismissed. Initially after Labour had won control of the LCC in 1934, the Webbs were full of his praise. 'Herbert Morrison' argued Beatrice,

> is the organiser of victory – the final victory doing endless credit to his doggedness, skill and masterfulness. He is a Fabian of Fabians – a direct disciple of Sidney Webb's: his method and purpose are almost identical with that of the Sidney Webbs of 1892; applied, of course, to existing problems of 1933. (14 March 1934)

A year later, however, the Webbs had grown more critical. Because of his great victory, Beatrice argued, Morrison's opinion of himself had increased. 'I admire him', she admitted,

> for his single-minded career as labour leader and careful student of events; I even like him. But he is not an attractive personality . . . he has neither personal magnetism, nor vision for social values . . . Morrison represents the highest level of the common-place politician and public administrator, without one spark of genius, and without a suspicion of personal charm. (27 July 1935)

Despite their infirmities, they also kept up with old friends. Occasionally they saw the Shaws. With great generosity, GBS had sent the Webbs a substantial cheque to help with Beatrice's hospital bills when she had her kidney operation. The money, Shaw told Sidney, was therapeutic; no-one could resist the 'lifting effect of £1000'. He expressed his warm affection for Sidney: 'The balancing instinct in nature is remarkable. Alarmed at her work in 1856, she produced you three years later as my complement. It was one of her few successes.'[3] After reading a book on Shaw a few years later, Beatrice commented,

> GBS is an eclectic; his breadth of vision is amazing; the whole world is his province. For the purpose of surveying and ascribing the whole field of human activies, he is always shifting his standpoint; he is always singling out the unexpected . . . he never stays put – partly because of intellectual restlessness . . . but also because of the clown or imp in him – a part he is always acting. Shaw is a charmer physically and mentally, but he fails to convert me to *all* his brilliant thinking for the good reason that he has no settled creed. (9 December 1939)

In the spring of 1937 the distinguished historian Elie Halevy and his wife visited the Webbs. Beatrice wrote,

> Where he and we differ, I think, is not so much in our understanding of the facts of the case, but in our scale of values. We value, almost fanatically, the equal presence of plentiful opportunity for a vigorous and varied life on the part of all men; he values the absence of restraint on the thought and expression of the intellectual elite. In a revolutionary period – a revolution revolving round the ownership or control of the instruments of production – the simultaneous enjoyment of both these social values seems impracticable. (11 May 1937)

At the beginning of 1937 they had seen Malcolm Muggeridge who had been working for the *Statesman* in Calcutta, for the first time for five years

> Is he mad, I wonder? He told us that he had become 'a mystic': and I can well believe it; he would need some escape from the reality of other people's human nature as he *visualises* it. It is this obsession for searching out all that is detestable in persons and institutions that is so odd and repulsive in Malcolm. (30 January 1937)

Kingsley Martin has left behind a memorable picture of weekends at the Webbs'.

> The pilgrimage to Passfield Corner was sometimes exhausting. The Webbs had been intensively working all the week, and their immense fund of argument and conversation was bottled up inside them. One arrived for tea on Saturday. Mrs Webb met one very graciously at the door. Sidney gave you a rather perfunctory handshake. You were taken upstairs and your part of the house, including your bathroom, was firmly indicated. You went down to tea where there were probably other guests. Serious talk began at once. The condition of the world and of the Labour and Socialist Movements, in particular, and immediate topics of the day, were systematically dealt with . . . After supper on Saturday night . . . Mrs Webb, with her skirts turned back over her knees and her fine hands extended over the fire . . . would allow herself to relax and talk about her family, and the early days of their marriage. Sidney, looking absurdly like a cockatoo, perched on a chair with his tiny feet scarcely reaching the ground and a high feather of hair standing up on his huge head, would break in now and then to correct or embroider an anecdote from a still more accurate memory.[3]

In June 1937 they gave a party at Passfield Corner for over a hundred Potter descendants as well as Fabian friends.

In the summer of 1938, the Nehrus spent most of a day at Passfield. 'Nehru, the leader of the India Congress and his lovely daughter, spent some hours here on Saturday . . . He is the last word of aristocratic refinement and culture, dedicated to the salvation of the underdog, whether in race or class; but I doubt whether he has the hard stuff of a revolutionary leader' (3rd July 1938).

The Webbs kept in close touch with the Russian ambassador Maisky, who had replaced Sokolnikov in 1932. 'Maisky,' she wrote in 1935, 'is not a personally attractive man – he is stocky and plain to look at – but he is trustworthy, hard-working and wholly devoted, and is a shrewd and lively companion – with no frills or pretentions' (16 March 1935). The Webbs liked him for all the characteristics other diplomats did not have. 'He is an open and genial propagandist of Soviet Communism . . . In spite of his lack of personal charm Maisky is certainly an active and efficient Soviet representative – wholly devoid of the well-bred aloofness from the common people of the typical diplomat' (23 January 1938). 'Maisky,' declared Beatrice a year later,

> is honest and self-devoted in character; acute, broad minded, witty and intelligent – a good husband, friend and citizen . . . I think he genuinely believes in the *new civilization* established in the USSR without being a fanatical Marxist . . . Maisky is an idealist – agnostic so far as the destiny of the human race is concerned – and a materialist and opportunist in the method of arriving at his appointed ends. (12 June 1939)

He was also a clever survivor, managing to end his days peacefully in retirement long after Stalin's death.

Their last years continued to be dominated by their enthusiasm for Soviet Communism. Their obsession astonished and infuriated their friends but they remained true to their new faith. They did not consider themselves to be Marxists. Indeed, despite the ineffectiveness of the Labour Party in the 1930s, they kept up their membership and argued that the British Communist Party should be wound up. But they genuinely felt that the Russian Communists had created a new civilization, based on common ownership, mass participation, and a dedicated selfless elite.

Even the show trials of the late 1930s failed to shake their belief in Soviet Communism. They convinced themselves that many of the accused were counter-revolutionaries and that the Western press was hopelessly biased. They continued to make excuses for the regime:

> One has just to shrug one's shoulders and mutter 'After all, the Soviet government has only just emerged from the Middle Ages', which is not quite consistent with welcoming Soviet communism as a *new civilization* . . . My own explanation is that all the leading men in the USSR have been brought up in the atmosphere of violent revolution, of underground conspiracies. (28 August 1936)

And in the last month of 1937, Beatrice admitted that they did not altogether accept the trials as inevitable themselves. 'There is always the lurking suspicion that Stalin and his clique *may* have lost their heads!' But, nevertheless, 'We console ourselves with the faith that the economics of Soviet Communism are so sound and the success of the system so apparent in the men and women concerned that even if there were a palace revolution, the new social order would be maintained' (6 December 1937). Four months later Beatrice acknowledged that the 'sickening vilification of all who differ from the policy of the government clique, the perpetual fear of innocent citizens being wrongly accused and convicted is a terrible social disease.' But she was still certain that the trials (of Rakovsky, Sokolnikov, Bukarin and others) was not a 'frame-up' (8 March 1938).

Whatever excuses they were able to put forward for the trials, the announcement in August 1939 of the German-Soviet Pact shook them considerably. As war began to draw ominously nearer, Beatrice became convinced that the underlying purpose behind the West's appeasement policy was to entrap the Soviet Union into war with Hitler. The Webbs believed that only some form of alliance with Russia could contain Germany and thus save Europe from a Second World War. The announcement of the German Soviet Pact devastated them: 'A day of holy horror!' Beatrice recorded, initially unable to accept the news. 'I am somewhat shaken as to the integrity of the international policy of the New Civilization' (23 August 1939). Two days later she was still shattered. 'The German-Soviet Pact seems a great disaster to all that the Webbs have stood for', she wrote sadly.

> Even Sidney is dazed and I am, for a time at least, knocked almost senseless! The manner of its making is even worse than its meaning . . . to become fervent supporters of collective security, to be missionaries of resistance against aggression and all attempts to extend territories by force . . . and then to conclude suddenly and secretly an alliance with Hitler's Germany is a terrible collapse of good faith and integrity . . . so far as our faith in Soviet communism is concerned, the last days have been tragic. I console myself with the thought of how rapidly currents of thought and feeling throughout the world change their course. Meanwhile, I am in a state of collapse. (25 August 1939)

When war was declared, the Webbs, away from it all at Passfield Corner, remained detached. After the first air-raid warning, which turned out to be a false alarm, Beatrice went into Sidney's room

> and saw him sitting up with his gas mask on! I suggested that he should take it off, which he promptly did. Mrs Grant had been in and was angry, '*you have no right* to tell Mr Webb to take his off' she said in a menacing voice. 'Pardon me,' I laughed – 'I am his wife

> and the mistress of this house. Keep yours on if you like. It is damned nonsense putting on gas masks out in the countryside. The Germans won't waste their gas on us. Our only danger – if there is one – is an explosive bomb. Even a quarter of a mile off I am told it might bring our house down!' (7 September 1939)

As the days went by, she began to feel better about the Nazi-Soviet Pact:

> It was a stroke of luck for the British and French governments it had neutralised, even antagonised the Japanese and Spanish governments against Germany, and enabled Mussolini to get out of supporting Hitler in the war; it had also produced a united front against Hitler's Germany (not only in British and French territories) but also in the USA and South American Republics. Finally, the USSR was justified in becoming overtly and decidedly neutral in a war between an enraged Germany and a hostile Poland on the one hand, and far away untrustworthy allies on the other. (11 September 1939)

During the first two years of the war the Webbs showed little concern about the hostilities between Germany and the allies, though as early as October 1939 Beatrice wrote that if 'only their old acquaintance (Winston Churchill) were the Prime Minister in the place of the reactionary and mechanical-minded Chamberlain, the prospect of a right and rapid ending of this murder and waste of the war would be more hopeful' (2 October 1939). What mattered to them was the fate of the Russians. They spent long hours patiently listening for Soviet news and broadcasts, were delighted by Soviet victories, and downcast by Soviet defeats. After the Russian invasion of Poland, Beatrice noted that 'the *power prestige* of the USSR has grown to win back territories without opposition from the inhabitants, for beaten Polish armies to greet the Red Army advancing as deliverers from aggression is horrid news for capitalist governments' (6 November 1939).

The Russian invasion of Finland was a set back: 'A mighty gain for the anti-Soviet fanatics' (10 February 1940), Beatrice sadly put it. She was soon heartened by the news that 'Moscow had made a triumphant peace with Finland' (11 March 1940). By November, Beatrice was looking presciently forward to peace:

> I still think that some form of co-operation between the USA and the USSR, in settling what should be the new international social order, is the one and essential guarantee for a permanent peace. For that reason, I want both these governments to keep out of the war and to be sufficiently tolerant of each other's organisation to agree as to terms of peace. (9 November 1940)

In June 1941 Hitler invaded the Soviet Union. The Webbs welcomed the new support for Russia expressed by British politicians but listened nervously as the German army swept across the Russian plains. Beatrice's last days were gladdened by the first news of German defeats at the hands of the Russians: 'It makes life worth living to those who believe in the living philosophy of scientific humanism and its application to international well-being' (22 January 1943). To the end both Webbs remained convinced by Soviet Communism.

> Soviet Communism is right in its idea of scientific humanism and in its method of planned production for communal consumption, based on its multi-form democracy . . . What it suffers from [she conceded] are the disease of orthodoxy arising from the herd instinct . . . and the *parrot* instinct, all of which violates its ideal of scientific humanism . . . I believe that these diseases are the result of, (1), the revolutionary period and, (2), the relatively primitive character of many of the races within the USSR; and, (3), the low standards of conduct inherent in the orthodox church and the autocratic and corrupt Czarist regime. To us, the progress made in the last twenty years by civilizing these millions of nondescript peoples is most encouraging as proof of the essential wisdom and rightness of the creed of Lenin, interpreted by the CP, led by the public spirited, and sensible group of whom Stalin is the acknowledged leader. The one feature that puzzles me is the institution of *Vocation of Leadership* and the consequent danger of the disease of orthodoxy? Free thought, free speech and a free press must be accepted by the *New Civilization*: it is the one contribution of Western Civilization which must endure and develop if permanent progress is to be maintained. (12 November 1940)

During these wartime years they were relatively isolated. They had a few visits from friends – Kingsley Martin, Stafford Cripps,

C. P. Trevelyan, the Maiskys, Carr Saunders, Herbert Reed, Hugh Gaitskell – but they spent most of the time alone, reading, listening to the wireless and going for walks. Beatrice worked as much as she possibly could on *Our Partnership*. In the spring of 1940 she wrote,

> Meanwhile I creep along with my work; tired by day and sleepless by night; looking after my dear one, except when I go with Peter (Mrs Grant's dog) for a walk of two or three miles – (I exhausted myself yesterday with a four-mile walk) whilst Sidney goes with Mrs Grant for one or two miles – sitting down on the camp stool which she carries. One day passes into another night rapidly; the week seems ended unexpectedly, the only time that drags are the hours in the night – that is why I scribble in this diary, with which I deaden my dislike of living, a dislike which becomes acute in the early hours of the morning before my cup of tea brings back a commonsense resignation to the decrepitude of old age. (3 April 1940)

Some eighteen months later she wrote,

> Yesterday afternoon when he and I were sitting in the garden, I asked Sidney, 'Do you wish to go on living?' He sat silent, surprised at the question and slowly said 'No' . . . he resents not being able to *think* and express his thoughts and not help the world he lives in. Then why not cease to exist? (6 October 1941)

In the last few months of her life, Beatrice's faculties began to fail. Her final diary entry, written on 19 April 1943 reflected her confused state of mind and her sense of approaching death.

> The most amazing fact is that the history of mankind is happening as I write these words. Tonight when we were listening to wireless, the BBC broadcast and the electric fire suddenly ceased. Sidney and Mrs Grant and Annie (the Webbs' housekeeper and servant) all asserted that it was accidental. But presently (as I write these words) the BBC ceased its activity, my cup of tea went cold, so did Sidney's glass of sherry. Annie came to tell me that the two British air machines has passed low over our house and that they had suddenly disappeared. At the same time I felt that I must go to the water closet and I had an action which seemed to clear away all unnecessary excreta, and I couldn't for the next few hours to get my feet warm and comfortable. But

> suddenly I ceased to exist, so did Annie and Jean, Mrs Grant and Sidney. So we are living/having a painless death as I had longed for. For if my reasoning is right we shall all disappear including *the Germans themselves from the territory which they have conquered.* There will be no Jews, no conquered people, no refugees. The garden will disappear and all our furniture, the earth and the sun and the moon. God wills the destruction of all living things, man, woman, and even a child. We shall not be frozen or hurt. We should merely not exist never even have existed. It all seems incredible and is therefore worth noting. Even Churchill and Roosevelt, states/Stalin and kingdoms would disappear! No-one would fear, it will be sudden and complete, so no-one need worry, and we can go on as long as we are conscious that we do exist. It is as ridiculous as it is terrifying. Annie, as she left me, said she would bring my breakfast and even offered to stay with me during the night so that I should not be lonely. So I kissed her and said 'good night'. I thought it kinder not to tell Sidney and Mrs Grant. We shall none of us suffer pain or discomfort: it will be sudden and complete as the wireless set was in its broadcast and the fire and the electric light, the chairs and the cushions, and the kitchen, the dining room, the study and the sitting room. What an amazing happening – well worth recording in my diary – but that also will suddenly disappear, even if I went on with this endless writing. As I turn out the light and heat up my tin kettle and hot water bottle, so my stomach may no longer pain me, I feel that this it is *inconceivable – and therefore that it will not happen.* (19 April 1943)

Eleven days later she was dead. Her ashes were buried in a glade at the bottom of the garden.

In his obituary in the *New Statesman*, Kingsley Martin wrote of the last time he saw Beatrice, a month before her death.

> I wish I had a photograph of her in this final stage of her extraordinary career. She looked incredibly distinguished; with a fine lace cap around her head and her face a fine mesh of wrinkles. Rembrandt would have loved to have painted her. She had lost nothing of her superb dignity, her austerity or her unique elegance. She was more like an eagle than ever, or, as Raymond Mortimer who was with me put it, she was like the most venerable abbess who has ever known what power was. As I left, I wondered

> whether it was the last time I should see Mrs Webb. She was, I am convinced, if you consider her as a character, as an intellect, as a writer and a sociologist, the most remarkable woman that this country has known.[4]

Living as an invalid at Passfield, Sidney survived her by four years to see the end of the war and the beginning of the cold war. In 1944 he was awarded the Order of Merit. Two years later Shaw sent him a letter which might serve as an epitaph: 'If anyone had asked me what I owed to you I should have said my entire education . . . I can also say that I never met a man who combined your extraordinary ability with your unique simplicity and integrity of character'.[5] Sidney died in October 1947. After his death, Shaw wrote on 14 October in *The Times* suggesting that their remains should be transferred to Westminster Abbey 'to commemorate an unparalleled friendship'. He was successful and a month later Beatrice and Sidney Webb became the first couple to be reinterred in the Abbey together.

Beatrice summed up her view of their marriage and partnership in a wonderful entry in her diary a few months before the war:

> Forty seven years today, we were married in a shabby little office of the Registrar of St Pancras Workhouse – a fitting spot for the opening of our recognised partnership, dedicated to the abolition of poverty in the midst of riches. Since that time we have been one and indivisible in work and rest, at home and abroad, in our private life and in our public career. Looking back on those forty seven years of companionship in thought and action, I remember no single note of discord; in stating our conclusions we have sometimes disagreed, it has ended either in a compromise or in a dismissal of the problem from our thoughts in order to hasten on the job and take on yet another task.

She then went on to discuss Sidney's Parliamentary career which entailed separation for the two of them.

> So far as I was concerned, this episode was wearisome and dispiriting owing to disillusionment with the British social system, and hopelessness about the future of western civilization. Watching from inside, our powerful governing class embracing

the labour leaders and their wives, our court with its flunkey Anglican Church, pandering to the landlord and financier, was not an inspiring spectacle! Then there was the renewal of hope through the USSR; and, in spite of my illness, owing to Sidney's continued strength, the authorship of *Soviet Communism: a New Civilization* – the crowning effort of Our Partnership. Today Sidney and I have ceased to work together. But we love each other more and more, and when one dies, I think, the other 'will die too". (23 July 1939)

The assessment of their contemporaries are a fitting tribute to the achievements of the Webb partnership. On Beatrice's death, Leonard Woolf wrote that,

> they did for both social thought and political practice in the twentieth century what Bentham had done in the nineteenth. There is, in fact, a clear resemblance between them and Bentham: their uncompromising intellectuality and rationalism; the aloofness, integrity, and asceticism of their lives; their emergence as national 'characters'; the way in which their theories influenced political practice by permeating or capturing the key politicians. The reason for this resemblance is, of course, that they, like Bentham were thoroughly British in mind, method and character; no other national tradition could produce that strange mixture of uncompromising ratiocination, practical common sense, and the courage of one's own absurdities. The Webbs developed a peculiar technique of social investigation. It was an attempt to apply the methods of science to the observation of human society, and in particular to contemporary social institutions, regarded not as static or historical phenomena but as social processes. As Beatrice Webb herself put it: 'Only by watching *the processes* of growth and decay during a period of time, can we understand even the contemporary facts of whatever may be their stage of development; and only by such a comprehension of the past and present processes can we get an insight into the means of change' . . . They owed much directly to Herbert Spencer, and to the great London investigation of Charles Booth, who, in Beatrice Webb's view, 'was the boldest pioneer . . . and the achiever of the greatest results, in the methodology of the social sciences of the nineteenth century'. But they differed from all other workers in their own field by the scale of their operations, the great intellectual power and imagination by which they

handled their material, and that breadth and steadiness of social vision which enabled them never to forget that the ultimate object of 'a comprehension of the past and present process' was always 'an insight into the means of change'. The result was that no British thinker or writer, no politician, no civil servant, however hostile to or critical of the Webbs he might be, could escape their influence, if he put a toe upon the territory which they had made their own. For over that territory, which stretched from Local Government to the Co-operative Movement, they ruled by right of conquest . . .

I do not believe it is possible to distinguish the contribution of each partner to this great work . . . All that one can say about their partnership is that by a rare miracle two great minds were enabled not merely to think the same thoughts, but to think them for a lifetime together and for a common purpose.

They achieved another thing of equal importance. It was their personal influence. I do not refer only to their influence upon politicians and upon the workers, in the Labour Party, the Trade Union Movement and the Co-operative Movement – that was great and of great importance. I am thinking rather of their personal influence upon an unending series of younger generations. And their interests in the young, in any one who showed the slightest gift for political thought or social investigation, was unsleeping and undenying. And they were tirelessly unselfish in offering any young man or woman of the kind opportunities of learning and working. In this way they exercised a profound influence upon the minds and work of several generations of the politically conscious young, and not least upon those who rebelled against, and sometimes affectionately ridiculed, the Webbs. They achieved this partly by the power of their minds and character, but also by a peculiar simplicity and integrity which made any little-mindedness impossible for them. I have never known anyone who met the opposition, violence, and ingratitude of youth with such complete fairness, sweetness and tolerance as the Webbs.[6]

Margaret Cole was equally enthusiastic in the *New Statesman*.

It does not often happen in the history of human affairs, that anyone attains equal eminence in the world of letters and in the world of action; succeeds, that is to say, both in writing books that will stand the test of time and (what may well be as significant) the

> setters of examination papers, and in blazing the trail of practical political activity. This was, however, the achievement of that amazing partnership . . .
>
> The bare list of titles of the Webbs' books is impressive enough; more impressive is it to count on one's fingers the number of them which are 'authoritative', 'exhaustive', 'indispensible to the student' . . . The proportion of the Webbs' published work which is really ephemeral, is astonishing low; . . .
>
> . . . from the very first, the partnership was not merely intellectual, but in the highest degree purposive; it sought to find out the facts, indeed, but still more to alter them, to mould English society in the right direction, the direction of Socialism . . . [they] . . . set to work in a manner which, for erudition combined with practical activity has only been paralleled, I venture to suggest, by the collaboration of Marx and Engels.[7]

R. H. Tawney summed up their personal qualities in a generous article in the *Proceedings of the British Academy*.

> Their long years of labour, and the persistence with which, unmoved by changing fashions, they held on their course, gave them the air of an institution. Disliking sciolism, they were cautious in expressing opinions on matters outside their own field. On those within it, the perplexed inquirer, whether student, official, trade unionist or politician, could appeal to them as an oracle, returning with collective wisdom – 'we think' – unambiguous answers from a wealth of experience no one else could command . . . The noblest of all titles, they used to say, is that of servant, and 'the firm of Webb' settled public causes with a concentration of purpose which few men bring to their own; but the partners were neither a card-index of facts nor bleak and arid doctrinaires. Their influence was not confined to public activities, and they impressed those who knew them not less by what they were than by what they did . . . To visit them at Passfield Corner was to share the company of two sociable personalities, with a psychological curiosity not too elevated to enjoy gossip, an engaging capacity for laughing at themselves and the appetite for physical exercise of a gryphon in the wilderness.
>
> Of the characteristics which they had in common, simplicity and magnanimity, were, perhaps, the most striking. The combination of worldly wisdom with personal unworldliness, though

> rare, is not unknown. The Webbs possessed it in more than ordinary measure. While they knew exactly what they wanted, and had few rivals in the business of 'getting things done', their achievements owed more to single-mindedness and integrity than to the artful astuteness ascribed to them by the credulous . . . It was easy to disagree with them, but difficult to stage a quarrel and, when friends insisted on nursing a grievance, they were indefatigable in seeking opportunities to re-knit broken links . . . They never lost . . . their faith in public spirit guided by knowledge as the architect of a better world. Their old age was free from disillusionment and cynicism. The Order of Merit conferred on Lord Passfield for 'eminent services to Social and Political Science' was an appropriate tribute to part of their joint work to which Mrs Webb, as well as her husband, attached most importance.

Practical intellectuals, tireless propagandists, dedicated democratic socialists, the Webbs' achievements are by any standard colossal. Founding the LSE and the *New Statesman* would have been enough for most people but in addition the partnership produced books of outstanding scholarship, helped lay the foundation of the welfare state, and, as we have seen, was a decisive force in the development of the Labour Party as an instrument capable of changing the face of Britain.

Above all, their Fabian approach – ethical, rational, evolutionary and democratic – has had a profound influence on British politics and society.

NOTES

1. S. Webb to E. Pease, 12 Jan 1939, FP.
2. G. B. Shaw to S. Webb, 30 Jan 1934, PP.
3. Kingsley Martin, *The Webbs and their Work*, op. cit. p. 295–296.
4. The *New Statesman*, 8 May 1943.
5. G. B. Shaw to S. Webb, 26 Mar 1946, Passfield Papers.
6. L. Woolf, *Economic Journal*, June/Sept 1943.
7. M. Cole, *New Statesman*, 28 May 1943.

Bibliography

This book is based primarily on the Passfield Papers, which is the collection of papers relating to Beatrice and Sidney Webb. They are deposited in the British Library of Political and Economic Science. The Library also holds some of the Shaw papers (the majority of which are housed in the British Library) as well as the Wallas collection. The Fabian Society papers are to be found at Nuffield College, Oxford; *Fabian News* and other Fabian publications are in the offices of the Fabian Society.

I have made full use of the relevant Cabinet and Cabinet committee minutes and papers at the PRO. The Ramsay MacDonald papers are also now deposited at the PRO. The Labour Party archives have proved indispensable.

Other papers which have proved to be of interest and which are to be found in the BLPES are: Broadhurst Papers; Lansbury Papers; Pease Collection; Bolton Papers; Beveridge Papers; Barnett House papers; Cole collection; Barrow House papers. The papers relating to the foundation of the London School of Economics are deposited with the LSE.

JOURNALS AND NEWSPAPERS CONSULTED

Clarion
Labour Leader
Labour Elector
Justice
Star
Fabian News
London
New Statesman
The Crusade
Workman's Times
The Times
Political Quarterly
Nineteenth Century
Victorian Studies
Manchester Guardian
St Martin's Review
Daily Chronicle
London Technical Education Gazette
Quarterly Journal of Economics

SECONDARY SOURCES: SELECT BIBLIOGRAPHY

Place of publication London unless otherwise stated.

Addison, P., *The Road to 1945*, 1975.
Allen, B. A., *William Garnett – A Memoir*, 1933.
Altrincham, *Kenya's Opportunity*, 1955.
Amery, L. S., *My Political Life*, 1953.
Arnot, R. P., *The General Strike*, 1926.
——, *History of the Labour Research Department*, 1926.
——, *The Miners*, 1953.
——, *The Impact of the Russian Revolution in Britain*, 1967.
Asquith, H., *Memories and Reflections*, 1928.
Barjour, A., *Chapters of Autobiography*, 1930.
Barker, R., *Education and Politics 1900–51*, Oxford, 1972.
Barnett, H. O., *Canon Barnett: His Life, Work and Friends*, 2 vols, 1918.
Bassett, R., *Nineteen Thirty One*, 1958.
Bealey, F., (ed) *Social and Political Thought of the British Labour Party*, 1970.
Bealey, F. and Pelling, H., *Labour and Politics*, 1958.
Beer, M., *A History of British Socialism 1919*, 1920.
Beer, S. H., *Modern British Politics*, 1965.
Bellamy, J. and Saville, J., (eds) *Dictionary of Labour Biography*, vol 1–2, 1972; 7.
Beveridge, J., *An Epic of Clare Market*, 1960.
Beveridge, W., *The LSE and its Problems 1919–37*, 1960.
——, *Power and Influence*, 1953.
Bolt, C., *Victorian Attitudes to Race*, 1971.
Brand, C. F., *British Labour's Rise to Power*, 1941.
Branson, N., and Heinemann, M., *Britain in the Nineteen Thirties*, 1971.
Briggs, A., and Saville, J., (eds) *Essays in Labour History Vols 1–3*, 1960, 1971, 1977.
British Blue Book: Report of the Commission on the Palestine Disturbances of August 1929. CMD 3530 1929.
British Blue Books: Report on Immigration, Land Settlement and Development by Sir John Hope Simpson, CMD 3686, 1930.
Brockway, F., *Inside the Left*, 1942.
Brown, E. H. P., *The Growth of British Industrial Relations*, 1960.
Brown, J., 'The Appointment of the 1905 Poor Law Commission.' *Bulletin of the Institute of Historical Research* XLII, (1969).
Brown, K. D., *Labour and Unemployment 1900–14*, 1971.
Bruce, M., *The Rise of the Welfare State*, 1973.
Bullock, A., *The Life and Times of Ernest Bevin*, Vol 1, 1960.
Burns, C., *A Short History of Birkbeck College*, 1924.
Caine, S., *The History of the Formation of the London School of Economics*, 1963.
Calcott, M., 'Sidney Webb, Ramsay MacDonald, Emmanuel Shinwell and the Durham Constituency of Seaham., *Bulletin 11, North East Group for the Study of Labour History*, 1977.
Carlton, D., *MacDonald versus Henderson*, 1970.
Castles, F. G., *The Social Democratic Image of Society*, 1978.
Caute, D., *The Fellow-Travellers*, 1973.

Citrine, Lord, *Men and Work*, 1964.
Clarke, P. F., *Lancashire and the New Liberalism*, Cambridge, 1971.
Clegg, H. A., Fox, A., and Thompson, H. F., *A History of British Trade Unionism since 1889*, Vol 1, Oxford, 1964.
Clynes, J. R., *Memoirs 1869–1924*, 1937.
Cole, G. D. H., *History of Socialist Thought*, 1953–60, 3 vols.
——, *World of Labour*, 1913.
Cole, M., *Beatrice Webb*, 1945.
——, *The Webbs and their Work*, 1949.
——, *The Story of Fabian Socialism*, 1961.
——, *Growing up into Revolution*, 1949.
——, *The Life of G. D. H. Cole*, 1971.
Cooke, C., *Life of R. S. Cripps*, 1957.
Courtney, K., Dairy (Unpublished) BLPES.
Cowling, M., *The Impact of Labour 1920–24*, 1971.
Crook, W. H., *The General Strike*, 1931.
Dalton, H., *Call Back Yesterday: Memoirs 1887–1931*, 1953.
Dangerfield, G., *The Strange Death of Liberal England*, 1936.
Donoghue, B., and Jones, G. W., *Herbert Morrison*, 1973.
Elton, Lord, *Life of James Ramsay MacDonald*, 1939.
Emy, H. V., *Liberals, Radicals & Social Politics 1893–1914*, Cambridge, 1973.
Fainsod, M., *International Society & the World War*, Cambridge Mass., 1935.
——, *How Russia is Ruled*, Harvard, 1970.
Feaver, G., 'The Webbs in Canada', *Canadian Historical Review*, vol LVIII, 3, September 1977.
Fishman, W. H., *East End Jewish Radical 1875–1914*, 1975.
——, *Trade Unions*, 1952.
Flanders, A., *Management & Unions*, 1970.
Fraser, D., *The Evolution of the British Welfare State*, 1973.
Freemantle, A., *This Little Band of Prophets*, 1960.
Galton, A. G., *Memoirs of My Life*, 1908.
Gardiner, A. G., *Pillars of Society*,
——, *Prophets, Priests and Kings*, 1908.
——, *John Benn & the Progressive Movement*, 1925.
Gilbert, B., *The Evolution of National Insurance in Great Britain*, 1966.
Glynn, S., and Oxborrow, J., *Interwar Britain: A Social and Economic History*, 1976.
Graubard, S., *British Labour & the Russian Revolution*, 1956.
Gregory, R. G., 'Sidney Webb & East Africa', History, vol. 72, California University Press, 1960.
Haldane, E. S., *From One Century to Another*, 1937.
Haldane, R. B., *Autobiography*, 1929.
Hamer, D. A., *Liberal Politics in the Age of Gladstone & Rosebery* Oxford, 1972.
Hamilton, M.A., *Arthur Henderson*, 1938.
——, *Sidney & Beatrice Webb*, 1933.
——, *J. R. MacDonald*, 1942.
Hansard's Parliamentary Debates 1922–1931.
Harlow, V., and Chilver, E. M., *History of East Africa*, vol 2, Oxford, 1965.

Harris, J. F., *Unemployment & Politics: A Study in English Social Policy 1880–1914*, Oxford, 1974.
——, *William Beveridge: A Biography*, 1977.
Harrison, J. F. C., *Robert Owen & the Owenites in Britain & America*, 1969.
Harrison, R., *Before the Socialists: Studies in Labour & Politics 1861–8*, 1965.
Harrod, R. F., *The Life of John Maynard Keynes*, 1951.
Hay, J. R., *The Origins of Liberal Welfare Reforms*, 1975.
Hewins, W. A. S., *Apologia of an Imperialist*, 1929.
Henderson, A., *The Aims of Labour*, 1918.
——, 'The New Labour Party Constitution' *Fabin News*, January 1918.
——, 'The Outlook for Labour' *Contemporary Review*, 23 February 1918.
Hinton, J., *The First Shop Stewards Movement*, 1973.
Hobhouse, S., *Margaret Hobhouse and her Family*, 1934.
Hobsbawm, E. J., *Labouring Men: Studies in the History of Labour*, 1964.
Holland, P., *Political Pilgrims: Travels of Western Intellectuals to the Soviet Union*, Oxford, 1981.
Holton, B., *British Syndicalism 1900–1914*, 1976.
Hunt, E. H., *British Labour History 1815–1914*, 1981.
Hurt, J. S., *Elementary Schooling and the Working Classes 1860–1918*, 1979.
Huxley, E., *White Man's Country*, 1965.
Hyams, E., *The New Statesman*, 1963.
Hyman, R., *The Workers Union*, Oxford, 1971.
Hynes, E., *The Edwardian Frame of Mind*, 1968.
Joint Committee on Closer Union in East Africa, H of C 156, 1931.
Jones, T., *A Diary with Letters, 1931–50*, 1954.
Judges, A. V., 'The Educational Influence of the Webbs' *British Journal of Education Studies*, 10 November 1961.
Kendall, W., *The Revolutionary Movement in Britain 1900–21*, 1969.
Kent, W., *John Burns; Labour's Lost Leader*, 1950.
Kimche, J., *There Could Have Been Peace*, New York, 1973.
Lacqueur, W., *A History of Zionism*, New York, 1972.
Lansbury, G., *My Life*, 1928.
Laurence, D. H., *Collected Essays: George Bernard Shaw*, 1965 and 1972.
Letvin, S. R., *Pursuit of Certainty*, Cambridge, 1966.
Lewis, G. K., 'Fabian Socialism: Some Aspects of Theory & Practice' *Journal of Politics*, August 1952.
Lichtheim, G., *A Short History of Socialism*, 1970.
Lyman, R., *The First Labour Government 1924*, 1957.
——, 'James Ramsay MacDonald & the leadership of the Labour Party' *Journal of British Studies*, 2, 1962.
MacDonald, J. R., *Socialism after the War*, 1917.
MacKibbin, R., *The Evolution of the Labour Party*, Oxford, 1974.
Mackenzie, N and J., *The Time Traveller*, 1973.
——, *The First Fabians*, 1977.
Mackenzie, N., *Letters of Beatrice & Sidney Webb*, 1980.
Marquand, D., *Ramsay MacDonald*, 1977.
Martin, K., *Father-Figures*, 1966.
Marwick, A., *Britain in the Century of Total War*, 1968.
——, *The Deluge*, 1965.
McBriar, A. M., *Fabian Socialism & English Politics 1884–1918*, Cambridge, 1962.

McCarthy, D., *Autobiography*, 1953.
Meinertzhagen, D., *Diary of a Black Sheep*, 1964.
Meinertzhagen, G., *Ploughshare to Parliament*, 1908.
Middlemas, K., *Politics in Industrial Society*, 1979.
Middleton, J. S., *Farewell*, 1944.
Middlemas, K., and Barnes, J., *Baldwin*, 1969.
Miliband, R., *Parliamentary Socialism*, 1961.
——, *The State in Capitalist Society*, 1969.
Minkin, L., *The Labour Party Conference*, 1978.
Morgan, K., *Keir Hardie*, 1975.
——, *The Age of Lloyd George*, 1971.
Morris, A. J. A., (ed) *Edwardian Radicalism 1900–14*, 1974.
Mowat, C. L., *The Charity Organisation Society*, 1961.
——, *Britain Between the Wars 1918–1940*, (2nd edition) 1968.
Muggeridge, K., and Adams, R., *Beatrice Webb*, 1967.
Musson, A. E., *British Trade Unions 1800–1875*, 1972.
Nicolson, H., *King George V*, 1952.
Olivier, M., *Sydney Olivier*, 1948.
Orage, A. R., (ed) *National Guilds*, 1914.
Orton, W. A., *Labour in Transition*, 1921.
Owen, D., *English Philanthropy 1660–1960*, 1965.
Pease, E., *History of the Fabian Society*, (3rd ed) 1963.
Peele, G., and Cook, C., (eds) *The Politics of Reappraisal 1918–39*, 1975.
Pelling, H., *A Short History of the Labour Party*, 1961.
——, *A History of British Trade Unionism*, 1962.
——, *Popular Politics and Society in late Victorian Britain*, 1968.
——, *Labour & Politics 1900–06*, 1958.
Pelham, M., *Lugard*, vol II, 1960.
Pierson, S., *Marxism & the Origins of British Socialism*, Harvard, 1973.
——, *British Socialists. The Journey from Fantasy to Politics*, Harvard, 1979.
Pimlott, B., *Labour & the Left in the 1930's*, Cambridge.
Pimlott, J. A. R., *Toynbee Hall 1884–1934*, 1935.
Polk, W. R., *Struggle for Palestine*, Boston, 1974.
Poirier, P., *The Advent of the Labour Party*, 1958.
Pribicevic, B., *The Shop Stewards Movement & Workers Control 1910–22*, Oxford, 1959.
Radice, G. H. and E. A., *Will Thorne, Constructive Militant*, 1974.
Reid, J. H. S., *The Origins of the British Labour Party*, 1955.
Renshaw, P., *The General Strike*, 1975.
Report of Sir S. Wilson on his visit to East Africa, CMD 3378, 1929.
Rose, M., *The Relief of Poverty 1834–1914*, 1972.
Rose, N., *The Gentle Zionist. A Study in Anglo-Zionist Diplomacy 1929–39*, 1972.
Roskill, S., *Hankey, Man of Secrets*, vol 2, 1972.
Royal Commission on Labour 1892 vol xxlx 4th Report.
Royal Commission on Palestine (Peel), CMD 5479.
Royal Commission on the Coal Industry, CMD 359, 1919.
Royal Commission on the Poor Laws & the Relief of Distress, CMD 5068, 1910.
Royal Institute of International Affairs, *Great Britain and Palestine 1915–39*, Information Paper No 20a.
Russell, B., *The Autobiography of Bertrand Russell*, 3 vols, 1967–68.

Russell, B., *Portraits from Memory & Other Essays*, 1956.
Samuel, Viscount, *Memoirs*, 1945.
Saunders, W., *The First London County Council*, 1892.
Searle, G. R., *The Quest for National Efficiency*, Oxford, 1971.
Selver, P. P., *Orage & the New Age Circle*, 1959.
Semmel, B., *Imperialism & Social Reform*, 1960.
Shinwell, E., *Conflict Without Malice*, 1955.
Skidelsky, R., *Politicians and the Slump*, 1967.
Simey, T. S., 'The Contribution of B & S Webb to Sociology'.
Simon, W. M., *European Positivism in the Nineteenth Century*, Ithaca, 1964.
Simon, B., *Education & the Labour Movement 1870–1920*, 1965.
Smith, H. L., and Nash, W., *The Story of the Dock Strike*, 1889.
Snowden, P., *Autobiography*, 2 vols, 1934.
Spencer, H., *Autobiography*, 1904.
Stedman-Jones, G., *Outcast London*, Oxford, 1971.
Shaw, G. B., *Sixteen Self Sketches*, 1949.
Sykes, C., *Cross Roads to Israel*, 1965.
Symons, J., *The General Strike*, 1957.
Tawney, R. H., 'Beatrice Webb', *Proceedings of the British Academy*, 1943.
Taylor, A. J. P., *English History 1914–45*, 1965.
——, *The Troublemakers*, 1957.
Thompson, L., *The Enthusaists*, 1971.
Thompson, P., *Socialists, Liberals & Labour*, 1967.
Tholfsen, T. R., *Working Class Radicalism in Mid-Victorian England*, New York, 1977.
Thorne, W., *My Life's Battles*, 1925.
Torr, D., *Tom Mann & his Times*, 1956.
Tsuzuki, C., *H. M. Hyndman & British Socialism*, Oxford, 1961.
——, *The Life of Eleanor Marx*, Oxford, 1967.
Ulam, A., *Philosophical Foundations of English Socialism*, Cambridge, Mass., 1951.
Vincent, J., *Origins of the British Labour Party*, 1967.
Wallas, G., *Human Nature in Politics*, 1908.
——, *The Great Society*, 1914.
Wells, H. G., *The New Machiavelli*, 1925.
——, *Experiment in Autobiography*, 1934.
Weizmann, C., *Trial & Error*, 1949.
Wertheimer, E., *Portrait of the Labour Party*, 1929.
Wiener, M., *Between Two Worlds: The Political Thought of Graham Wallas*, Oxford, 1971.
White Paper: Disturbances in May 1921, CMD 1520, 1921.
——: Palestine: Statement with Regard to British Policy, CMD 3582, 1930.
——: Palestine: Statement of Policy by H. M. G., CMD 3692, 1930.
——: Jerusalem: The Western or Wailing Wall Incident, CMD 3229, 1928.
——: Future Policy with Regard to East Africa, CMD 2904, 1927.
Williams, F., *Ernest Bevin*, 1952.
Williams, G., *The Coming of the Welfare State*, 1967.
Winter, J. M., *Socialism & the Challenge of War*, 1974.
Wolfe, W., *From Radicalism to Socialism*, Yale, 1975.
Woolf, L., *Beginning Again*, 1965.
——, *Downhill all the Way*, 1967.
Wright, A. W., *G. D. H. Cole and Socialist Democracy*, 1979.

PUBLISHED WORKS OF BEATRICE AND SIDNEY WEBB

Sidney Webb: books and pamphlets

The Difficulties of Individualism, Fabian Tract 69, 1884.
Facts for Socialists from the Political Economists and Statisticians, Fabian Tract 5, 1887.
The Progress of Socialism, Hampstead Society for the Study of Socialism, Tract No 1, 1888.
Wanted, a programme: an appeal to the Liberal Party, 1888.
What Socialism means: a call to the unconverted, 1888.
An Eight Hours Bill, Fabian Tract 9, 1889.
Facts for Londoners, Fabian Tract 8, 1889.
Socialism in England, American Economic Association, 1889.
English Progress Towards Social Democracy, Fabian Tract 15, 1890.
Figures for Londoners, Fabian Tract 10, 1890.
Practicable Land Nationalisation, Fabian Tract 12.
The Workers Political Programme, Fabian Tract 11, 1890.
The Case for an Eight Hours Bill, Fabian Tract 23, 1891.
The Eight Hours Day (with Harold Cox), 1891.
Fabian Municipal Program, Fabian Tracts 30–37, 1891.
The Fabian Society: its Objects and Methods, 1891.
The London Programme, 1891.
Questions for London County Councillors, Fabian Tract 26, 1891.
Questions for Parliamentary Candidates, Fabian Tract 24, 1891.
Questions for School Board Candidates, Fabian Tract 25, 1891.
The Reform of the Poor Law, Fabian Tract 17, 1891.
The Truth about Leasehold Enfranchisement, Fabian Tract 22, 1891.
The Reform of London, 1892.
The London (Vestries), Fabian Tract 60, 1894.
Socialism: True and False, Fabian Tract 51, 1894.
The Difficulties of Individualism, Fabian Tract 69, 1896.
Labour in the Longest Reign 1837–97, Fabian Tract 75, 1897.
The Economics of Direct Employment, Fabian Tract 84, 1898.
The London County Council Election, 1898.
The London Polytechnic Institutes, 1898.
The Education Muddle and the Way Out, Fabian Tract 106, 1901.
Twentieth-Century Politics: a Policy of National Efficiency, Fabian Tract 108, 1901.
The Education Act, 1902: How to Make the Best of It, Fabian Tract 114, 1903.
London education, 1904.
The Decline in the Birth Rate, Fabian Tract 131, 1907.
Paupers and Old Age Pension, Fabian Tract 135, 1907.
The Basis and Policy of Socialism, 1908.
The Necessary Basis of Society, 1908.
Socialism and Individualism, 1908.
The Place of Co-operation in the State of Tomorrow, 1910.
Grants-in-aid: a Criticism and a Proposal, 1911.
How the Government Can Prevent Unemployment, 1912.
The Legal Minimim Wage, 1912.
What About the Rates? Fabian Tract 172, 1913.
The War and the Workers, Fabian Tract 176, 1914.

Great Britain After the War (with Arnold Freeman), 1916.
Towards Social Democracy?, 1915.
When Peace Comes: the Way of Industrial Reconstruction, Fabian Tract 181, 1916.
The Reform of the House of Lords, Fabian Tract 183, 1917.
The Restoration of Trade Union Conditions, 1917.
The Works Manager Today, 1917.
The New Constitution of the Labour Party, 1918.
The Teacher in Politics, Fabian Tract 187, 1918.
The Root of Labour Unrest, Fabian Tract 196, 1920.
The Story of the Durham Miners, 1921.
The Constitutional Problems of the Co-operative Society, Fabian Tract 202, 1923.
The Labour Party on the Threshold, Fabian Tract 207, 1923.
The Local Government Act 1929 – How to Make the Best of It, Fabian Tract 231, 1929.
What Happened in 1931: a Record, 1932 Fabian Tract 237, 1932.

For articles in periodicals and contributions to composite works please see British Library of Political and Economic Science, *Publications of Sidney and Beatrice Webb: An Interim Check List*.

Beatrice Webb: books and pamphlets

The Cooperative Movement in Great Britain, 1891.
The Relationship between Co-operation and Trade Unionism, 1892.
Women and the Factory Acts, Fabian Tract 67, 1896.
The Relation of Poor Law Medical Relief to the Public Health Authorities, 1906.
A Crusade Against Destitution, 1909.
Socialism and the National Minimum, 1909.
The Minority Report in its Relation to Public Health and the Medical Profession, 1910.
The New Crusade Against Destitution, 1910.
Complete National Provision for Sickness: How to Amend the Insurance Act, 1912.
A Woman's Appeal: Personal Expenditure in Wartime, 1916.
The Abolition of the Poor Law, Fabian Tract 185, 1918.
The Wages of Men and Women: Should they be Equal?, 1919.
My Apprenticeship, 1926.
The Discovery of the Consumer, 1928.
A New Reform Bill, Fabian Tract 236, 1931.
Our Partnership (ed Barbara Drake and Margaret Cole), 1948.
Diaries, 1912–24, (ed Margaret Cole), 1952.
Diaries, 1924–32, (ed Margaret Cole), 1956.
American Diary 1898 (ed David Shannon), 1963.

For articles in periodicals and contributions to composite works see British Library of Political and Economic Science, *Publications of Sidney and Beatrice Webb: An Interim Check List*.

Sidney and Beatrice Webb: books and pamphlets

The History of Trade Unionism, 1894.
Industrial Democracy, 2 vols, 1897.
Problems of Modern Industry, 1898.
English Local Government from the Revolution to the Municipal Corporations Act, 11 vols, 1906–1927.
The State and the Doctor, 1910.
The Prevention of Destitution, 1911.
The Principles of the Labour Party, 1918.
A Constitution for the Socialist Commonwealth of Great Britain, 1920.
The Consumers Co-operative Movement, 1921.
The Decay of Capitalist Civilisation, 1923.
Methods of Social Study, 1932.
Soviet Communism: a New Civilisation?, 1935.
Is Soviet Communism a New Civilisation?, 1936.
Soviet Communism: Dictatorship or Democracy?, 1936.
The Truth about Soviet Russia, 1942.

For articles in periodicals and contributions to composite works see British Library of Political and Economic Science, *Publications of Sidney and Beatrice Webb: An Interim Check List*. Sidney Webb's unpublished lectures are to be found in the Passfield Papers at the British Library of Political and Economic Science.

Index